The Vichy Syndrome

HENRY ROUSSO

The Vichy Syndrome

History and Memory in France since 1944

Translated by Arthur Goldhammer

HARVARD UNIVERSITY PRESS

Cambridge, Massachusetts
London, England

This translation is based on the second, revised edition of
Le Syndrome de Vichy: De 1944 à nos jours, copyright © 1987 and
1990 by Editions du Seuil, Paris.

First Harvard University Press paperback edition, 1994

Library of Congress Cataloging-in-Publication Data

Rousso, Henry, 1954–
[Syndrome de Vichy.   English]
The Vichy syndrome : history and memory in France since 1944 /
Henry Rousso ; translated by Arthur Goldhammer.
p.   cm.
Translation of: Le syndrome de Vichy.
Includes bibliographical references (p.) and index.
ISBN 0-674-93538-1 (cloth)
ISBN 0-674-93539-X (pbk.)
1. France—Politics and government—1945–   2. France—History—
German occupation, 1940–1945. 3. World War, 1939–1945—France.
4. Pétain, Philippe, 1856–1951—Influence. I. Title.
DC397.R7314   1991
944.082—dc20   90-20006
CIP

Contents

FOREWORD

Stanley Hoffmann

French historians, in the past ten years, have turned to an important, complicated, and difficult issue: memory. What is it that groups, elites, nations, remember from their past? What do they *want* to remember, and what do they repress? What places, monuments, and works of art do they select in order to commemorate past events? To what contemporary uses are memories put? How divisive are these remembrances and concealments—a question that is unavoidable, indeed primordial, in a country such as France, torn not only, as de Gaulle once put it, between appeals to renewal and sirens of decline, but between nostalgia for the great rare moments of unity and the many instances of Franco-French internal conflict.

Henry Rousso's meticulous and provocative study is one of the most original manifestations of this interest in the traces, dreams, and scars left by the past. It is also the first comprehensive attempt to deal, not with the most dramatic and traumatic episode of contemporary French history—the period between France's fall in June 1940 and the liberation four years later, when the Vichy regime and de Gaulle's Free French competed for legitimacy, and collaborationists and resisters fought each other without mercy—but with the way in which the postliberation French have faced that episode, the skeletons in the nation's closet, and the cataclysmic collapse of a regime, the Third Republic, and of a social order that seemed so stable and safe. What myths have the French developed in order to appease their consciences and restore their self-esteem? How have they, over time, judged Vichy and their own behavior? How deep and lasting are the wounds? This is the unexplored and mined terrain fearlessly trod by a young historian who belongs to the generation of postwar France and is thus well placed, insofar as he is close enough to the drama to be passionately concerned and distant enough to be equitable.

What he shows, explicitly and vividly, is how the French chose to believe that Vichy had been the creation of a small group of rather wicked (but still more misguided than evil) men, that the crimes com-

vii

mitted were crimes of the Germans and of very small bands of collaborationists, and that most of the population had resisted the Occupation in some degree. The Resistance represented French continuity—the continuity of the republican regime and of a patriotic nation—saved France's honor, played a major role in the liberation, and was the secular arm of the savior, Charles de Gaulle. It was not only de Gaulle who promulgated this myth. The political classes of postwar France, from the far left to much of the far right, had come out of the internal or external Resistance, and while their acceptance of de Gaulle was often flickering or conditional, and while some of the internal resisters challenged the Gaullist version of the myth, in general they rallied around it. De Gaulle himself always knew that it was a myth—he told an aide that after June 1940 he always "acted as if . . ."—but he was a firm believer in pedagogical sublimation: the French had to be turned forward, to effort and greatness, not backward to a morose and divisive analysis of their failings or crimes. By and large, France's elites agreed, either out of compassion and a fervent desire to bury an ugly past or out of self-interest to avoid embarrassing scrutiny; and the general public, which deep down knew that the myth was a cavalier interpretation of reality, pretended that it was indeed the truth. Thus for many years, as Rousso shows, the Vichyites were treated as the scapegoats for the nation's flaws, and they themselves argued that they had nothing but the best intentions, the noblest motives, and the worst luck. What this meant, not so incidentally, was that collaboration with Nazi Germany was not, so to speak, given its due: the Vichyites had no interest in evoking it or in doing anything beyond presenting it as imposed by the Nazis; and the sharers of the official myth had no wish to stir the ashes in order to find the embers of shame.

What is striking in this respect is the continuity of the Fourth Republic and the de Gaulle period of the Fifth. But the myth could not last forever. May '68 saw young people challenging all the established verities and taboos of their elders. It was no coincidence that Marcel Ophuls and the other makers of *The Sorrow and the Pity* had been "sixty-eighters." President Pompidou had not been in the Resistance and was personally exasperated by the "resistancialist" mythology. Inevitably a reaction began, which, like all reactions, went too far in reverse. It seemed to assume that, at the root of the collective repres sion of reality, there had to be the fact that the French, far from fighting on the good side, were either cowards or stinkers (to use the famous categories devised by Sartre, himself a prime example of the gap between the official myth and the truth). Instead of a (false) version in black and white, there now prevailed a picture in uniformly dirty grays. For a while, myth and countermyth coexisted. Even as Ophuls' incisive inquest was making its way to the moviegoing public, Robert Paxton's *Vichy France* came out in translation. The book demonstrated the willingness of Vichy to collaborate and the purely domestic origin of much of Vichy's most hideous legislation (especially against the Jews)—and thus stressed the continuity between Vichy and prewar French conservatism, reaction, and profascist sympathies. There was a firestorm of criticism and disbelief. But this was the last hurrah of the older myth.

What about the countermyth? It has, by now, faded somewhat. It had its useful function in showing that the national good conscience was not justified, that misdeeds and injustices had been committed, that many people, especially on top, had either dirtied their hands or looked the other way in order to keep them clean. But it was ultimately discarded, not because it offered an unflattering mirror to the French but because it was even more inaccurate than the resistancialist tale. The patient work of historians, especially the colleagues of Henry Rousso at the Institut d'Histoire du Temps Présent, has shown, first, that the reality of those four dark years—during which the French were splintered in every conceivable ideological and geographical way—was infinitely more complex than either myth suggests and, second, that public support for Vichy was short-lived, public support for political repression, racial genocide, and collaboration with the Nazis was minimal, and public hope for liberation was steadily growing. The French had not all been active or vicarious heroes—but they had not been docile culprits either.

Rousso's book provides a subtle answer to those who still accuse the French of not having confronted their past, of not having faced their crimes and prejudices as deeply as the West Germans have. This certainly has not been true for the past twenty years, and Rousso documents the confrontation just as he unsparingly indicts the earlier avoidance of the truth. His book is thus a significant contribution to our understanding of postwar French political culture; it is also a contribution to our understanding of the dominant role in French consciousness played by de Gaulle (whose birth in 1890, death in 1970, and radio appeal for resistance on 18 June 1940 were all celebrated in 1990). It ought to stimulate an equally ambitious, painstaking, and painful study of the memory of the Resistance in postwar France (today we know more about Vichy and collaboration than about the Resistance). Rousso, especially in his penetrating analysis of the Barbie trial, shows how difficult such a self-examination would be (it may well have to wait until the chief survivors of the Resistance have passed away). Finally, this book ought to provoke American readers into thinking about their own memories of troubled periods of their past, about evasions, myths, and distortions, and about the way in which the past never ceases to color and to disturb our behavior in the present.

ABBREVIATIONS

ACJF   Association Catholique de la Jeunesse Française (Catholic Association of French Youth)

ADMP   Association pour Défendre la Mémoire du Maréchal Pétain (Association to Defend the Memory of Marshal Pétain)

ANACR   Association Nationale des Anciens Combattants de la Résistance (National Association of Resistance Veterans)

ANMRF   Association Nationale des Médaillés de la Résistance Française (National Association of French Resistance Medalwinners)

CDJC   Centre de Documentation Juive Contemporaine (Center of Contemporary Jewish Documentation)

CED   Communauté Européenne de Défense (European Defense Community)

CFLN   Comité Français de Libération Nationale (French Committee for National Liberation)

CHGM   Comité d'Histoire de la Deuxième Guerre Mondiale (Committee on the History of World War II)

CHOLF   Commission d'Histoire de l'Occupation et de la Libération de la France (Commission for the History of the Occupation and Liberation of France)

CNE   Comité National des Ecrivains (National Writers' Committee)

CNIP   Centre National des Indépendants et Paysans (Independents' Party)

CNR   Conseil National de la Résistance (National Resistance Council)

CPL   Comité Parisien de Libération (Parisian Liberation Committee)

CRIF   Conseil Représentatif des Institutions Juives de France (Council of French Jewish Institutions)

FANE   Fédération d'Action Nationaliste Européenne (European Nationalist Action Federation)

xi

FFI	Forces Françaises de l'Intérieur (French Forces of the Interior)
FFL	Forces Françaises Libres (Free French Forces)
FNDIRP	Fédération Nationale des Déportés et Internés Rêsistants et Patriotes (National Federation of Deportees and Prisoners)
FNSP	Foundation Nationale des Sciences Politiques (National Political Science Foundation)
FPLP	Front Populaire de Libération de la Palestine (Popular Front for the Liberation of Palestine)
FTP	Francs-Tireurs et Partisans (Sharpshooters and Partisans)
IHTP	Institut d'Histoire du Temps Présent (Institute for the History of the Present)
JOC	Jeunesse Ouvrière Chrétienne (Christian Working Youth)
LICRA	Ligue Internationale contre le Racisme de l'Antisémitisme (International League against Racism and Antisemitism)
LVF	Légion de Volontaires Français contre le Bolchevisme (Legion of French Volunteers against Bolshevism)
MRAP	Mouvement contre le Racisme et pour l'Amité entre les Peuples (Movement against Racism and for Friendship among Peoples)
MRP	Mouvement Républicain Populaire (Popular Republican Movement)
OAS	Organisation Armée Secrète (Secret Armed Organization)
PCF	Parti Communiste Français (French Communist Party)
PSF	Parti Socialiste Français (French Socialist Party)
RPF	Rassemblement du Peuple Français (Rally of the French People)
RPR	Rassemblement pour la République (Rally for the Republic)
SFIO	Section Française de l'Internationale Ouvrière (French Section of Workers' International)
STO	Service de Travail Obligatoire (Obligatory Work Service)
UDF	Union de la Démocratie Française (Union for French Democracy)

The Vichy Syndrome

INTRODUCTION: THE NEUROSIS

The idea for this book began with a discovery that could have been surprising only to the naive young scholar that I was. In the late 1970s I began research on the history of the Vichy regime, obviously still a subject of heated controversy. Nevertheless, in all innocence, I thought sufficient time had elapsed to allow me to wield my scalpel. But the corpse was still warm. It was too soon for the pathologist to begin an autopsy; what the case called for was a doctor qualified to treat the living, not the dead—perhaps even a psychoanalyst.

What surprised me most was not the passionate reactions—even among historians—to everything written about the "dark years" of the war but the *immediacy* of the period, its astonishing presentness, which at times rose to the level of obsession: witness the constant scandals, the endless invective and insult, the libel suits, and the many affairs that attracted the attention of all of France, such as the trial of Klaus Barbie and the arrest of Paul Touvier. The cultural sphere, moreover, was inundated by images of a troubled yet fascinating past, as during the period of reappraisal I shall call the "forties revival" (*la mode rétro*).

I sensed an urgent need for something more than the usual scholarly approach. Alongside the history of Vichy, another history took shape: the history of the *memory* of Vichy, of Vichy's remnants and fate *after* 1944 and to a date that is still impossible to determine.

Born ten years after the war, I belong to a generation that grew up in the rather burdensome shadow of remembrance and mimickry of May '68. For us there was no "founding event" to rally around, nothing comparable to the Occupation with its pro- and anti-Resistance commitments or the Algerian War or the feverish events of May. Moreover, we of the post-May generation witnessed repeated attempts to overcome those old divisions, the most serious of which were those stemming from the 1940s. Forty years after the fact, many politicians and intellectuals, young as well as old, were still playing at "Phalanges de l'Ordre Noir" [Phalanxes of the Black Order, the title of a well-known comic strip by Christin and Bilal in which former Franco supporters engaged in fanciful battle with former republicans in the 1970s, some forty years after the end of the Spanish Civil War—trans.].

The Field of Memory

Thus subjective factors played a part in my choice of subject. For some years now, historians have been taking an increasing interest in "phenomena of memory." At first glance it would seem that history and memory are two clearly different ways of looking at the past. The difference has frequently been analyzed, most recently by Pierre Nora.[1] Memory is a living phenomenon, something in perpetual evolution, whereas history—as understood by historians—is a scholarly and theoretical reconstruction and as such is more apt to give rise to a substantial, durable body of knowledge. Memory is plural, moreover, in that distinct memories are generated by different social groups, political parties, churches, communities, language groups, and so on. Thus "collective memory" might seem to be a figment of the imagination, or at any rate little more than a misleading composite of disparate and heterogeneous memories. By contrast, history has a more universal, if not more ecumenical, purpose. For all that history may be controversial, it remains a fundamental instrument for the education of citizens. Memory at times lives on in a religious or sacred key; history is critical and secular. Memory is subject to repression, whereas nothing in principle lies outside the historian's territory.

Yet the distinction between history and memory is a characteristic trait of the twentieth century, first identified as such by Maurice Halbwachs, a disciple of Bergson, and exemplified by the evolution of contemporary historiography, whose goal is no longer legitimation but the advancement of knowledge. In the nineteenth century the difference was all but nonexistent, particularly in France. The function of history then, of what Nora has called "history as memory," was essentially to legitimate the nascent Third Republic and to forge a national feeling. Today no such confusion is possible: the disintegration of rural society and of the ancestral traditions it embodied, the proliferation of sources of information and, concomitantly, new approaches to social reality, the weakening of nationalist sentiment in Western Europe since World War II, and the depth of internal divisions including those born of Vichy—all these have caused history and memory to evolve in different directions:

> As "society" has taken the place of "the nation," legitimation based on the past and therefore on history has given way to legitimation based on the future. The past could only be understood and honored, and the nation could only be served; the future, however, must be prepared for. The three terms have regained their autonomy. No longer is the nation something to be fought for; it is a given. History has become a social science, and memory a purely private phenomenon. The "nation as memory" will have been the last incarnation of "history as memory."[2]

Thus a new field of study has been opened up for historians: the history of memory, that is, the study of the evolution of various social practices and, more specifically, of the form and content of social practices whose purpose or effect is the representation of the past and the perpetuation of its memory within a particular group or the society as a whole.

This history is rooted in what Nora and his colleagues have called *lieux de mémoire*, or mnemonic sites, embodying concrete traces of the past, visible and durable signs of its celebration. The history of memory can arise out of the memory of a particular group: the Camisards, for example, as studied by Philippe Joutard,[3] or combat veterans, as studied by Antoine Prost.[4] But it may also be associated with certain key events, whose memory survives long after the last flames have been extinguished and whose influence extends over the whole of society: examples include the French Revolution, of course,[5] the wars in the Vendée that grew out of it and have attracted renewed attention,[6] and World War II.[7] Historians are interested not only in ascertaining the facts about such events but also in comprehending their persistence.

It is no accident that these events were all associated with times of deep crisis for France's national unity and identity. These are the times

tional feeling. Today no such confusion is possible: the disintegration of rural society and of the ancestral traditions it embodied, the proliferation of sources of information and, concomitantly, new approaches to social reality, the weakening of nationalist sentiment in Western Europe since World War II, and the depth of internal divisions including those born of Vichy—all these have caused history and memory to evolve in different directions:

> As "society" has taken the place of "the nation," legitimation based on the past and therefore on history has given way to legitimation based on the future. The past could only be understood and honored, and the nation could only be served; the future, however, must be prepared for. The three terms have regained their autonomy. No longer is the nation something to be fought for; it is a given. History has become a social science, and memory a purely private phenomenon. The "nation as memory" will have been the last incarnation of "history as memory."[2]

Thus a new field of study has been opened up for historians: the history of memory, that is, the study of the evolution of various social practices and, more specifically, of the form and content of social practices whose purpose or effect is the representation of the past and the perpetuation of its memory within a particular group or the society as a whole.

This history is rooted in what Nora and his colleagues have called *lieux de mémoire,* or mnemonic sites, embodying concrete traces of the past, visible and durable signs of its celebration. The history of memory can arise out of the memory of a particular group: the Camisards, for example, as studied by Philippe Joutard,[3] or combat veterans, as studied by Antoine Prost.[4] But it may also be associated with certain key events, whose memory survives long after the last flames have been extinguished and whose influence extends over the whole of society: examples include the French Revolution, of course,[5] the wars in the Vendée that grew out of it and have attracted renewed attention,[6] and World War II.[7] Historians are interested not only in ascertaining the facts about such events but also in comprehending their persistence.

It is no accident that these events were all associated with times of deep crisis for France's national unity and identity. These are the times that have left the most lasting, most controversial, and most vivid memories—all the more so in that each new crisis has fed upon its predecessors: the Dreyfus Affair on the French Revolution, Vichy on the Dreyfus Affair, the Algerian War on Vichy, and so on. Memories of the past have themselves become components of the crisis, albeit at times of secondary importance.[8]

An "event-oriented" approach is useful in that it allows giving due weight to the tensions involved in any would-be collective representation of the past. Such tensions arise, first of all, among rival social groups, each jealous of its own reconstruction. An ex-POW will not share the same memories as a former partisan or a person deported to a concentration camp. There may also be tensions between such group memories and what might be called the "dominant memory," that is, a collective interpretation of the past that may even come to have official status; here, for example, I am thinking of Gaullist or Communist memory. There may also be tension between, on the one hand, the "voluntarist" memory that builds monuments, decorates graves, and buries heroes and, on the other hand, latent or implicit memory, subject to repression and therefore to slips, lapses, or silences—manifestations of the return of the repressed. For study reveals that, even at the social level, memory is a structuring of forgetfulness.

These same tensions also exist in the writing of history. Whether professional or amateur, the historian is always a product of his own time and place. He stands at a crossroads in the byways of collective memory: on the one hand he, like any other citizen, is influenced by the dominant memory, which may subconsciously suggest interpretations and areas of research; on the other hand, he himself is a "vector of memory" and a carrier of fundamental importance, in that the vision he proposes of the past may, after some delay, exert an influence on contemporary representations.

As a result, the history of the Revolution, Vichy, or the Algerian War cannot really be called universal. Now that history no longer has the purpose of forging a national identity, it has no therapeutic value, and in the short term, at least, it often has the effect of perpetuating old divisions, as a glance at the controversial nature of the so-called *guerre franco-française,* or Franco-French internal war, will show. And of those wars none has been more divisive than the war over Vichy.

Why Vichy?

Krzysztof Pomian writes that "when the time is right, an era of the past may serve as a screen on which new generations can project their contradictions, controversies, and conflicts in objectified form."[9] Something like this seems to have happened in the early 1970s with respect to memories of the Occupation. It has therefore been necessary to return to the source in order to locate those aspects of the event itself that were likely to survive the crisis and resurface once it had passed.

Why have memories of the Occupation (1940–1944) proved so enduring and controversial? The first reason is of course that the tragedy that France suffered in those years was one of unprecedented gravity. The country, already shaken by the events of the 1930s, was subjected within a few short years to a series of terrible blows. The war of 1939–40 was brief but disastrous: some 90,000 French soldiers died, and nearly two million French troops were taken prisoner. Crushing and unexpected military defeat led to a humiliating and ferocious occupation by foreign troops. Metropolitan France was divided into separate zones, and the Empire disintegrated as Vichy and de Gaulle vied for control of its component countries. Within France, civil war attained its peak in 1944 but continued after the Liberation in the form of the so-called *épuration,* or purge of those alleged to have collaborated with the Nazis. Finally, France rejoined the Allied war effort in 1944–45 as it also began to face the problems of economic, political, and moral reconstruction. Such well-known facts scarcely bear repeating except to emphasize that these wrenching events were squeezed into a period roughly equal to the term of a single legislature in peacetime; the French had no time to grasp, come to terms with, and mourn what had befallen them in one catastrophe before they found themselves caught up in yet another. It was under Vichy, and with Vichy, that people first began to take the measure of the defeat, and it was through the purge that the majority of Frenchmen became aware of what the Pétain regime had been.

Furthermore, the fall of France in 1940 undermined an imperial power, a state that appeared to rest on solid underpinnings. In the space of a few weeks, the country's institutions crumbled along with its military, political, and local elites. The normal channels of trade and distribution were suddenly cut off. Authority seemed to have evaporated somewhere between Paris and Bordeaux: nothing of the kind had ever been seen in the history of a major modern state.

The very name given to the regime that succeeded the Third Republic and administered its coup de grâce focuses attention on this sudden power vacuum. For the new regime was called *l'Etat français*, or French State (as opposed to *la république française*), an appellation that has about it something of a magical incantation. The "state" allegedly created in a casino in Vichy on 10 July 1940 was precisely what was just then crumbling to pieces. *L'Etat français* was from the beginning a nonstate. Its program of internal reconstruction and modernization grew out of this vacuum. As has often been pointed out, the tragedy of Vichy lay in its belief that it could somehow fill the abyss that had suddenly opened up beneath the feet of the French in June 1940, and that it could do so under the watchful eyes of the occupying forces. The people of France, left to their own devices and to the Germans, buffeted between Pétain's reassuring words and the harsh realities of the Occupation, and subject to various authorities all of questionable legitimacy, would long remember the bitter taste of this collapse, much as they would have liked to forget it.

No doubt the crucial feature of the Vichy regime, however, was the large number of internal conflicts that erupted between 1940 and 1944, conflicts that make Vichy the very archetype of the *guerre franco-française*. Already in the 1930s there had been clashes over the nature of the dangers threatening France: some people, especially on the left, saw the principal danger as fascism and Nazism, even within France's own borders; others believed that the chief threat came from the Popular Front and the Communists. The only point these opposing views had in common was their emphasis on the "enemy within," particularly on the right. First the Munich crisis and then the armistice led to a solidification of these positions, although there were of course some who changed sides or views at the last minute. Eventually the line came to be clearly drawn between the Collaboration and the Resistance, groupings diverse in themselves though clearly differentiated.

But this major division masked others that sometimes ran deeper still. Old but never-effaced differences stemming from the Revolution and the Dreyfus Affair resurfaced during the Occupation: the battle against republican institutions, from the constitutional acts to various

6

clerical proposals made in 1940 and 1941, was a Vichyite obsession, even if the conflict was less bitter than it seemed at the time. Similarly, Vichy's antisemitism, which had concrete, official ramifications in law and justice, was inspired not by Nazism but by French antisemitic traditions.

At the same time, social antagonisms stemming from the events of 1936 erupted with violence. As is well known, the Vichy regime was in many respects—from the organization of production to the abortive Riom trials—a form of revenge against the Popular Front. Not all leading industrialists were collaborators, any more than all workers were members of the Resistance. Nevertheless, awareness of the gulf separating the two sides was sufficiently acute at the time that it gave rise, justifiably or not, to persistent hatreds.

So numerous were these internal divisions that it is not unreasonable to refer to them collectively as a civil war. To some the use of the term may seem shocking: in France there was nothing comparable to what took place in Spain in 1936 or in Greece during and after the war or in Yugoslavia, to say nothing of Germany and Italy. Yet France was a country steeped in a democratic and republican parliamentary tradition, and this was the first time since the Commune that its internecine struggles had taken on so murderous and radical a character.

The Vichy regime and the collaborationists were directly responsible for the imprisonment of 135,000 people, the internment of 70,000 suspects (including numerous political refugees from central Europe), and the dismissal of 35,000 civil servants.[10] As victims of exclusionary laws, 60,000 freemasons were investigated, 6,000 harassed, and 549 (of 989) died in the camps.[11] The French governmental apparatus, together with parties in the pay of the Germans, abetted the deportation of 76,000 French and foreign Jews, fewer than 3 percent of whom survived. They also worked to send 650,000 workers to Germany as conscript labor and waged unremitting battle against the Resistance and all other opponents of the regime. Admittedly, Vichy and the collaborationists were not directly responsible for all the executions, extortions, and deportations. Today, however, there can be no doubt that many victims of the era were claimed not by the foreign occupation or military conflict but by internal struggles in which Vichy figured as the initial issue: this is a fact, not an ideological prejudice.

7

It is also true that the struggle waged by Free French and resistance forces left bloody traces as well. Roughly 10,000 people were killed without trial or other legal authorization by the Provisional Government; a good half of these summary executions were carried out prior to 6 June 1944 (D-Day), thus *en pleine Occupation*. Of 160,287 cases examined by military and civilian courts, 45 percent ended in dismissal or acquittal, 25 percent in *dégradation nationale* (national dishonor) and loss of civil rights, and 24 percent in prison terms, a third of these being terms at hard labor for a limited period or for life. Finally, 7,037 people were sentenced to death, and perhaps 1500 were actually executed. In addition, the purge of the professions, while not equally thorough or equitable in all sectors of the economy, affected some 150 business executives and managers, some of considerable importance, as well as some 700 educators, to cite just these two figures.[12]

To this total must be added the thousands of deaths resulting from battles in western Africa and Syria between soldiers who remained loyal to Vichy and others who rallied to Free France. In sum, then, the fratricidal struggles of the Occupation were by no means a "cold" or merely "verbal" civil war but a civil war *tout court*, at least when seen within the context of French history. And civil wars have always been the hardest to deal with afterward, for in a foreign war the enemy goes home when hostilities end—in a civil war the "enemy" remains.

These factors stemming from the domestic situation in France were compounded by the general characteristics of World War II. To begin with, it was an ideological war, unlike World War I. In this sense, divisions within France largely overlapped worldwide divisions born of the confrontation between the century's three great political systems: fascism/Nazism, communism, and representative democracy, a confrontation whose echoes would continue to resound long after 8 May 1945 (V-E Day).

Second, the war produced profound upheavals everywhere, including France. The Blitzkrieg of 1940 and the bombings of 1943–1945 demonstrated the power of technology to a panicky population. Most people were obsessed with memories of the trench warfare and wholesale bloodletting of World War I and therefore failed to grasp the

significance of changes in the scale of warfare. But a few did, as
General de Gaulle's appeal to the French nation on 18 June 1940
makes clear: "Devastated today by mechanical force, we will be able
to conquer in the future by a superior mechanical force: therein hangs
the fate of the world." Panic at the collapse of state and society was
accompanied by a growing awareness that only a strong state could
cope with serious difficulties ranging from economic crisis to war itself, deal with the new technologies, and above all ensure the security
of its citizens: such was the inevitable corollary to be drawn from the
disorders engendered by these profound changes. The American historian William H. McNeill has even gone so far as to suggest that the
"welfare state" was a direct product of the "warfare state."[13]

Finally, after the Armenians, Manchurians, Germans, Russians,
Spaniards, and Jews of Europe, the French during the war came face
to face with the brutality of the twentieth century: mass terror, concentration camps, the systematic use of death as a political weapon.

But the ubiquitous state, technology, and organized violence are
only one side of the coin; the other involves the globalization of trade,
the unification of the marketplace, and the convergence of people's
outlooks over a large portion of the planet. So it makes sense to claim
that to a large extent it was World War II that gave birth to the world
as we know it today. The birth occurred not only in pain but in alien-
ation and division. And these circumstances, too, are part of the reason why the French (and others) have had such a difficult time coming
to terms with this period of the past.

Why approach the problem by way of Vichy? Why not, for example, ask the same kinds of questions about the remembrance and
memory of the Resistance? The Resistance and resistance fighters are
of course present in these pages, but whole aspects of the story have
been deliberately left out. Nor have I dealt with the Communist memory of the war (which would require more than one book) or with
the memories of various groups having a special attachment to the
period, a subject that has been studied by others.[14]

My working hypothesis is this: the civil war, and particularly the
inception, influence, and acts of the Vichy regime, played an essential
if not primary role in the difficulties that the people of France have
faced in reconciling themselves to their history—a greater role than
the foreign occupation, the war, and the defeat, all things that, though

they have not vanished from people's minds, are generally perceived through the prism of Vichy.

Rather like the unconscious in Freudian theory, what is known as collective memory exists first of all in its *manifestations,* in the various ways by which it reveals its presence. The Vichy syndrome consists of a diverse set of symptoms whereby the trauma of the Occupation, and particularly that trauma resulting from internal divisions within France, reveals itself in political, social, and cultural life. Since the end of the war, moreover, that trauma has been perpetuated and at times exacerbated.

A chronological ordering of these symptoms brings into focus a four-stage process of evolution. Between 1944 and 1954 France had to deal directly with the aftermath of civil war, purge, and amnesty. I call this the "mourning phase," whose contradictions had a considerable impact on what came afterward. From 1954 to 1971 the subject of Vichy became less controversial, except for occasional eruptions in the period 1958–1962. The French apparently had repressed memories of the civil war with the aid of what came to be a dominant myth: "resistancialism." This term, first coined after the Liberation by adversaries of the purge, is used here in a rather different sense. By resistancialism I mean, first, a process that sought to minimize the importance of the Vichy regime and its impact on French society, *including its most negative aspects;* second, the construction of an object of memory, the "Resistance," whose significance transcended by far the sum of its active parts (the small groups of guerrilla partisans who did the actual fighting) and whose existence was embodied chiefly in certain sites and groups, such as the Gaullists and Communists, associated with fully elaborated ideologies; and, third, the identification of this "Resistance" with the nation as a whole, a characteristic feature of the Gaullist version of the myth.

Between 1971 and 1974 this carefully constructed myth was shattered; the mirror was broken. This was the third phase of the process, which is analyzed here as a "return of the repressed." In turn this inaugurated a fourth phase, continuing to this day: a phase of obsession, characterized on the one hand by the reawakening of Jewish memory and, on the other, by the importance that reminiscences of the Occupation assumed in French political debate.

The first part of the book thus attempts to trace the contours of a "neurosis." What is borrowed from psychoanalysis is simply a metaphor, not an explanatory schema. No attempt is made to sort out different types of symptoms: an offhand remark by a French president is treated on the same level as the scandal triggered by a film or a notorious political trial. At this stage of the argument, all that matters is the patent topicality of a reference to the past, however insignificant it may be in itself.

In the second part, however, I attempt to establish a hierarchy of symptoms by investigating the vectors of the past, particularly those that played a decisive role in the history of the syndrome: commemorations, film, and historiography (including both historical research and teaching). I consider commemorations because of their apparent failure to construct an official memory of the past; film because visual images seem to have had a decisive impact on the formation of a common, if not a collective, memory; and historiography because historians and their books are a primary vector of memory.

Finally, after analyzing the vectors of memory and studying the formulation of the signs used to represent the past (or reveal its existence), I turn my attention to the recipients, to what might be called "diffuse memory" as opposed to the organized memory of groups and political parties and of scholarly re-creation. This is, indeed, the ultimate winner in the contest among representations because it cannot by itself formulate a coherent and operational vision of the past that is anything other than individual. The question here is: were French people of various ages and outlooks influenced by the representations offered to them?

Based on the idea that the past survives in an active form in the present and on the assumption that such survival can be studied historically, this book is intended to be open-ended. So I make no claim to have said the last word on the subject. And one final remark: I have tried within the limits of my power not to become a prisoner of the syndrome I am describing.

Part I

Evolution of the Syndrome

I

⟶⟨⟨◉⟩⟩⟶

Unfinished Mourning
(1944–1954)

An objective (and optimistic) view of the postwar period customarily sees it as divided into two successive phases: Liberation and Reconstruction. First night, then light. Yet the decade that followed the end of the Occupation was a difficult period of mourning, one that involved not only the usual and traditional grieving for those killed or wounded in the war, as had occurred after 1918, but also a more complex and controversial coming to terms with France's internal injuries. The "crises of memory" that would repeat themselves in later years originated in this period, when the French nation found itself incapable of dealing fully with the trauma it had suffered.

The Liberation: A Screen Memory

When the nightmare finally ended, France experienced a joy so profound that memory of those first "fair days" lingered on through two generations. According to a poll carried out in 1983, the Liberation of 1944 and the Armistice of 1940 ranked first and second on the list of "the most important events of the last forty years" (cited, respectively, by 51 and 31 percent of those polled).[1] Despite all the subsequent upheavals, the war thus retained its paramount significance in the minds of the French. Logically, however, the armistice (and therefore the defeat) should have ranked first: the cause precedes the effect. In retrospect, however, the hierarchy of representations, in which the positive or negative character of an event is allowed to color its historical importance, has supplanted the hierarchy of the facts.

That, at any rate, is the way a positivist historian might view these poll results. In fact, however, the years 1944 and 1945 were of crucial importance, not only in themselves (that is a subject for another

15

book) but as the period when retrospective visions of the Occupation first began to take shape. Because of the need to limit the repercussions of the war, and because rival political forces attempted to exploit an ambivalent heritage to their own advantage, collective memory of still fresh events quickly crystallized around a small set of central ideas and images:

> Paris! Paris humiliated! Paris broken! Paris martyrized! But Paris liberated! Liberated by itself, by its own people with the help of the armies of France, with the support and aid of France as a whole, of fighting France, of the only France, of the true France, of eternal France.

With these few sentences, spoken on 25 August 1944, Charles de Gaulle established the founding myth of the post-Vichy period. His legitimacy unchallenged, the General subsequently lost no opportunity to write and rewrite the history of the war years. The vision he proposed sprang solely from his imagination.

According to this vision, the rest of France, like the city of Paris, had liberated itself. In his 25 August speech at the Hôtel de Ville, General de Gaulle did not mention "our beloved and admirable allies" until near the end. Neither did he have much to say about the Resistance or resistance fighters (résistants), whose contribution had been merely circumstantial. Salvation came from "eternal France," an abstraction that became a keystone of Gaullist symbolism. Thus one powerful image, the military defeat of 1940, was effaced by arms and by the nation as a whole. And like all representations with collective value, this one was not entirely devoid of objective significance: it was true that, thanks to de Gaulle's efforts, a French division had been the first to enter Paris; it was also true that vast tracts of French territory, particularly in the southwest, had seen virtually no Allied troops.

If, however, "France" thus remained inviolate, what role in this vision of events was to be accorded Vichy and collaboration? This question was answered as rapidly as the other. On the same day, 25 August 1944, Georges Bidault, flanked by the members of the Conseil National de la Résistance (CNR), which he chaired, and by the Comité Parisien de Libération, came to request that the leader of Free France "formally proclaim the Republic before the people here assembled." Bidault received this sovereign reply:

> The Republic has never ceased to exist. Free France, fighting France, [and] the French Committee of National Liberation have by turns embodied it. Vichy was and is null and void. I myself am the president of the government of the Republic. Why should I proclaim it?[2]

This response was of course political. In memoirs published after the Algerian War, Bidault stated that, since neither he nor any other member of the CNR knew what de Gaulle intended to say on the balcony of the Hôtel de Ville, they had wished "from the outset to avoid any possibility of misunderstanding."[3] Nevertheless, de Gaulle's statement illustrates the way in which Vichy was simply enclosed in parentheses.

On 2 April 1945, Flag Day, when regimental flags were returned to the units of France's resurrected army, de Gaulle continued in much the same vein, this time attempting to blur the specificity of the Nazi occupation:

> France is gaining a clear idea of what needs to be done to repair the damage wrought by this war, begun some thirty years ago . . . In the moral realm, seeds of dissension subsist and must be eliminated at all cost. We have paid dearly for those seeds, sown by countless internal conflicts and coupled, of course, with repeated invasions, for our domestic battles have never failed to invite quick foreign intervention.[4]

This concept of a "thirty years' war" was another major component of Gaullist symbolism. Combining the two world wars in a single unit made it possible to focus on military matters and thus divert attention from unique aspects of World War II: the role of irregular partisans, ideological conflict, and the genocide. True, the deportees had yet to return, and the war, in which elements of the regular French army were participating, was not yet over. De Gaulle's statement was also an attempt to overcome internal divisions through a call for unity, indeed for *union sacrée*. Closely linked to the "invasions," France's internecine struggles would have no reason to continue once the enemy was defeated. Of course the General did not wish to deny the existence of conflict between supporters and adversaries of Nazism, but his interpretation obscured the specific internal causes of that conflict. Finally, it anticipated ultimate victory, echoing the victory of 1918 when joy was unalloyed, without any hint of discomfort or shame.

17

This coherent, relatively self-contained view constitutes what I shall call the "Gaullist resistancialist myth." This myth did not so much glorify the Resistance (and certainly not the résistants) as it celebrated a people *in resistance,* a people symbolized exclusively by the "man of June Eighteenth" (de Gaulle), without intermediaries such as political parties, movements, or clandestine leaders. [It was on 18 June 1940 that de Gaulle broadcast his appeal to the French nation, calling on the people of France to resist the Nazi invasion.] This image was to be superimposed on the far more complex and inconsistent realities of the Occupation. Its unavowed objective was to present an interpretation of the past in light of the urgent needs of the present. Yet de Gaulle by himself could not cope with the demands of restoring the republican order while at the same time providing a smoothly polished image of complex events that had been experienced by millions of people in very different ways. The Gaullist myth was launched, but it did not really take hold until much later and even then for only a short time.

Although resistance fighters often were missing from de Gaulle's speeches, they occupied, in the immediate postwar period at any rate, a prominent place on the political scene. The history of France from 1944 to 1947 has been explored by many, and I do not wish to reexamine it here. Suffice it to say that the entire right wing of French politics, including the traditional rightist parties, was totally discredited in these years. Indeed, the collapse of the Vichy regime had come close to signaling "its irrevocable doom."[5] To give some specific examples: 302 deputies and senators were made ineligible for election to public office because they had voted to grant "full powers" to Marshal Pétain or had participated in the Vichy regime; of these, 163, or more than half, had belonged to the parliamentary center or right in 1936; 79 others came from the Radical family of parties, and 52 from the SFIO (Socialists). In the daily press, communist, socialist, and resistance papers accounted for more than half the circulation, and the readership of communist dailies had quadrupled compared with prewar figures. Finally, a sample of a thousand legislators elected to office during the Fourth Republic shows that two-thirds had been associated with formations of the Resistance or Free France.[6]

The country's political leaders, their ranks partially replenished, would henceforth make a fetish of the Resistance, which, despite its rather vague definition, became a quasi-sacred symbol. Membership was claimed as a coveted prize, a key that could open all doors. The Resistance was integrated into all the political ideologies of the day as an essential motif. But the left was perhaps keener than the right to install the Resistance in the pantheon of republican values. It therefore developed its own version of the "resistancialist myth," which differed from the Gaullist version in that it incorporated political parties and movements. Keenest of all were the Communists, who before long were describing themselves as the "party of 75,000 *fusillés*," those shot dead by the Germans.

But the resistance aura (one sign of whose potency can be seen in the way former résistants have kept up personal ties for more than forty years despite growing ideological differences) proved more useful within party caucuses than out on the stump. In the first postwar elections, the winners were largely the same men who had been politically prominent before the war, regardless of whether they had played an active role in opposing the Germans. The Resistance changed the composition of the upper strata of France's political class but had no apparent effect on the lower levels:

> Of the 90 percent of the French population that applauded the Liberation in August 1944, how many, even in the popular classes, felt, because of the Resistance, a commitment to envision in its image entirely new structures of political participation? No doubt very few. Classical republican democracy was so deeply rooted in French habits that the party organizations (even in parties that had been faint-hearted or absent between 1940 and 1944) were probably more genuinely popular in 1945 than were the committees of unknown heroes.[7]

A novel tension is evident in this passage. The postwar citizen clung to the reassuring image of a resisting France, but the desire for a return to normality and the wish to forget the exceptional circumstances of the Occupation stood in the way of any real consecration of the Resistance. This contradiction became evident with the failure, in the summer of 1945, to establish a grand "Party of the Resistance." The triumph of the triparty system indicated not only a refusal to experiment with institutional change, something of which both de Gaulle and the various resistance movements dreamed (each in a different way), but also a consecration of the traditional parties, which had gained strength in the struggle against the occupying forces or found other ways to exploit the resistance heritage.

This ambivalence—between an emotional commitment to the idea of the French people united in resistance coupled with a refusal to accept the résistants as the postwar political elite—was a crucial feature of the still inchoate view of the past I am attempting to describe. It calls attention to certain central complexities and ambiguities in the concept of resistance, a concept that embraces not only a historical phenomenon with political and military aspects but also the individuals behind that phenomenon and attitudes shared by large numbers of people.

After the war, some sort of purge (*épuration*) was inevitable. The postwar "purification" affected not only political parties but also professions and ideologies. It also marked a milestone in the representation of the Occupation, for it was on the basis of values stemming from those dark years that judgments, including death sentences, were handed down.

While some collaborators were charged with crimes, torture, or slander under provisions of the standard penal code, most were prosecuted under Article 75, a provision adopted in 1939 that made "intelligence with the enemy" a crime. Although this article stood on fairly solid legal ground, it was politically less secure. Nothing was said about ideological commitment, of which patriotism was not the sole determinant. How were the courts to judge men who laid claim to "a certain vision of France," though obviously not the same as de Gaulle's? Did the European fascists have a "fatherland"? Was not the anti-Nazi struggle a war with no frontiers?

The sentences meted out by the courts varied widely. The severity of punishment depended, first of all, on the nature of the court: military tribunals were generally more lenient than civilian courts and were willing to consider the "sincere convictions" that may have motivated individuals to join the Milice (Vichy's paramilitary arm) or the LVF. Another factor was the social status of the defendant: businessmen and engineers were treated more leniently than journalists because the former were less in the public eye and, even more important, because their services were indispensable to postwar economic recovery. Still a third factor was the date of the trial: it was better to appear in court after 1945 than before.

As was only logical in what was in effect a civil war, a *guerre franco-française,* the purge itself gave rise to deep divisions, which grew even deeper as the Liberation receded into the past. In a book published in 1953 and awarded the Prix de la Résistance in the following year, Jean Cassou, one of the first to join the Resistance, voiced a bitterness typical of a whole generation of resistance fighters:

> The judgments of the courts were generally nothing but shams, which never got to the heart of what was fundamentally a simple issue. No one learned anything from the trials of Pétain and Maurras, neither those unwilling to learn nor those who needed to learn. Maurras was convicted for having slandered a neighbor in one of his last articles. But what about all the people he slandered in countless other articles? What about a half century of [the extremist rightwing political organization] Action Française?[8]

From another part of the political spectrum, Charles Rist, a political moderate but fiercely anti-Pétain, spoke for many whose commitments were less than categorical. In his diary on 28 January 1945 he wrote:

> Most people were disgusted by the arbitrariness and groundlessness of the arrests and by the jailing of men with spotless reputations . . . Special courts flourished as they had done under Vichy . . . Drancy [a prison camp] operated as it had in the time of the Boches.[9]

The purge thus made everybody unhappy, because it had proved impossible to strike a satisfactory compromise between traditional justice, which was what most moderates (as well as those with most to lose politically) were calling for, and the need to root out fascism. The dilemma was not merely moral: the law versus legitimate revenge, short-term memory versus persistent bitterness. It was also political, and the most intransigent of all were the Communists. The purge had a major influence on all subsequent memory of the Occupation—in many ways a new conflict supplanted the old one. A purely domestic affair, trumpeted by a free and unfettered press, this new division was no less virulent than the one it replaced. It too gave rise to derogatory myths: it was alleged, for example, that 100,000 people had been summarily executed (in fact the number was one-tenth that large[10]) or that "red soviets," particularly in southwestern France, were making political threats.[11]

21

Given these competing myths and the resurgence of internal dissension, the first official celebrations of the Resistance could hardly have been expected to unify the nation.

World War I, a cataclysm without precedent, had claimed nearly a million and a half lives and left millions of others maimed—visible walking reminders of the slaughter. The memory of the trenches had found symbolic embodiment in a universally admired archetype: the combat veteran. As Antoine Prost has forcefully demonstrated, the principal message bequeathed by the survivors of that conflict was one that spoke to the senses; it was a message first of physical suffering and then of mental anguish. Indeed, pain could assume an exemplary and even edifying character for future generations. The crucial values were "love of life, pride at not having buckled under, and a sense of having stood by one's comrades and having been able to count on them."[12] After this national sacrifice, which had gone virtually uncontested until 1917, the French were joined in mourning. As a result, the countless statues of *poilus* (infantrymen) that embellish village squares throughout France have the same features carved into their limestone or marble, and the heroic victory is uncontroversially marked by a single date each year: 11 November, Armistice Day.

The end of World War II brought forth no similar outpouring of grief. Of the 600,000 French dead, only a third had died weapon in hand. The rest had vanished in bombardments, executions, massacres, and deportations or had fallen victim to internal combat in France or its colonies. Traditional forms of commemoration were inappropriate to such circumstances. Hence the authorities maintained a discreet silence about the war and its memories. On 7 July 1946, in the presence of Paul Reynaud, Léon Blum, Edouard Daladier, Albert Sarraut, Joseph Paul-Boncour, and thousands of others, Alexandre Varennes, representing the government, unveiled in the forest of Fontainebleau a monument to Georges Mandel, who had been executed by the Milice. Engraved on the face of the stone were the words: "Here died Georges Mandel, murdered by the enemies of France on 7 July 1944." Those enemies remained nameless and faceless; they might have been not *miliciens* but Germans, and in the mind of today's casual tourist they probably are.[13]

This is hardly an isolated example. Monuments to the dead of World War II are extremely rare. Most of the memorial steles honor

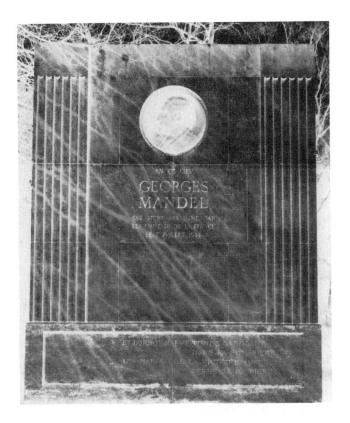

Memorial to Georges Mandel

South of Fontainebleau on National Highway 7, the Georges Mandel memorial was dedicated on 7 July 1946. Attending the ceremonies were Paul Reynaud, Léon Blum, Pierre Cot, Edouard Daladier, Albert Sarraut, Joseph Paul-Boncour, and the son of Winston Churchill. The monument was designed by the architect Nicod and the sculptor François Cogné, known for his statues of political leaders including the one of Clemenceau that stands on the Champs-Elysées. The stele marks the place where Mandel was killed by French miliciens, who had previously taken him from the Santé prison where the Germans had sent him after his deportation to Germany. The inscription reads:
"And when he fell bloody in the dust, Victory's hands closed his eyelids.
—Tristan L'Hermite." (Photo Constant Anée)

the victims of "the two wars," with the names of those killed between 1939 and 1945 added to the longer as well as more prominently placed list of those killed between 1914 and 1918.[14]

After the war hundreds of associations were formed, establishing what amounts to a veritable hierarchy of suffering: the volunteer resistance fighter did not wish to be confused with the "racial" deportee; the deportee did not wish to be mistaken for a prisoner of war; the prisoner of war was careful to distinguish himself from the "*déporté du travail*," the laborer "deported" to work in Germany for the Reich (and here the quotation marks are meant to signify a fierce battle, still raging today, over the precise significance of STO service). As for the victims of the purge (whether executed or simply murdered), their memory lives on in every corner of France—but nowhere is it inscribed in stone.

The period 1944–1946 saw many celebrations of the Liberation or victory, in itself proof that France was incapable of constructing a unified national memory of the event. The series of celebrations began in the autumn of 1944, when the Communist Party honored the victims of the clandestine war in ceremonies at Père-Lachaise in Paris, in Ivry, and in Chateaubriant. The party even managed to take charge of the 1944 Armistice Day celebration "in homage to the soldiers of 1914–1918, to the heroes who for four years have been fighting outside France as well as on the very soil of the fatherland," as one National Front brochure put it.[15] (The National Front was a Communist mass organization.) Of course those who had been fighting "outside France" included not only the Free French of London and Algiers but also Communist leader Maurice Thorez, in Moscow during the war. Similarly, the "four years" in question were already being presented as a monolith, with a discreet veil drawn over the party's "dialectical" attitude between 1939 and 1941.

In January 1945 a dispute erupted over which of three men would be added to the Pantheon, the Paris monument to deceased heroes of the republic: Romain Rolland, supported by the Communists; Charles Péguy, backed by *Le Figaro;* or Henri Bergson, favored by the MRP. Which choice would be most significant: the antifascist intellectual, the patriot of 1914, or the Jewish philosopher? As it happens, none of the three was admitted. It was not until 1964 that the "Ecole Normale des Morts" would induct a wartime hero, none other than Jean Moulin.[16] On 12 February 1945 the left celebrated the anniversary of the antifascist strike of 1934 and thus a civil war that had raged for eleven years, from the dawn of the Popular Front to the Liberation, while on 2 April, Flag Day, de Gaulle, whose vision was always more farsighted than most, celebrated the "thirty years' war." July Fourteenth, Bastille Day, was celebrated mainly as a day of popular rejoicing, from which politics was temporarily absent.

Given this logic of events, it is not surprising that the only ceremony that took on any genuine importance was Armistice Day, 11 November 1945. Even the celebration of 8 May 1945, the day Germany officially surrendered, was relatively quiet, according to reports of the prefects.[17] On Armistice Day, however, the government had decided that the remains of fifteen French citizens would be brought to the tomb of the unknown soldier: two who had fought with the Resistance inside France, one man and one woman; two deportees, one man and one woman (both combatants rather than "racial" deportees); one prisoner shot while attempting to escape; one member of the Forces Françaises de l'Intérieur (FFI); and nine soldiers from various branches of the military and theaters of operation. The ceremony was grandiose, a sort of condensation of all war commemorations past and future, and what it revealed was a real consensus for this date, the true national holiday of 1945.

Spectators at the earliest French parades had glimpsed the striped pajamas worn by deportees, but these were soon banished from official commemorations. The return of victims from the Nazi concentration camps was the event most quickly effaced from memory. The earliest informed articles about the camps had appeared in the winter of 1944: in the 15 December 1944 issue of *Action* Roger Vaillant described the liberation of the Struthof camp in Alsace, and in the 10 January 1945 issue of *Ce soir* Georges Soria relied on Soviet army dispatches to depict the freeing of Maidanek.[18]

The most terrible shock, however, came in April, when the first trainloads of camp survivors arrived in Paris. Many expected to find the returnees in roughly the same condition as the prisoners of war. Olga Wormser-Migot, who was involved in the process of repatriation, attests to the abyss between expectation and reality:

When the Gare d'Orsay was suggested as a place to receive the survivors, no thought was given to their condition. It was assumed that after completing the necessary formalities, they would be able to return home and resume normal life . . . Could we have known?[19]

Ultimately it was not Orsay that was chosen, but the Hôtel Lutétia (which had served as Abwehr offices during the Occupation). "The victims are still a nuisance," Emmanuel Mounier ironically observed in September 1945. "Why, some of them are even disfigured. Their complaints are tiresome for those whose only wish is to return as quickly as possible to peace and quiet."[20] Many of the returnees had managed to survive only because they hoped to bear witness to what they had endured, yet they were met with rejection and repression. It was another missed opportunity, and one that proved to be the source of much bitterness and misunderstanding. It was not until 1954 that France established a Journée de la Déportation (Day to Commemorate the Deportation), and it would take thirty years for memory to be rekindled in those Jews who had escaped the genocide.

The Liberation thus represents an intermediate stage between the Occupation and the memory of the event. It contains in embryonic form the chief characteristics of the Vichy syndrome, which initially took the guise of ambivalences and rivalries.

Between the darkest episodes in this history—the civil war and the deportation—and the most heroic chapters, there was an unresolved tension. This tension gave rise to an ambiguous attitude toward the Resistance, and it left feelings of fear, bitterness, and dissatisfaction about the postwar purge. Official commemorations created symbols that only partially captured the memory of the war. Many important issues were ignored. Memory of the war would therefore develop largely outside this official framework, which had gained acceptance only at the cost of distorting the realities. At the same time, partisan memories and rivalries blocked the formation of a more accurate "official" memory.

The Communists, for instance, emphasized the clandestine struggle, the antifascist war, and the class war against a "treasonous" elite. In their view the resistance fighters were the heirs of 1793 and the Commune, whereas Pétain was an emulator of Bazaine, the traitor who surrendered to the Prussians in 1870.

The Gaullist view stressed military aspects and republican legitimacy. The resistance fighters had been heroic, to be sure, but they had done no more than their duty as soldiers. The "resistance," for its part, had stemmed from France as a whole, from the France of Joan of Arc and the *poilus*. This rewriting of history responded to a widely felt need, but it did not suit everyone. In particular it irritated many *anciens résistants,* who came to feel a lasting bitterness against de Gaulle. Some were frankly outraged: "De Gaulle uttered these criminal words: 'The time for tears is over. The time of glory has returned.' We will never forgive him," wrote the novelist Marguerite Duras as she waited in anguish for her husband to return from Dachau.[21] It should come as no surprise, then, to discover that the Gaullist view did not displease the segment of the public that remained loyal to Marshal Pétain, those Fred Kupferman has dubbed the *pétaino-gaullistes* who, frightened by an already distorted image of the purge, dreamed of a different epilogue: "Reciprocal amnesty, maintenance of what was good in Vichy's legislative accomplishments, [and] a common war against Germany."[22] Was not Pétain an essential part of de Gaulle's "eternal France," and was he not also—indeed, supremely— a "member of the resistance"? This new myth caught on more quickly than anyone could foresee: it may be that no new heroes were actually inducted into the Pantheon, but there was no shortage of candidates.

The Cold Civil War

Events moved quickly. The historical sequence that had begun in Munich, continued through the war, and culminated in the Liberation finally came to an end in 1947. The beginning of the cold war raised new fears of global conflict. Shortages led to social tensions, and people were impatient for the "rutabaga era" to end. Meanwhile, the dismissal of Communist ministers from the government on 14 May cut short that misbegotten legacy of the Resistance, triparty rule. Anticommunism quickly became the dominant force in French politics, as the right dropped its mask and raised its true colors.

In this context the Occupation took on a new cast. It became, as the Liberation suggested it would, a vast reservoir of symbolic references upon which the political parties drew as issues of the day required. The nation had endured a rocky period of mourning between

1944 and 1947. Now the premature rebirth of internal divisions ended that mourning before it was complete.

As government after government drifted rightward, France witnessed the revival of "neo-Vichyite" sentiment, despite the fact that the Vichy era had once been presumed permanently discredited. As early as 1945, right-wing reactionaries had braved the purge and attempted to reestablish their presence. Several more or less clandestine newsletters began publication: *Les Documents nationaux,* of Maurrassian inspiration; *Questions actuelles,* the paper of the self-styled "national opposition"; and *Paroles françaises,* edited by André Mutter, a former member of Croix-de-Feu and onetime resistance fighter who was elected as an independent deputy for Aube and who became a cofounder of the short-lived Parti Républicain de la Liberté, which engaged in violent attacks on Mutter's former "comrades." Although *Paroles françaises* achieved a circulation as high as 100,000, none of the other publications ever had more than a few thousand readers.[23]

In 1947 this neo-Vichyite current broadened with the publication of the first issue of René Malliavin's *Ecrits de Paris* and the reemergence of a regular publication with the official sanction of the Action Française, *Aspects de la France.* In 1951 Malliavin also launched *Rivarol,* named in honor of the counterrevolutionary who had fought the Terror as Malliavin and his friends had fought the purge. Its pages contained articles by some of the leading writers of occupied Paris, such as Alfred Fabre-Luce and Marcel Jouhandeau, along with such promising young talents as François Brigneau, the future editorial writer for *Minute.*

In the same year, 1951, a new concept was formed, highly prized on the right: *résistantialisme,* spelled with a *t* rather than a *c* (as in what I have been calling "resistancialism"). The difference is crucial. The word *résistantialisme* has a pejorative connotation aimed directly at the résistants, especially those whose bravado was allegedly displayed only in the final days of the war. The Resistance itself, ever more vaguely defined, thus remained inviolate. In directing its attack against individuals, the neo-Vichyite right sought to coopt a symbol that still had positive value in the eyes of the public while at the same time denouncing the evils perpetrated by those responsible for the purge. And was it not de Gaulle himself who had first proposed this abstract and disembodied idea of the Resistance?

Michel Dacier put it this way in the first issue of *Ecrits de Paris:* "The word [*résistantialisme*] seems excellent, for it offers the very great advantage of excluding from the debate entirely the Resistance itself, which was a manifestation of the moral health of the nation."[24] What a strange notion: a Resistance without résistants. Dacier went on to develop an argument that some rightist extremists consider definitive. Because defeat was inevitable, he claimed, Vichy was also inevitable. It had been a fully legitimate government, which resisted the Nazis as much as it could. Alongside the resistance of the left, which had been "infiltrated" by Communists and was in many ways disreputable and dishonest—in a word, "revolutionary"—there had grown up a resistance of the right, frequently anti-Gaullist, aligned with Pétain, Weygand, and Giraud, and faithful to the French military tradition. Finally, Dacier charged that since 1944 unnamed "others" had plunged France into civil war, and as a result the French had "become habituated to hatred and, even worse, suspicion."[25] This charge has often been repeated by admirers of Vichy. Around the same time, Louis-Dominique Girard, who had served on Pétain's staff, coined the phrase *guerre franco-française* to refer not to the fratricidal struggles of the Occupation but to the civil war alleged to be raging in France in 1950.[26]

The Maurrassians went even further, attempting to deny the crucial distinction that lay at the heart of all ideology in the period 1940–1944: "To those who remember, 'Resistance' and 'Collaboration' were, during those terrible years, two survivals of the 'regime of opinion,' both aimed squarely at the authority, sovereignty, and unity for which the Marshal stood."[27] With one stone the Maurrassians wanted to kill two birds: the memory of collaboration, in which they were implicated (Maurras had denounced collaborationists but had largely supported Vichy policy and state collaboration); and the Resistance, in which they clearly had had no role whatsoever (except for a few isolated individuals).

Yet there were rightist attempts to revitalize French nationalism that did not bear the stigmata of the Occupation. Roger Nimier, for example, was perfectly willing to jettison outmoded ideas:

Our friends are dead. Our hopes are ruined. Those who once dreamed of a new order have found fraternity in the ruins, suffering in impoverished nations, and, among corpses heaped on rubble, this century's only true Europeans. Less imaginative, the rest of us have only France. We endure this interlude with blank expressions. We do not understand our elders' allegiances: it is only right that they should live for once-beloved comrades, but that they should also live for old flags, drenched in honor but also in senseless shame, can only be termed weakness. The lights of June 1940 and of the summer of 1944 are now fused; despair and joy balance each other in a shameful equilibrium, which we repudiate. Vichy, Gaullism, Collaboration—these belong to history. Neither victory nor defeat: the situation as it exists in 1945 has left us free. I am well aware that some would dig up the cadavers beneath our feet to tell us that we must carry on along the one and only path to glory. But in the absence of humanity—and that is precisely what is most sorely missed—comes fatigue.[28]

"Is a right wing without nostalgia possible?" asked Raoul Girardet.[29] With all due respect to Nimier and his "*hussards*," the answer would seem to be no. These revisions of history can be seen as part of a sweeping attempt to recast the image of the right. One way or another, Vichy had to be dealt with, whether to claim its legacy or to deny its relevance. *Rivarol* called on its readers to forget the past.[30] Not everyone on the right went that far. Yet the Occupation obsessed counterrevolutionaries as well as nationalists, and its presence loomed behind both the parliamentary right and the Gaullist RPF.

A large segment of the moderate right joined the nostalgic extremists in opposition to the purge: the substitution of one civil war for another was in full swing. Consider one example. An ecclesiastic by the name of Desgranges, a deputy from Morbihan affiliated with the Popular Democratic Party, founded a confraternity (associated with the Order of Our Lady of Mercy) for the purpose of aiding victims of the new "Terror." In 1948 he published a best-selling pamphlet entitled *Les Crimes masqués du résistantialisme:* "Resistantialism is to the Resistance what clericalism is to religion, what liberalism is to liberty, and, as Sartre might say, what nausea is to life. It is the exploitation of a sublime epic by the tripartite gang under Communist leadership."[31] Father Desgranges denounced the purge for its errors, lack of principle, and injustice. He shed tears for the members of France's elite who were sacrificed, "compromised by the Marshal and abandoned by the General."[32] No doubt he was thinking of his own career: he had voted to grant full powers to Pétain on 10 July 1940 and, like many other Catholics, appears to have succumbed to the Pétainist temptation only to declare after the war that he had been deceived.[33] Whether a shrewd psychologist or a man with a lucid vision of the future, he proposed expunging the terms "Vichyism" and "collaboration" from the French vocabulary, because ultimately his greatest fear was of anti-Vichyism and of "the deception through *words* that has claimed the lives of so many innocents."[34]

Yet his break with Vichyism was not total. In 1946 Desgranges helped found the Association des Représentants du Peuple de la IIIe République. Its membership included mayors and deputies declared ineligible for office, among whom were some former resistance fighters (elected in the October 1945 municipal elections after their ineligibility was lifted) as well as once-prominent figures in the defunct government such as Paul Faure and Pierre-Etienne Flandin. In March 1948 the association staged a Banquet of 1000, in reference to the banquets of 1848. Speakers at this affair championed the idea of an amnesty and defended the actions of the "honest and sincere guerrilla fighter" as well as of the Vichy ministers "who signed secret treaties with England" while condemning collaborators and criminals who had posed as members of the Resistance.[35] What was odd was that the association worked for the rehabilitation of purged political leaders and yet claimed to be staunchly in favor of the Third Republic. In its view, Vichy had been nothing more than a creation of the Third Republic's own institutions, a consequence of the parliamentary vote of 10 July 1940; the new regime, it claimed, had directed its fire primarily against the deputies, senators, and mayors of the Third Republic by declaring them ineligible. In 1948 many members of the association joined the Centre National des Indépendants, a new political party.

Attacks on résistants in this period were not only verbal. Some former members of the Francs-Tireurs et Partisans (FTP) and the FFI were suspected, in some cases with good reason, of having engaged in extortion during the Liberation and were prosecuted for their alleged actions. In the fall of 1946 a sordid affair involving an escape route for German prisoners came to light. Among those implicated in this so-called affair of La Queue de Renard (the name of a place) was Robert Leblanc, the former leader of the Surcouf *maquis* (guerrillas) in Normandy. Leblanc attempted to avoid the summons to appear before the investigating magistrate by fleeing into the country, just as he had done as a guerrilla. A few years later, in 1953, came the Guingouin affair. Georges Guingouin, also known as "the Limousin Tito," formerly head of the FFI in Limoges and a legendary figure in the clandestine Communist Party, was arrested on 24 December 1953. From then until June 1954 he was held in prison, where he suffered mistreatment and may have been the victim of a murder attempt. Accused of having instigated the murder of peasants in Corrèze, he became the target of bitter animosity. In fact, he had been instrumental in setting up a military tribunal in Limoges in August 1944. Acting under the authority of the Fifth Military Region, this court was responsible for some forty executions. Supported by comrades from the Resistance, including Claude Bourdet writing in *France-Observateur*, he was ignored by the Communist Party, from which he had resigned a few months earlier. Guingouin failed to understand that the party, for reasons of its own, had also decided to draw a veil over the 1940s. In the face of the most vicious slander, Guingouin would later come to the defense of André Marty and Charles Tillon. The case against him was dismissed in 1959. His attorney, the young Roland Dumas, was well aware of the symbolic importance of the charge against his client, which "on the pretext of attacking the 'red terror' was gradually expanded to a wholesale indictment of the maquis and the Resistance."[36]

To many people it seemed as if the world had been turned upside down. Former collaborators were amnestied in the name of national unity, while former resistance fighters were prosecuted. The most surprising thing in this reshuffling of the deck was the role played by those who changed sides. A small number of those who had fought against the occupying forces went over to the camp of the *épurés*, the alleged victims of the purge. Some, like Desgranges, claimed to be motivated by Christian beliefs, while others, like Colonel Rémy, a close associate of de Gaulle, probably acted out of beliefs that were more political than religious.

The General's Archer

The "Rémy affair" was exclusively a matter of words—words imputed, borrowed, and endlessly rehashed. It was also a debate over the meaning of the past that implied a choice between historical and political truth. Hence it illustrates the Vichy syndrome to perfection.

On 11 April 1950 Colonel Rémy published an article in the weekly magazine *Carrefour*. "The France of June 1940 needed both Marshal Pétain and General de Gaulle," he wrote, and added that he, a Gaullist loyalist, was offering to "reach out to the Marshal's supporters, who had been as quick as the Marshal himself to place themselves at France's disposal." These few sentences immediately sparked a heated controversy.

In this period of amnesty and ideological recentering, there was nothing new about the sentiments expressed—what was novel was the identity of their author. Born in Vannes on 6 August 1904, Gilbert Renaud, who took the nom de guerre Rémy, had been before the war a businessman and movie producer; he became, as the phrase goes, "a leading figure of the Resistance." His sympathies for the Action Française did not prevent him from rejecting the armistice, and in July 1940 he joined the secret service of Free France under the command of Colonel Dewavrin, later known as Colonel Passy, another legendary figure of the Resistance. As founder of the Réseau Confrérie Notre-Dame (Notre Dame Confraternity Resistance Network), he was responsible for the effort to link up with the FTP, and in January 1943 he accompanied Fernand Grenier, a representative of the Communist Party, all the way to London.

In 1945 he began publishing a series of works about the clandestine struggle. These were widely read, and Rémy became the archetypical Resistance hero, "a jumbled image that combined elements of the secret agent, the vigilante, or outlaw made popular by the western, and the dauntless knight of spotless reputation who, tommy gun in hand, blows up countless factories and trains."[37]

Rémy in April 1947 was one of the founders of the RPF, the postwar Gaullist party. He became a member of the party's executive committee and, as he himself phrased it, served as "unofficial coordinator of Gaullist ceremonies."[38] His article was published at a rather delicate moment: one year later, in June 1951, the RPF would participate in legislative elections, the first real electoral test the party had faced since its sweep of the municipal elections in October 1947. But that was not all. It was surprising, but still possible to accept, that Rémy in his article had come to the defense of Marshal Pétain. But he went further and quoted the words of de Gaulle, allegedly uttered in private conversation in December 1946:

> Remember that France has always had two strings in its bow. In June 1940 it needed the Pétain "string" as much as the de Gaulle "string."[39]

Here we see what was truly at issue in the ambiguous (to say the least) attitude of de Gaulle and the RPF toward Pétain.

As the man chosen to receive this "revelation" of the General's thinking, Rémy had apparently been touched by grace. In June 1940, however, the same Rémy had reached the point of "hating the very name Pétain."[40] In 1945 his feelings remained much the same as they had been in 1940, and in his memoirs he had denounced "the Vichyite morphine."[41] De Gaulle's confidential remarks in 1946 had "dumbfounded" him, he said, but had not altered his position. In 1949, through a friend who was a close associate of General Weygand, Rémy had met Admiral Paul Auphan, who had served as secretary of state for the navy under Vichy and was an ardent defender of Pétain. It was Auphan who had converted Rémy and made him a believer in the Pétainist "resistance." Among other things, Auphan claimed that Pétain had sent secret telegrams to Darlan encouraging him to throw his support to the Americans when they landed in North Africa on 8 November 1942.[42] In March 1950, Father Desgranges, the Morbihan deputy for whom Rémy had voted for many years and whom he had come to know well, persuaded the colonel to make a public statement denouncing the "crimes" of the Liberation and blasting the special tribunals. A month later he published his article.

It would be a mistake to view Rémy's conversion as an isolated occurrence, an individual decision. As Rémy himself stated more than once, he had simply followed the example of de Gaulle himself. After leaving the government in January 1946, the General indeed found frequent occasion to mention the name of Pétain, and for essentially political ends. In June 1948 he referred to "the great leader of the Great War . . . swept away by the effects of old age [and] the torrent of desertions."[43] During a March 1949 press conference, the General raised the issue before an attentive but discreet audience of reporters. Pétain's conviction had been necessary, de Gaulle said; there was little

34

choice, for had he said anything else, he would have been contradicting himself. The conviction was necessary because Pétain "had symbolized capitulation and, even if he did not wish it, collaboration with the enemy." In 1945 this had been a valid judgment of the man. "Today," however, "there is an old man in a fortress, [a man] who I and many others acknowledge has rendered great service to France."[44] Finally, on 16 March 1950, the General spoke once again to the press: "If proof of the government's failure is wanted, it can be found in this burning and bitter issue . . . It is a disgrace (*opprobre*) to allow a man of nearly ninety-five to remain in prison."[45] Less than a month later, Rémy used the same word in the title of his article, "La Justice et l'opprobre."

Clearly the situation had changed considerably since the Liberation, when public statements generally omitted all mention of the Vichy regime. Step by step the notion that Pétain bore some inescapable guilt for his actions had been abandoned, first on grounds of old age, then because it was alleged that his collaboration was more or less involuntary, and finally because of tender concern for the welfare of the man held prisoner on the Isle of Yeu. But it is highly unlikely that de Gaulle had really changed his mind about Vichy. It is certain, moreover, that his concern for Pétain the man was sincere: had he not attempted to prevent the Marshal's trial? Yet it is always difficult (and pointless) to separate Charles de Gaulle the individual from Charles de Gaulle the politician.[46] In his battle against the Fourth Republic, the leader of the RPF coolly and systematically played an important trump card, seeking to arouse indignation in a segment of the electorate, indignation that was all the more legitimate because it was expressed in the first instance by Pétain's chief adversary.

With de Gaulle, however, nothing is simple. At no time did he become aware of Rémy's plan to publish his article with the help of Emilien Amaury. Rémy repeatedly insisted that de Gaulle had always allowed him to operate with a free hand. The General made no protest, for example, when Rémy took part in a 1950 meeting to promote the rehabilitation of Charles Maurras. Therein lies the crux of the matter: while it is obvious that de Gaulle was using Pétain's detention to provoke the government, there is no evidence that he was prepared to carry revisionism to quite the same lengths as Rémy, or to let it be believed (even if he privately agreed) that the man of 18 June was made of the same stuff as the man of 16 June and 10 July.

After publication of the article, de Gaulle reacted vigorously:

> Nothing can justify the policy of the regime or men of Vichy, namely, surrender to an enemy power in the midst of a world war and deliberate collaboration with the invader. The nation has condemned that policy. It had to do so for the sake of France's honor and future.[47]

In a letter to Rémy the General reiterated his "unalterable" friendship but deplored his associate's initiative, which was particularly embarrassing because Rémy was also an official of the RPF.[48] In answer to the many letters he received voicing astonishment at his alleged statement, de Gaulle repeatedly expressed anger over the words attributed to him by Rémy:

> I was under the impression that, from 18 June 1940 on, what I said and did about Vichy was known to everyone. I believed that such knowledge would be enough to contradict a million times over the slanderous remark about the "two strings." I am chagrined to discover the apparent doubt on this score expressed in your letter of 2 May, and which coming from you I find inexplicable.[49]

In another letter de Gaulle expresses outrage at the fact that Rémy had drawn a parallel between "what *we* did, namely, the war, and what *Vichy* did, namely, to put it in a word, surrender." And he stated his position in the strongest possible terms: "Leniency and clemency, which I favor, have nothing to do with the question of principle, which will never change."[50]

This position would appear to be quite clear, were it not for the climate of the period, certain ambiguities in the General's speeches, and the fact that de Gaulle never *publicly* denied that he had made the private statement to Rémy. Furthermore, there are indications that the tenor of de Gaulle's remarks, made in December 1946 out of earshot of possibly indiscreet listeners, was very close to what Rémy claimed.

In 1947 Rémy was delegated by de Gaulle's aide, Claude Guy, to draft a pamphlet lauding the exploits of the RPF's leader. There we find the now notorious 1946 statement:

> I recently had occasion to discuss with the General the attitude of Pétain in those brilliant yet hazy summer days of 1940. Our discussion took place in Paris, in the evening, on avenue Victor-Hugo. After dinner, the General invited Captain Guy and myself to take a walk with him. He wore civilian clothes, happy once again to be able to walk freely on the streets of Paris (Guy later told me that this was the *second* time since the Liberation that he had taken the opportunity to stroll about the city) . . . He answered me calmly and objectively, as though the issue concerned another hemisphere and was not one whose consequences he would be the first to bear. I am deeply chagrined that I was unable to record our conversation in detail, but I do not believe that I will be misrepresenting the General's thoughts if I sum them up as follows: once the armistices were signed, once our country was confronted with the fait accompli, it was not a bad thing that France should have two strings in her bow, one in the hands of de Gaulle and the other in the hands of Pétain, provided of course that both would be in accord with the sole benefit of the nation.[51]

The first point to note is that this text dates from 1947, or prior to Rémy's conversion and from a period when, by his own admission, he still clung to his anti-Pétain and anti-Vichy positions. The text, moreover, was corrected by de Gaulle himself. In the first draft Rémy had written: "France must always have two strings in her bow. At that time it needed the de Gaulle string, but it also needed the Pétain string." The General eliminated the implication of a timeless need from the passage, limiting the need for "two strings" to the special circumstances of the Occupation, and he added the concluding proviso. Then Rémy produced a new draft, maintaining the literary subjunctive (*il n'était pas mauvais que la France disposât de deux cordes à son arc*), which leaves some doubt as to whether the phrase should be read as expressing a retrospective wish or an established fact, and preserving the final clause, which appears to moderate the statement but which can be interpreted in different ways.[52] Whatever corrections may have been made, the fact remains that it was de Gaulle who, if he did not actually formulate the two-string parable, was prepared to allow the words to be imputed to him.

Another revelation came in the memoirs of Georges Pompidou, who disclosed that he had prompted the General to delete a sentence from his closing speech to the RPF's third convention at Porte de Versailles on 25 June 1950. Originally de Gaulle had intended to invoke the two-string parable: "I pointed out to him that he seemed to be making a confession. Stung, he agreed."[53] In the speech de Gaulle acknowledged that few elected officials of the Third Republic had "the courage to refuse complete abdication," but he also stressed the fact that the country's institutions were then in a state of collapse. Pompidou further contends that de Gaulle, referring to Rémy, said: "He failed to grasp the essential point." In the General's mind, Rémy had gone too far in pursuing the logic of the RPF position, while Pétain, regardless of his presumed popularity and ideological correctness on certain issues, symbolized surrender in the face of the enemy.

The political consequences of the *Carrefour* article were not long in coming. Rémy resigned from the RPF leadership committee; the RPF emphasized that his statements represented only his own personal views; and de Gaulle tried to revert to the anti-Vichyite tone of earlier years. But all in vain: the storm had been unleashed. In the Socialist Party paper *Le Populaire* (12 April 1950) Robert Verdier accused the RPF of rallying Vichy's forces to destroy the republican regime. On the same day *L'Humanité*, the Communist paper, denounced Rémy's words as the premise for "imperialist aggression against the Soviet Union." *Libération* fulminated against the "de Gaulle-Pétain axis." Even *L'Epoque,* the organ of the moderate right, deplored (also on 12 April) what it saw as a campaign ploy in the words of Rémy and, even earlier, of the General: "It is too easy, after sentence is pronounced, to discover where justice lies in order to win the votes of the condemned," a cheap shot intended to remind readers of de Gaulle's responsibility for Pétain's imprisonment.

Even if Rémy's action was truly his own and not a reflection of the RPF's official position, it nevertheless revealed an unavowed—indeed unavowable—facet of the party's makeup. Although publicly repudiated, Rémy received unofficial support from certain members of the Gaullist movement. On 9 November 1950, moreover, during debate on a proposed amnesty bill, Louis Terrenoire and Edmond Michelet, deputies of the MRP who had joined forces with the RPF, filed an amendment calling for Pétain's release from prison. Although their motion was rejected on technical grounds by a vote of 466 to 98, it received the backing of right-wing elements whose debt to the legacy of the Resistance was minimal.[54]

There can be no doubt that there was pro-Pétain sentiment within the RPF, although it is difficult to say whether those who leaned in this direction had been captivated by the magic of the Marshal's rhetoric or were convinced of its impact on public opinion. The appeal to the presumed partisans of Pétain's "National Revolution" is a concrete illustration of René Rémond's shrewd remark: "In fact, in all the history of Gaullism, the RPF chapter, so multifarious in its manifestations, came closest to what people in France have become accustomed to refer to as fascism."[55] It is difficult to question Rémy's good faith. Like so many others, he succumbed to the mystical charm of the Pétain myth. A convinced royalist and Catholic, his anticommunism led him to reject a certain view of the Resistance. As for de Gaulle's attitude, we must disentangle it from the literal meaning of his words. He cannot deny having been the author of the two-strings parable, since he repeated it on several occasions. Yet de Gaulle rejected the far-reaching interpretation given by his loyal aide Rémy, because at the time the General was playing a double game. In calling for a pardon for Pétain, he was not only voicing his own personal sentiments but also distancing himself from the excesses of the purge and, like other political leaders, sought to shift the blame to the Communists alone. In continuing to condemn Vichy on principle, however, he remained the supreme résistant. In reality, it was de Gaulle who needed two strings in his bow, the Resistance and Pétain, as an indispensable element of what was then the basis of his political platform, the call for national unity. The invective that he simultaneously reserved for Vichyites, not only in public but even more in private, was certainly directed more against adversaries on his right, whose hatred of de Gaulle had continued uninterrupted since the Occupation, than against the vague current of sympathy for Pétain and Pétainism.

De Gaulle thus gave voice to all the ambiguities in a past that was being remade to suit the present situation: in 1940 Pétain was the enemy; in 1944 he posed a problem; in 1950 he furnished a weapon, but one that cut two ways. It should come as no surprise, then, that of the long list of maledictions that would be applied at one time or another to virtually all of France's political leaders, the first was launched by the "man of June Eighteenth."

The Legend of the Marshal

The revival of Pétainism culminated in 1951. In the June 1951 legislative elections the Union des Indépendants Républicains (UNIR) received 288,089 votes. This loose political association had been founded by Pétain's attorney, Jacques Isorni, who once described himself as the only man still collaborating at a time when most people in France were trying to join the Resistance (that is, in 1945), and by Odette Moreau, another attorney who had represented Gabriel Péri, the Communist scholar shot by the Nazis during the Occupation, and who later represented Jean de Bassompierre, a milicien executed after the Liberation. Elected to the National Assembly were three adherents who openly proclaimed their admiration for the Marshal's ideas: Jacques Isorni in Paris, Roger de Saivre in Oran, and Paul Estèbe in the Gironde. De Saivre and Estèbe had been members of Pétain's cabinet. In addition, Jacques Le Roy Ladurie, elected on another list of independent candidates, had served as minister of agriculture in the Laval government.

A month later, on 23 July 1951, Marshal Pétain died at the age of ninety-five on the Isle of Yeu. The event might have been treated as a kind of apotheosis, the ascension of the martyred Marshal, and it was indeed envisioned in such terms by Pétain's supporters, who imagined all of France bidding farewell to the victor of Verdun with one final salute. In actuality, however, Pétain narrowly escaped unceremonious burial in a corner of Fort Pierre-Levée. The government of Henri Queuille, which had formally resigned on 10 July, decided as one of its final acts that the body could be buried in the cemetery at Port-Joinville on the tiny Isle of Yeu, which hardly lent itself to a ceremony of great pomp.

On the night of 24 July, veterans of Verdun began a funeral vigil. Beneath the mortuary windows were stationed four young women dressed in the traditional costume of the Vendée, the province of

The Pétain myth: Brochure distributed by *Aspects de la France* after Pétain's death

France that had risen in rebellion against the Great Revolution and had stood ever since as the very symbol of counterrevolution. From the small crowd of a few hundred onlookers rose the powerful voice of a Vendean peasant reciting the words: "Saints of France, pray for our old leader." When the prayer was over, the same voice cried out: "Monsieur le Maréchal, forgive France!"

On the following day the island became quite a bustling place. A colorful crowd of summer tourists and curious local fishermen formed on the dock to watch the arrival of generals Weygand and Hering, Admiral Fernet, and a host of other personages, military and civilian. Elsewhere former Vichy functionaries and other "purge victims" passed around a small hagiographic brochure. The atmosphere was not unlike the revanchist political demonstrations in the years after the Franco-Prussian War. When the religious service began, however, the ceremony regained its dignity. The service was relayed throughout the island by a network of loudspeakers. Then the coffin was conveyed to the cemetery. As it was lowered into the grave, General Weygand tossed in a small image of a croix de guerre that had been given him by a Vendean veteran. Someone then shouted "Vive la France!" and the crowd took up the cry, while someone else attempted, less successfully, to start a chant of "Vive le Maréchal!"[56]

Although two masses were celebrated in Paris and a wreath was laid at the Arc de Triomphe, the event did not live up to expectations. It would be an exaggeration to say that Pétain's death was greeted with widespread indifference. The prevailing sentiment was rather one of relief. Hubert Beuve-Méry put it this way:

> May it please heaven that this debate be laid to rest along with the man who wished to shoulder sole responsibility for it. But the wound persists, and perhaps it is one that must be opened and drained to diminish its purulence . . . As Frenchmen stand at this graveside and await the next swing of the pendulum, will they find the wisdom to reflect honestly on their past and present faults, often quite serious on both sides, so as to comprehend, jointly and more fully, the harsh conditions that lie ahead in the future they all share?[57]

Wise words whose pessimism was justified. Pétain's death did nothing to assuage the lingering damage of wartime divisiveness. In fact, it only fanned the flames. Already a figure of legend—infamous to some, sacred to others—Pétain would continue to divide the French after his death, especially since that event spurred his supporters to new activity.

In April 1948 Pétain's attorneys had formed a so-called Committee of Honor, chaired by Louis Madelin, to work for the Marshal's release from prison. In response to protests from outraged resistance groups, the committee was quickly banned. At the time the Marshal had been more than a little reluctant to endorse the actions of this high-profile group: "He could not permit any consideration of or request for his release while others, guilty only of having obeyed his orders, remained in prison."[58] After Pétain's demise, however, his supporters were free to celebrate his memory.

On 6 November 1951 the Association pour Défendre la Mémoire du Maréchal Pétain (ADMP) was founded. It was never banned and remains active to this day. Let us interrupt our chronological account long enough for a brief tour of the sanctuary.

The Guardians of the Temple

The ADMP, of which General Weygand served as honorary chairman until 1965, sought to attract all Pétain supporters, primarily those who had worked with the Marshal during the Occupation. The association's board of directors was headed by General Hering, former military governor of Paris, until 1960; then by Jean Lemaire, one of Pétain's lawyers, until 1968; then, from 1968 to 1973, by General Lacaille, who had served as Huntziger's chief of staff; and from 1973 to 1976 by Admiral Auphan. In 1976 the post of board chairman became a four-year position occupied in succession by three former Vichy ministers: Jean Borotra, Georges Lamirand, and, most recently, François Lehideux. Clearly the ADMP has been an association of prominent figures from the beginning. Between 1951 and 1971 its board of directors counted among its members thirty-six high-ranking officers, twenty-two former ministers, twelve members of the Académie Française, a number of prefects, and other top officials. One of the first to join (in 1951) was, not surprisingly, Colonel Rémy, who remained a member until his death and who enticed many "Pétaino-Gaullists" into the organization.

43

N° 81   N° 81 - Janv.-Février 1971

LE MARÉCHAL

ORGANE DE L'ASSOCIATION POUR DÉFENDRE LA MÉMOIRE DU MARÉCHAL PÉTAIN

Direction et Rédaction : A.D.M.P., 6, rue de Marengo, PARIS (1er) • C.C.P. 6459-26 PARIS • Tél. : 231-39-50 (poste 114)

« AI-JE DONC VRAIMENT MÉRITÉ UN TEL SORT ? » Philippe PÉTAIN

La mort du Général DE GAULLE
Le problème de la translation des Cendres du Maréchal PÉTAIN

La mort du Général de Gaulle a provoqué une vive émotion en France et dans le reste du monde. On a célébré à cette occasion la carrière exceptionnelle de celui qui, après la terrible défaite de 1940, maintint notre pays dans le combat et lui permit d'être présent à la table de la victoire grâce à la valeur des soldats de la France Libre, de ceux de l'Armée d'Afrique préparée par Weygand et conduite par Juin puis par de Lattre, de ceux de Leclerc et des combattants sans uniforme de l'intérieur.

Au moment où l'on évoque cette période dramatique de notre histoire, l'A.D.M.P. se doit de rappeler qu'un Maréchal de France, après toute une vie consacrée au service de la Patrie, s'est à cette époque sacrifié pour elle afin de lui éviter de plus dures épreuves, qu'il fut ensuite injustement condamné par un Tribunal d'exception pour un crime de trahison qu'il n'avait pas commis, et qu'il mourut en prison à 95 ans, après six années de cruelles souffrances matérielles et morales... La France, incontestablement, doit réparation au Maréchal Pétain.

La translation de ses cendres à Douaumont auprès de ses anciens soldats, conformément au vœu qu'il a exprimé en 1938 dans son testament, et à celui formulé en 1966 par 800.000 anciens combattants, symboliserait cette réparation. Le passionnant récit (publié ci-contre), qu'a bien voulu nous adresser au sujet le Colonel Rémy, montre que le Général de Gaulle y pensa en 1958, et qu'elle aurait pu se faire à cette date dans un climat d'unanimité nationale. Il y pensait certainement le 10 novembre 1968, lorsqu'il fit solennellement déposer une couronne sur la tombe de l'Ile d'Yeu et quand, dans son discours des Invalides le même jour, il rendit un hommage tout particulier au Maréchal Pétain.

Comme le Colonel Rémy, l'A.D.M.P. regrette profondément que cette translation n'ait pas eu lieu en 1958, ni depuis lors. Elle reste indispensable, pour l'honneur de la France et pour l'union des Français. L'A.D.M.P. ne cessera de le rappeler.

Le Président :
Général LACAILLE

Les Vice-Présidents :
J. BOROTRA, A. FOUGERET, P. HENRY, G. RIVOLLET.

DÉDICACE AU MARÉCHAL PÉTAIN PAR LE GÉNÉRAL DE GAULLE DE SON LIVRE « LE FIL DE L'ÉPÉE »

CET ESSAI, MONSIEUR LE MARÉCHAL, NE SAURAIT ÊTRE DÉDIÉ QU'A VOUS, CAR RIEN NE MONTRE, MIEUX QUE VOTRE GLOIRE, QUELLE VERTU L'ACTION PEUT TIRER DES LUMIÈRES DE LA PENSÉE.

C'est par cette phrase que le général de GAULLE dédia au Maréchal PÉTAIN son ouvrage « Le fil de l'épée ».

En outre le n° 1 d'une édition de tête porte la dédicace manuscrite ci-dessous :

« HOMMAGE D'UN TRÈS RESPECTUEUX ET TRÈS PROFOND DÉVOUEMENT » signé C. de GAULLE.

Le Colonel Rémy a bien voulu nous adresser le texte historique ci-dessous, qui fait écho à la préoccupation majeure de l'A.D.M.P.
Nous l'en remercions chaleureusement.

Un certain jour de l'année 1953, le Général Weygand me dit tout à coup : « Rémy, la France glisse vers l'abîme. Il faut faire quelque chose pour empêcher cela. Avez-vous une idée ? »

L'idée me vint à l'esprit par le fait même que la question m'était soudainement posée. « Oui, mon Général, répondis-je. Mais je ne sais si elle vous conviendra. »

— Eh bien, quelle est-elle ?

— Mon Général, si une délégation d'anciens combattants de Verdun vient vous prier de vous rendre à Douaumont pour y recevoir solennellement la dépouille mortelle du Maréchal Pétain, quelle sera votre réponse ?

— Quelle- question ! Je serai là-bas, à côté de n'importe qui.

— Il ne s'agit pas dans mon idée de n'importe qui, mon Général. Si cette délégation vous disait qu'en sortant de chez vous elle ira faire la même demande au Général de Gaulle, et que celui-ci accepte, que ferez-vous ?

Le Général Weygand se raidit légèrement dans son fauteuil, et plongea son regard dans mes yeux. Puis il déclara d'une voix contenue : « Rémy, c'est vous qui avez raison. J'y serai, moi aussi. »

Je fis part de cette conversation au Général Hering, Président de l'A.D.M.P., qui m'honorait lui aussi de son amitié, et dont je savais que le Général de Gaulle lui témoignait une affectueuse déférence. « L'idée est excellente ! s'écria-t-il. Je vais m'occuper de la réaliser. »

Le Général Hering est mort, et c'est seulement à lui qu'il eût appartenu de dire pourquoi ma suggestion n'aboutit pas. Je suis cependant en mesure de déclarer que le Général de Gaulle n'y fut pour rien.

Peu après le retour du Général de Gaulle au pouvoir, en 1958, j'eus l'occasion de déjeuner à la table de mon ami Emilien Amaurry en compagnie de notre ami commun Edmond Michelet. « Quand le Général m'a fait appeler pour me proposer le Ministère des Armées, sans que j'eusse rien sollicité. Dans l'ordre des valeurs, c'était une sorte de rétrogradation. Ce qui me fit dire au Général :

« Bien entendu, mon Général, je suis tout à votre disposition, mais je ne vois qu'une signification au poste que vous me m'assignez : vous voulez que je sois le Ministre qui conduira le Maréchal Pétain à Douaumont ? »

« Le Général de Gaulle sourit, ne me répondit pas. Mais j'interprétai ce sourire comme un acquiescement. Je crois que cela se serait fait sans une sorte de mise en demeure qui parut dans la presse. Chacun sait que le Général n'aimait pas qu'on prétendît le mettre au pied du mur. De ce jour, il n'y eut plus d'espoir. »

Qu'on me permette de dire que ce fut un malheur pour la France. Le transfèrement de la dépouille mortelle du Maréchal Pétain à Douaumont eût pris, au plan national, toute sa signification si la cérémonie avait été présidée par le Général de Gaulle, Président de la République.

Je suis de ceux qui ne croient pas à la nécessité d'un procès en réhabilitation, qui est déjà fait dans l'esprit du Français, mais à un geste constituant une réparation, qui eût mis fin à ce qui, tout bien considéré, fut une mauvaise querelle de famille, en scellant la réconciliation entre des Français qui furent animés par un même amour de la Patrie. Ce geste sera fait, je n'en doute pas, mais l'amour que je porte à mon pays me fera mourir avec le regret au cœur qu'il n'ait pas été accompli par mon ancien chef dont, quoi qu'on puisse en dire, le prestige était tel dans le monde qu'à travers sa personne c'est un hommage à la France que le monde entier, ou presque, a rendu lors de la cérémonie qui fut célébrée à Notre-Dame le jour de ses obsèques. Comment douter que le monde entier eût été à Douaumont pour y voir le Général de Gaulle accueillir celui qui fut son chef ?

Colonel RÉMY.
Janvier 1971.

The headline reads: "The Death of General de Gaulle. The Issue of Moving Marshal Pétain's Ashes"

Soon after its foundation the ADMP embarked on a major propaganda campaign directed at the "forty million Petainists" of 1940, or what was left of them. The first appeal for new members, already defensive in tone, shows how totally divorced from reality the ADMP was:

> If our membership included all who saw in the armistice of June 1940 an act of salvation and in the Marshal's presence as head of the French state a protective guardianship, then the ADMP truly would include all French citizens, all who, along with the victor of Verdun, waged the politics of presence on our invaded and occupied territory.[59]

Yet for all the favorable circumstances of the 1950s, the ADMP never had a chance of becoming a popular movement. By its own estimates, its 1955 membership amounted to some 7,000 individuals (a figure that included family members); in 1961 there were still only "several thousand," while in 1971 a sudden jump to "tens of thousands" was reported; in 1976 a figure of 2,500 was mentioned, while in 1983 the secretary-general of the organization claimed that membership totaled nearly 20,000.[60] But numbers are relatively unimportant. The ADMP's impact was primarily ideological. Modest but stubborn, its action comprised three fundamental objectives.

Judicial Review

The association's first objective was to secure a judicial review of the record of Pétain's trial. This legal battle, led by attorney Jacques Isorni, raged on for thirty years. Between 1950 and 1981 each new minister of justice found the inevitable Pétain dossier awaiting him the moment he took office. In all, eight requests were filed asking the minister to rule not on the substance of the case but on the legality of the petition for review by the high court. Through 1972, five of these petitions were accepted, but actual review was denied. A sixth petition was filed with René Pleven in 1972 and a seventh with Alain Peyrefitte in 1979, but both were rejected on the grounds that judgments of the Haute Cour were not open to review. In 1981 Robert Badinter broke with his predecessors and submitted the eighth petition for review. But Isorni's hope that a colleague, himself familiar with "judicial errors," might repair the injustice was soon disappointed when the petition for appeal was denied. Could the attorney really have hoped to mobilize public opinion behind such an issue in 1985? This hesitation waltz shows that no government, no matter what its political hue, had an accurate idea of the importance of the Pétain myth in public opinion. The ADMP exploited this ignorance by turning its petition for review into a regular ritual, primarily thanks to the efforts of Isorni.

Relocation of the Remains

In similarly ritual fashion, the ADMP called for the Marshal's casket to be transferred to Douaumont. In May 1954 a petition bearing almost 70,000 signatures and supported by numerous World War I veterans' organizations was submitted to the government. The pretext for such a move was still "national reconciliation."

According to the Pétainists, the government on two occasions came close to swallowing the symbolic bait. In the summer of 1958, just after de Gaulle's return to power, the General allegedly approved of a relocation ceremony to be organized by Edmond Michelet, whose son Claude wrote:

> My father's diary makes clear how concerned General de Gaulle was to put this difficult matter behind him. He delegated to this minister for veterans' affairs the task of organizing the ceremony in which Marshal Pétain would be buried, as he had a right to be, at Verdun. The ceremony was to be neither grandiose nor humble. It was essential to honor the Great War leader without ignoring the old man's attitude in Vichy. The mission was not an impossible one because, as my father said, "No one can accuse me of Pétainism. I will certainly come up with three *poilus* from 1914–1918 and three deportees willing to escort the Marshal's remains, and everyone will see the thing for what it is: reconciliation."[61]

Oddly enough, it was Jacques Isorni who was accused, by Rémy among others, of having sabotaged the plan by writing to de Gaulle in terms that appeared to force his hand:

The statesman desirous of complementing his renown by adding the one element it still lacks cannot refuse to make this gesture of civic piety, in which the people of France will see nothing but a symbol of concord and reconciliation, like the symbol you have just offered, in Algeria, to all of France, including her adversaries.[62]

But as Isorni rightly points out, it is highly unlikely that the plan had really advanced very far, and still more unlikely that a letter from him precipitated the final decision: "As if de Gaulle had waited for me to say something—one way or the other, he made up his own mind!" The second failure, according to Isorni, involved Georges Pompidou, who allegedly abandoned plans to relocate Pétain's remains in the face of strong pressure from some long-time Gaullists.[63] In such matters, the participants have all convinced themselves that they are in possession of the truth, and for the time being it is difficult to verify their claims. Whatever the truth may be, the important point to note is that the transfer of Pétain's casket was actually intended to alter his memory. Claude Michelet's opinion to the contrary notwithstanding, the point was indeed to *forget* the marshal of 1940 in order to enhance the image of the general of 1916, and to use the memory of World War I veterans, for whom Pétain was still linked with the slogan *On les aura!* (We'll get them!), in order to promote an ideology.

Reconciliation

The project of the ADMP and the Petainists was also in part ideological: its goal was to resurrect Pétain's ideas and the values of his so-called National Revolution. From 1951 to the present, and with even greater intensity during the Algerian War, the ADMP has served as a breeding ground for the nostalgic extreme right, which has remained peripheral to political conflict in France and yet serves as a kind of sounding board for radical ideas. Although it has concealed its identity behind a "manifesto of reconciliation," its true colors have frequently been revealed in displays of unchecked bitterness. In May 1977, for example, just after the municipal elections and with the Union of the Left [an alliance of the Socialist and Communist parties together with part of the Radical Party] threatening to win the coming legislative elections, Admiral Auphan did not shrink from injecting his group into the political debate:

> So long as France remains a country in which one can say what one thinks—which may not be for long—nothing prevents us from proclaiming . . . that this sentence [of Pétain's], bewildering to so many people, must be revised, and that all of us, loyal to the principles embodied in his speeches, and despite the many threats that have been brandished against us, prefer the commonsense slogan "Work, Family, Fatherland" [the motto of the Vichy regime] to materialism in all its forms, whether liberal or collectivist. What is happening in France now is but the price to be paid for the refusal of reconciliation thirty-three years ago.[64]

Furthermore, many members of the ADMP belonged to extreme right-wing groups, including Georges Rouchouze, former bodyguard of Francis Bout-de-L'An (secretary-general of the Milice), member of the National Front, and a supporter of Front leader Jean-Marie Le Pen, who served for some time as chairman of the ADMP's Saint-Etienne chapter. Politically, the ADMP has been divided into two factions, which have successively dominated the organization's affiliates: the anti-Gaullists, led by Jacques Isorni, who never forgave de Gaulle for either the purge or his Algerian policy, and the Pétaino-Gaullists, led for a time by Rémy. The latter were always fascinated by the General, who was of course an enemy but even more a rival, whose model of French society was not unlike their own. Had it not been for the dramatic events of 1944–45, Pétain might have chosen de Gaulle as his political heir and thus reaped the benefit of the aura that so thoroughly protected the man of June Eighteenth. Thus in January 1971, following de Gaulle's death, the ADMP's newspaper published an astonishing panegyric by its president, General Lacaille:

> The death of General de Gaulle has given rise to considerable emotion in France and throughout the world. The occasion is an opportunity to celebrate the extraordinary career of the man who, following the dreadful defeat of 1940, kept our country in the battle and permitted it to take its place at the victory table, thanks to the courage of the soldiers of Free France, of the Army of Africa trained by Weygand and led first by Juin and later by de Lattre, of Leclerc's troops, and of irregulars inside France.[65]

In its own way this was a touching homage, but it failed to please all members of the ADMP. The two factions continued to struggle bitterly until 1985, shortly before the death of Colonel Rémy, and it appears that the hard-core Pétainists had gained the upper hand.

These vulgar temporal battles did little to detract from the more spiritual aspects of the ADMP. During the first general assembly in 1951, General Hering urged members to view their role as an "apostolate." The calendar of every subsequent year was marked by sacred anniversaries. On 24 April, the date of Pétain's birth, pilgrims visited Cauchy-la-Tour, Pétain's birthplace in the north of France. On 23 July they set sail for the Isle of Yeu, their Golgotha. On 1 May they simultaneously honored the Charte du Travail (the Labor Charter, representing Vichy's "good works" in the social realm) and Saint Philippe, whose "day" was actually the third. Last but not least, they commemorated 10 November, the date of victory in 1918, although the ceremonies were carefully postponed one day to allow members to participate in the official ceremonies of 11 November. In some cases this "apostolate" came close to being an obsession. In *Le Maréchal* for March 1959 we read: "Statistics regarding first names given to children in 1958 [the year of de Gaulle's return to power] . . . show that the name most frequently chosen was Philippe." Such nonsense may be amusing, but it was not without effect, particularly on certain elements in the Catholic hierarchy. Had not Pétain himself, at the beginning of his trial, claimed to represent "a certain tradition, that of French and Christian civilization"? In 1950 Rémy, on advice of Monsignor Beaussart, dean of the chapter of Notre-Dame, even went to Rome to attempt to enlist the support of Pius XII in the Marshal's behalf.

The apostles' road was not always an easy one. Hopes born in the context of the cold war faded with time. Today the question that most troubles the ardent keepers of the Pétainist flame is this: who will take the place of the octogenarians who return each year to the sanctuary on the Isle of Yeu?

Legal Oblivion

At the time the ADMP was born, turmoil still swirled around the dark years of the war, which remained fresh in people's minds. Ultimately

49

this turmoil crystallized in a major battle over the question of amnesty, of which the Pétain case was one aspect. This fierce ideological struggle was an essential stage in overcoming the effects of the Occupation. Historians for some time now have been attentive to controversies among intellectuals in the late 1940s over the fate of writers who lent their pens to the German cause. The debate between Albert Camus and François Mauriac, for example, is well known. Camus, writing in *Combat,* sought to persuade himself of the need for "humane justice." Mauriac, writing in *Le Figaro,* quickly came to advocate pardons for those writers who had "gone astray." Inaugurating an era of petitions, Mauriac in 1945 sought in vain to save Robert Brasillach from execution, and many members of the intellectual and artistic elite, Camus included, joined him in the attempt. A few years later, Jean Paulhan, an editor at Gallimard who had worked with the Resistance during the Occupation, voiced his disapproval of the purge and in particular of the policy of the Comité National des Ecrivains (CNE); in his book *Lettre aux directeurs de la résistance* he criticized them for having condemned without judgment.[66]

If we focus exclusively on intellectuals, however, we may easily lose sight of the forest for the trees. While writers wounded one another with words, the battle over amnesty soon engaged all political parties. Amnesty was a serious matter because it touched on questions of morality and memory as well as law. In French law, amnesty is actually defined as "legal oblivion" (*oubli juridique*). Hence it had the potential to alter the country's very perception of the Occupation, because the courts would be empowered to impose silence concerning all judgments covered by the amnesty.

The issue was also one of major importance for the renascent right, which wished to cleanse itself of allegations of collaboration and Pétainism and which found in the amnesty issue a place to attack political organizations that claimed the legacy of the Resistance. The amnesty question thus became a gauntlet thrown down to the left, and especially to the Communist Party.

The offensive was launched in 1948. In the frontlines, of course, were those singled out in the purge, as we saw earlier with the Banquet of the One Thousand. In the National Assembly, however, the attack was led by the Christian-Democratic MRP and the RPF, while de Gaulle's statements about Pétain loomed over the whole discussion. On 24 October 1950 the first major debate on the issue began, after bills were filed by Georges Bidault, Edmond Michelet, and Louis Rollin. Proponents of amnesty cited five major arguments: clemency, reparation for the injustices of the purge, national reconciliation, the political nature of certain offenses committed during the Occupation, and finally the example set by Germany and Italy, which had already embarked on national reconciliations of their own. On the other side, the Communists, who vigorously opposed any kind of amnesty, attacked pell-mell the rebirth of neofascism, the political tactics of the right, and the connection between German rearmament and the wish to absolve collaborators. The Socialists, for their part, accepted the principle of pardon but waved a menacing finger in the direction of any attempt at rehabilitation.

With only a minority in the Assembly, the left could not prevent enactment on 5 January 1951 of the first amnesty law, which had passed on second reading by a vote of 327 to 263. This law granted amnesty to all those who had committed acts for which the punishment involved loss of civil rights (*dégradation nationale*) and a prison sentence of less than fifteen years. The law also provided for individual remedies for those who had been forcibly conscripted, minors below the age of twenty-one, and those who had already served most of their time. Though broad in principle, this law did not apply to grave crimes or to decisions of the Haute Cour, which had been abolished along with the other *cours de justice* the previous year.[67]

This act represented the first serious attack not on the ideology of the Resistance, which five years after the war's end was already moribund, but on its memory. The new law allowed notorious fascists and Vichyites not only to resurface but to reclaim their civil rights and especially to run for office, without having to appear, as Antoine Pinay had done, before a *jury d'honneur*. Prisoners jailed during the purge began to be released.

The right, emboldened by this initial success, pressed its advantage. A second debate began in July 1952, this time over total amnesty. The slogan of "national unity," by which was meant a holy alliance against the Communists, loomed large in the speeches of right-wing deputies. The external danger now was not German but Soviet: "The Fourth Republic is strong enough to demonstrate understanding and humanity. It must do so, particularly since, in the face of rising perils, union of all Frenchmen is more desirable than ever. If the fatherland is in danger tomorrow, all its children will not be too many for its defense."[68] When one rightist deputy alluded to the amnesty of the communards in July 1880, the Socialist Daniel Mayer responded angrily:

> How tactless you are to cite Victor Hugo at length in order to draw a parallel between the soldiers of the Commune and the collaborators of 1940–1944. The Commune's soldiers—and I do not speak of their social designs or their economic experiments—were those who, right up to the Wall of the Fédérés, sought to do battle with the adversary to which you surrendered in 1940.[69]

Mayer's intent, of course, was to point out that the Resistance had been a patriotic response and that the collaborators, whatever else they may have been, were *also* traitors and judged as such. As for the need for national unity:

> We had it at one point, and if you are determined at all cost to unite all men and all parties, then take [Nazi victims] Gabriel Péri, Pierre Sémard, Pierre Brossolette, Marx Dormoy, Estienne d'Orves, Gilbert Dru . . . and all those who, on the benches of this chamber, and whatever they may have been thinking, embodied what André Malraux once called "a moment of human dignity."[70]

In 1952 amnesty was undeniably an act of clemency and an attempt to calm political passions and salve old wounds. The problems of the purge, political as well as legal, had considerably prolonged the *guerre franco-française,* which by 1952 had been raging for eight, twelve, or eighteen years, according as one traced its beginning back to 1944, 1940, or 1934. Like any political "reconciliation," however, this one involved its share of ulterior motives and misunderstandings. Numerous bills, for example, had proposed granting amnesty simultaneously to collaborators and to those found guilty of criminal offenses during strikes in 1947 and 1948, a linkage that provoked howls of outrage from the Communists although it had previously been made in the partial amnesty law of 1947.

The battle between right and left thus supplanted solidarities born of the Resistance. But the change did not come about without incident. When Deputy Roger de Saivre, formerly assistant chief of staff under Pétain, was elected to the National Assembly in 1951, he urged his colleagues to eliminate "forever from our discussions and our public life that which has been poisoning it for so long," namely, debates about the collaboration and therefore about the Resistance. Georges Bidault, of all the deputies one of the staunchest supporters of amnesty, stood up and shouted, "Vive la Résistance!" His words were greeted with thunderous applause.

After a year of polemics and consideration of hundreds of amendments, the second amnesty law was passed on 24 July 1953 by a vote of 394 to 212. In a reflection of the law's ambiguities and the deputies' misgivings, the first article broke with customary practice and set forth the legislators' grounds for adopting the new law:

> The French Republic pays homage to the Resistance, whose combat both inside and outside our borders saved the nation. It is out of fidelity to the spirit of the Resistance that the Republic today wishes to grant clemency. Amnesty is neither rehabilitation nor revenge, nor is it a criticism of those who, in the name of the nation, bore the heavy burden of judgment and punishment.[71]

This preamble does little to hide the Assembly's paramount concern with justification. The first sentence, included at the behest of the Communist deputies (who voted against the law), was voted on separately and unanimously approved.

All remaining prisoners of the purge, except those guilty of the most serious crimes, were now released. The 1953 law thus marked the end of France's *épuration*. Although the Haute Cour was reconvened in 1954 and again in 1960 to try escaped criminals who had returned to France, including Abel Bonnard, its sentences were henceforth only symbolic, as were those of the military tribunals that replaced the *cours de justice*. Of the 40,000 individuals sent to prison in 1945 for acts of collaboration, the number remaining in jail progressed as follows.[72]

1945	40,000
1948 (Dec.)	13,000 (amnesty 1947)
1949 (Oct.)	8,000
1950 (Apr.)	5,587

1951 (Jan.)	4,000
1952 (Oct.)	1,570 (amnesty 1951)
1956	62 (amnesty 1953)
1958	19
1964	none

It therefore took less than a decade for the ostracism to end. The bitterness evident in some quarters is not difficult to understand:

> Why and how was this country betrayed? What about treason? What treason? Where was the treason? How, under what law, to what end, and with what concerns did the people of this country live during that time? What did they do, and why did they do it? Everything went up in smoke, in exactly the same way as a little village called Oradour.[73]

A political victory for the right, the amnesty was a missed opportunity for the nation to remember. Yet it was no more capable than all the official ceremonies of preventing buried bitterness from erupting in recurrent, polemical fashion, not least because the divisions of the Occupation were not always ideological.

Feverish Reminiscences

It was not within the power of the legal amnesty to quell all reminiscence of the Occupation, and in the early 1950s numerous eyewitness accounts and memoirs began to appear. These revealed fault lines that separated not opposing political ideas but different religious beliefs, community values, and sentiments born of the peculiar geography of the Occupation itself.

The Finaly Children

On 3 February 1953 the so-called Finaly affair first captured the attention of the public. Two Jewish children, aged twelve and thirteen, whose parents had died at Auschwitz, were "kidnapped" by the woman who had been taking care of them, Antoinette Brun. The children had been entrusted to her by the nuns of Notre-Dame-de-Sion, who had saved them and many others like them from the slaughter.

54

Claimed after the war by relatives living in Israel, the children became the focus of an emotional and religious dispute. When a member of the Jewish community came to check on the children, Brun is alleged to have said: "I turned them into little Catholics." Meanwhile, the Catholic hierarchy attempted to justify their ill-timed baptism, which triggered a heated response from the rabbinate. The affair lasted until 26 June 1953, when the children were handed over to their family.

The Jewish community, however, had many questions about the matter. Did the role of certain Christian organizations in saving Jews justify the church's attitude? What about the children's actual parents, who had been cremated in the ovens? André Kaspi summed up the issues succinctly: "Are [French Jews] now considered to be full-fledged French citizens? In claiming their identity, can they count on the sympathy of others, Catholics first and foremost?"[74] Caught up in a complex tissue of memories, this incident erupted into a major drama with symbolic value: when the Finaly children arrived in Israel in July 1953, they were greeted with flowers and banners. The episode revealed all that was unique about Jewish memories of the war, distinct from the memories of other deportees. In the symptomatology of the Vichy syndrome, Jewish memories occupy a place of their own, about which I shall have more to say later.

The Children of Oradour and Alsace

On 12 January 1953 an unusual trial began before the military tribunal of Bordeaux. Twenty-one survivors of the Das Reich division of the SS were charged with a crime that had become the symbol of Nazi military barbarity: the massacre of 642 residents of the village of Oradour-sur-Glane in the Haute-Vienne department.

There were no German officers among the accused and only two NCOs, minor players. The case might have been the occasion for a new war-crimes trial that would have meted out some justice, however inadequate, for the countless crimes committed by the occupying forces. In the event, however, it became a national drama. "Was it an accident or a dreadful paradox," Jean-Pierre Rioux asked, that fourteen of the twenty-one accused were French nationals, natives of Alsace, twelve of whom had been conscripted "against their will" into the Waffen SS, along with one volunteer and one person whose status was unclear?[75]

The case is extremely complex, not least from a legal standpoint. After deserting the SS, most of the indicted Alsatians had joined either the FFI or the FFL. After the war the charges against them were dismissed. In 1953 they returned home, married, and began to forget about the drama in which they had been involved. Yet they were brought back into court under a retroactive law of 15 September 1948, which established the principle of "collective responsibility" for war crimes. The president of the court, whose task was arduous, made no reference to this law, however, for fear of drawing too blatant a parallel between the German and the French defendants. What emerges clearly from the case is the reluctance of the postwar authorities to deal with the thorny problem of the so-called *malgré-nous*, those who claimed to have been forced to serve in German units against their will. During National Assembly debates on the Bordeaux trial, certain deputies were quick to point this out: "Surely what emerges from the midst of this drama is the problem of the forcible conscripts . . . Unfortunately, this issue appears to have been ignored in the past. The least that can be said, in any case, is that governments faced with many other postwar concerns failed to consider and deal with this one."[76] What this deputy considered to be an act of omission looks remarkably like political repression (in the Freudian sense), although eventually the repressed material tragically resurfaced in the course of the judicial process.

The political aspects of the case were also complex, because it burst on the scene just as the countries of Europe were making progress toward reconciliation. In Bonn Chancellor Adenauer was afraid that the trial might damage the credibility of the young West German democracy. In France the Communists, the only party not divided on the issue, noted the coincidence of calls for amnesty with the proposal for a European army and denounced both in their customary language. One Communist deputy, Marcel Rosenblatt, challenged his opponents in these terms: "You know full well that the Americans have called the SS the best European soldiers. That's why you need them."[77]

The last and crucial point was that the case involved two conflicting sets of memories, both belonging to victims who had suffered yet incompatible with each other. Groups representing the families of the Oradour victims called for justice, while organizations in Alsace, particularly the Association des Déserteurs, Evadés, et Incorporés de Force (ADEIF), which represented deserters, escapees, and forcible conscripts, argued that the province had already paid dearly during the Occupation. André Moser, an attorney representing the Alsatians, made this point in his closing argument:

> For us, these young people are the living embodiment of our tragedy. We are afraid of the hurricane that is gathering strength above our plain. It is Alsace that will either bear the brunt of the winds of condemnation or breathe the fragrance of hope. Remember that beyond the cries of the 642 Limousin victims ring now and forever the shouts of the thousands of Alsatian victims, who died for the same cause.[78]

The Alsatian case initially met with success. On 28 January 1953 an amendment to the 1948 law drained it of its content by allowing the trial of the French defendants to be severed from that of the Germans at Bordeaux. After tense deliberations, however, the court handed down its verdict on 13 February: the two NCOs were sentenced to death, and the remaining French and German soldiers received terms at hard labor. France was in a state of shock.

Seizing the initiative, René Mayer, president of the Council of the Republic, filed a bill calling for amnesty for forcible conscripts. Debate on this measure proceeded in parallel with debate on amnesty for collaborators, but was less polemical. On second reading the bill passed by a vote of 300 to 228. All the Communists, a majority of the Socialists, and a third of the Radicals voted against it.[79] Like the amnesty act of July 1953, the first draft of the new bill contained a preamble in which the victims of Oradour received special mention. This preamble was eliminated from the second reading, however, after it was rejected by the Council: on questions of pardon, the deputies had a decidedly bad conscience. On 21 February 1953 the Alsatians were freed.

This case sheds light on two additional factors that influenced memories of the war. The courts had proved incapable of reaching an equitable verdict. This was even more true now than it had been during the purge, which had proceeded in an atmosphere of civil war. (Indeed, the bad memories left by the purge may have been at least partly responsible for the courts' difficulties now.) Whenever the judicial system was called upon to resolve an issue stemming from the Occupation, the courts found themselves, on the one hand, prisoners of their respect for the law, which often was ill equipped to deal with the situation, and on the other hand hamstrung by the political consequences of their decisions, when those decisions were not purely and simply preempted by the government. Thus the courts, to no surprise of jurists, proved incapable of writing history, while the decision to grant amnesty was a direct consequence of a symbolic inscription of the past in the present.

The courts were further hampered by the fact that this story was told differently depending on whether the teller was a "collaborator" or a "résistant," on the right or on the left, in Strasbourg or Limoges. We thus come to the second factor mentioned above. The Oradour affair demonstrated that the fault lines created by the Occupation were not simply ideological. They were also geographical, a reflection of the different situations existing in different parts of occupied France. As calm returned to Alsace, turmoil continued in the Limousin and bitterness grew. Like other victims of the war and the Occupation, the region felt that it had been a casualty twice over.

Unfinished mourning? Insuperable political contradictions halted the mourning process before it was over. Constant calls to forgive, to reconcile, even to forget the past clashed with an urgent need to deal with the spontaneous return of repressed material. Even with all the ceremonies and all the trials, old memories simply could not be contained; old wounds were reopened and the dead were hauled into court. Official symbols could not make shattered memories whole.

Furthermore, the idealized image of the Resistance contrasted sharply with the fact that actual résistants were being expelled from political organizations. The Communists quickly weeded out those who had been leaders in the clandestine struggle. The SFIO, meanwhile, turned its back on offers of help from elements of the Resistance and became the "party of the system," a symbol of the ambiguities of the Fourth Republic.[80] Although most deputies, particularly in the Fourth Republic's first legislature, had been leaders in the

Resistance, their real influence decreased steadily, especially after 1951. The traditional right based its new legitimacy more on the battle against resistantialism (with a *t*) and the purge than on values born of the war. Even the Gaullists of the RPF hesitated to allude to wartime heroism. This was the period in which the defining elements of the syndrome took shape: the Resistance became an ambiguous founding myth, while résistants were dismissed as troublesome individuals. Stripped of their memories, these résistants became all the more sensitive about the past.

In the mid-1950s the direct consequences of the Occupation began to fade as other urgent issues came to the fore (the colonial wars, the instability of the Fourth Republic, international tensions). Reference to the *années noires* never stopped, however. During the heated debates on the CED (European Defense Community) from 1952 to 1954, opponents of an alliance with Germany denounced the "new collabos" and enlisted the support of Resistance associations and groups. In the words of Jean-Pierre Rioux, this marked "a first, sudden reawakening of torments repressed since 1945."[81] Indeed, it was one of the first battles in which the memory of the Occupation began to act as a distorting mirror in controversies that had less and less direct connection with the fateful year 1940.

2

―――⊷◉⊶―――

REPRESSIONS
(1954–1971)

The year 1954 marked a turning point. France had only recently embarked on its first period of economic expansion unperturbed by wor-
ries about monetary instability. Growth had just begun to make its
mark. Perhaps it was only now that the Occupation could begin to
recede into the past. Previously, shortages and economic difficulties
had prolonged memories of the lean wartime years just as effectively
as the political aftermath had done. In 1952 Jean Dutourd had im-
mortalized the alimentary humiliations of the dark years in his fic-
tional diatribe against profiteering grocers, *Au Bon Beurre.*

Other hatreds and conflicts supplanted those of World War II. At
Dien Bien Phu in May 1954, the defeat of French forces by the Viet
Minh seriously undermined the tenuous reconstruction of the French
army that began in 1941 in Africa, continued in France in 1944, and
culminated in Germany in 1945, where the French contribution to
the downfall of the Third Reich helped the nation forget the debacle
of 1940. The inglorious end of the Indochina war and the beginning
of yet another war in Algeria once again compromised "French grandeur."

The year 1954 also marked the high point in the career of Pierre
Mendès France. Once again the nation had found a "providential
leader," one who might justifiably claim to be carrying on the resistance legacy and the struggle against "neo-Vichyite" politicians whose
renewed antisemitic attacks often were aimed personally at him. Yet
Mendès, though profoundly marked by the war, led a generation that,
while being a product of the Resistance, had little desire to rehash old
quarrels. Later, to be sure, Mendesist intellectuals did found the Club
Jean Moulin—named in honor not only of Moulin the Resistance
leader but perhaps even more of Moulin the republican prefect—but

this was only after de Gaulle's assumption of power on 13 May 1958 and was intended as a warning against hypothetical "fascist" temptations. Under Mendès the CED issue was finally laid to rest, with all its echoes of Munich. Ultimately, the battle over the CED did not prevent Franco-German reconciliation, which proved easier to obtain than reconciliation within France.

The Oberg-Knochen Trial

One of the last great postwar trials also began in 1954: that of Karl Oberg, commander of the SS in France from 1942 and 1944, and his adjutant Helmut Knochen. These two men bore ultimate responsibility for the battle against the Resistance and for implementation of the Final Solution in France. The trial therefore should have been an event of major symbolic importance.

In retrospect, however, one is struck by the fact that the case of Klaus Barbie, brought to trial some thirty years after Oberg, aroused a much greater furor even before it went to court than did the relatively sedate Oberg case. Only a few years earlier, the last trials of French officials had stirred up more controversy than the Oberg affair. Yet the Oberg trial had revealed the scope of collaboration and repression under Vichy. René Bousquet, Vichy's chief of police, had been called as a witness and allowed to testify freely in his own defense.

As *Le Monde* correspondent Jean-Marc Théolleyre remarked at the time, much had been expected of this relatively rare testimony by a former Vichy official. Bousquet, a "young, elegant man looking quite trim in his gray suit, his face still tan from vacation sunshine,"[1] had been sentenced in 1949 to loss of his civil rights for a period of five years, this being the sentence automatically meted out to Vichy's ministers by the Haute Cour. He carefully delineated the scope of the agreements he had worked out with Oberg and Knochen between 2 and 4 July 1942 setting forth the terms of cooperation between the French police and the SS. (Among other things, these agreements had allowed the French police to arrest Jews in the summer of 1942, most notoriously in the so-called Vel d'Hiv roundup, named for the stadium in which Jewish detainees were held.) Caught up in the logic of his defense, Bousquet described these accords with the Germans as a victory, much as others have claimed that the earlier Montoire accords amounted to a "diplomatic Verdun." The former Vichy minister even went so far as to exonerate the accused Nazis: "I owe it to the truth to say that on most issues, the General gave me what I wanted. On the others, Berlin did not allow him to go any further than he did."[2]

Oberg's French attorneys sought to defend their client by preparing a summary of Vichy's responsibilities in the enforcement of anti-Jewish laws and edicts, a summary that in many ways anticipated historical findings of the 1970s and 1980s. The facts, however, did not speak for themselves. The trial was not a suitable context for bringing to light the truth about the past. And the revelations were necessarily tainted, since the lawyers were bound, as defense attorneys, to insist that their clients were "honorable" men.

The Oberg-Knochen trial thus served as a screen, a salve for guilty consciences. On 9 October 1954 the military tribunal of Paris sentenced the two Nazis to death, but the death sentences were commuted by René Coty in 1958 and in 1962 General de Gaulle freed the two men after eighteen years in prison. This was much harsher punishment than was meted out to most collaborators, many of whom were freed before the end of the fifties; it was less severe than that of Adolf Eichmann, who was hanged in Jerusalem—also in 1962, the same year that Oberg and Kochen were released.

The Syndrome in the Chamber

Over the next few years the visible signs of the wartime legacy gradually vanished. Occasionally a figure with a dubious past would surface, reopening old wounds. In politics and intellectual life such cases were not uncommon, though few attracted much notoriety.

There was, for example, a stormy debate in the National Assembly on 18 April 1956. Jean Legendre, an Independent (right-wing) deputy from the Oise department, asked that the January election of Robert Hersant, a Mendesist Republican, be declared invalid. Legendre's case was based on Hersant's past, shady aspects of which were brought to light for the first time.

In August 1940, at the age of twenty, Hersant had founded a small political movement known as Jeune Front (Young Front), not unlike other small political groups that sprang up in the early stages of the Occupation. In 1941 he became the director of a so-called Marshall Pétain Youth Center in Brévannes and later launched a newspaper known as *Jeunes Forces*. On several occasions he published articles in the collaborationist press.[3] In April 1945 he ran for municipal office in Paris but was indicted in June for acts harmful to state security and collaboration. He spent a month in jail and in 1947 was stripped of his civil rights for ten years for having briefly served as director of the Young Front; in 1952 his civil rights were restored under the terms of the amnesty.[4] Had he not become, in later years, a highly controversial figure and powerful press magnate, his past probably would not have created as much of a stir.

The attack on him in 1956 was a purely political maneuver. With his back to the wall, Hersant did a poor job of defending his record. To justify his role in establishing Pétainist youth centers, he alluded to the unemployment that had existed at the time and claimed that the centers had been run by officials of the Jeunesse Ouvrière Chrétienne (JOC, or Christian Working Youth). This allegation incurred the wrath of another deputy, Fernand Bouxom: "The leaders of the JOC were being arrested at that time! There's a small difference there!" Hersant admitted his role in establishing Jeune Front but denied that it was a collaborationist movement. He also claimed that he had received a relatively light sentence in 1947, at a time when "judgments were particularly severe for those who had collaborated" (which was inaccurate, the trend having been toward lighter sentences). When Jean Legendre reminded him that the court in rendering judgment had alluded to alleged propaganda activities on behalf of the LVF, Hersant's reply was even more inept: "That is completely ridiculous. The alleged incidents occurred in 1942, and the LVF was only established two years later."[5]

But such details are not what make the case interesting. Branded a "collaborator," Hersant was denied his seat in the chamber by a vote of 125 to 11. The Communists, along with most Socialists and Radicals, abstained from voting, however. Most of the hostile votes came from the Poujadists, Independents, and segments of the MRP, while the eleven votes in favor came from Republican colleagues. In other words, elements of the right with the closest ties to Pétainism enjoyed the rare luxury of skewering a "collabo" in the ranks of the left. The judgment was political, not moral. Jean Legendre, "stentorian spokes-man for the [anti-Mendesist] sugarbeet growers," cared not a jot about Hersant's collaborationist past. It was the Mendesist he went after, just as he had previously gone after Mendès' interior minister, François Mitterrand, for allegedly leaking classified information in a case involving "anticommunist counterintelligence activities."[6] In any case, the invalidation of Hersant's election did not last long; he was reelected deputy for the Oise on 18 June 1956, and this time there was no protest.

The Hersant affair shows the mechanism underlying accusations of collaboration. The condemnation of the man's past had nothing to do with the acts he was alleged to have committed. In 1956 the attack on him was launched by the right. In the 1970s it would be renewed with even greater vigor by the left, partly because Hersant had by then become a powerful press baron and partly because people had become more attuned to the realities of the 1940s. In both cases, however, the attack was merely a ploy, a distortion of the past for tactical purposes.

The Syndrome in the Académie Française

On 20 April 1958 a scandal erupted in the Académie Française. Word that writer Paul Morand would seek election to that august body provoked a wave of indignation among those *immortels* who had been part of the Resistance. Here, at least, there was no ambiguity: Morand had joined the Nazi camp even before the fall of France.

In *France la doulce* (first published in 1934 and translated into German in 1939) Morand had denounced what he called, in veiled terms, the *pègre cosmopolite* (cosmopolitan underworld). After the invasion the German Propaganda Abteilung mentioned him, along with Jacques Chardonne and Robert Brasillach, as an exemplar of the "new French literature," whose attitude toward the occupying power was deemed "extremely positive."[7] A career diplomat, Morand served in 1943 as Vichy's ambassador to Rumania. In July 1944 he was named ambassador to Switzerland with the help of Jean Jardin and over the objections of the Swiss. He wrote for collaborationist papers such as *Combats,* the organ of the Milice, to which he contributed along with other well-known writers including Colette and Pierre

Mac Orlan.[8] At the Liberation he was removed from his post. In 1953, however, the Conseil d'Etat revoked this decision, and two years later he was readmitted to the diplomatic service. In *Le Flagellant de Séville* (1951) he described the occupation of Spain by Napoleon's army in terms that seemed to justify collaboration and to lampoon resistance.

Given this history, it may seem surprising that he would have attempted to gain entry to the Académie, but it should be borne in mind that this institution had been a bastion of respectable Pétainism since the Liberation. In 1944–45 it had been threatened with dissolution by General de Gaulle, who forced cancellation of its 1945 elections. Quite a few admirers of Pétain's National Revolution had once gathered under the cupola of the academy, and four of the most prominent of them had been forced out during the postwar purge: Charles Maurras, Pétain himself, Abel Bonnard, and Abel Hermant. Bonnard and Hermant were replaced in 1946 by Jules Romains and Etienne Gilson, but the other two seats were to remain vacant until after the deaths of Maurras and Pétain.

In 1958 only thirteen of the Académie's forty chairs were occupied by men elected prior to 1940, the year of the last pre-Occupation election; during the Occupation no elections had been held. Between 1944 and 1946 twenty-odd new members were elected, including quite a few writers and other prominent figures associated with, or reputed to have been associated with, the Resistance, among whom were Louis Pasteur Vallery-Radot, Jules Romains, and André Siegfried. Despite this wholesale change of personnel, however, the Pétainist clan remained quite powerful, not least on the several occasions when the influence of Pétain and Maurras had made itself felt. In 1953 former ambassador André François-Poncet was elected to Pétain's chair. It is customary for new members of the Académie to deliver a eulogy to their predecessors, and François-Poncet's speech was, for obvious reasons, anxiously awaited. The diplomat proved equal to the challenge, which he faced with not a little courage and considerable rhetorical skill: he expounded the view that Pétain had served as a "shield" for France and shifted all blame to Laval, while at the same time insisting on his admiration for de Gaulle (who was nevertheless greatly irritated by the shield metaphor): "Though I do not mistake the intentions of the man who wished to cover France with a shield, I have often paid silent homage, as here in your presence I pay public homage, to the man who picked up the sword that had fallen from our hands."[9]

Traditionally the new member's eulogy is followed by another academician's response, and in this case the respondent was Pierre Benoit, who spoke on the theme of reconciliation, a favorite topic of the Pétainists: "My impression is that nothing is left for us to do but to congratulate ourselves for having done our best to bring about this union."[10] In the following year Robert Aron published his *Histoire de Vichy,* a book that develops even more fully the theme of the shield and the sword, a variation on the parable of the two strings.[11] In 1956 François-Poncet was again called upon to address the Académie, this time to welcome Jérôme Carcopino, who had served as minister of education under Vichy. On this occasion the ex-ambassador felt at liberty to ignore the more controversial aspects of the new member's career and to concentrate his praise on Carcopino's achievements as a student of Roman history.

For Paul Morand in 1958, however, equivocation was more difficult; the writer's past commitments could not simply be swept under the rug. It was not Morand the friend of Proust and Giraudoux who stood as a candidate for election, but Morand the man of Vichy, not to say the collaborator—a term that had been carefully avoided until then, except when François-Poncet used it to blacken the name of Laval. Morand's candidacy was taken as an act of political provocation. André Siegfried, who published an anonymous (but transparent) article in the *Revue française de science politique,* viewed it as such and named the man he believed to be behind it: Jacques de Lacretelle.[12] Along with ten of his colleagues, led by Mauriac and Romains, Siegfried signed a letter in the form of a petition from the "résistant" clan to François-Poncet, who was acting director of the academy for the current trimester:

> The undersigned members of the Académie Française do not question the candidate's literary credentials. But his name and his role during the last war remain associated with memories and grievances whose nature is such as to revive old controversies and conflicts better settled by the passage of time.[13]

They walked into a trap, one that had no doubt been carefully laid, for there was no way to exclude Morand without provoking precisely the kind of controversy that the petitioners had wished to avoid—Morand's past would have to be brought out and, with it, all the bad memories alluded to in the petition. Jules Romains, who was in the United States during the war, made a more sharply political case against Morand in *L'Aurore*. To elect Morand, he argued, would signify "the revenge of the Collaboration on a France that had first spurned the enemy and then driven it from French soil and on an intellectual elite that had preferred to incur the hostility of the government and to run the risks of resistance or exile rather than accept the favors of the occupying power."[14]

Jacques de Lacretelle took up Morand's defense, citing the testimony of Jews whom the writer had allegedly saved and using as a pretext the Conseil d'Etat's decision to reverse Morand's dismissal from the diplomatic service.[15] Interestingly, Lucien Rebatet rose to Morand's defense in *Rivarol* (8 May 1958): "This liberal, this unwavering 'good European,' at one glance took the measure of de Gaulle and his clique in London in 1940, returned to France, and agreed to represent French interests in a country enmeshed in battle with Stalin." The paper, however, took the position that the opposition to Morand was not really political at all but a settling of personal and literary scores led by Jules Romains, Georges Duhamel, and above all François Mauriac.

The Morand case clearly demonstrates the failure of the purge to establish a clear definition of the crimes and misdemeanors of collaboration. The Pétainists capitalized on this failure: why should Morand be excluded when he had not been found guilty of violating any law? The charge seemed to have merit because it was difficult to admit that the judicial system had not been equal to the task assigned to it.

The academy election of 22 May 1958 was thus an extremely tense occasion. In a clever stratagem, two elections were conducted simultaneously: one to fill the seat of Edouard Herriot, for which Jean Rostand was the favorite, and another to fill the seat of Claude Farrère, for which Paul Morand and Jacques Bardoux vied for the favors of the right. The deal was supposed to be that the right would give the left Rostand in exchange for Morand, but this shrewd bargain went disastrously awry. Faced with outspoken hostility to its candidate, the Pétainist clan blocked the election of Rostand, who, like Morand, received only eighteen of the nineteen votes required to don the academician's sword. Furious, Pierre Benoit, organizer of the election, declared that he would never again set foot in the Académie. "He was never seen again," the duc de Castries laconically reports.[16]

Stubbornly, Morand stood for election again in 1959. This was his third try, for he had also failed back in 1936. The affair came to the attention of the new head of state, however. Reverting to the argument made by the petitioners in 1958, de Gaulle disapproved of Morand's candidacy "because of the partisan hatreds the writer would arouse within the Académie."[17] Morand was forced to withdraw. The author of *L'Homme pressé* (The Man in a Hurry) would have to wait nine more years for a place under the cupola, which he finally won in October 1968, after the General withdrew his veto. Morand was elected to the chair of attorney Maurice Garçon, one of those who had signed the petition against him in 1958. In 1975 another writer, Félicien Marceau, provoked a new controversy over his work for Belgian radio during the Occupation, in spite of which he was elected to the chair of Marcel Achard. This time it was Pierre Emmanuel, an authentic member of the "intellectual elite" alluded to by Jules Romains, who stalked out of the Académie, never to be seen again.

May, June, July

General de Gaulle's return to power in 1958 reminded many people of his radio appeal to the French on 18 June 1940. Among Gaullists, the memory of that day was directly relevant to the situation of France eighteen years earlier, for behind the Algerian question loomed the specter of the 1940 defeat and the collapse of the state. At times these reminiscences took on an almost surreal quality. Corsica, for example, had been the second department of France to be liberated in 1943, just after Algeria, and the Corsica landing of 24 May 1958 (Operation Resurrection) was preceded by broadcast messages reminiscent of the clandestine radio of the wartime years.

The General's return also stirred memories among his adversaries, who recalled the controversial vote of 10 July 1940 granting Pétain full powers to govern France. The political legitimacy of de Gaulle's call for resistance rested on the questionable legality of this vote. The left was quick to draw the analogy. On 1 June 1958, the day of the brief ceremony marking de Gaulle's investiture by the National Assembly, Mendès France spoke in terms reminiscent of Danton: "The people believe we are free, but we no longer are. My dignity prevents me from giving in to this pressure from the factions and the streets."[18] He might well have uttered these same words in the casino of Vichy, breaking a certain lugubrious silence there, had he not been captured while attempting to leave France and thus found himself imprisoned in Rabat on that fateful day. René Rémond makes a similar point about the attitude of François Mitterrand: "Who can say that Mitterrand, in declaring himself an unalterable opponent [of the new Gaullist regime] on 1 June 1958, was not convinced that he was the authentic heir of the spirit of 18 June?"[19] Later, in *Le Coup d'état permanent*, Mitterrand would deplore the "illicit profit" that the General derived from his glory: "Before going on, shall I cede to custom and hail the man of 18 June 1940, the leader of wartime France, the liberator of the Fatherland, and bemoan the misunderstanding that today pits him against former comrades who remain republicans?"[20]

The extreme right, and especially the Pétainists, also found it expedient to exploit the parallel between 1940 and 1958, which gave rise to some disturbing comparisons. On 3 June 1958, the date of a vote to amend article 90 of the constitution so as to allow the new government to introduce further amendments, one deputy, Tixier-Vignancour, a supporter of Pétain during the Occupation and leader of the extreme right, argued that the Assembly had no business delegating the power to revise the constitution to de Gaulle. Only a few days before, Tixier had voted in favor of de Gaulle's investiture, just as he had voted for and still defended the granting of full powers to Pétain. A formidable debater, Tixier justified his negative vote on article 90 by invoking the precedent of 1940:

> Monsieur le Président du Conseil, some years ago [during the Occupation] you convened in Algiers a commission of jurists among whom, if memory serves, was M. Edgar Faure, whom it pleases me to see today seated in this chamber . . . Now it so happens that this commission informed me and other deputies and senators of the

Third Republic—those who had voted on 10 July 1940 to approve a motion stating that the government would proceed to draft a constitution to be ratified by the nation and applied by such assemblies as it might create—that we had no right to delegate such constituent authority, and that therefore we 580 deputies and senators had committed a grave error for which we were to be punished by being declared, as it was termed, ineligible for elective office.

Amid thunderous protest Tixier concluded:

You will forgive me for thinking that never in my wildest dreams would I have imagined that I would be asked twice in my life to delegate the fraction of constitutive authority that I held and, what is more, that for this second occasion I would be asked to do so by the very same man who punished me for having done it the first time.

Perhaps the most savory aspect of the whole episode is that Edgar Faure by no means lost countenance at the derogatory allusion to his role, as this exchange between the two men shows:

Faure: Monsieur Tixier-Vignancour, may I interrupt?
Tixier: Certainly.
Faure: I thank you for your courtesy . . . I must say that the question of delegation of constituent authority is indeed a delicate one. But, Monsieur Tixier-Vignancour, as it seems that both of us, searching our memories, have followed a similar path, at least up to a certain point, it so happens that I have with me this evening a journal published in Algiers at the time when—under your supervision, Monsieur le Président du Conseil—I had the privilege of heading the legislative services of the Committee of National Liberation.
Tixier: I was aware that you had brought that journal with you.[21]

Vichy was indeed on everyone's mind. A debate on constitutional law ensued, in which Tixier, supported by Jacques Isorni, attempted to use contemporary Gaullist arguments to prove that the vote of 10 July 1940 had been perfectly legal:

Tixier: The text that was approved [in 1940] explicitly did not provide for any application of the constitution, as its wording

70

shows: "It will be ratified by the nation and applied by such assemblies as it may create."

J. Minjoz: You are overlooking the essential point: the preceding assemblies had been abolished.

Tixier: That is precisely what is going to happen to you, my dear colleague, precisely that![22]

What a strange debate, with its bewildering shifts from past to present and back again. Roles were reversed and political bearings were lost in a storm of withering wit. The debate certainly had its comical side, which might seem inappropriate given the momentousness of the issue being debated before the Chamber. The whole controversy served more than anything else to confuse the past and destroy the organic unity of the event. The past was plundered by both sides to provide historical justification for action in the present, but at the same time it was shown to be infinitely malleable, manipulable at will for rhetorical effect and slanderous purpose. Had the symbols being invoked become mere political instruments, or did they still have real emotional significance? It would scarcely matter if the Occupation were of concern only to the politicians, but in fact it was a trauma from which the whole society still suffered. False analogies and, later, the abusive use of certain words (such as "genocide") did not deceive anyone who had lived through the events, but they probably did induce a certain fatigue in people less keenly attuned to the issues.

The Gaullian Exorcism

De Gaulle's vision of the Occupation took shape in five stages. At the time of the Liberation the General laid the two main cornerstones: the obliteration of Vichy and the redefinition of the Resistance as an abstraction, an achievement not of the résistants but of "the nation as a whole." From 1946 to 1950 he chose, as a political tactic, to appeal to a segment of the electorate by plucking the Pétain "string," a choice that had the effect of stirring up pro-Pétain sentiment. With the Rémy affair, however, things got out of hand, and the General dropped the hot potato. By then, moreover, Pétain was dead and the symbol had lost much of its potential value; after the Marshal's death, de Gaulle resumed his anti-Vichyite tone. Between 1954 and 1958, he returned to an earlier interpretation, one that he had first tried out in 1944 and now resurrected in the sixth chapter of his *Mémoires de guerre:* that the history of France from 1940 to 1944 had been made in London and Algiers. Prior to the final crystallization of the resistancialist myth in the 1960s, he would once again attempt—in the fifth and final stage—to exorcise the year 1940.

On 30 December 1958, as part of budgetary economies under the Pinay-Rueff plan, veterans' retirement benefits were eliminated, a measure that affected many former résistants and provoked a public outcry. A year later, shortly before Armistice Day, de Gaulle explained his action: "Veterans are entitled to be first in line for honors; they are not entitled to be first in line for claims on the state."[23] Significantly, he alluded only to the situation of World War I veterans and said nothing about veterans of World War II or the colonial wars. Retirement benefits were quietly reinstated. Clearly this was a symbolic gesture, "whose financial significance was not great and whose expediency was not obvious."[24] The General appears to have had little desire to share his heroic legacy with others, no matter how distinguished their war record.

On 11 April 1959 came another insult. De Gaulle issued an order changing the date of the celebration of victory in Europe from 8 May to the second Sunday of the month. The reason given was that the proliferation of nonworking holidays was injurious "not only to the national economy but to certain occupational groups."[25] On Sunday, 9 May 1959, the government honored not just the Allied victory but also Joan of Arc, whose feast day happened to fall on that date. The ceremony, spurned by most veterans' organizations, thus lost something of its special significance.

In the same year, 1959, other celebrations took on new importance: on 18 June the General paid a visit to Mont Valérien; on 29 August he commemorated the liberation of the capital along with members of the Conseil National de la Résistance and the Comité Parisien de Libération; and finally, on 11 November, de Gaulle paid his respects to the dead of both world wars, just as in 1945.[26]

Yet while the General sought to highlight his personal idea of the Resistance, he took care, even as he promoted what he considered the essential unity of the nation, to show sensitivity to all schools of thought, not least through small gestures. In April 1959, just before the first senatorial elections of the Fifth Republic, de Gaulle visited Auvergne. It was an occasion for reviving old memories. On the eighteenth the president and his entourage stopped in Vichy. From the first it promised to be an interesting visit. The General exchanged a few words with Mayor Coulon:

—Since Albert Lebrun's visit in 1933, no president of the Republic has come to our city. [This was incorrect: the mayor "forgot" the fact that President Lebrun had come to Vichy in July 1940.]
 —My presence here has a somewhat unusual aspect owing to past events of which you are aware as well as to events of today.

De Gaulle then spoke to the citizens of Vichy, "queen of spas," whose municipal council had asked, in September 1944, that any allusion to the Vichy regime be stricken from the language:

I am going to make a confession that I must ask you not to repeat, but I have to tell you that it's a rather emotional occasion for me to be making an official visit to Vichy. You will understand the reasons why. But history is a continuous thread. We are one people, and whatever ups and downs we may have suffered, whatever events we may have seen, we are the great nation of France, the one and only French people. I say this in Vichy. I am bound to say this in Vichy. The past is finished. Long live Vichy! Long live France! Long live the Republic![27]

This was an astonishing speech, every bit as astonishing as the General's famous "Vive le Québec libre!" (a phrase he uttered during a speech in Montreal, provoking a furor in Canada). De Gaulle's "confession" with its lofty view of history enabled him to allude to the unspeakable past and its not yet forgotten horrors. He even played the sorcerer's apprentice by broaching the subject of national unity in the former capital of Pétain's France, knowing full well the negative significance still implicit in the word "Vichy," which he repeated emphatically, as if uttering a magic incantation. One of the ministers traveling with him spoke of "exorcism."[28]
 On the same day de Gaulle also paid homage to the people of Moulins: "I know all that was done here, and it was all the more meritorious because you here were on the periphery of the action . . . on that

73

gash in our territory known as the line of demarcation."[29] A short while later, on 6 June 1959, on his way from Clermont-Ferrand, the General stopped at Mont-Mouchet at the site of a monument to the French maquis. Between 16 and 20 June 1944 some three to four thousand guerrillas under the command of Colonel Gaspar had clashed in open battle with German forces and, before breaking off the engagement, left several of their number dead on the battlefield. For this visit de Gaulle was in uniform. With veterans of the United Resistance Movements lined up before him, the General walked forward alone toward their ranks and shouted, "Gaspar!" Gaspar stepped forward and bowed to the General, who again uttered Gaspar's name in an "emotional" voice before treating the leader of the maquis to "an affectionate thump in the pit of the stomach."

> While in Auvergne I was keen to pay my respects to those of our men who died at Mont-Mouchet. What happened here was a moving episode of the French Resistance which deserves to be more widely known. The attack was made when it had to be made, and those who fought here did not fight in vain. I am glad to participate in this ceremony with you, our maquisards, and their leader, Gaspar.[30]

This tribute was remarkable, if belated. On 1 July 1945 General de Gaulle, in the company of the Sultan of Morocco, made an official visit to Auvergne during which he refused to visit Mont-Mouchet. In Clermont he shook hands with several officials, including Gaspar, of whom he took no special notice.[31] At the time de Gaulle wished to minimize the influence and popularity of maquis leaders. Nor did he wish to stir up still fresh memories of the errors and weaknesses of the FFI's leadership at the time of the Allied landing. Local resistance fighters resented this omission. By 1959 the context had changed: it was not so much the maquis leader as the résistant that de Gaulle was honoring.

Within a few weeks the General had visited several memorial sites along a symbolic itinerary. He had exorcised the civil war, reminded people of the geographic (but no other) divisions enforced by the occupying powers, and, in his own way, celebrated the Resistance while refusing to grant it privileged status. New divisions stemming from the war in Algeria were too deep, however, to permit a definitive crystallization of the past.

Old Divisions Resurface

The historian must take care lest he too succumb to the charms of anachronism. When viewed in hindsight and with strict objectivity, the Algerian War has only a tenuous relation to the Occupation. But contemporaries did not see it that way. In their imaginations and slogans and at times in their actions, the most prominent figures in this new *guerre franco-française* identified with the men and events of 1940. Many of them, and especially the leaders, had been active during the Occupation. Hence the real anachronism is not to confuse the two sets of issues but to ignore memories of World War II as a factor in the Algerian conflict.

During the Algerian War historical analogy took on a new dimension. It became more than mere reminiscence and more than just a tactical device for blackening the reputation of one's enemies. Analogy became a way of laying claim to a political heritage. But the history in question was a tangled skein. The new divisions did not coincide exactly with those of 1940. The new fault line did not pass precisely between the camp of the résistants and that of the collaborators. Reclassifications in this area defined reclassifications in other areas as well, all of which depended to one degree or another on memories of the past. One consequence was that people were reminded of the fact that the choice between resistance and collaboration was insufficient to capture the true complexities of the divisions that existed in France during the Occupation.

Recently Pierre Vidal-Naquet has drawn a broad distinction among three ideal types of opposition to the Algerian War: the "bolsheviks," including neo-Leninist revolutionaries and dissident communists; the "third-worldists," including some of religious and some of secular bent; and the "Dreyfusards," whose allegiance was not so much to an idea of Algeria as to an idea of France.[32] Obviously it was among this third group that the resistance analogy took on symbolic value, particularly insofar as the Resistance was, in part, a continuation of a long-standing struggle against anti-Dreyfusard nationalism.

Initially this segment of the left denounced the resurgence of what it called fascism. This was evident in 1957, in the struggle against Algerian torture, and again in 1958 when, as we saw earlier, de Gaulle's assumption of power in May was likened to Pétain's acceptance of power on 10 July 1940. "The fascist plague and its imitations always draw strength from exacerbations and perversions of national feeling. The liberal state is collapsing at the very moment when it ought to be taking charge of the destiny of a menaced and humiliated nation," wrote Michel Winock.[33] The fascist label was applied not only to the ultranationalists but also to France's new "savior." Fascism was bandied about as a generic concept more than as a term having specific reference to the history of the 1930s and 1940s: anything that posed a threat to the republic and to democracy was fascist.

Two years later, however, the principal danger seemed to come from the OAS (Secret Armed Organization), whose struggle to keep Algeria French was only "a pretext, a way . . . of achieving what has always been their supreme objective: the conquest of power, the installation of a fascist regime."[34] As a result, General de Gaulle, the OAS's prime target, became for some people a bulwark against that particular fascist threat. Michel Winock remembers having been scandalized at the time when certain opponents of the war switched their support to the General: Roger Stéphane and Maurice Clavel, for example, tried to see de Gaulle as a providential leader, as the man not of 13 May but of 18 June. "Once again the General cast his shadow over editorial offices."[35]

Nevertheless, there were limits on the left to the use of the 1940 analogy. Once one started looking to the past, it was natural to go back beyond 1940 to the Dreyfus Affair. Furthermore, the 1940 analogy was inadequate to account for certain dimensions of the Algerian War: one man who has studied these issues, Bernard Droz, emphasizes that "the true civil war was that which devastated the Algerian people."[36] The obvious truth of this statement highlights the sometimes farfetched character of historical analogies based on France's internal conflicts. Finally, and what was no doubt the most crucial factor, the resistance heritage was not the sole possession of those who opposed the war in Algeria. Among those who favored keeping Algeria French, memories of the dark years were at once more imperious and more contradictory.

After World War II the extreme right in France evolved in a complex fashion. The Poujadists, after scoring an electoral success in 1956, saw their influence decline with the fall of the Fourth Republic. Although the left saw the Poujadists as heirs of Pétainism and fascism, those antecedents appear to have had little impact on the movement, whose ideological roots were shallow. There was an attempt to build a consensus around the notion of *nationalisme renouvelé,* modernized nationalism, an idea promoted by Pierre Boutang and his newspaper *La Nation française,* aimed at "men who wish to keep faith with the old Marshal whom they served and others who fought in the ranks of the Resistance and in the uniforms of Free France and who refuse to renounce anything in their past."[37] Only the Pétainists (Tixier-Vignancour, Jacques Isorni, and others) and the neofascists, such as Maurice Bardèche, remained loyal to the political traditions of the Occupation: the National Revolution for the former, the "new European order" for the latter.

De Gaulle's return in 1958 gave rise to considerable dissension. Among the hard-core Pétainists, Jacques Isorni refused to support the General in any way after the investiture vote of 1 June 1958: "The memories to which I am faithful, some of them stained with blood that has yet to be effaced by word or deed, prevent me from doing otherwise." Tixier-Vignancour, as we saw earlier, voted for investiture but against delegation of the power to draft a constitution. Finally, other Pétain supporters rallied behind de Gaulle: among those voting *oui* was the Marshal's wife.

The hesitant attitude of *Rivarol* is illuminating in this connection. A nostalgic Vichyite organ, *Rivarol* at first maintained its usual hostility toward the General: an editorial in the 15 May issue approved of "a government of public safety, yes, but not de Gaulle." In the following week, however, the paper published two photos side by side on its front page: one of Pétain, the other of de Gaulle. Each was captioned with a quotation: "To alleviate the suffering of France, I make a gift of my person" (Pétain, 16 June 1940); "I am a man who belongs to no one and to everyone" (de Gaulle, 19 May 1958). Having drawn this parallel, the editors with some reluctance found it possible to support de Gaulle, who, in spite of his "disastrous" actions in the past, was preferable to "keeping in power a pack of pretentious babblers" (editorial of 22 May 1958). Through July *Rivarol* stuck to this position, which can be summed up as follows: support de Gaulle out of loyalty to Pétain, and better de Gaulle than another Popular Front.

Unfortunately, the evolution of the Algerian conflict threw everything into turmoil once again. Hostility to the General created new support for a neofascism that had more than one thing in common with its model. The Mouvement Populaire Français (whose very name was an explicit allusion to Jacques Doriot's Parti Populaire Français) called for a war on both "capitalist plutocracy" and the Marxist class struggle, conducted Nazi-style parades, and paid solemn homage "to the great Europeans who knew how to live and die for the great cause of the white peoples of the world: José Primo de Rivera, Marcel Déat, Drieu La Rochelle, Jacques Doriot, Robert Brasillach, Marcel Bucard, and others."[38] Jeune Nation, one of the most active movements, was founded by three brothers, François, Pierre, and Jacques Sidos, sons of an inspector-general in the Milice who was executed in March 1946. François Sidos enlisted in the Forces Françaises Combattantes in 1940 and fought the Nazis, while the other two, Pierre and Jacques, were incarcerated at the time of the Liberation for having collaborated with them.

The battle to keep Algeria French briefly encouraged illusions of unity among these nostalgics for Vichy:

> The liquidation of France's colonial empire brought forces to the national opposition that had been lacking since 1945. Relieved of the heavy burden of Vichy, it could once again appeal to the nationalism, indeed to the pure and simple patriotism of the French people, to oppose the abandonment of an important segment of the nation's territory. The army became receptive to its propaganda, and a million *pieds-noirs* [Algerian-born Frenchmen] constitute what is apparently the largest force of shock troops that the national opposition has commanded since the purge.[39]

This vengeful spirit was widespread among those who had been ostracized in 1945. On 6 December 1960 a branch of the Pétain association was established in Algiers. In the group's first official act, members swore to continue the struggle for "French land" with "arms in hand if necessary" and to see to it that "all sell-outs and traitors to the fatherland" would be brought to trial before the Haute Cour; they also swore to ensure that the remains of "the man who twice saved the Fatherland and who, in 1940, despite the defeat and the Occupation, was able to keep France's territory and national treasure intact" would be transported to Douaumont.[40] Note the familiar inversion of logic and the use of false analogies: the traitor de Gaulle is to be tried before the Haute Cour for selling out an empire saved in 1940 by Pétain and the Armistice, making it possible to mount a military resistance (the only legitimate resistance) in Africa. Advancing the same argument, General Weygand broke his silence in October 1959 to proclaim that Algeria was French, a declaration that would lead de Gaulle to write of "an occasion for giving vent to the rancors of Vichy."[41]

Yet allusions to the Occupation sustained attitudes other than hostility and revenge. Authentic former résistants, many of them well known, numbered among the most intransigent opponents of Algerian independence. Château-Jobert, a leader of the OAS and zealous defender of the "Christian West," was a veteran of the FFL and Compagnon de la Libération, as were Jacques Soustelle and Georges Bidault. Bidault's case is especially noteworthy, because in 1962 he did not hesitate to support the OAS by founding what he called the Conseil National de la Résistance, a name that evoked memories of the organization of which Bidault became the head in 1943 after the death of Jean Moulin.

Bidault attempted to justify his action in his memoirs. He argued, not inaccurately, that the empire had been the principal preoccupation of wartime Gaullism, pretending not to notice any difference between the geopolitical situation of 1940–1944 and that of 1958–1962. What is interesting about his argument, however, is not so much its polemical aspect as its fidelity to a certain *sensibility*, which sheds some light on the complex posterity of resistance participation:

> Among those who had truly been resistance fighters, who had faced real dangers, there were not a few who judged me guilty of bad taste for plucking the Resistance out of the museum for a purpose which, though identical to our primary aims, no longer enjoyed the good fortune of pleasing them. The fact must be faced: many résistants had gone into retirement ... Many were convinced that the epic they had known firsthand could not and should not be repeated. In their minds the Resistance was such a beautiful thing that it must remain a unique memory, never to be seen again. Its place was in the Old Soldiers' Museum. What they liked about it was what would never recur.[42]

Coming from the leader of the MRP, the principal architect of the amnesty and pardon, this call for commitment on behalf of a memory of the past has a rather strange ring. In some ways it echoes the sentiments of those adversaries of an *Algérie française* whose commitment stemmed from memories of their youth in the Resistance and who, like Bidault, had resisted the temptation to rest on their laurels as old soldiers. Yet Bidault's loyalty to the past did not prevent him from drawing the logical implications of his hatred of de Gaulle. In 1965, even as he was drafting the above lines, Bidault in exile addressed a message to supporters of Pétain on one of the many occasions when it was thought the Marshal's ashes might be transferred to Douaumont and a few months before the 1965 presidential election:

> Without renouncing or changing anything that I did or said in those darkest of times, and speaking as one who has never owed Pétain anything, who never fought him half-heartedly, who was neither his protégé nor his godson, but who was his enemy, I say that today, at this very moment, it is the right of those who have known, as I have known, the hardships, horrors, and rigors of combat in the Resistance on French soil to say, and to say out loud, [that] Pétain had the Germans on his back and that he saved the Empire. And it was the man who, in opposition to Pétain, demanded that the Empire join the war and who proclaimed that Pétain was about to deliver it to the enemy, who, once the victory was won, and in spite of solemn commitments, made a gift of that same Empire to the scum who deported our families and ruined North Africa . . . The summit of Marshal Pétain's life was Douaumont. The summit of General de Gaulle's life was London and Algiers . . . Pétain died at Douaumont; de Gaulle died in Algiers.[43]

Let me make my position clear: the Algerian War, as I said earlier, was not governed solely by the logic of reminiscence. From it, however, we can derive a useful catalog of the various ways in which the past can be mobilized for political purposes:

—*As heritage.* Some of the arguments put forward on both sides of the conflict clearly sprang from roots in the past. Some ultranationalists emulated the men of Vichy in their desire to destroy the republic and even emulated collaborators in their desire to install a fascist regime. These goals did damage to the cause of the extreme right. The army did not, in its entirety, favor the "counterrevolution" of the OAS—far from it. And most of the proponents of a French Algeria were not attracted by the idea of a French-style fascism. According to René Chiroux, many were embarrassed by the bad image that attached to their cause.[44] On the left, the struggle against the Algerian War brought forward new ideas and new leaders, often from outside the established parties, much as the struggle against the German Occupation had done.

—As *nostalgia*. Some of the men and women on both sides of the Algerian conflict forged their commitment out of memories of the Occupation, hence of their youth and earliest battles, which set the pattern for subsequent commitments. Nostalgia thus played a direct role, as in Bidault's appropriation of the CNR name, as in the memories of wartime Gaullism that motivated some on the left, and even, to take an extreme example, as in the emulation of Nazism by certain small groups. Neither the right nor the left could do without nostalgia.

—As *fantasy* (or the Maurras complex). In January 1945 Charles Maurras, upon receiving a life sentence and true to his certainties and dogmas, exclaimed: "This is Dreyfus' revenge!" Four decades after the Dreyfus Affair, these angry words were intended as an unambiguous declaration of Maurras' belief that the enemy condemning him in 1945, ironically to the same sentence as Dreyfus, was structurally the same enemy he had always been fighting, the republican government that he contemptuously called *la Gueuse* (the trollop). This belief only enhanced his legitimacy in his own eyes and reinforced his identity. As Mona Ozouf wrote of the Action Française's homage, on the occasion of the hundred-and-fiftieth anniversary of the French Revolution in 1939, to Charlotte Corday [who murdered Marat during the Revolution] and to the Vendean rebels [who rose against the First Republic in 1793]: "If those on the other side are always the same, how could those who oppose them be anything but what they had always been, yet even more so?"[45] In order to exist through time, to keep the faith despite duration, an enemy must be invented, an enemy that is also impervious to the effects of time. (Similar kinds of behavior could be seen in the 1960s.) The enemy must take on the traits of the devil; the crisis is too grave, the stakes too high, to permit anything less. The enemy becomes an abstraction, the absolute adversary with whom no compromise is possible. For those who felt themselves victims of the postwar purge, the enemy, after some vacillation, became de Gaulle, the one and only de Gaulle, the everlasting de Gaulle. For Bidault the enemy was the "spirit of surrender," the same spirit that had led France to give up the fight in 1940 and to abandon the empire in 1962. On the left the enemy was the specter of an anti-Dreyfusard reaction and of course of fascism, which, real or mythical, was frequently brandished in order to attract recruits and unify the ranks.

The war in Algeria, observed from the metropolis, was indeed a reprise of the *guerre franco-française,* but only insofar as old cleavages reproduced themselves in people's minds. What they saw, then, was not an image of the past but a transformation of that image to suit contemporary conditions.

An Invented Honor

The French love anniversaries, especially twentieth, twenty-fifth, thirtieth, and fortieth anniversaries. Such dates always take on a particular luminosity: round numbers are reassuring because they stir memories. The year 1964 was no exception. It was both a turning point and a culmination. France's new wounds from the Algerian War and old Occupation wounds that Algeria reopened had begun to heal (although they too would leave scars in memory). Nostalgia for the past gave way to optimistic dreams of a future planned by cheerful technocrats.

The time had come for Gaullism to leave its troubled past behind and to establish its legitimacy on a sublimated version of history. Exorcism was no longer the order of the day; now the challenge was to bestow on France an "invented honor."[46]

The problem was not just to bury memories of the *guerre franco-française* once and for all but to orient all future memory, to forge an official version of the past appropriate to the country's newfound "grandeur." It was in 1964 that this new version of the Occupation—a version most comforting to French sensibilities—achieved its definitive form: France was now cast as a nation that "forever and always resists the invader," whatever uniform he might wear, be it the gray-green of the German army or the paraphernalia of the Roman legions. In 1959 René Goscinny and Albert Uderzo, two little-known cartoonists working for the new newspaper *Pilote,* reinvented the immortal Gaul in the character of Astérix. In 1963 Astérix was made to conquer the Goths and give a pasting to several Gallo-Roman "collaborators." But it was not until the end of 1980, after Goscinny had died, that Uderzo openly alluded to the "great divide" that cut the village in two.

Since 1964 a prize has been awarded each year in every school in France for the best essay on "the Resistance and deportation." Along with grammar and the history of the republic, the heroic deeds of the previous generation were to help shape today's pupil and tomorrow's citizen. The Resistance became a common theme of films, novels, and historical treatises, while Vichy and collaboration fell under a taboo that was rarely violated. Such a diversion of memory called for a consecration with full Gaullian pomp, and in due course a suitable occasion was found: the transfer of Jean Moulin's ashes to the Pantheon.

The idea was first broached in the spring of 1963. It was proposed not by the government but by the Union des Résistants, Déportés, Internés, et des Familles des Morts of the Hérault, a group formed in March 1960. (Jean Moulin was born in Béziers, departmental seat of the Hérault, in 1899.) At the same time, Raoul Bayou, socialist deputy for the Hérault and secretary of the National Assembly, made a similar suggestion: "No one," he maintained, "will question the especially heroic nature of the work of Jean Moulin, the true founder and first leader of the Resistance on French soil."[47] Moulin was indeed a plausible figure around whom to build a consensus. To the left, moreover, he offered one great advantage: his role demonstrated that General de Gaulle was neither the first nor the only résistant.

Despite the fact that the suggestion emanated from the opposition, it made headway within the government, which apparently had formulated no plans of its own prior to the Hérault proposal. On 30 May 1963 André Malraux, then minister of cultural affairs, discussed the matter with Prime Minister Georges Pompidou. The only problem that arose was whether to proceed by executive order or by parliamentary legislation, "the custom being to leave it to the legislature to bestow such honors on behalf of the nation." The minister of the interior noted that, while it was "highly desirable to associate the parliament with so solemn a public manifestation of respect and gratitude," the new constitution permitted the executive to act without legislative approval.[48] The decision was ultimately made by the head of state, and on 11 December 1964, several days in advance of the ceremony, an executive order was issued by the Elysée.[49] It is interesting to observe that the matter was never debated in either the Assembly or the Senate; the only notice taken in the legislature was a written question submitted by one deputy, Bayou, to which a laconic response was issued by the minister of veterans' affairs.

The Gaullists thus not only coopted the opposition's proposal but also avoided parliamentary debate. A debate would have given opponents of the government a role in what was intended to be an official occasion. Furthermore, the vote would not have been unanimous, and thus symbolic unity would have been spoiled by factors of a partisan political order. Once the decision was made, moreover, the opposition raised no real objection to the staging of the ceremony. On this issue the consensus was genuine.

By contrast, the choice of date was apparently the result of chance and not a little haste. The Pantheon, undergoing renovation at the time, would not be available up through November 1964; that left only one month before the end of the designated year, the twentieth anniversary of the Liberation. The most suitable dates seemed to be the eighteenth and nineteenth of December, a few days before the Christmas holiday. The only connection with the career of Jean Moulin was that it was on the night of 1 January 1942 that he parachuted into France as the representative of General de Gaulle.

The ceremony was a two-day affair conducted according to precise protocol. The plans were approved at a meeting held on 8 December in the office of the president and attended by representatives of the *direction de l'Architecture*, responsible for overall organization, and of the ministries of the army and veterans' affairs.[50] Not a single detail, down to the uniforms to be worn by each unit in the parade, was left to chance. Timing was worked out to the second. To avoid any slipups, the directive issued by the military governor of Paris ended with a reminder to all recipients to synchronize their watches with the telephone time service, the number for which was printed at the bottom of the document.

The first day of the ceremony, Friday, 18 December 1964, was devoted to the exhumation of the remains and the transfer of the funerary urn. On Friday morning the urn was placed on display in the crematorium at Père-Lachaise cemetery in Paris. General de Gaulle appeared at 12:15 to pay his respects before anyone else. The protocol specified that this was to be "a strictly private ceremony with no formalities of any kind."[51] The container, wrapped in a tricolor flag, was then placed in a casket bearing the simple inscription "Jean Moulin." At 2:45 the casket was transported to the Ile de la Cité and, to the accompaniment of a funeral march, placed in the crypt of the Monument to the Martyrs of the Deportation with military honors. The protocol for the ceremony indicates that the detachment from the 76th Infantry Battalion was to return to its vehicles only "after the departure of the official authorities," that is, the representatives of the government.

Following the homage of the head of state in the morning and the military honors in the early afternoon came the turn of the Resistance, the résistants, and the public. From 3:00 until 9:30 an honor guard stood watch. Members of the guard were replaced initially at half-hour, and later at ten-minute, intervals. The guard consisted of 194 Compagnons de la Libération along with political leaders of every stripe: Jacques Baumel of the UNR, Marcel Paul of the Communist Party, Colonel Rol-Tanguy, Eugène Claudius-Petit, Emmanuel d'Astier de la Vigerie, and many others. Members of the Conseil National de la Résistance were present, along with representatives of various interior resistance movements and of Free France. Throughout the ceremony the great bell of Notre-Dame pealed forth.

At 10:00 in the evening a cortege was formed, led by a regiment of the Garde Républicaine of Paris and followed by the flags of various resistance groups. Behind them, an armored reconnaissance vehicle carried the casket, flanked by torchbearers. Concluding the procession were former resistance fighters and their families. In the darkness of a Paris winter night and to the accompaniment of drums decked with crepe, the cortege made its way toward the Pantheon along the quai de l'Archevêché, the rue du Cloître-Notre-Dame, the courtyard of the cathedral, across the Pont Saint-Michel and up the boulevard of the same name to rue Soufflot and the Pantheon. There the dead hero was honored with another rifle salute, and a vigil of Compagnons de la Libération and resistance fighters was organized to stand watch over the remains. Throughout the night red, white, and blue antiaircraft searchlights played across the sky over the Pantheon.

The ambiguities of the ceremony are apparent in this first day's events. The day was to have been an occasion for the Resistance as a whole and the people of Paris to pay their respects to Moulin. All movements and parties were represented, including—the point is important—the Communists and the rest of the left. In addition, the ceremony was designed to involve the city of Paris, and every aspect of the procession route had a precise significance. From Père-Lachaise to the crypt was simply a matter of covering ground: the dead hero was plucked from among the other remains buried at Père-Lachaise and reunited with the martyrs of the underground struggle. From the crypt to the Pantheon the procession passed through the heart of the capital, in a sense the heart of France "outragé, brisé, martyrisé, mais libéré" (in the words of de Gaulle). Here it was the people rather than officialdom that paid its respects. Yet two important aspects of the ceremony cannot be ignored. First, from the beginning of the day to the end, events were enveloped in military symbolism. Second, the first person to pay his respects to the martyr was General de Gaulle, ostensibly as a "private individual." Discreetly by comparison with what would take place on Saturday, Jean Moulin was thus linked to the man of June Eighteenth and the military aspects of the Resistance, and thus placed within a tradition more martial than political. In short, the government, in advance of the real ceremony, conceded the privilege of honoring the soon-to-be resident of the Pantheon to partisans of the Resistance and to the people of Paris.

But on the following day, Saturday, 19 December, it was General de Gaulle, this time in his guise as head of state, who presided over the ceremony. The celebration of the dead hero gave way to republican pomp. In front of the casket, still lying on a catafalque at the foot of the Pantheon, two reviewing stands had been erected: one, the presidential stand, stood in front of the Faculty of Law (to the left as one faces the Pantheon from the rue Soufflot); the other stood before the *mairie* of the Fifth Arrondissement, to the right. Together the two reviewing stands formed parts of an extended letter V, as in the V for Victory (see diagram).

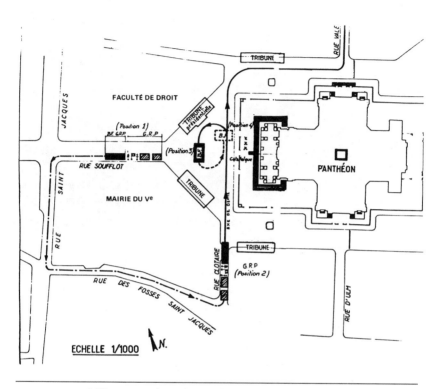

Military parade at the Pantheon, 19 December 1964

There were six companies of marchers: one representing the Garde Républicaine of Paris, whose buglers led the march; three representing the Army; one representing the Air Force; and one representing the Navy. While André Malraux delivered his eulogy, the marchers waited on rue Soufflot at position 1. Then they moved to the parade's starting point, position 2. The parade got underway as the president of the republic and members of the government left the presidential reviewing stand to take up positions to the right of the catafalque holding the casket, which stood directly in the center of the Pantheon's facade. In this way the marchers were able to pay their respects "in a single moment" to both Moulin and de Gaulle. When de Gaulle accompanied the casket into the Pantheon, the parade halted. When he emerged it resumed, and the lead marchers headed down rue Valette. (The drawing is taken from the notes of the military governor of Paris, dated 11 December 1964 and preserved in the Archives des Palais Nationaux.)

Jean Moulin at the Pantheon, ceremony of 19 December 1964

The catafalque stands at the right of the picture, as the Garde Républicaine, followed by companies representing the various arms of the military, salutes General de Gaulle, flanked by Georges Pompidou (on his right) and André Malraux (on his left).
(Photo AFP)

The minister of the army, Pierre Messmer, and the minister of veterans' affairs, Jean Sainteny, arrived shortly after noon and were welcomed by General Dodelier, military governor of Paris. De Gaulle arrived a few minutes later, accompanied by Georges Pompidou and André Malraux. Following a salute by the Garde Républicaine, the four ministers and the president went up and bowed to the casket before returning to the presidential reviewing stand. At 12:30 Malraux delivered the eulogy, which ended with "Le Chant des partisans" (The Partisans' Song). Next came a carefully organized military parade. Leading the way were elements of the Gardes Républicaines of Paris, followed by units of the three branches of the service, army, navy, and air force. Starting from the rue Clotaire, the troops moved from right to left across the facade of the Pantheon, passing first in front of the catafalque and then in front of the chief of state and government ministers, who for this part of the ceremony stood to the right of the casket so that the troops, as they passed by, could "salute in one single motion both the mortal remains of Jean Moulin and the president of the Republic" (see photograph).[52]

Next the casket was moved to the center of the Pantheon and placed on a temporary altar (*reposoir*) under the cupola. The base of the altar was draped in veils of violet, the color of mourning, while in the choir beyond hung an immense tricolor flag, similarly draped in violet. Here, the General, the four ministers, and the Grand Chancelier de l'Ordre de la Libération came to pay their last respects to the hero and to salute his family. Neither the president nor the prime minister was present when the casket was carried down into the Pantheon's northern crypt in preparation for the final interment, which was to take place later. The official ceremony ended in the center of the Pantheon.

Broadcast live on one of the state-owned television channels, this second day of the ceremony was completely unlike the first. Everything revolved around the General, who all but upstaged his former subordinate. Resistance veterans, particularly those representing the interior resistance, that of movements and parties, were relegated to a secondary role. The office of the minister of veterans' affairs had even forgotten to issue an official invitation to the ANACR, a major resistance group, which, despite the ideological diversity of its membership, was considered to be fairly close to the Communist Party. Was this omission deliberate? In any case, the ANACR, in a press release dated 15 December, called on its members to participate in the "popular homage," that is, the Friday ceremony, but made no mention of the following day's events: "By paying solemn homage to the august figure who symbolizes their union in the combat for the Liberation, résistants of all movements, fraternally assembled, will bear witness to their common loyalty to the ideals of liberty, justice, and peace, which the Conseil National de la Résistance expressed in their name." In the end, however, the error was rectified, and Pierre Villon, a Communist deputy and president of the ANACR, took part in the ceremony along with other notable members of the group, including

Jacques Debû-Bridel and Léo Hamon.[53] Still the incident clearly reveals the difference between Friday's celebration and Saturday's: the latter was intended to focus attention on the connection between the dead hero and the General, a connection that was historically quite real, of course, but that was portrayed as virtually exclusive, as André Malraux's celebrated speech makes clear.

Malraux's relatively short speech, roughly fifteen minutes long, situated itself at the crossroads of history, memory, and epic. Beyond the striking imagery and vibrant evocation of a "people of the night," Malraux's speech was an ideological tour de force, a proof of the fundamental axiom of Gaullian resistancialism in a series of equations: the Resistance equals de Gaulle; de Gaulle equals France; hence the Resistance equals France.

De Gaulle and France

"The General," Malraux argued, "took upon himself the *non* of the first day, the continuation of combat whatever the means, and, last but not least, the *destiny* of France . . . France, and not some legion of French combatants." This was the man, the incarnation of the wounded nation, that Moulin met in London to relay the latest news and urge him to organize a secret army. In this way of looking at things, the Resistance was composed of many movements, each of which followed its own course, but only the leader of Free France was capable of effecting a "synthesis." The forces that engaged in clandestine struggle and in combat outside France constituted a potential for resistance that became operational thanks to de Gaulle alone:

> Each group of résistants could claim legitimacy for itself through the ally [England, the United States, or the Soviet Union] that armed and supported it or even on the basis of courage alone; only General de Gaulle could call upon the movements of the Resistance to form a *union* among themselves and with other forces, for it was through him alone that France waged one combat.

This organic unity of de Gaulle with France, to which each of the separate resistance movements subscribed, explains Moulin's role in the Gaullian mythology. For it was Moulin—not the prefect who went to London but the emissary who returned—who made that unity possible. He was merely the disciplined instrument of a mission that transcended and predated him. (Indeed, he was perceived that way by many people at the time, and there were some who, for that very reason, harbored serious doubts about him.) The mission was to restore France's "liberty and grandeur," to borrow a phrase from the speeches of June 1940.

The Resistance

"After twenty years, the Resistance has become an exotic world, a place where myth coexists with organization . . . [Resistance was once a] deep, organic, apocalyptic sentiment, which since then has taken on the character of a myth." In Malraux's rhetoric, résistants and Resistance are two very different things. The fighters belong to the realm of contingency, concrete reality, history as it is lived. The Resistance subsists in the sphere of immanence, epic and edifying abstraction, history as it is dreamed. This is the realm of the Idea, not of flesh and blood. At this altitude men are merely pawns, important to be sure but secondary.

> Jean Moulin has no need of a usurped glory: it was not he who created Combat, Libération, Franc-Tireur, but Frenay, d'Astier, Jean-Pierre Lévy. It was not he who created the many movements in the Northern Zone, whose names history will record. It was not he who made the regiments; it was he who made the army.

Again we come back to this constant of Gaullist thinking: the Resistance was above all a military action, a continuation of combat after the 1940 defeat and in the tradition of Verdun. Accordingly, Moulin was honored with parade after parade in the two-day ceremony marking the transfer of his ashes.

This view offered two notable advantages: the civil war could be forgotten because the mission of the army is to fight foreign enemies, not handfuls of domestic traitors (about whom Malraux has virtually nothing to say); and the political and ideological diversity of the actual Resistance could be ignored.

The Nation: Yesterday, Today, Tomorrow

Malraux, in his passion, could not refrain from a direct allusion to the present:

> To attribute little importance to so-called political opinions when the nation was in mortal peril—the nation, not a nationalism then crushed by Hitler's tanks, but the invincible and mysterious fact that was to pervade this century; to believe that the nation would before long vanquish the totalitarian doctrines with which Europe then resounded; to see in the unity of the Resistance the most important means of fighting for the unity of the nation—to hold these views was perhaps to affirm what has since been called Gaullism. It was certainly to proclaim the survival of France.

And so, presto, Moulin became a Gaullist, vintage 1964. This would be his last heroic act. Therein lies the crux of the ceremony. The French, yesterday a people of the night, had survived a long and overcast dawn and now at last could see the light. The Pantheonization of Jean Moulin was to mark a point of no return: "May the commemorations of the two wars culminate today in the resurrection of the people of shades whom this man set in motion and symbolized, and whom he now invites to stand humble watch over his remains." Then "Arise ye dead!" and erase all memory of individual sacrifice to make room for the higher spirit that motivated each one and that ought now, twenty years later, to motivate all.

Malraux's evocative description of a personal encounter with this army of shades (during funeral ceremonies for Alsatian partisans in the Corrèze) and his biblical use of the familiar form of the second-person pronoun to address the dead hero and recount for him, in halting phrases, all that he did not live to see—Normandy, Leclerc at the Invalides and later in Strasbourg—made this an exceptional speech. And the speaker's talent, the talent of a man keen to reach out to the younger generation, helped to veil its ideological and partisan character. The fact remains that the transfer of Jean Moulin's ashes was a political act.

To begin with, the speech was made in a particular context. The ceremony took place three days after the vote on an amnesty for relatively minor offenses committed during the Algerian War and one week after the vote on a law suspending the statute of limitations on crimes against humanity. The dynamics of national memory had created a very special set of circumstances. The time had come to forgive crimes committed in the latest *guerre franco-française,* a time for the nation to pardon those wayward children who had once again gone astray. Meanwhile the nation solemnly affirmed that the most spectacular of the Nazis' crimes would never be forgotten, but in a law aimed primarily at German war criminals, at foreigners. Rather than repress the past in its entirety, a selection was made to further national unity.

Second, people of all political persuasions were satisfied by this arrangement, and the satisfaction accounts for the absence of conflict prior to the transfer of Moulin's remains. It also explains why Jean Moulin was the right figure and the Pantheon the right place for carrying out such a maneuver.

Before 1964 Jean Moulin was not the legendary and symbolic figure he would soon become. Each party and movement had its own heroes: the Communists had Danièle Casanova, Jean-Pierre Timbaud, and Georges Politzer; the Socialists had Pierre Brossolette; the right had Honoré d'Estienne d'Orves; and the names of countless others, chosen to reflect local ideological allegiances and wartime memories, adorn streetcorners and squares in every town and village in France. Given this plethora of partisan and regional memories, with each group and locality jealous of its own martyr, the unifier of the Resistance was frequently lost in the crowd. In commemorations of World War II he did not always enjoy a place of honor.[54] A complex figure whose eminently political mission was just as complex as the man himself, Moulin played a role that is still hotly debated by veterans of the Resistance. He certainly did not enjoy the reputation of "universally acknowledged hero" that some would bestow on him in 1964. The Gaullists, in a transparent anachronism, chose him as a symbol. The man who, though obedient to the General, stood above the parties and movements in 1943 was to serve exactly the same cause twenty years later, at a time when France was fighting, again as always, for its national independence.

In the ceremonies marking the transfer, therefore, care was taken to distinguish between the commemoration of a unified resistance and the commemoration of the roots of Gaullism, which now traced its origins back to World War II and sought to identify itself with France in its entirety. Nobody was deceived. The Gaullists knew perfectly well that the public could be persuaded to accept this identification only with the tacit agreement of others with a legitimate claim to the heritage of the Resistance. And those others, the Communist Party above all, were glad to have their heroic exploits recalled: for to do so, even if it was only to be coopted, reinforced their own legitimacy.

In this respect the Communist reaction to the ceremony was typical. The party used the occasion, once again, to denounce collaborators, meaning Pétainists who were clamoring, not without arousing sympathy among some Gaullists, for the Marshal's remains to be transferred to Douaumont. Furthermore, by taking an active part in the Friday ceremonies, the party recalled the meaning of the clandestine struggle:

> Jean Moulin in the Pantheon means that France is honoring the man who understood that, in the struggle against Nazi power, the liberation of our people depended on unity, just as it does today in the struggle against the power of money. Jean Moulin in the Pantheon means that France pays homage to the leader of the CNR, whose program included nationalization of banks and trusts. Jean Moulin in the Pantheon means that the fatherland is grateful to great men who keep their word.[55]

André Wurmser, the author of this editorial, noted that the ceremony placed the accent on Moulin's activities after his meeting with de Gaulle (the second meeting, in February 1943, from which he returned with the mission of setting up the Conseil National de la Résistance) and paid little attention to the efforts in France that "would lead to the trip to London where, with the consent of the Resistance from Jean Moulin to Fernand Grenier, General de Gaulle became president of the provisional government of the French Republic." In other words, "the focus is much more on Jean Moulin *mandaté* than on Jean Moulin *mandatant*," that is, on the Moulin who persuaded resistance elements to accept the head of Free France as their supreme authority rather than on the Moulin responsible for unifying a segment of the internal resistance movement. Yet Wurmser concludes with these words: "All of this matters very little, however. Honor to Jean Moulin! Honor to those who, following his example, died for their country! Honor to the French Resistance!" Clearly Communist and Gaullist memories of the Resistance had been reconciled to permit sharing of power over the past.

Similarly, the choice of the Pantheon was no accident. The Pantheon was, from its inception, a monument for the celebration of the republic, "designed to dramatize the national consensus in an almost religious fashion."[56] The choice was therefore inevitable in the wake of the Algerian turmoil and one year (to the day) before what was to be the first election by universal suffrage of a president of France, an event that many considered to spell the end of the republican ideal. And yet, if Mona Ozouf is correct, the Pantheon has also been "a focal point of divisions within France; it still bears the original scars of the French Revolution, which have never been effaced."[57] Pantheonizations have always been occasions for memorable controversies, such as the one that erupted over the interment of Jean Jaurès on 23 November 1924 or the debates, mentioned earlier, that followed the Liberation. In the event, however, the organization of the ceremony in two phases, as well as the choice of Moulin as the hero to be honored, helped to circumvent conflict; consensus was achieved around a least common denominator.

Another question remains. The Pantheon was a place of oblivion as well as remembrance. It has never rivaled the Invalides as a monument to martial glories, nor has it welcomed beneath its cupola France's "truly great men," those who assumed responsibility for the nation (such as de Gaulle himself). Was Jean Moulin forgotten? In many respects the answer is yes. His identity was bestowed upon de Gaulle: the remains honored were those of a man described as the General's spokesman, the leader, to be sure, of the people of the night but a *delegated* leader. The dead man was honored in such a way as to honor even more the living head of state. Adversaries of Gaullism pretended to see Moulin only as the "unifier" of the internal resistance forces. After he was Pantheonized, not to say fossilized, partisan groups began once more to hone their weapons, though in time of crisis or in the wake of a dramatic election they might have occasion to allude to his memory. Under the cupola the symbol became unusable; or at any rate it was little used.

There were other signs after 1964 that Moulin had lost some of his aura. In May 1969 a memorial was erected at the spot in Salon-de-

Provence where he had parachuted into France in January 1942. Funds for this monument were raised by local groups, and the ceremony was quite small. True, the ANACR does regularly stage important ceremonies at the site. One such ceremony was held on 22 October 1972, just after the outbreak of the Touvier affair, and it ended significantly with an oath to "continue to fight for France by defending the Resistance and résistants."[58] Still the Salon monument has not become an important memorial site, as was noted by Maurice Agulhon who, on a visit to Salon, found the place run down: all there was for tourists to see was a "sewer," and on the day of Agulhon's visit the tourists happened to be Germans.[59] On the day the monument was inaugurated, de Gaulle left public life, and the memorial failed to attract all the attention it deserved. But it would appear that the ecumenical character of the figure of Moulin has faded somewhat since his Pantheonization; or at any rate it had faded until the heroic myth was revived by the new president, François Mitterrand, in 1981. Since 1964 Moulin's name has figured not so much in ecumenical celebrations as in heated polemics having to do with his role in the difficult unification of the Resistance or with the circumstances of his arrest (such as those surrounding the Barbie trial and the publication of Daniel Cordier's biography).

Twenty years is time enough for one generation to pass and another to arrive on the scene. The wartime generation, which held most of the reins of power, rewrote history for the consumption of a new generation that had not known the worst of its parents' suffering. But twenty years was also the time required for the statute of limitations to take effect for crimes committed in 1944. And oblivion has its limits.

In June 1964 a bill was filed in the National Assembly suspending the statute of limitations for crimes against humanity as defined by the Nuremberg Trials and the United Nations Charter: "Murder, extermination, enslavement, deportation, or any other inhuman act committed against an entire civilian population before or during the war, or persecution for political, racial, or religious reasons." The bill was a response to an announcement by the West German government that the statute of limitations would take effect for all war crimes, including crimes against humanity, as of 8 May 1965 (this action was later postponed). The bill was passed unanimously by both houses on first reading (26 December 1964).[60] In contrast to the amnesty-law debates of the 1950s, the discussion went without a hitch. Both Raymond Schmittlein of the UNR and Marie-Claude Vaillant-Couturier of the Communist Party were applauded by deputies on all benches in the chamber. Partisan insults were held in check. Harmony this time was indeed a reality. Of course the only war criminals discussed were Nazis. Although the 1945 United Nations Charter explicitly mentioned accomplices, the possibility of applying the law to French war criminals and collaborators was never raised.[61] Ten years later, however, when the law was invoked for the first time, it was to indict French citizens.

Despite some repression of wartime memories in the 1960s, memories of the Resistance were thus widely discussed, but largely within the framework established by the Gaullist version of the past. Yet that epic vision did not establish its priority until rather late in the day and was never able to silence all doubt or eradicate all bitterness. Not even the General himself was entirely exempt from vengeful impulses: when Weygand died on 28 January 1965, de Gaulle refused to allow the funeral to be held, as was the custom for general officers, in the Eglise Saint-Louis des Invalides—"a petty action that can only do a disservice to the regime."[62]

As early as the mid-1950s many French people clearly wished to lay controversy about the past to rest, and the invented honor of the Gaullists seemed perfectly tailored to fill the bill. Hence de Gaulle was able to build a consensus around his version of resistancialism, a concept broad enough to make room for other partisan views. A generation undeniably embraced the Gaullist image and ignored what few discordant voices remained.

> So long as the Resistance might pose as a pretender, it had to be struck down, if need be with the help of the parties. When the parties began grasping for power, the dead Queen once again became ripe for the taking . . . Many people were and are convinced that the new republic was founded by de Gaulle, that is, by the Resistance, the troubled interlude of the Fourth Republic having virtually disappeared from memory. [This founding myth] is shocking to historical consciousness and vexing for those involved as actors, who become suspect if they hint that the Resistance and de Gaulle were not identical; [yet] it is politically effective.[63]

3

THE BROKEN MIRROR
(1971–1974)

In May 1968 a generation noisily proclaimed its repudiation of a certain type of society and therefore, implicitly, of a certain vision of its history. In April 1969 Charles de Gaulle bade farewell to public life, this time without hope of return, having stepped aside in favor of his tranquil dauphin, Georges Pompidou. The epic was over. On 9 November 1970 he died, leaving the people of France an album of souvenirs that from then on belonged definitively to the past. Here we have three major events in the history of France and three important dates in the evolution of collective representations.

May '68 might have been just one more in the recurring series of *guerres franco-françaises*. Two Frances did indeed clash in May: right against left; a party of order versus liberal and libertarian tendencies; a culture attached to tradition versus a culture eager for reform and change, not to say revolution. This time, however, civil war was not on the agenda, or at any rate was so only briefly, in episodes that received great attention at the time but were quickly forgotten. The events of May were more a family affair than an affair of classes or parties. In a break with custom, moreover, the principal antagonists were not old adversaries whose ranks had simply been replenished by an infusion of young blood; they came instead from a new generation less likely than its predecessors to invoke the well-known, established camps, long inured to perennial battle. Disconcerted, the traditional political organizations at first failed to see their place in this new rebellion. The students of May did not share their memories or their historical guideposts.

Still memories of the Occupation were not altogether absent. In the heat of the uprising with its myriad slogans, "antifascism" was a frequent reference. Students shouted "CRS equals SS" [Compagnies Ré-

98

publicaines de Sécurité, the riot police, equal the Nazi SS] or "Nous sommes tous des juifs allemands" (We are all German Jews). Somewhat later the Maoists launched the concept of a New Resistance. All these were bridges spontaneously laid down between the past and the present, across which passed the abstract and rather fantastic idea of a fascist threat. In hindsight it seems possible that, beyond the natural inflation of ideological discourse, such slogans were intended as a kind of supreme provocation, for they had the power to reawaken complexes long dormant in the elder generation. Indeed, the slogans would have been particularly irritating to their chosen targets, who, after all, were Gaullists.

Furthermore, influential aspects of extreme leftist thought had grown out of the Algerian War and other anticolonial struggles and were thus steeped in the tradition of civil warfare. In the May '68 crisis, however, reference to the past did not play so large a role as in other conflicts. The students of May were challenging a government that saw and presented itself as the heir to the Resistance. Their challenge was aimed as much at its present identity as at its history. They were also at odds with a society that had taken refuge behind "invented honor." Indeed, it was because the students sensed something invented in de Gaulle's attempt to substitute himself for the Resistance that it left them unmoved. Unlike their parents, they did not need to grasp at straws. On the contrary, they had every reason to denounce such a revision, because the heroic image did not fit the men they chose to attack, Molotov cocktails in hand.

Still the year 1968 marked a turning point in France's thinking about the Occupation. The change did not come about immediately— the battle over the past was waged below the surface. Memory resembled not a paving stone hurled in anger but a "cultural time bomb": "By refusing to acquire the means necessary to seize power, the sixty-eighter (that creature as mythical and yet as necessary as the 'average Frenchman') ensured that his actions would affect not the realm of power but the realm of representation."[1] And this was true no matter how "political" he wished his rhetoric to seem. The truth of this observation is confirmed by a glance at the new interpretations of Vichy that would blossom a few years later. These new images of the past, the work of a handful of writers and filmmakers, marked a fundamental break with what had gone before.

"The father is dead. The time has come to draw up an inventory of the estate."[2] The parental voice had fallen silent; its mythical language had ceased to capture the imagination. Having first exorcised the memory of Vichy, de Gaulle had gone on to concoct a sacred and edifying history of the Resistance. For a time his charisma had forestalled all agonizing or provocative questions. After his death, however, the public suddenly found itself confronted with a confused image of the past, "unable to find the thread of its history and anxious about not living up to its heroic dream."[3] Under Pompidou, who succeeded de Gaulle as president, political Gaullism replaced ideal Gaullism.

Pompidou died in 1971. Ten years later, several newspapers followed the lead of *Figaro Magazine* in hypocritically lamenting those years of calm, "the good old days" when France was governed by a tranquil president who "kept faith with his roots." It was then 1981, and France had entered a period of economic crisis (and socialist rule). Suddenly a new nostalgia emerged, nostalgia for a "strong and peaceful France," a unified country happily savoring the fruits of economic growth. According to a March 1984 opinion poll, nearly four-fifths of the population, people of every generation and of all political persuasions, had an image of the short Pompidou years as a time when "the living was easy."[4]

Let us cast a backward glance at the reality of that time. Youth protest did not end with the final fireworks of 1968. At the first sign of a stink bomb, the riot police invaded lycées and schools where students were still mobilized in opposition to muffled drumbeats from America's war in Vietnam. France was laboring under the heavy weight of nearly a decade and a half of Gaullist rule. Yet 1968 had marked a cultural divide; seeds of change, sown seemingly at random during the great student fest, had begun to sprout.

By 1971 *la doulce France* had once again begun to feel aftershocks of the 1940s. But now the blows were felt in literature, film, and scholarship.

Pitiless Sorrow

The first explosion, if not the first symptom, was *The Sorrow and the Pity,* a film directed by Marcel Ophuls and produced by André Harris and Alain de Sédouy.

The title, misleading or perhaps ironic, has little to do with the general tone of the film. It is taken from a phrase uttered by Monsieur Verdier, the pharmacist in the film and a typical bourgeois, a man whose characteristic perch, firmly on the fence, is almost a caricature. Ophuls' film became a kind of countermyth to the official Gaullist myth. At the time it provoked all kinds of reactions: hostility, self-flagellation, shame, indignation, surprise, disbelief, even sorrow—everything but retrospective pity. Toward whom would such pity have been directed?

Ophuls, spurning the epic realism of the 1960s,[5] chose instead to film, in high-contrast halftone, a documentary of daily life in Clermont-Ferrand, a city allegedly typical of France under the Occupation. In this way he managed to capture the doubts of a country that had shown little inclination to take a stand until the "moment of choice" finally came in 1942. Without didacticism the film shows us a range of characters, actors in a drama: Pétainists, some presentable, others less so, collaborators, and prominent leaders who stiffly protest that their consciences are clear are shown side by side with nameless as well as illustrious resistance fighters and others—many others, of every sort. *La grande histoire,* the history of textbooks and official ceremonies, makes only brief appearances. With a Stendhalian eye, keen for telling detail, Ophuls all but ignores the great figures that had traditionally dominated images of the period, foremost among them General de Gaulle, who is virtually absent from the film.

An Eyewitness Account

Ophuls, Harris, and Sédouy have always insisted on the creative and artistic aspect of their work. Their many technical innovations no doubt contributed greatly to the success of the film, which has become a model for documentary filmmakers. For the first time, eyewitness testimony is given precedence over archival footage. In a total of 260 minutes of film, clips from French newsreels and German propaganda films account for only 45 minutes. The rest is devoted entirely to interviews with witnesses, many of whom are questioned in surroundings of high emotional charge: Christian de la Mazière, former member of the Waffen SS, is interviewed in Sigmaringen, the Mecca of collaborators in exile; René de Chambrun, Laval's son-in-law, is interviewed at Chateldon on Laval's own estate; Colonel du Jonchay of the army resistance organization is interviewed at Vichy; and so on.

This imbalance between interviews and archival footage is no accident. The dramatic power of the film depends on the distance between the objective image of the event, of the news, and the subjective version of the actors. Each person's testimony is thus punctuated by a kind of call to order, a constantly repeated imperative: "Remember!" This accounts for the apparent contradiction between two orders of truth: that of the past and that of memory. Caught up in the dynamic of the film, the spectator's immediate impression is that many of the witnesses, particularly those from the Pétainist camp, are baldfaced liars, which is not always the case. When Georges Lamirand is asked about the meaning of the National Revolution, he exclaims: "That's only a word!" But the image shows him in 1942 addressing a crowd of young people beneath a portrait of Pétain, and suddenly it takes on the character of an indictment. There is nothing particularly reprehensible about the speech, compared with certain other actions. Yet the film gives the impression that one is catching a witness in the act of telling a lie, for the gap between yesterday's actions and today's words is very wide. When teachers at the Lycée Blaise-Pascal try in vain to evade a question about their Jewish colleagues of the time, we hear and see Vichyite antisemitic propaganda that not only undercuts the credibility of the witnesses but also deprives them of all dignity.

These procedures, along with the choice of witnesses, were widely criticized. Of the thirty-six witnesses who speak in the film, twenty-six are French, five German, and five English. In some ways this selection makes perfect sense, but it also calls attention to a controversial aspect of the work: since the action is set in the Southern Zone, it necessarily emphasizes French domestic issues; the occupying forces play only a modest role.

A second point worth mentioning is that testimony by prominent figures is far outweighed by testimony given by unknown or merely local personalities. Only Pierre Mendès France, Jacques Duclos, Georges Bidault, and Emmanuel d'Astier de la Vigerie—all authentic résistants—were of national stature. A few others were important, though not well-known, figures: Marcel Degliame-Fouché, former member of the CNR; Emile Coulaudon, known as "Gaspar," leader of the Auvergne maquis; René de Chambrun, Laval's son-in-law; and Georges Lamirand. The other seventeen witnesses were "average" Frenchmen, suddenly plucked from anonymity.

A third point is that there are far more résistants than there are collaborators. In addition to the six résistants already mentioned, we find the two Grave brothers, M. Leiris, the mayor of Combronde, and Claude Lévy, former member of the FTP, all résistants or described as such. In the same camp we may also place Roger Tounze of the newspaper *La Montagne* and Henri Rochat, Mendès' attorney. On the other side the list is shorter: one out-and-out Pétainist, Georges Lamirand; one Lavalian, René de Chambrun; one collaborationist, de la Mazière; and two personalities who, regardless of what they actually did or thought during the Occupation, are presented as an antisemite (the milliner) and a Pétainist (the hairdresser whose head was shaved at the time of the Liberation and who is the *only* woman in the film to testify as a participant in the events). One case is open to discussion: Colonel du Jonchay, who seems as much a résistant as a Pétainist and anticommunist. All in all, the balance clearly tilts toward the résistant side, especially if the quality of the testimony, particularly that of Mendès France, is taken into account. Ophuls comes to a somewhat different conclusion by examining the film as a whole, including the archival footage: "After underlining every line in the manuscript [it would appear] that 20 percent of the film is devoted to describing the Resistance, 20 percent to the collaboration and to Vichy politics and propaganda, while 55 percent does not refer directly to either."[6]

Finally, on the Resistance side, various ideological tendencies are unevenly represented (not allowing for the quality of the testimony in each case). The Communists are represented by Duclos, and the FTP is briefly described by Claude Lévy (not portrayed as a Communist in the film). The noncommunist left-wing resistance includes d'Astier, Mendès, Degliame-Fouché, and the Grave brothers, known to be affiliated with the Socialist Party. The right-wing nationalist resistance finds an exponent, albeit an ambivalent one, in Colonel du Jonchay. The other witnesses are hard to place politically simply on the basis of what they say in the film. The great omissions are of course the Gaullists and Free French. Yet even this bald summary of the film's contents speaks eloquently of a dramatic change in the way the Occupation was interpreted.

A French-Centered View

The German occupier—the foreign element—plays little role in the film. The viewer learns—or is reminded—that until at least November 1942 the German presence was not the sole or constant determinant of the actions of Vichy France. Champion cyclist Raphael Géminiani is portrayed, misleadingly, as having been uncertain about whether Germans were actually present.[7] Previously unchallenged assumptions are thus called into question. Two judgments, never before emphasized, suddenly loom large. First, the Vichy regime—its laws, actions, and policies—was governed by a logic that flowed as much from internal considerations, from political and ideological factors peculiar to the history of France, as from the defeat and occupation. Second, the foreign war (what the General had called the thirty years' war) left fewer scars than the civil war, as the interviewees' silences and slips make clear.

Antisemitism

Among the vast areas of amnesia revealed by the film, French antisemitism ranks among the most important. We see manifestations of antisemitism among the French of the Southern Zone, which owed nothing to the Nazis. The point is crucial, since the 1970s also witnessed a notable reawakening of Jewish consciousness and memory in France. It might be objected that the film fails to speak of instances of sympathy toward persecuted Jews, which were quite common, particularly in the Southern Zone, from the summer of 1942 on. But the criticism loses some of its force in the context of the 1970s. Traditional representations had literally obliterated the existence of a French antisemitism that was encouraged by official policies, with both official and unofficial forms having deep roots in French tradition. Generally all persecution of Jews was laid at the door of the Nazis. The film might have been more balanced had it spoken of opposition to antisemitism as well, but that would have been to weaken its main thrust. Only today, now that official antisemitism in Vichy has been studied, mapped, and measured, can we judge the distance between the government and the public in this regard, and for this some credit should go to *The Sorrow and the Pity*.

The Collaborators

The most striking and novel testimony (apart from that of Mendès) is without doubt that of Christian de la Mazière. The filmmakers took particular care with this witness, moreover, exploiting his natural photogenic qualities and dramatizing his words by filming them against the fantastic backdrop of Sigmaringen. A man steeped in military and nationalist tradition, de la Mazière typifies only a small minority of the Waffen SS's Charlemagne Division, most of whose men (as opposed to officers) were of modest background. Viewers get no notion of this, however. The man's sincerity and open admission that he wished to wear the German uniform reveal a forgotten or neglected aspect of French collaboration: the pro-Nazi commitment of some collaborators. Collaborators were not simply traitors. Some, particularly the most extreme, acted as they did out of political and ideological fervor. Their commitment brought them no dividends, and many paid with their lives after embracing what they knew to be a lost cause. This picture is a far cry from the classic image of the "collabo" who betrays his country for money or out of intellectual or moral turpitude. To be sure, that kind also existed. But with de la Mazière suddenly a reassuring image collapses. It is simply not true that there had been only two kinds of Frenchmen, good and bad. There were those who consciously chose the camp of fascism and Nazism, and there were those who were willing to die for a certain idea of France—indeed, of democracy and the republic. Implicitly, in other words, the film recognizes that nothing could be taken for granted about the choice of one side or the other; it recognizes that France was divided by a split that ran through all the countries of the world, and that World War II was not simply a conflict between nations but also a bloody ideological struggle. In 1971 there was still something novel about this realization.

There was also something dangerous, something apt to trouble young people inclined to respect commitment for its own sake, and something that would reinforce visceral anticommunist feelings in the wake of France's discovery of Solzhenitsyn and the Gulag archipelago. While the film in no way denies the criminal nature of fascism *and* of fascists, it does place that criminality in a wider context.

The Résistants

In the ensuing reaction, the Resistance lost its status as a purely patriotic movement and came to be seen instead as a form of commitment. Therein lies the crux of *The Sorrow and the Pity*. No doubt the
film is one-sided and incomplete. The two major components of the
Resistance, the Communists and the Gaullists, are deliberately neglected. The absence of de Gaulle is so glaring that the credibility of
the film suffers. The reason for these major omissions is that the filmmakers wished to emphasize the noncommunist internal resistance,
especially at the grassroots level. Nothing is said about the University
of Strasbourg, which had been evacuated to Clermont-Ferrand; this
omission too distorts reality by overlooking nonmilitary forms of resistance. Part of the population, in Clermont as elsewhere, became
caught up in the spirit of rebellion. The Verdiers are hardly typical of
the French population as a whole, and the hairdresser and the milliner
still less so. D'Astier's definition of the Resistance ("we were misfits")
drew hostile reactions from other veterans, who noted that resistance
units drew many more recruits from among prominent local officials,
blue- and white-collar workers, and other well-integrated groups than
from among marginals; this sentiment has since been confirmed by
careful scholarly studies. Finally, the film simply obliterates one whole
aspect of the history of the Resistance: the establishment of a clandestine government with an executive branch (the GPRF), a legislative
branch (the Assembly in Algiers), an army, and, even more important,
a structure that was as democratic as it could be in the circumstances,
the CNR, a council representing all factions and unique among European resistance movements. In other words, the film ignores the
comforting (and to some extent accurate) image of a well-oiled resistance organization, an alternative *state*, which in fact and in memory
supplanted the illegitimate legality of Vichy.

The Scandal

It is worth noting that critics of the film agreed that it deserved credit
for its work of demystification. The Communist press was fulsome:

> This film is a giant: Thanks to the mass of evidence and testimony
> that it gathers together, stirs up, and lays bare. Thanks to the excep-

tional way in which it is put together. And last but not least, thanks to its power to shock, its stunning lucidity. This film hits you in the gut, in the heart, and in the mind.[8]

L'Humanité spoke of "a political act—not depressing but purifying."[9] Although the Communist papers complained in passing of the limited role accorded to Communist résistants, clearly the party was delighted to see its Gaullist rivals deflated. The tacit consensus between Gaullists and Communists concerning the war had broken down in 1968. Meanwhile the Pompidou government defended itself against attacks in the film and elsewhere but did nothing to revive the resistancialist myth.

At the other end of the spectrum, *Rivarol*, the Pétainist paper, was also delirious with joy: "'Colonel Gaspar,' the hilarious hero of the Auvergnat maquis and a dead ringer for Podgorny, has long since shed his guerrilla costume. He drives a Mercedes and sells TV sets, smiling at all his customers, including former 'fence-sitters' and 'collabos.'" The extreme right-wing newspaper praised the film's account of the National Revolution and even the way it portrayed the Germans:

> The German veterans interviewed were a far cry from the stereotype of the "dull-witted brute" . . . For these veterans the French were not, and could not be, adversaries in the full sense of the word—so that it is hardly surprising that the regime born of the "resistantialist" myth was taken aback by this revision of history.

The paper went on to note that one of the Grave brothers who had been sent to Buchenwald reported that there was a movie theater in the concentration camp. The article concluded with a long-repressed wish: "Despite the banning of the film from television, will those who saw it in Paris and, one hopes, in the provinces finally understand that the often misrepresented collaboration was the least of the Occupation's evils?"[10]

Between these extremes, all the critics praised the quality of the film, the power of its images, the sincerity of its witnesses. Amid this chorus of praise, however, a few discordant voices were heard. Alfred Fabre-Luce, one-time adept of the "New Europe," lashed out at the film's anti-Pétainism. Pointing accurately to certain omissions, he criticized the filmmakers for their tactlessness in dealing with "the Jewish question," for "it is always embarrassing," he said, "to see survivors [Jews] pouring scorn on the very man [Pétain] to whom they owed their lives."[11] Germaine Tillion, a former resistance fighter, responded with outrage to this declaration, but her criticism of the film was no less harsh than Fabre-Luce's: "What emerges from all of this is the profile of a hideous country." Aware of widespread disaffection with the Resistance, she attacked the film for preferring "a scandalous quarter truth to the timeworn version that tells the other three quarters."[12] With great prescience Tillion sensed that the rediscovery of collaborationism and fence-sitting would only hasten disillusionment with the resistance fighters themselves, already victims of a myth they had done nothing to create.

Claude Mauriac acknowledged the value of the film but lamented the absence of de Gaulle, who is barely glimpsed at the end of the picture: "The heart is missing. Ours suffers."[13] Finally, Jean-Paul Sartre, writing in *La Cause du peuple*, also turned up his nose. Wearing his blinkers of the moment, he denounced, as always, the "dominant ideology" without grasping the degree to which the spirit of May permeated *The Sorrow and the Pity,*

> a film that speaks of neither political truth nor life in the concrete. It thus fails of both its goals, the only goals it could have set for itself. This is a film that makes you smile constantly, but the Occupation was by no means all laughs. Hence it is an inaccurate representation, deliberately so. It is a film for television, commissioned for television. Therefore the people who made it knew what TV could accept. And so they made a film that in its entirety is "beneath" the truth, but with little winks of the eye so that those who know what the Occupation was like can say: Yes, when he says that, he means more. But for people who don't know, or who aren't used to this kind of wit, it gives a very different impression.[14]

Oddly enough, Sartre's rejection of the film was matched by the government's refusal to allow it to be shown on television: both were inclined to treat potential television viewers as children, illiterates, or deviants. If *Sorrow* failed to satisfy the philosopher, it struck the government, more clearsighted in its reactions than Sartre was in his criticisms, as intolerable. Those "winks of the eye" must have been lethal indeed to have drawn the wrath of officialdom for more than a decade!

The conflict between the makers of *The Sorrow and the Pity* and the French state television networks was to continue from 1971 to 1981, a symptom of the deep gulf that separated the governments of Georges Pompidou and Valéry Giscard d'Estaing from the mood of the public. Guardians of official memory, the government and the television authorities did all they could to stem the tide this heretical film had set in motion.

Shot in 1967 and 1968, *The Sorrow and the Pity* was the second of a trilogy of films dealing with contemporary French history. All three filmmakers belong to the "generation of sixty-eight," not in terms of age (all were in their thirties by May '68) but in terms of cultural values shared not only by students but also by many intellectuals, young and not-so-young.

In 1965 Harris and Sédouy had produced two television documentaries, *Zoom* and *Sixteen Million Youths,* that marked a sharp break with the starchy traditions of the ORTF [the state agency responsible then for all broadcasting in France]. Their conception of journalism was utterly at odds with the philosophy of President Pompidou, who said that "television journalists are not like other journalists; they are a little more." In 1976 Harris and Sédouy produced the first film in the trilogy, *Munich ou la Paix pour cent ans,* which was directed by Marcel Ophuls, the son of Max Ophuls, a world-renowned director who had fled the Nazi regime. The subject of the film was a clear indication of the filmmakers' intentions: Munich was not only a point of departure for World War II but a crucial episode in the French civil wars of the 1930s and 1940s, a controversy that prefigured the later controversies over Vichy:

> Marcel Ophuls: From the beginning we started out in a certain direction, and we have continued along the same line.
> André Harris: All the symbolism associated with the word Munich implied that—
> Marcel Ophuls: —that we would become muckrakers—
> André Harris: —that we would be airing dirty linen. At the time we were all irritated by the linearity and total unreality of historical programs and films, by the notion that History is something to be nailed to the wall for people to look at.[15]

After the success of their first attempt, the filmmakers started on *The Sorrow and the Pity,* whose fate would be quite different (though it aroused less hostility than the third film, *Frenchmen, If Only You Knew*). Already, however, misunderstandings were accumulating between the three filmmakers and officials of the ORTF: "What we envisioned more and more as a history of the Occupation continued to be labeled a history of the Resistance by the bureaucrats."[16] After May '68, Harris and Sédouy were asked to leave the ORTF, and Ophuls went to work for German television. Their project was revived by new financing, this time from the video department of the Swiss publishing house Rencontre of Lausanne and by the Norddeutscher Rundfunk of Hamburg. After nine months' work and fifty-five hours of filmed testimony, the film was finally ready for distribution in 1969.

At this point the filmmakers became involved in a complicated series of exchanges with the ORTF. After showings in West Germany, Switzerland, the Netherlands, and the United States, it seemed only natural that the film would at last air on French television. For ten years, however, the ORTF imposed what Marcel Ophuls has called "censorship through inertia," refusing to acquire rights to the film. In 1971, the head of the ORTF, Jean-Jacques de Bresson, himself a former résistant (who, in 1985, would be elected president of the Association Nationale des Médaillés de la Résistance Française), explained to the Senate's committee on cultural affairs that the film "destroys myths that the people of France still need."[17]

In April 1971 *The Sorrow and the Pity* was shown in the Saint-Séverin, a small theater in the Latin Quarter, and later in a much larger theater on the Champs-Elysées. Although customers were turned away from every showing, the film was seen by some 600,000 people; during eighty-seven weeks of exclusive screening in Paris, 232,000 people came to the theater. The unusually long run was due to the limited number of daily showings.[18] In 1972 Arthur Conte, the new head of the ORTF, promised to broadcast the film but later changed his mind. According to Ophuls, René de Chambrun, a Laval flunky as well as a descendant of the Marquis de Lafayette, may have influenced the decision after being contacted by Conte in connection with preparations for the celebration of the bicentennial of the American Revolution.[19] In 1979, after the American miniseries *Holocaust* was shown on French television, the possibility of broadcasting *Sorrow* was again raised. Nothing came of it. This time Simone Veil, the minister of health, used her influence to tip the balance. Meanwhile the film was rereleased for theater viewing, but by this time it was already considered an "academic" classic and drew only 30,000 spectators. It is interesting to consider the significance of Veil's opposition to broadcasting the film. As one who had been deported to Auschwitz during the war, she had made a powerful impression when she spoke courageously of her experience in a televised panel discussion that followed the airing of *Holocaust*.[20] Yet she remained staunchly opposed to Ophuls' film. Earlier, as an ORTF board member in 1971, she had used her influence to prevent its airing.

In 1981 the minister and the director traded accusations. "What is intolerable about *The Sorrow and the Pity*," the minister argued, "is that it purports to present a comprehensive view of occupied France. . . . To depict all Frenchmen as bastards is a form of masochism."[21] Ophuls responded by asking what kind of government it was that arrogated to itself the right to decide "what millions of our fellow citizens can and cannot see on their television screens."[22]

Finally, twelve years after the film was first released, it was shown on 28 and 29 October 1981 on Network FR3, where it was seen by an audience of fifteen million. Despite the change in the political climate since the film's original release, the critics were still lavish in their praise, but most of those who had been hostile then remained unalterably opposed. Fabre-Luce proposed that the title be changed to "Animosity and Gloating." Simone Veil still felt that the film "portrayed a cowardly, selfish, nasty France and that it terribly blackened the reality." She reiterated her disappointment that one saw "very few résistants."[23]

The troubled history of *The Sorrow and the Pity* raises a fundamental question: how could a film viewed by only a minority of the population (700,000 prior to the 1981 broadcast, or fewer spectators than would have attended a major hit during the first few weeks in Paris theaters alone) have had such a major impact on people's attitudes? Certainly the scandal stirred up by the film played a part. But that cannot be the whole story.

To begin with, the film was a deliberate effort of demystification on a vast scale. The men who made it were quite frank about their purpose: "What irritated me was not the Resistance but 'resistancialism,' which, though it misrepresented the reality of history, nevertheless littered literature, film, casual conversation, and children's textbooks."[24] The camera was moved so as to shed light on hitherto shadowy areas of history, but at the same time it darkened what had previously been overexposed. Thus, as Stanley Hoffmann points out, the danger was that one myth would be replaced by another, and indeed this was precisely what happened: the image of a France united in resistance was supplanted (wrongly, we can now say in all serenity) by the image of a France equally united in cowardice.[25]

This partial demystification was open to challenge and criticism, and the film was in fact assailed for its unflinching partiality. With hindsight, however, the critics seem to have missed their mark. *The Sorrow and the Pity* was intended to be *a* film about the Occupation; it never claimed to capture the whole complex reality in a few hours of images. It is perhaps an unintended homage to the filmmakers' achievement that this is what was expected of them after the fact. Paradoxically, the film became an important historical touchstone for the public and historians alike precisely because of its shortcomings and the questions and controversies they aroused.

A further reason for the film's impact has to do with the originality of its form. The preponderant role of the interview and the simultaneous contradiction of some spoken testimony by images on screen made *The Sorrow and the Pity* seem rather like a conversation around the family dinner table; the story is told in familiar terms and open to challenge by all who hear it. French viewers responded in highly emotional ways. In this sense, *Sorrow* was surely the first film about the memory, as distinct from the history, of the Occupation. The authors aimed their spotlights not at the 1940s but at the late 1960s, after a decade of Gaullist government. On this point too they were quite frank:

> [During a screening at the ORTF] Michel Cournot criticized us for asking questions thirty years after the fact. Had I been able to respond, I would have said: "If you had invented a time machine and offered to rent it to us, I'm not sure that we would have accepted." For us, in fact, the interesting thing was to compare the historical reality—and all its attendant ambiguity—with the memory of people today.[26]

Still another reason for the film's impact was an unintended consequence of the censorship. More than the film itself, the attempt to block its broadcast revealed the fragility of the official myth. The ORTF in 1971 was fighting a rear-guard action. It refused to face facts: the idyllic marriage of France with de Gaulle and the Resistance was on the rocks. Once again, though, it was the myth, the contemporary politicized image of the Resistance, that was at issue, not the Resistance as such, much less the résistants or their history.

After the election of Giscard d'Estaing in 1974, the new government, which can hardly be suspected of wishing to defend Gaullism's historical image, nevertheless perpetuated the habit of silence so deeply ingrained in the halls of power. The policy of silence found support even among liberals like Simone Veil. It proved even more effective (if less sensational) than the president's alleged wish (alluded to in the film) to protect his family's image. When it comes to memory, however, silence is never fruitful. Recollections and fantasies about the dark years were so common in the period 1974–1981 that the effect of the censorship was like rubbing salt into an open wound. And ultimately it turned out to benefit only the opposition: the Socialists, who came to power in 1981, allowed the film to be shown on television, thus creating the impression that they, at least, had nothing to hide.

Finally, *The Sorrow and the Pity* openly confronted the issue of how historical memory should be passed on. Those most hostile to the film (outside the government) remained implacable in their opposition, from 1971 to 1981. It was no accident that Fabre-Luce, onetime proponent of a German Europe, and Simone Veil, onetime deportee, should have found themselves in agreement on the issue. All who criticized the film for favoring one side or the other, all who saw its shortcomings and nothing else, had one thing in common: they belonged to a generation that had lived through the war, that had profoundly suffered from it, and whose behavior ever since had been greatly influenced by the experience of the Occupation. This remark applies even to Sartre's ideological pseudo-critique. The man who published the article in *La Cause du peuple* was not the editor of that newspaper but the author of *Les Mouches* (1942), whose "complex" on the subject of commitment to the Resistance is well known. The differences between these hostile critics and their younger colleagues reflect a generation gap. Those born after the war recognized their own questions in *Sorrow* and thus applauded, regardless of their political tendency, when the mirror was broken.

Those who lived through the war found themselves ensnared in memories of their own and instinctively reacted against the film.

But not without a certain blindness. For in the film it is generally the witnesses from that same generation who raise the most controversial issues: Mendès France and Claude Lévy discuss antisemitism; Coulaudon (Colonel Gaspar) alludes to the many people who like to tell him stories about their "resistance experience" but "who never did what had to be done"; the Pétainists, for their part, extol the National Revolution. All these issues were raised by the witnesses, not by the filmmakers.

What would a woman like Simone Veil have said if she had been interviewed for the film? What résistants would Germaine Tillion have mentioned? And how would they have reacted? Mendès, interviewed in 1971, criticized the film for its omissions, its occasionally farfetched interpretations, and its lack of balance. But his attitude was by no means hostile.[27] Those who were also actors in the drama and therefore potential witnesses themselves fail to identify with those who actually appear in the film, because the truth as it appears to them intersects only by chance with the images and testimony recorded by the camera.

The Sorrow and the Pity thus disclosed a structural tension: the transmission of a history so full of conflict depends on an alchemy whose secret no one possesses—not the actors, not the historians, not the filmmakers. Nor can anyone claim exclusive possession of the truth. The truth is partial in both senses. History is not the mortar out of which an artificial unity can be created—unless the mortar is mixed with that express purpose in mind. *Sorrow* avoided just that.

The Touvier Affair: Episode One

Ophuls' film would not have caused such a scandal when it was released if it had been an isolated symptom. On 29 August 1971 the *New York Times Magazine* published a piece on President Georges Pompidou by Keith Botsford, a writer who lived in Europe. Botsford described without embellishment the new president's modest career during the Occupation and reported these words of Pompidou's on the subject of the Resistance:

"I hate all that business," he said with a quick wave of his hand and sharp displeasure in his bright eyes. "I hate medals, I hate decorations of all kinds."[28]

At the time these words passed almost unnoticed. A few months later, controversy erupted. On 13 December 1971 Maurice Clavel, a philosopher, writer, and filmmaker, caused a scandal during a televised debate with Jean Royer, the deputy mayor of Tours and proponent of a new "moral order." Clavel had made a short film, *Life Protests,* that was shown just before the debate and from which a word had been cut without his permission. Furious, he stood up and, before leaving the studio, denounced his "censors" on the air. In the film Clavel makes a rather wild appeal to his audience to let their consciences be stirred and to rise up in protest against routine and conformity—in short, to embark on a new resistance. He explicitly related this plea to what Pompidou had said in the *Times:* "At a time when the president of the republic can speak to a leading American newspaper of his revulsion (*aversion*) and irritation at the thought of the Resistance." The ORTF cut the word "revulsion."[29]

There is no question that Clavel put his own interpretation on what Pompidou actually said. The best proof of this is that he uses two words—the harsh "revulsion" and the relatively mild "irritation"—where the president had used only one ("I *hate* all that business"). Yet he knowingly put his finger on the crucial issue of Pompidou's ambivalence toward the Resistance, since the president could hardly have been unaware of the ways in which his admission lent itself to misinterpretation. The president's remark was ambiguous, because it could be interpreted as expressing irritation with the Resistance and résistants as well as with the phenomenon of resistancialism. How could one fail to draw the conclusion that the president was referring to the history and not the myth, since he was simultaneously ordering (or failing to block) censorship of *The Sorrow and the Pity,* which was as hostile to the myth as he could possibly wish?

Pompidou, moreover, had difficulty formulating a response, since he was caught between his personal feelings (which were fairly similar to those of the filmmakers, though for different reasons) and the duties of his office: "I'm sure you can understand my unwillingness to be drawn into a discussion of this subject. To do so would be contrary not only to the dignity of my office but also to the force and longevity of my convictions, which no one can question."[30]

This minor scandal shows the degree to which memory of the Resistance had lost its coherence in 1971: Clavel, himself a former résistant, resurrected the resistance legacy in a typically sixty-eightish outburst, while at the same time another sixty-eighter was attacking a resistancialist myth also disapproved by the president, whose thoughts were at bottom not so different from those of his critic.

In the Clavel affair, the Resistance was once again called to the rescue in the face of Royer's reactionary (one would like to say Pétainist) tendencies and of what Clavel perceived as indifference on the part of his fellow citizens. For Ophuls and the producers of *Sorrow*, the problem lay rather in the idealization of the Resistance. Clavel and Ophuls, in their determination to be nonconformists, were both members of the generation of '68—each of course in his own way. Yet one reminisced openly about his combat experience during the Occupation and the Algerian War, and this estranged him from the other, who exhibited less reverence toward the past and greater preoccupation with the neglect of antisemitism and collaboration. Meanwhile President Pompidou attempted to enforce silence, aided in his efforts by zealous television executives—yet even he was incapable of quieting his subconscious, his deep-seated emotions.

These obvious contradictions became even more acute in the early stages of the so-called Touvier affair, which marked a major turning point in the government's attitude toward memories of the Occupation. On 23 November 1971 President Pompidou quietly granted a pardon to a former official of the Milice, Paul Touvier. Twice, on 10 September 1946 by a court in Lyons and on 4 March 1947 by a court in Chambéry, Touvier was sentenced to death (in absentia, having eluded the police), but by 1967, when the statute of limitations took effect, he had yet to be captured. Although the death penalty then lapsed, Touvier was still forbidden to reside in the twelve departments of southeastern France, barred from enjoyment of property he owned in the region. The presidential pardon eliminated these secondary penalties and permitted Touvier to show himself openly in the town where his family home was located, Chambéry, nestled between the Glières highlands, where in March 1944 the Milice helped the Nazis destroy resistance units, and the mountains of Vercors, where the largest partisan battle of the war was fought.

This presidential act gave rise to a heated controversy, which was to consume Pompidou's "tranquil" France for many months and which resurfaced more than twenty years later. On 5 June Jacques Derogy published an article in *L'Express* in which he reported that he had "discovered the whereabouts of the butcher of Lyons," an appellation that would later be applied to the German Klaus Barbie. The press was unleashed in one of the most spectacular outbursts of journalistic attention to the Occupation since the 1950s: 350 articles appeared in the month of June alone, 2,000 in 1972, and some 5,000 through 1976.[31] With a series of "exclusive reports," "revelations," and "new documents" added to an already thick dossier, the media kept up constant pressure.

Part of the reason for the intense interest in the case was political. The "new society" touted by Prime Minister Jacques Chaban-Delmas was encountering increased hostility from the UDR and orthodox Gaullist quarters, while on the left long-suppressed hopes had been revived by Mitterrand's assumption of leadership of the Socialist Party on 16 June 1971. When the affair erupted, therefore, the president found himself somewhat isolated. He had suffered a personal defeat when a record number of voters abstained in the referendum of 23 April 1972 concerning enlargement of the European Community. In these circumstances the Touvier pardon, which had been granted without publicity, crystallized a broad spectrum of opposition after word leaked out. Certain of the president's rivals seized on the opportunity to mount a campaign intended to unseat General de Gaulle's beleaguered heir.

The Sorrow and the Pity had exhumed the memory of "German France." But to illustrate the concept, the film had found a presentable collaborator, Christian de la Mazière, and made him into something of a film star.[32] But now, just as the film was being shown around the country, a "real" collaborator appeared almost like a ghost—a collaborator with real crimes and authentic victims to his credit. Suddenly reality outstripped misleading fiction. And Touvier, the real collaborator, was by no means presentable.

Paul Touvier was born in 1915. Raised in a traditional Catholic family, he had joined the ACJF (Association Catholique de la Jeunesse

Française, France's Catholic youth organization) as an adolescent. Heeding the advice of his father, a veteran of World War I, Touvier joined Colonel de La Rocque's French Social Party (an extreme right-wing group of which his father was already a member) just before the war. Mobilized, he fought in Norway in April 1940. After the armistice he quite naturally (given his background) enlisted in Vichy's National Revolution. He became a member of the Légion Française des Combattants, the regime's propaganda spearhead, and in 1942 joined the legion's Service d'Ordre. Because his patriotism "commanded him to follow the Marshal," he changed as the government changed. Apparently, under pressure from his father and a priest, Touvier joined what would become, in January 1943, the Milice.[33] He became head of the Milice's S-2 (intelligence and operations) branch for Savoy and later for the Rhone under the command of Joseph Lécussan. In this capacity he was intimately involved in the murder of Victor Basch and his wife, who died on 10 January 1944 near Lyons, although no investigation, including the official prosecution begun in 1989, has been able to establish Touvier's direct responsibility for the crime.

At the time the Basch murders were seen not as an instance of police brutality but as a bloody revival of the Dreyfus Affair, because the victim had been a former president of the Human Rights League and an impassioned Dreyfusard. This background served only to focus even greater attention on the pardon that was granted twenty-eight years after the fact to one of the presumed accomplices in the murder, a crime that in many ways typified the fratricidal passions of the time.

Theft, extortion, and murder all figured in the daily activities of the miliciens in a region where a relatively high percentage of the population was involved with the maquis. When the debacle came, Touvier did not follow the remnants of Darnand's Franc-Garde into exile. Somehow miraculously avoiding the police, who might have offered him protection in exchange for help against the Communists, he began an underground existence that would last for twenty-seven years.

Thus Touvier was no minor bit player or misfit like the eponymous central character of the film *Lacombe Lucien*. He typified the extremist wing of the collaboration as a member of a paramilitary unit created by Vichy for the express purpose of combatting the Resistance. There is no air of European romanticism about him, only an odor of blood, French blood, stemming from crimes in which he participated personally and directly. Hence Pompidou's reduction of Touvier's sentence was widely seen as a provocation.

Over the next few years, quite a few escaped collaborators would resurface in France, men who had been sentenced to death in absentia but who had eluded justice. Yet the case of Touvier stands out. From the first he had received support from the Catholic Church, support that was systematic and continuous: a priest officiated at his marriage, held in secret just after the Liberation; Touvier then found refuge in any number of monasteries, mainly in Savoy, and on 24 May 1989 he was arrested in a monastery run by fundamentalist Catholics (*intégristes*). The list of clergymen who provided him with assistance is impressive: it ranges from the chaplain assigned to prisoners of the Milice to the Jesuits of Lyons and includes many Dominican and Benedictine monks. The satirical newspaper *Canard enchaîné* alluded to an "ecclesiastical connection."[34] From the time of the purge, a small segment of the clergy had, out of "Christian charity" and ideological conviction, offered effective protection to former Pétainists and collaborators sought by the police. Touvier was one of the most important figures to receive such protection, a kind of prize specimen: for a time he was even given quarters in the official residence of the archbishop of Lyons. It was there that he was served, not without difficulty, with official notification of the ban on his residence in the region (although no further action was taken).[35]

One man supported Touvier with all the considerable influence at his disposal: Canon Duquaire, onetime secretary to Cardinal Gerlier and later to Monsignor Villot, whom he followed to the Vatican when Villot was named secretary of state. After making Touvier's acquaintance in 1957, he submitted a first application for pardon to de Gaulle in 1963 after garnering the considerable support of Edmond Michelet, a noted resistance fighter, former minister of justice, and member of the Conseil Constitutionnel. This application pertained to the death penalty itself, but it was rejected in view of the fact that Touvier was still at large and unlikely to be executed. After the statute of limitations took effect in 1967, Duquaire again filed a request for pardon, which reached Pompidou in 1969. Now the only issue was the secondary penalties, including the confiscation of property. One of the arguments raised was that Paul Touvier's children were deprived of the fruits of an estate that had been bequeathed to them by Paul's father. The application for pardon made its way from the ministry of the interior to the State Security Court and the chancellery. On 28 January 1970 the prosecutor of the State Security Court asked Jacques Delarue, a former member of the Resistance and a historian specializing in the Occupation who had been involved in the investigation of many collaborators since the Liberation, to prepare a report on the case. Delarue submitted his findings on 10 June 1970. After calling attention to Touvier's frequent lies, Delarue noted the man's rather unsavory character and characterized his activities during the Occupation as "nefarious, unscrupulous, and inexcusable." The first death sentence handed out to Touvier in 1945, Delarue concluded, had been fully justified as punishment for "a series of crimes and offenses unparalleled in amplitude."[36] He recommended that the application for pardon be rejected: "I said that if he were pardoned, there might well be demonstrations, particularly in Lyons, by people who had suffered from his crimes."[37] Meanwhile Pierre Arpaillange, at that time director of criminal affairs and pardons and later, at the time of Touvier's arrest in May 1989, minister of justice, also recommended that the application be denied, adding only that "because of the length of time elapsed since the crimes" the residential restrictions on Touvier be relaxed in order that he might "find work."[38]

Various people now came forward in support of Touvier, following the lead of Charles Duquaire, Edmond Michelet, and others, including Jacques Brel, who had been deceived by Touvier. One of these was Colonel Rémy, faithful to the logic of his battle against the purge and his conversion of 1950.[39] Another was the philosopher Gabriel Marcel, who had been persuaded to join the cause by his colleague Marie-Madeleine Davy, a former member of the Resistance. In a letter to the president of the republic dated 17 November 1970, Marcel wrote that Touvier "spared no effort to fight against what he deemed crimes against humanity by a segment of the Milice, such as the appalling execution of Victor Basch and his wife." Marcel continued: "I even believe that he remained in the Milice only to combat its excesses."[40] Marcel, born a Jew, had converted to Catholicism and was one of the leading Christian existentialist philosophers. Though untainted by any hint of compromise during the Occupation, he was nevertheless criticized for certain of his positions. In October 1944, for example, before the liberation of the camps, he published a highly controversial article in *Témoignage chrétien* in which he called upon Jews to be discreet in their demands when their persecution finally came to an end and criticized "the strident tone [adopted] . . . by some who had only recently become French citizens [and who] in many cases had been leading lives across the Channel or the Atlantic that were far less harsh and above all less dangerous than the lives that others of their race (*leurs congénères*) had been obliged to lead in France."[41] Marcel was a friend of Edmond Michelet and after the Liberation had shared Michelet's hostility to the purge; both men were literally "mouse-trapped" by Touvier, as Marcel publicly acknowledged in *L'Express* on 19 June 1972, when he also revealed that he had realized his error well before Pompidou's decision and that his change of heart caused Touvier to panic, as witnessed by Touvier's urgent letter of 10 January 1971, which the philosopher now made public.[42] Still this intervention in the case by well-known intellectuals and prestigious former résistants probably had an influence on President Pompidou's decision. When the scandal finally came to light, this aspect made the whole issue more complex and tortuous than it might otherwise have been.

The underside of the affair would not be exposed until May 1972. Rejecting the advice of Delarue, the State Security Court, and the minister of justice, Pompidou granted the controversial pardon. His action was to be kept quiet, even confidential, yet the police were required by law to publish the information throughout the country. "Under such conditions how could [the pardon] remain secret?"[43] In the event it attracted considerable attention, owing to the hidden role of the church, the personal involvement of Pompidou, who knew all the facts before reaching his decision, and the personality of Touvier, who soon found himself the object of constant attention from reporters prepared to publish his version of the truth. In an interview with *Paris-Match,* for example, Touvier declared: "I never killed anyone. I never ordered that anyone be killed. I never tortured anyone."[44]

Naturally the most vehement reaction came from resistance groups, already in an uproar over *The Sorrow and the Pity.* Demonstrations were staged throughout France. On 18 June 1972 in Paris 1,500 marchers gathered at the Monument to the Deported. Among them were Compagnons de la Libération, several former ministers, including some Gaullists, résistants, representatives of the Jewish community (including Pierre Bloch, president of the Antisemitic League, and Rabbi Bauer), and Catholics (including Father Riquet and Father Braun, both former resistance fighters), whose presence was interpreted as a condemnation of the support given Touvier by some elements within the church.[45]

At the same moment, Pompidou was in Colombey-les-Deux-Eglises to dedicate the Croix de Lorraine erected there in memory of General de Gaulle. The ceremony was ill timed. The presidential pardon had created a broad opposition front, ranging from the left-wing Gaullists of the Union Travailliste to the Communist Party. In Chambéry a member of the regional council observed: "The most recent demonstration by Savoyard résistants against the pardon granted to the milicien Touvier, which drew more than 4,000 participants, had a much greater impact on local opinion than the announcement that same day of Mr. Chaban-Delmas's resignation."[46] (Chaban resigned as prime minister on 5 July 1972.)

To make matters worse, the Touvier pardon contradicted the government's policy toward Klaus Barbie. The former head of the Lyons SD (Sicherheitsdienst, or German security service) had been arrested on 2 March 1972 by the Bolivian police in response to a request from France for his extradition (a request that would take eleven years to bear fruit). On 26 May 1972, in a rare atmosphere of national unity, Jean de Lipkovski, secretary of state for foreign affairs, addressed the National Assembly: "Nothing but unanimity is possible in the state of rage that grips us when we see this abject figure still walking about a free man." Lipkovski affirmed the government's determination to seek justice.[47] Now, as it happens, Barbie and Touvier exercised similar responsibilities, one with the SD, the other with the Milice; both served in Lyons, the capital of the Resistance; they may even have met. In any case, their names were frequently linked in the public mind. Why pardon for one and furor toward the other, when both were part of the same criminal system? Pierre Bourgeade issued a stinging denunciation: "In taking the action he did in the Touvier affair, Mr. Pompidou demonstrated that his judgment of Nazism, a system with which Touvier was intimately associated, does not coincide with the judgment of the vast majority of French people."[48]

After four months of polemics, the president finally broke the silence and ended his isolation. When questioned about the Touvier affair by Jacques Fourneyron of the newspaper *Progrès de Lyon* at a press conference on 21 September 1972, Pompidou squarely confronted the facts of the case. He pointed out that the pardon applied only to the secondary penalties and did not restore all of Touvier's civil rights (including the right to vote). The former *milicien* was "still subject to what is called *la mort civile*" (literally, civic death, meaning loss of many of the rights of citizenship). Alluding to the terrible responsibility that goes with the right of pardon, the president denied that he had in any way absolved Touvier of his guilt. His action, he said, had been "purely and simply an act of clemency, and that is all." Furthermore, he would not alter his decision. Yet conscious of the fact that his explanation was somehow inadequate to the gravity of the protest aroused by the decision, he ended by making a clean breast of his feelings on the question of the Occupation, about which he acknowledged having received many letters of protest:

> Over the past thirty years or so, our country has lived through a series of dramatic events. The war, the defeat and its humiliations, the Occupation and its horrors, the Liberation, and in reaction the purge and—let us be frank—its excesses, the war in Indochina, and then the dreadful Algerian conflict and its horrors, on both sides, and the exodus of a million French citizens driven from their homes, followed immediately by the OAS and its murderous attacks and violence, and then, in reaction, the repression. As one who was denounced by the men of Vichy to the German police and who twice escaped assassination attempts by the OAS, once at General de Gaulle's side and once in an attack aimed directly at me, I feel I have the right to ask if we are going to keep the wounds of our national discord bleeding eternally. Hasn't the time come to draw a veil over the past, to forget a time when Frenchmen disliked one another, attacked one another, and even killed one another? I say this not out of political calculation, although I see that there are some sharp minds here, but out of respect for France.[49]

"Forget." Once again the word was uttered openly. But Georges Pompidou could not claim the authority of his illustrious predecessor. He was heir to the founder of the Fifth Republic, not to the man of June Eighteenth. As he himself candidly acknowledged, he had lived through the Occupation largely "by remaining passive."[50] Although he made some attempts to join his intellectual friends in the Resistance, he had avoided all-out commitment: "I did enough imprudent things to risk being deported, which, dead or alive, would have made me a hero. But clearly I lacked an adventurous spirit."[51] As a result, Pompidou had always harbored a certain suspicion of the résistant mentality. As a member of the commission that awarded the Resistance Medal to employees of the ministry of education, he had an opportunity to appreciate the difference between the true resistance fighters and those who only joined up at the last minute. "Later on, that experience probably made me somewhat skeptical of certain resistance credentials and indulgent toward the targets of the purge, particularly those whose files I had to examine as secretary of the Conseil d'Etat."[52]

When he uttered the word "forget," Pompidou was exhibiting a reflex reaction common to many who had lived through the war. Many contemporaries had complex feelings about friends and colleagues who had committed themselves totally to the Resistance. Pompidou's act might even be called courageous, because it made so much of the distinction between those who were really "in it" and those who were not. (Pompidou, incidentally, was indeed denounced by Abel Bonnard's office in 1944, but nothing came of it.)

The Touvier pardon was also a political act. In the first place it came in the wake of other pardons. In 1966 de Gaulle had granted pardons to certain collaborators: Jacques Vasseur, who had served with the Gestapo in Angers, and Jean Barbier, who was accused of having betrayed members of the Resistance. But the General had acted only to prevent two executions, which, despite the seriousness of the charges, were unthinkable twenty years after the end of the war. In both cases, moreover, the former collaborators would remain in prison until 1983.[53] In addition, as we saw earlier, the Germans Oberg and Knochen were released in 1962, during de Gaulle's presidency. Unlike Vasseur and Barbier, Touvier's life was no longer in jeopardy. All that was at stake was his property. What is more, it was clear that he had not been forsaken by everyone. In the circumstances, the argument that the pardon had been granted as a "humanitarian gesture" did not seem convincing.

Pompidou's decision also sent a message to the extreme right, which since 1969 had supported the new president. Somewhat earlier, at the time of the Clavel affair, the Action Française newspaper *Aspects de la France* had bestowed on Pompidou the title of "liquidator of Gaullo-Resistantialism" (spelled, please note, with a *t*).[54] According to Jacques Delarue, Pompidou may also have been courting the favor of the Catholic hierarchy, which would have given him a not inconsiderable political advantage in the upcoming elections. One question remains unanswered, however: why would the Church have invested so much in such an unprepossessing protégé?[55]

These personal and political considerations go some way toward explaining Pompidou's decision. But the explanation of the scandal it provoked must be sought elsewhere—in the contradiction between the desired goal and the existing state of public opinion. For all his sincerity, Pompidou probably did not fully grasp the degree to which his decision ran counter to public sentiment. He thus handed the press, which did appreciate the extent of public interest in the matter, a golden opportunity. At the same time, he exposed his flank to attack by adversaries within the governing coalition. In superficial ways the Touvier affair was exploited politically, as were other scandals of the day (in real estate, morals, and the so-called Marcovic affair).

In another sense, though, the magnitude of the response is best explained in terms of a series of fundamental issues concerning the organization of memory. How could Pompidou have hoped to draw a veil over internal dissension at a time when people's consciences were being reawakened, when *The Sorrow and the Pity* was raising new questions, and when debate was being revived? Was it really possible, with a single act, whether quietly discreet or publicly symbolic, to silence a new generation's questions and doubts? Was it really possible to ignore the concerns of former resistance fighters and deportees, whose great fear was that the past might be forgotten?

What Pompidou faced was the backlash from the Gaullian myth. Convinced that that myth had been fabricated, Pompidou sometimes gave the impression of wanting nothing more to do with either résistants or resistancialism. Yet at other times he defended the myth of a unified Resistance and gave the impression that, now more than ever, it was essential to forget the conflicts of the past. The contradiction between the presidential pardon and the official censorship of *Sorrow* thus served as a catalyst, reinforcing the effects of both: the government that was suppressing the truth about the collaboration was at the same time granting a pardon to a former collaborator.

There can be no doubt that the pardon was a logical consequence of the official tradition of forgetfulness and silence. In the—all things considered—rather minor case of the milicien, Pompidou had really tried to achieve the same thing as de Gaulle, but he failed because the expectations of the French people had changed. The General's "invented honor" had marked a fortuitous encounter between a political will and a cultural and intellectual need. By contrast, Pompidou's "reconciliation" ran against the tide at a moment when the French had just been reminded of how much they had been wronged. The proposed reconciliation failed to offer, as de Gaulle had been able to do, a satisfactory interpretation of history to go with it. Worse still, it heightened suspicion of the still serviceable Gaullist myth of a unified Resistance. In the end it left the French with no defenses to confront their own past.

"Forget." In retrospect it seems incomprehensible that a man like Pompidou could fail to appreciate the consequences of an action that he appears to have weighed solely in tactical political terms, unless—and this is highly unlikely—he did not really wish to bring about the reconciliation he recommended. Still questions remain as to the reasons for the Touvier pardon, which may be answered if the trial actually goes forward. What is striking, however, is that the effects of the pardon were precisely the opposite of what was intended. Not only were old wounds reopened, but the whole affair, unintentionally revived by the presidential action, would take on even greater importance after Touvier's arrest in 1989. Charges of "crimes against humanity" filed against Touvier by groups of former résistants and deportees, the first such charges to be filed after the law of 1964 suspending the statute of limitations for these crimes, finally, after a lengthy legal battle, bore fruit, leading to the first actual indictment (of Jean Leguay) and to the first trial (of Klaus Barbie)—an odd fate indeed for a pardon intended to "draw a veil" over the past.

The Forties Revival

By 1974, three years after the release of *The Sorrow and the Pity*, France was once again "occupied," this time by films, books, discs, newspaper articles, and swastikas on page one. The country had experienced a "forties revival," a *mode rétro* as it was called in a seemingly innocuous phrase that might have been applied to a fad for any era of the past. Was this fad as innocent and superficial as it seemed? Hardly. It was too extravagant to have been mere amusement. What it was, in fact, was the third piece of the broken mirror, the most jagged expression of the return of the repressed.

The mode began in 1971 with the release of *Sorrow*, although this was neither the first nor the only symptom of a new interpretation of the Occupation. Suddenly writers and filmmakers found a public, potential supply met with pent-up demand. There had been no shortage of precursors in the preceding years. Patrick Modiano, one of the leading writers of this new wave, had published *Place de l'étoile* with Gallimard in 1968. Any number of novelists and screenwriters had produced pieces whose action was set in the period 1940–1944. Michel Drach, who made the film *Violons du bal*, had scurried about frantically for fifteen years trying to get it produced. Paul Guimard had long been seeking a producer for his novel *L'Ironie du sort*, published in 1960. Both films were finally shot in 1974. Guimard's book even enjoyed a resurgence of popularity fifteen years after its first publication: between 1971 and 1974 there were three new printings and sales of 150,000 copies.[56]

There were ambiguities about this new fashion, however, and some of the works that came out of it were not exactly what they seemed. The Occupation may have been their common subject, but it appeared in many guises. In 1971 Pascal Jardin, a well-known screenwriter, published a brief account of his "dark years" entitled *La Guerre à neuf ans* (The War at Age Nine, whose sequel *Le Nain jaune* [Yellow Dwarf] was published in 1978, after the forties revival had subsided). Pascal was the son of Jean Jardin, who had been Laval's chief of staff in 1942 and a close associate of Raoul Dautry, a top civil servant before the war and an influential figure afterward. The elder Jardin had thus been an éminence grise behind these powerful men, who, when plucked from the shadowy corridors of power, proved frightening to a public always ready to find *synarques* (Vichy technocrats associated with the Synarchy movement) lurking behind the scenes. Recently Pierre Assouline has revealed how surprised Jean Jardin had been by his son's memories: "When you write a novel of that sort, you tell true stories but change the names. But he—he used real names and told whatever stories he pleased!"[57] But the accuracy of the novel is beside the point. What mattered was Pascal Jardin's impressionistic style, which was faithful if not to history then at least to his memory.

The novel is brisk, lively, and disrespectful. Seen from a boy's height of four feet and a few inches, the turbulent capital of Vichy is an amusement park full of dubious and fascinating characters: Paul Morand, who diverts himself with the narrator at the tennis club; Robert Aron, who while making his getaway inadvertently runs into Consul Krug von Nidda; Coco Chanel, Yvonne Printemps, and many others. There is nothing apocalyptic or evil about the place, just the ordinary antics of the affluent who, scarcely disturbed by events, enjoy evenings such as this:

> Herr Rahn [a Reich counselor to Vichy] and the minister Jacques Le Roy Ladurie sat down at the piano after dinner. Two colossal men, they improvised four-hand piano. They played mock Bach, mock Mozart, jazz Bach, and Beethoven-Armstrong with such force that the strings of the piano snapped one after another. It was repaired the next day by a piano tuner with a white cane, who pretended to be blind and who stuck a bouquet of microphones to the tail of our Pleyel concert grand. The problem with people of this sort was that you never knew whether they were working for the Resistance or the Gestapo.[58]

The tone was undeniably new. It did not violate taboos; it simply ignored them, as Emmanuel Berl, who wrote a preface for Jardin's book, was well aware: "In my estimation [this book] sheds more light on May '68 than does Mr. Marcuse's Eros." In other words, the revolution in memory was somehow implicit in the sexual revolution.

Pascal Jardin was the first of the "children of the collaboration" to lay his memories on the table. He was followed a short time later by Marie Chaix, who published *Les Lauriers du lac de Constance* in

1974. In a less jubilant tone she recounted the career of her father, Albert Beugras, the official in charge of the underground activities of the Parti Populaire Français, from the sumptuous feasts of occupied Paris to his twilight years as an exile in Germany. In the same vein, but later, Jean-Luc Maxence settled a score with his father's ghost in *L'Ombre d'un père*. The father, Jean-Pierre Maxence, had been an extreme right-wing militant, a book reviewer for *Aujourd'hui*, and an occasional contributor to *La Gerbe* and to *La Nouvelle Revue française* when it was under the editorship of collaborationist Drieu La Rochelle. All these writers stated an obvious truth, which gradually took hold in the public mind: that whatever crimes these collaborators might have committed, whatever opinion one might hold of them, they could not remain internal exiles forever. They too were part of France's national heritage. And what is more, people "discovered" that many of them had already resumed their place in society. Thus, with their words, their sincerity, and their very different styles, these authors helped to overcome legitimate opposition and rehabilitate their parents in the collective consciousness of the nation.

At the same time, other children—the children of genocide—were also exhuming old images: of roundups, repression, and antisemitism. Typical works in this vein include Joseph Joffo's *Un Sac de billes* (1973) and the films of Michel Drach and Michel Mitrani (see Chapter 5).

Finally, Patrick Modiano must be placed in a category of his own, so great was his influence in those years. Nearly all his books exhibit a fascination with the murky, shadowy ambiguities of the Occupation. In *La Place de l'étoile* (1968) he portrays a Jewish collaborator in a parody of the literary hallucinations of Céline and Maurice Sachs. In *La Ronde de nuit* (1969) and the screenplay for Louis Malle's film *Lacombe Lucien* he plays with the ambiguity of commitment, reacting strongly, almost too strongly, against any notion of ideological determinism and portraying his characters as stooges without conscience or morality.

Modiano's work is an anguished, frenetic meditation over the shards of a mirror that he himself helped to smash. He clings to these fragments of reality and even seeks refuge in them; yet he seems to be saying that no logic, no rational and reassuring organization, can restore to memory its lost coherence. For Modiano, the Occupation has lost all historical status. It is a puzzle that must never be solved, for it is only through the gaps in the picture that the truth can emerge.

Even from this brief look at the forties revival, it should be clear that it is misleading to describe the phenomenon as a fad, because the various cultural signs of which it is composed point in different directions. Those children who revived memories of their parents' past succeeded in laying bare the stark divisions of those dark years: a whole generation—sons of collaborators and sons of deportees alike—had to cope with the bloody legacy. In 1974, however, it was difficult, in an emotional, visceral sense, to establish an equitable hierarchy. The previous generation had encountered the same difficulty at the time of the Liberation. How could the younger generation be expected to improve on their work thirty years later? Collaborators remained fascists, not to say criminals, and deportees remained victims. But what about their children? Thrust into the public eye against their will, the collaborators, who had previously been cropped out of images of the past although not banished from social intercourse, suddenly assumed a different guise: that of the father. But this discovery was traumatic because meanwhile other fathers (and mothers), parents who had also disappeared but in Hitler's ovens, had returned to haunt the collective memory.

Modiano's wide-eyed journey through time aroused curiosity. The success of his work, which cannot be explained solely by his admittedly considerable literary talent, is evidence of this. Yet people were also curious about works that emulated *The Sorrow and the Pity* by denouncing, justifiably if with varying degrees of success, the magnitude of Vichy's crime and the reality of France's attraction to fascism. Which path to follow? Modiano or Ophuls? To *decompose* reality or to *recompose* it?

The impact of the forties revival (leaving aside commercial exploitation of the phenomenon, a logical consequence of the public's intense interest) stemmed from these tensions, which only added to France's confusion about its past.

The forties revival played an essential role in the history of the Vichy syndrome. Artists anticipated the evolution of the public's attitude. They made new trends intelligible to large numbers of people by casting them in aesthetic form. Pascal Ory observes that "once again it was the artists who 'innocently' laid down the first explosive charges." But "the revival probably would not have attained the proportions it did if it had not received additional impetus from a rather unusual source: namely, the various 'affairs,' major and minor, whose content and dramatic staging periodically revived debate."[59]

My interpretation is somewhat different: that the "explosive charges" and the "affairs" were both manifestations of the same underlying phenomenon. The change first became apparent between 1971 and 1974 in the cultural sphere, from which emanated the most significant and visible signs of a new outlook on the past. But these cultural changes were as much revelation as catalyst: the forties revival became a social fact only because the ground was already prepared and a demand for the new cultural product already existed. This hypothesis has at least one merit: it explains why the public exhibited a new sensitivity to the Touvier affair and other scandals. Resistance veterans and the Jewish community did not need Ophuls or Modiano to jog their memories; the rest of the public probably did.

Fresh memories, new questions, a rekindled fascination with the past: in the four years since the mirror was first broken, the fragile equilibrium that had held since the 1950s was destroyed. Had people stopped talking about the Occupation? They were about to begin again. The gates were opened to obsession.

4

Obsession (after 1974): Jewish Memory

Since the early 1970s memories of the Occupation have taken on a new dimension. Each year has brought its share of revelations, revivals, scandals, and battles over how the past should be remembered. After 1974 open and explicit references to 1940 became a constant of the cultural scene.

No doubt the economic crisis that followed the 1973 oil embargo evoked nostalgic thoughts in many Frenchmen suddenly faced with an uncertain future that made the past seem more vivid in their eyes. People began to look to the past rather than the future, a change that was reflected in a new appetite for works of history.

Still, while economic factors may have influenced what I have called the Vichy syndrome, other factors had a more direct bearing on its evolution. Foremost among these was a reawakening of Jewish memory, a phenomenon by no means confined to France. In the wake of a series of crises in the Middle East and the emergence of new forms of antisemitism, Jewish consciousness was heightened around the world. Memories of the genocide—the Shoah—were at the heart of this change. In reaction, it was inevitable that France would witness a resurgence of Vichyite and collaborationist reminiscence as well as one of the most serious outbreaks of antisemitic sentiment in recent years. In exploring the fourth phase of the national neurosis, the reawakening of Jewish memory will serve as a touchstone.

Meanwhile, political debate in France erupted into a kind of verbal civil war. The vitriolic nature of the debate was reminiscent of the 1940s: the only thing new about this bluster and invective was that the bitter words were now brandished by politicians too young to have experienced the war first hand. At the same time, the extreme right rediscovered its racist roots and resurrected ideas, or rather ide-

132

ologies, that resembled (or were thought to resemble) the racist ideologies of the wartime years.

Finally, it was in this context that the Barbie trial took place, an
event that at one time seemed to offer the prospect of being both
climax and catharsis. But that was before other scandals erupted and
other trials got under way, making it clear that the France of the
1990s will still have to go on coping with the aftermath of the 1940s.

A Period of Malaise

"In November 1940 I was eight years old, and already a Jew."—
Claude Berri, *Le Vieil Homme et l'enfant* (1967)

Between 1978 and 1981 France was convulsed by a series of events
in which the antisemitism of the dark years played a central role: the
Darquier de Pellepoix affair, the indictment of former Vichy officials
for crimes against humanity, the polemic over broadcast of the miniseries *Holocaust,* and the Faurisson affair. All these symptoms appeared, not by chance, within a brief period. Their common root lay
in a nervousness that had been growing within the French Jewish
community since the 1960s.

In 1945 that community had been deeply scarred by the deportation: one-fifth of the Jewish population (including Jews of foreign as
well as French birth) had vanished into the camps. France had been
a refuge for Jews before the war, so the wartime antisemitism of the
French government had a terrible demoralizing effect. A minor incident like the Finaly affair could, as we saw earlier, easily degenerate
into a religious war or an affair of state. The silence surrounding the
tragedy of the camps (for Jews and others) only served to widen the
gap. Despite all this, the Jewish community reaffirmed its identity
within French society. In this the fact that some French citizens had
demonstrated sympathy and solidarity with the Jewish plight during
the dark years played a part. But the bad memories could not be
wiped out overnight.

Antisemitism, widely viewed after the war as a freak of history, was
openly avowed only in certain quarters of the extreme right: neo-
Nazis and Poujadists in search of a scapegoat. According to Béatrice
Philippe, even the repatriation of some 300,000 North African Jews

between 1956 and 1967 failed to provoke any major resurgence of antisemitism among the French population, although it did disrupt the internal equilibrium of the Jewish community. The Sephardic Jews of North Africa, uprooted from their native lands, fought hard to preserve the distinctive features of their religion and culture. In this respect they resembled other *pieds noirs* (repatriated French citizens from North Africa) but differed from the more assimilated Ashkenazy Jews.[1]

The creation of the state of Israel in 1948 had altered the whole picture. The governments of the Fourth Republic, encouraged by the pro-Israeli views of a majority of the French public, supported the Jewish state and thus facilitated the reconciliation of the Jews with the rest of the nation. On the other hand, a new form of antisemitism emerged, ideological in essence and more pernicious than other forms because it was more ambiguous: anti-Zionism. The Communists, ensnared in their Stalinist logic, were the first proponents of this new ideology, especially at the time of the Slansky trial and the alleged "doctors' plot" against Stalin (1952–53).

The Franco-British military intervention in Suez in the fall of 1956 was an important milestone. While the background of the intervention lay in developments in Algeria and in the international situation, it was not without domestic consequences in France. The episode revealed a shift in France's "Jewish problem" from the right to the left. A majority of the public backed the government's initiative, but out of "imperialist ardor" rather than philo-Semitism.[2] The army and the right also approved the government's action owing to a resurgence of nationalism in the wake of defeats in Indochina. On 10 November, when Pierre Mendès France rose in the Assembly to denounce what he considered an act of pure folly, one deputy shouted "A mort!" (Kill him!) and another "A Moscou!" (Send him to Moscow!). Meanwhile, Pierre Poujade kept up his attacks on "the Jew Mendès," echoing the courts of Vichy. But on the same day Tixier-Vignancour, who had never distinguished himself for his love of Judaism but who approved of the expedition, was heard to shout: "A Tel-Aviv!" (On to Tel Aviv!).

After the Communist Party declared its hostility to Zionism, another part of the left, this one noncommunist and traditionally a supporter of Israel, also changed its position radically, although for very different reasons:

> A new left, composed mainly of intellectuals and defined by its anticolonialist positions, has begun to look at the Jewish state with new eyes. What it sees is no longer the promised land of asylum for victims of persecution and survivors of the camps but rather an ally of colonialism.[3]

The Jewish community thus found itself in a new situation. Antisemitism of the populist, nationalist, or religious type that had been free to express itself openly during the Occupation had not completely disappeared, but it had lost much of its virulence. Support for Israel as a "Western nation" temporarily concealed this antisemitism from view. Anti-Zionism, on the other hand, raised more delicate issues: under its banner gathered not only people genuinely committed to decolonization, including many Jews, but also others who hid old reflexes behind an ideological alibi. By all appearances, however, it was not the antisemitism of the Nazis or Vichy that shaped the views of this latter group, at least not in any direct way.

The Six-Day War, launched by Israel on 5 June 1967, marked a true turning point. Although the French government continued to express sympathy for Israel, it adopted a position favorable to the Arab countries. After repeated warnings to Israeli leaders, France on 2 June suspended arms shipments to eight countries in the region, including Israel; strict enforcement of the embargo on arms for Israel began in January 1969. Eleven days after the 10 June cease-fire, de Gaulle condemned the Israeli attack. Then, on 27 November 1967 in a press conference called to set forth the position of the French government, the General let slip an unfortunate phrase:

> Some people even feared that the Jews, hitherto dispersed, but who had remained what they had always been, an elite people, sure of itself and domineering, might, once reassembled on the site of their former grandeur, transform into ardent and conquering ambition the very moving wishes that they had been formulating for nineteen centuries: "Next year in Jerusalem."[4]

These few words provoked a considerable uproar, especially since the government's policy failed to sit well not only with French Jews but with the vast majority of the population, which polls showed to be immensely pleased with the Israeli victory. Several times de Gaulle tried, uncharacteristically, to soften the effect of his words through messages to the chief rabbi of France and to David Ben Gurion. But the press conference, and even more the shift in French policy, aroused great anxiety among Jews in the country.

In an emotional but lucid article written on 28 December 1967, in the heat of the controversy, Raymond Aron identified the perverse effects of de Gaulle's disingenuous phrase. Aron refused to join the chorus of those who charged the man of 18 June with antisemitism, but he did denounce his Machiavellianism:

> Let us not fall into the trap that has been laid for us. By inserting a phrase about the "Jewish people" into a historical set piece about the birth of Israel, the head of state was deliberately soliciting two responses, one in defense of the state of Israel, the other in protest against the succinct, not to say insulting, characterization of Jews as such. Taken together, these two responses would have provided a new foundation for the implicit accusation [that French Jews hold a] double allegiance. Inevitably, Jews would be divided.[5]

Aron then went on to criticize the idea of a homogeneous, well-defined Jewish people as well as the idea that there was any such thing as a Jewish community, particularly in France:

> This community does not exist as such. It has no organization; it can and should have none. I am not aware of the proportion of those whom the Vichy government designated Jews who were practicing or nonpracticing or who continued to belong to the "domineering people."[6]

Although Aron considered himself "dejudaicized," he acknowledged the reality of a "collective emotion" on the part of France's Jews, an emotion that he fully shared. Surely his first major complaint against de Gaulle was that the head of state had forced French Jews to take a stand with regard to Israel—on orders of the Prince. His second, and more serious, complaint was that de Gaulle had violated the taboo that held antisemitism in check:

> Knowingly, deliberately, General de Gaulle has inaugurated a new
> phase in Jewish history and perhaps in the history of antisemitism.
> Once again anything is possible. It is back to square one. The issue,
> of course, is not persecution, but only "malevolence." The time for
> contempt is past, but the time for suspicion has arrived.[7]

The proof was quickly forthcoming. Following his remarks on 27 November, de Gaulle received a flood of criticism, but among the expressions of support was a rather embarrassing one from Xavier Vallat, who had been the first commissioner for Jewish questions under Vichy and the man in charge of enforcing antisemitic measures in 1941 and 1942. In the Action Française newspaper Vallat asked:

> Why should I hide the fact that the passage on the Middle East was
> the one that pleased me most? . . . In the past, when some poor sap
> who had stumbled into journalism happened to say that the Jews
> were an exclusive, unassimilable people convinced of their superiority and, ever since Jehovah's promise to Abraham, persuaded that
> it was their destiny to rule the world, M. Bernard Lecache [president
> of the League against Antisemitism] issued an urgent appeal for application of the Marchandeau law, which as everyone knows doubles the penalty for libel when a Jew is the object of attack . . .
> Charles de Gaulle said enough to find himself suddenly transformed
> into a disciple of Hitler, and really it's about time! Now it's Bernard
> Lecache's move, and we'll just stand by and watch how he scores![8]

Even in Israel the comparison with Vichy seemed perfectly natural, and a leading daily newspaper did not shrink from running the headline "Charles Pétain."[9]

Aron's views were hardly typical of Jewish opinion in general. Claude Lévi-Strauss, though largely in agreement with Aron, pointed out to him in a letter written in April 1968 that during the Six-Day War certain prominent Jewish leaders and newspapers had made misleading statements. While admitting to an "ineradicable antipathy to the Arab world," Lévi-Strauss took note of the plight of oppressed minorities, ranging from the Indians of America to the Palestinians.[10]

This restrained and friendly controversy shows that it was not only among antisemites that taboos had collapsed. From now on, the specter of Nazism, genocide, or Vichy could not be used to cut off debate about the specific policies of the Jewish state. Not all the anti-Zionists were racists, but the tendency on all sides to demonize the enemy increased the danger that certain distinctions simply would not be made.

The year 1967 thus marked a turning point in the debate on decolonization and the development of the Third World. A segment of the Jewish community, convinced that old demons had resurfaced, once again found itself isolated. Some felt that they had again been cast as French Jews rather than Jewish Frenchmen. Elements within the Jewish community also appealed to history to bolster their own claims to authority and to silence opposition from Jews reluctant to grant Israel unconditional support.

In the 1970s official Jewish community organizations regained influence as French policy turned unambiguously pro-Arab. One sign of this was the promulgation on 25 January 1977 of the charter of the Conseil Représentatif des Institutions Juives de France (CRIF). Originally called the Conseil Représentatif des Israélites de France, this organization was established in 1944 for the purpose of defending the common interests of the Jewish community. In opposition to the Union Générale des Israélites de France, which had been established by Vichy in 1941 (and was in some ways akin to the Judenräte of occupied central Europe), Communists, Bund socialists, and Zionists reached agreement with the Consistoire Israélite (the official governing body of the French Jewish community) concerning a charter setting forth the broad goals of the community, of which the CRIF declared itself to be the sole legitimate representative.[11] In 1977 the CRIF reaffirmed its original goals for the first time since 1944 and added certain new aims to its charter. It pledged to recognize diversity within the Jewish community but at the same time to foster solidarity and unity; it promised to combat racism in all its forms and to defend human rights; and it pledged unconditional support for the state of Israel. Furthermore, the CRIF asked that the cultural and religious presence of Judaism in France be acknowledged. It also formulated what it called a legitimate demand, and one that would be repeated frequently in the years to come: that French public schools offer instruction in Jewish history, particularly that of the Holocaust.[12]

This concern with education coincided with similar concerns on the part of resistance and deportee groups, which were also calling for better instruction about what happened in the years between 1939 and 1945 (see Chapter 6). Underlying these concerns was a deep desire that neglect of the past give way to remembrance—and not remembrance of the sudden, accidental kind that could be evoked by a few phrases in a speech but a deeper, calmer reflection on history that would allow the legacy of the past to be passed on to subsequent generations. In other words, history was to substitute for suppressed memory and repression; the past was to be recorded under scholarly control in a form that could be accepted by everyone.

Yet this call for education could not conceal the fact that the Jewish community had entered a new phase in coming to terms with its historical memories. Thus, even as the scandals of the late 1970s were raising questions about the role of the French government in the persecution of Jews, within the Jewish community itself a heated controversy erupted over reactions to Nazi persecution. The debate was triggered by the publication in 1966 of Jean-François Steiner's highly controversial book about Treblinka, and it would continue into the 1980s in the form of repeated debate about the notion of "Jewish resistance." Even more than the rest of French society, Jews were obliged to reconsider the history of the 1940s.

The Darquier Affair

On 28 October 1978 began a long saga with many unexpected twists and turns. That day the magazine *L'Express* published a startling scoop. Journalist Philippe Ganier Raymond had found in Spain, and interviewed, Louis Darquier, known as Darquier de Pellepoix, Xavier Vallat's successor as the head of Vichy's Office for Jewish Affairs, a position he held from May 1942 to February 1944. The interview was published in its entirety without comment or cautionary introduction under a sensational title: "At Auschwitz Only the Lice Were Gassed." This was only the most provocative of many outrageous statements made by the bedridden octogenarian, who clearly had seized the occasion to vent hatred stored up since the Occupation. A dyed-in-the-wool Nazi and zealous antisemite since the 1930s, Darquier was the very embodiment of the most violent, irrational, and sinister aspects of Vichy's anti-Jewish policy. Thanks to friends in Franco's Spain and to the absence of any demand for his extradition, Darquier had lived a comfortable life in exile, despite his having been sentenced to death in absentia in December 1947.

Thirty-five years later, Darquier had forgotten nothing and renounced nothing. In the interview, torrents of antisemitic hatred poured from him in a diatribe that seemed to belong to another era. Certain of his statements were particularly shocking, however. In the first place, he denied that there had been a Final Solution in which millions had died: "Pure and simple invention—Jewish invention, of course." Then, minimizing his own role, he accused René Bousquet, the former head of the French police, of having organized the repression of Jews in the Northern Zone and in particular the Vel d'Hiv roundup, which was carried out by Bousquet's men. This assertion was confirmed by documents produced by Ganier Raymond, documents that, while by no means unknown, provided a devastating indictment of the Vichy government.[13] Darquier added, not entirely disingenuously, that he "met very few Germans" in the course of his work. He gave the impression of being a tranquil man but rather surprised that no one until now had disturbed his quiet existence. Of course, as the ministry of justice was quick to point out, Darquier had been condemned to death for intelligence with the enemy, not for crimes against humanity, and his death sentence had lapsed in 1968 when the statute of limitations ran out.

Darquier's statements were bound to cause a furor. The ensuing debate, however, covered a vast territory and had innumerable ramifications. Yet there is something surprising about this reaction, since Darquier was hardly unknown and his misdeeds had not been forgotten. Under severe attack for its decision to publish the article, L'Express pointed out that Jean-François Revel had described Darquier's role in the Final Solution much earlier, in another article published in May 1967.[14] In February 1972 Jacques Derogy, also writing in L'Express, had detailed the activities of the former commissioner for Jewish affairs.[15] Darquier had in fact wanted to return to France in the weeks following the death of Vallat on 6 January 1972. (Vallat's funeral was the occasion of clashes between former Vichyites and Jews.) At the time, emotion over President Pompidou's antiresistancialist statements was still running high. Darquier, interviewed by the Madrid correspondent of *Le Monde*, stated: "It is not true that I took part in the expulsion of foreign Jews who were living in France." This was one of several lies that he would reiterate in 1978.[16] Some of Darquier's wartime activities had been disclosed by a number of writers over the previous twenty years.[17] But none of this history, and none of Darquier's earlier statements, had aroused anything like the storm of protest that erupted in 1978.

The Grand Orient de France (a Masonic lodge), the Fédération Nationale des Déportés et Internés Résistants et Patriotes (FNDIRP), the Association Française des Juristes Démocrates, and many other groups called for Darquier to be extradited from Spain or at least indicted for inciting racial hatred, a crime under the law of 1 July 1972. In view of that law, the minister of justice ordered an investigation, but no indictment had yet been handed down when Darquier died on 21 August 1980. (His death was not confirmed until three years later.)

On 2 November 1978 the Darquier affair became the subject of debate in the National Assembly. The majority of deputies followed the lead of the government and of President Giscard d'Estaing by attacking *L'Express*. The Rassemblement pour la République (RPR, Jacques Chirac's neo-Gaullist right-wing party) alluded to "sacrilegious texts," and the Union pour la Démocratie Française (UDF, Giscard's center-right group) accused the magazine of "surreptitiously favoring rehabilitation [of a man guilty of] abominable crimes." On the opposition side, the Communists attacked the government for, among other things, failing to ask for Darquier's extradition, while Alain Savary, representing the Socialist Party, demanded to be allowed to speak on radio and television on behalf of the "voice of truth, that is, of the Resistance."[18] Prime Minister Raymond Barre also intervened in the debate with an open letter to the presidents of the three television networks:

> Over the past few months I have noted a tendency on the part of certain press and news organs to produce articles and broadcasts dealing, directly or indirectly and at times indulgently, with Nazism

and its more serious manifestations . . . Naturally there can be no question of drawing a veil over these events and personalities. No one is more aware than I of the importance and requirements of historical research, and in my view it is essential that the generations born since the war have a precise and clear understanding [of that period] . . . In our country, however, where memories of the war and the Occupation are ineradicable, those responsible for the news . . . must remain vigilant as to the manner in which history is presented. As I see it, it is desirable that undue emphasis not be given, out of a taste for sensation and novelty, to programs that might be perceived as rehabilitation.[19]

The government was not unanimous in its hostility, however. Minister of health Simone Veil appeared on Europe 1 on 30 October and stated that she regarded the *Express* article as "a cry of alarm," while Lionel Stoléru, the secretary of state responsible for the condition of manual laborers, wrote to the magazine that it had "done well to publish this exhibit for the prosecution in the battle against racism."[20] Public reaction, as reflected in *L'Express,* was equally contradictory. The CRIF denounced Darquier's attempt "to murder even the memory of his victims." The MRAP condemned the "partisan and incomplete account" of the genocide. Henri Amouroux protested against all forms of censorship and defended his journalistic colleagues; the French, he said, were an "adult people" and could face the truth about their past. Finally, any number of former deportees spoke out with radically differing views: some were outraged by the insult to the victims, while others congratulated the magazine for "having awoken the entire country."[21]

The reasons why *L'Express* chose to publish the article seem fairly simple, although the decision to publish an interview with Darquier rather than a commentary no doubt contributed to the uproar. Raymond Aron, who chaired the magazine's editorial committee, was not informed of the project, about which he did not hide his misgivings. Nevertheless, in the face of attacks on the magazine, he chose to write a postscript to the article in which he defended the good faith of the journalists and backed editor-in-chief Jean-François Revel on grounds of journalistic ethics.[22]

Revel's judgment that the time was ripe for the publication of such an article was quite correct. A few months earlier, Kurt Lischka had been indicted for war crimes. Although his whereabouts in Germany had been discovered earlier by Robert Werner, a reporter for *Paris-Jour*, he was rediscovered in 1971 by Beate and Serge Klarsfeld. Formerly an SS lieutenant-colonel in charge of the Gestapo's Department of Jewish Affairs and later Knochen's principal assistant, in which capacity he served in the Reich Security Office in France, Lischka had been living in quiet retirement in West Germany, but in 1975 his status changed abruptly when the Bonn parliament ratified a Franco-German treaty on Nazi war crimes in France. His trial in Cologne was marked by several incidents, including a demonstration by a thousand French Jews, but it ended in conviction and a ten-year prison sentence on 11 February 1980. Two other war criminals, whose names were notorious in France, were also sentenced at the same time: Herbert Hagen, assistant to Oberg, the head of the SS in France, and Ernst Heinrichsohn, assistant to Dannecker, head of the Anti-Jewish Section, who received sentences of twelve and six years respectively. *L'Express* was therefore simply following a natural reflex, which was to ask about French war criminals whenever the question of German war crimes was raised.

Another interesting aspect of the Darquier affair was the personality of Philippe Ganier Raymond, the *Express* reporter who broke the story and who, seven years later, would again emerge as one of the key figures in yet another symptom of the Vichy syndrome, the so-called Manouchian affair. The author of a book about the Affiche Rouge, in 1975 he published an anthology of documents relating to antisemitism during the Occupation. Like many of his contemporaries, Ganier Raymond saw the forties revival as a covert rehabilitation of fascism and denounced it as such. He was also a bitter critic of what he regarded as France's current "authoritarian regime," and he had some very unflattering things to say about Jacques Chirac: "Is the prime minister a fascist? Sure, no doubt about it, and with the characteristic ferocity of those who want to blot out memories of an extreme leftist youth, of people like [Marcel] Déat, [Jacques] Doriot, and Gitton."[23] He described his work as a diatribe against the right, under which head he indiscriminately lumped Vichy, the Algerian torturers, and the governments of the 1970s:

> Right-wingers, you are not innocent. You and your fathers before you have committed unexpiable crimes. This is the record of what you did, said, and thought over a four-year period. This is not an

anthology. It is scarcely more than a sample, a glimpse at what you are capable of when you are given free rein. Stay on the right if you like, but people should know: you are murderers, and of the worst kind, murderers by proxy. Cowards.[24]

Thus the man who, three years after publishing the book that contains this preface, tracked down Darquier was no ordinary journalist in search of a scoop. He was one of a group of writers, reporters, and columnists obsessed with the Occupation, some for ideological reasons, others for family, personal, or emotional considerations, still others out of a wish to be provocative. Whether one approves of them or not, and whether or not their motives were honorable, these writers played a crucial role in prolonging the syndrome. Often they blew up minor affairs into issues of major importance, and at times they led their readers off on wild goose chases, which they were able to do only because of the government's official policy of silence.

Holocaust

The Darquier affair soon gave rise to another involving equally powerful passions. A week after the Darquier interview appeared, writer Marek Halter issued an appeal calling on the French television authorities to broadcast the American miniseries *Holocaust*. Disturbed by the French authorities' lack of interest in the series, Halter took advantage of the opening provided by the interview: "With stupefaction France learned from the interview with the former commissioner for Jewish affairs under the Occupation that fascism is not dead and that its most reliable allies are ignorance and neglect."[25]

Directed by Marvin Chomsky, who had previously done the highly acclaimed series *Roots,* and based on a novel by Gerald Green, *Holocaust* told the story of two German families, one Jewish, the other Nazi, in the years from 1933 to 1945. The makers of the series, violating the taboo on images of the Holocaust, did not hesitate to show the horrors of the Final Solution on the screen, complete with reconstructions of the setting and associated dialogue. More important than the message was the form of the presentation: a televised miniseries aimed at reaching the broadest possible audience, a true turning point in the portrayal of the Shoah. When broadcast in the United States in April 1978, the series was viewed by an audience of 120 million people. Broadcast rights were immediately purchased by West Germany and twenty-eight other countries, but not by France.

Besieged with questions, the three public television networks justified their decision as best they could. Network FR3 claimed that the series was too expensive, when in fact it cost 135,000 francs per hour, the usual price for the countless American series favored by the French viewing audience. Jean-Louis Guillaud, head of Network TF1, argued that the French had done better work on the same subject, in particular Alain Resnais' film *Night and Fog,* an admirable short documentary but by now more than twenty-three years old. His counterpart at Network Antenne 2, similarly afflicted with the chauvinist virus, spoke of promoting a French production rather than buying the American one. Everyone naturally thought of *The Sorrow and the Pity*—mistakenly, since it was not a French but a German-Swiss production—which had still not been shown on French television. Were the French authorities simply displaying their usual ticklishness or their reluctance to broadcast a trans-Atlantic import dealing with this delicate subject? No, just the usual silence. Had not Raymond Barre given clear warning to the network heads? The upcoming elections for the first European Assembly, scheduled for June 1979, further complicated the issue. The UDF aimed its criticism at both the RPR and the Communist Party, alleging fears that broadcast of the series might be used to mount "an anti-German campaign," while the Communists replied that "the champions of a supranational Europe (run by the trusts) are prepared gleefully to sacrifice the memory of Hitlerism's thousands of victims to their political calculations."[26]

Antenne 2 finally decided to purchase the rights to the series in November 1978, eight months after the Americans made their first proposal. "The controversy over the Darquier de Pellepoix interview had an impact on our decision," network head Maurice Ulrich declared in an interview with *L'Express.*[27] The producer Armand Jammot offered the opinion that "this document must be shown, and a great debate must be held to remind people of the reality of the camps, about which some people know nothing and which others deliberately refuse to see."[28] Even the government seemed to change its attitude, for Christian Beullac, minister of education and acting minister of culture and communication, urged parents and teachers to take advantage of this "remarkable material." After the long official silence, television was thus to be used as a powerful teaching device.[29]

Holocaust was broadcast between 13 February and 6 March 1979. Once again controversy erupted. This time the issue was the content of the series. The style was "too Hollywood," the camp inmates "too well fed." There were errors and omissions concerning the complicity of local authorities, ranging from Polish policemen to French miliciens, with the Nazi death machine. Charlotte Delbo wrote:

> When I sat down in front of the TV set, I had a lump in my throat. Based on the articles I had read I was afraid that I would feel uncontrollable emotion at the sight of truly unbearable things. Almost immediately the lump disappeared. I was not moved—and don't think that I am inured to such things because I'm an Auschwitz survivor.[30]

To conclude the series of broadcasts on 6 March, Antenne 2 staged a great debate in the format of one of French television's warhorses, the *Dossiers de l'écran*. The show had virtually patented a formula for dealing with thorny issues: a film was screened, followed by a debate in which people representing every conceivable shade of opinion were free to argue. This had once been a pioneering device for dealing with controversial topics, but by now the format was old hat. The network invited representatives of different generations to discuss the series and thus was able to gauge the reaction of a cross-section of the population. Jammot stated that the debate would be conducted "with great dignity [and] with the approval of survivors' organizations."[31] Among those represented were "young people," carefully supervised to prevent any intemperate outbursts, along with eyewitnesses and survivors of the camps, including a Gypsy and such prominent personalities as Marie-Claude Vaillant-Couturier of the FNDIRP and Simone Veil. The occasion was undeniably an emotional one. Veil said that "*Holocaust* is too optimistic a film because the inmates still treat each other nicely. In reality we became true animals." But the hoped-for dialogue between the younger and the older generation never took place. One of the youths, speaking for his comrades, remarked: "We were supposed to represent the reactions and impressions of young people, but instead we've been given the impression that what's really going on is a debate among old veterans, which is just what we don't want to become." Worse still, legitimate questions were evaded. When another young person asked Veil about Robert Hersant's past, which *Le Canard enchaîné* had just exposed in a series of articles, she peremptorily warned against confusing the terms collaborator and Nazi, thereby suggesting implicitly that one of the two was appropriate to the case of Hersant. When the impertinent questioner read an excerpt from a newspaper article published at the time about a demonstration of the Jeune Front, the organization to which Hersant belonged, Veil struck a pose of dignified silence that was anything but apolitical.[32]

Such misunderstandings and telescopings of past and present were typical of the national debate that followed the broadcast of *Holocaust*. Once public uproar had succeeded in changing the network's mind, there was a profusion of criticism about what the film did not discuss. *Holocaust* would prevent discussion of other massacres, it was alleged, or would somehow deflect criticism of ordinary racism. In *Le Monde* for 27 February 1979 Tahar Ben Jelloun published a lesson in linguistics: the term "genocide," he argued, could equally be applied to the American Indians and the Armenians, the victims of Sétif and the fellaghas tortured in Algeria. *Libération* was critical of what it called the "establishment of a hierarchy" of genocides, as a result of which only certain people (read: Jews) "are entitled to official condolences." During the debate Guy Darbois had made a clumsy allusion to homosexuals among the deportees: "A simple mention will suffice." As a result, *Libération* resorted to a facile irony that only served to conceal its customary ignorance (happily the newspaper has since improved). Guy Hocquenghem intimated that the failure to discuss deportees other than political prisoners and Jews was somehow the work of the latter, the reflection of "a hierarchy no doubt based on that of the camps."[33]

Similarly, *L'Humanité*, while recognizing the qualities of the film, was critical of the "exclusive focus on the Jewish problem" and proposed to remedy the situation by speaking of "holocausts," in the plural.[34] In short, after public insistence that "these things must be talked about," some people now began to sing a different tune: "Let's change the subject." The controversy raged on for five months.

Leguay, Bousquet, Touvier: Episode Two

After the Darquier and *Holocaust* affairs came yet another dark episode. On 12 March 1979, following the debate on *Dossiers de l'écran*, Jean Leguay, a man of sixty-nine living in quiet retirement and unknown to most people in France, was indicted by investigating magistrate Martine Anzani for crimes against humanity. This new case was an outgrowth of the Darquier and Touvier affairs, the latter somewhat forgotten since the grant of a pardon by Pompidou in 1972. Following the pardon, however, various groups of former résistants and deportees, acting at the behest of attorneys Serge Klarsfeld and Joe Nordmann (president and founder of the Association Internationale des Juristes Démocrates), filed several complaints of crimes against humanity against Touvier (on 9 November 1973 in Lyons and 27 March 1974 in Chambéry). On 12 February 1974 and 6 June 1974 respectively, the investigating magistrates in the two jurisdictions ruled that they had no authority to pursue the charges, and these decisions were upheld on 30 May and 11 July 1974 by courts of appeal in Lyons and Chambéry on the grounds that the charges alleged concerned only war crimes, not crimes against humanity. The statute of limitations had taken effect in 1967, and the last time Touvier had been convicted (in absentia) was 1947. On 6 February 1975, however, the criminal division of the Cour de Cassation (supreme appellate court) overturned both decisions on the grounds that the investigating magistrates had not looked into the charges closely enough to determine whether crimes against humanity were involved. In actuality, this fundamental ruling was made partly because of the influence of the Association Internationale des Juristes Démocrates, particularly through the attorney Lyon-Caen and the president of the criminal division, Judge Rolland.[35] But then, on 27 October 1974, a criminal court in Paris ruled that it was competent to hear the charges but that the complaints were inadmissible because the statute of limitations had taken effect. On 30 June 1976 the criminal division of the Cour de Cassation once again overturned this ruling.

At this point the case entered a different channel. On 17 December 1976 the charges were brought to the attention of the foreign ministry on the grounds that prosecution of crimes against humanity was a matter of diplomatic interest, given France's subscription to the London accords of 1945 and to the charter and statutes of the international tribunal at Nuremberg. Hence the case was partly a matter of international law. The Quai d'Orsay issued its response on 19 June 1979. At this stage, two cases—Touvier and Leguay—were combined, one strengthening the other. On 15 November 1978, after publication of the Darquier interview, Klarsfeld filed a complaint against Jean Leguay alleging crimes against humanity, and these charges led to Leguay's indictment on 12 March 1979. As in the Touvier case, Judge Martine Anzani brought the matter to the attention of the Quai d'Orsay (writ of 20 February 1979). Having mulled the matter over since the first request on December 1976, the foreign ministry apparently found religion and on 19 June 1979 issued its opinion that the statute of limitations did not apply. After the indictment of Leguay, the same investigating magistrate, Anzani, was asked to pursue the Touvier case, now also exempted from the statute of limitations. On 28 November 1981 an international warrant was issued for Touvier's arrest. But Touvier was already well known because of the 1972 scandal and his unsavory personality; Leguay was not.

From May 1942 to the end of 1943 Jean Leguay had been René Bousquet's representative in the occupied zone. Under the agreement between Oberg and Bousquet, Leguay was thus responsible for the deportation of large numbers of Jews from both the occupied and unoccupied zones. On 25 May 1945 the purge commission of the interior ministry dismissed Leguay from his official post of prefect, but this was a purely administrative, not a criminal, matter. In December 1955 the Conseil d'Etat reversed this 1945 decision on the ground of "acts of resistance," as a result of which Leguay was rehabilitated and permitted to pursue a career in business. Meanwhile Bousquet, like all Vichy ministers and general secretaries, was brought before the Haute Cour on 23 June 1949 and given a symbolic sentence (five years' loss of civil rights), which was immediately suspended for acts of resistance. He too went on to a career in business, most notably with the Bank of Indochina. In a press conference held on 12 March 1979, Serge Klarsfeld made no secret of his intention to see to it that Bousquet would also be indicted.[36]

The milicien Touvier, the commissioner for Jewish affairs Darquier, the prefects Leguay and Bousquet, and Maurice Papon (who would be indicted on 19 January 1983)—five former French government officials whose pasts came back to haunt them. That is all they have in common, except of course for the most important thing: all of them, to one degree or another, contributed to Vichy's involvement in the Final Solution. Yet the differences are striking between fascists like Touvier and Darquier, both apparently sadists and criminals unambiguously on the side of the Nazis, and top civil servants like Leguay, Bousquet, and Papon. These differences are reminiscent of the dichotomy (as well as the reciprocal influences and de facto solidarity) between the Paris collaborationists and the men of Vichy. While Touvier went underground, Darquier, who had nothing to lose, did not hesitate to proclaim his sympathy for Nazism thirty-five years after the fall of the Third Reich. By contrast, the former prefects had reentered society and government and could even point to "services rendered to the Resistance." On 13 March 1979, following his indictment, Leguay was quoted in *Le Figaro:* "I have no apprehension when I consider the indictment just handed down . . . because from 1940 to 1944 my only concern was to defend and protect the French people from the occupying power."

Nevertheless, the indictment of Leguay was an essential step in the prosecution of related cases. It was literally a historic event, of far greater importance than the grumblings of an antisemitic derelict which attracted so much more attention from the media. The Leguay indictment marked the first time that the suspension of the statute of limitations for crimes against humanity was applied to a *French* citizen; in 1983, of course, it would also be used against the German Barbie. Thus the Touvier and Leguay cases set legal and historical precedents that marked a strange turn of affairs. Although the 1964 law was passed at a time when memory of Vichy was at a low ebb and for the purpose of ensuring that Nazi war criminals would be brought to justice, its effect was ultimately to reopen French wounds and to involve the courts in complex affairs that seemed, however great the moral satisfaction they may have offered, to revive the purge trials of thirty years before. And that was effectively the case, because no collaborator or Vichy official had been indicted at the time of the Liberation for acts pertaining to the deportation of Jews; crimes committed in connection with the Final Solution had been left out of the debate altogether.

Note, however, that the Leguay case, by far the most important of those investigated in the 1980s given the scope of Leguay's responsibilities under Vichy, failed to arouse emotions or passions comparable to those seen in the Darquier, Touvier, and Barbie affairs. Leguay's indictment was handed down amid widespread indifference, and it took ten years for his case to come before the courts, in the summer of 1989, when Leguay was dying and after the trial of Barbie in 1987 and the arrest of Touvier in May 1989. The investigation was complete, and the case about to be sent to a Paris court, when Leguay died on 2 July 1989. In a break with custom, the statement declaring the case closed by virtue of the defendant's death alluded to Leguay's *guilt:* "The investigation established that Leguay, Jean, did participate in crimes against humanity committed in July [the Vel d'Hiv roundup], August, and September 1942."[37] The prosecutor's final report to the court, submitted on 26 July 1989, included no fewer than thirty-three pages detailing the charges against the deceased.[38]

Negationism

In the course of his antisemitic ravings, Darquier denied the existence of gas chambers at Auschwitz. A few days after his interview, the newspaper *Le Matin* published a brief excerpt from a letter received on 1 November 1978, which expressed the following wish:

> I hope that certain of the statements that journalist Philippe Ganier Raymond has recently imputed to Louis Darquier de Pellepoix will at last lead the general public to discover that the so-called massacres in "gas chambers" and the alleged "genocide" are both part of the same lie.[39]

Robert Faurisson carefully chose his moment to enter the fray. First noticed in January 1978, when he proved to be a disruptive presence at a colloquium on the churches during the war, the professor from Lyons had until then been only the subject of rumors as strange as the statement in his letter was outrageous. But now the public discovered the weird world of the "revisionists," as they called themselves without challenge. Revisionism, however, usually refers to a normal phase in the evolution of historical scholarship, and I prefer to call those who would deny the existence of the Holocaust "negationists," for what is at issue is a system of thought, an ideology, and not a scientific or even critical approach to the subject. What ensued was a veritable cultural epidemic sustained by lies and deceptions, an epidemic that availed itself of the impact of the media, of inadequate responses from a variety of quarters, and of the very sensitivity of Jewish memory.

In 1980 Noam Chomsky, the renowned linguist and vehement adversary of American policy in Vietnam, supported Faurisson's right to publish views on the grounds that freedom of speech would otherwise be threatened.[40] Haled into court, Faurisson was nevertheless sentenced on 8 July 1981 to pay a symbolic franc in damages to nine organizations representing former inmates of the camps, as well as to the MRAP and the LICRA, which had joined the plaintiffs by bringing charges of racial slander. The courts refused to take a position on the substance of the case, however, arguing that "tribunals have neither the competence nor the jurisdiction to judge history," much less to "decide how a particular episode in national or world history ought to be represented." This judgment was upheld on 26 April 1983 by the Paris court of appeals, which also found that Faurisson's work "could be characterized as a sweeping exoneration of Nazi war criminals." While the case was before the courts, Faurisson and his followers were aided by extreme right-wing groups, glad to have their views backed by "scientific texts." Maurice Bardèche was the first to publish such texts in his *Défense de l'occident* (June 1978). Then, in June 1985, at the University of Nantes, a doctoral degree was awarded to Henri Roques, a former member of Charles Luca's French Phalange, by a jury of extreme right-wing examiners, who, incidentally, were totally incompetent in the subject matter; the degree was revoked one year later.

The negationists received even more active support from a sectarian ultraleftist group, the Vieille Taupe (Old Mole) of Pierre Guillaume, Jean-Gabriel Cohn-Bendit, and Serge Thion, among others, which became the official publisher of negationist works. The motives of the extreme rightists are fairly clear, since Faurisson and his followers were simply elaborating lies first told by the Nazis themselves, intended to conceal the reality of the Final Solution. The motives of the leftists, on the other hand, remain obscure. According to Alain Finkielkraut, the group consisted of fundamentalist Marxists whose anti-Stalinism, anti-Zionism, and denunciation of western values as imperialist allegedly led them to deny a historical reality that could not be accommodated within their shrunken worldview.[41]

Negationism gave rise to numerous controversies involving such issues as freedom of speech, the need to discuss and refute absurd theses, the role of intellectuals and historians in particular, and of course the most pernicious forms of antisemitism. These controversies are only peripherally related to the Vichy syndrome, but they do raise two important questions. Why did scandal erupt at this particular time? And why was there such an outpouring of emotion over statements that, on any other subject, would have been dismissed out of hand?

The denial of the genocide was by no means new. As early as 1948, Paul Rassinier, a Socialist resistance fighter who was deported to Buchenwald and Dora (concentration camps where conditions were atrocious, to be sure, but which were not extermination camps), took it into his head to denounce alleged lies about the Nazi camps.[42] After being expelled from the SFIO in 1951, Rassinier (like Faurisson later on) made contact with pacifists and libertarians and garnered support from such outspoken antisemites as Henry Coston, director of the Librairie Française; charges were filed against him on several occasions. When, in October 1964, he was accused of neo-Nazism on the basis of statements published in *Rivarol*, Rassinier filed suit for libel against Bernard Lecache, head of the LICA. He lost his suit, became an object of ridicule, and was permanently discredited.[43] Despite the bizarre nature of the case, Rassinier never became as renowned a figure as Faurisson, whose allegations were reported in the media and whose work was called meticulous and scientific. Furthermore, though the earlier scandal was similar in nature to the Faurisson affair, it never attained the same dimensions: the courts were not obliged to hand down an unprecedented statement on the writing of history, nor was the secretary of state for universities forced to take administrative action against a group of professors. In any case, there were others besides Rassinier who, from the moment the war ended, more or less openly asserted that the Nazis should bear no guilt toward the Jewish people. Finally, Faurisson and his followers were only the French representatives of an international network of negationists, which with other groups in the United States as well as Germany was generally supported by extreme right-wing groups, neo-Nazi organizations, and anti-Zionists from the Middle East: it has been established that the activities of the Vieille Taupe were financed by the Iranian embassy.

In France the controversy at first found historians at a loss for a response. Should they peremptorily declare that Faurisson's allegations had no basis in fact, or should they offer a detailed refutation? In February 1979 a petition was signed by many illustrious professors of the Collège de France, the Centre National de la Recherche Scientifique, the Ecole des Hautes Etudes en Sciences Sociales, and other leading academic institutions. Most of those who signed the petition, at the behest of historians Léon Poliakov and Pierre Vidal-Naquet, were not specialists in the history of World War II. The signers granted that anyone had the right to interpret Hitler's genocide with complete freedom, but they refused to allow its existence to be questioned:

> The question is not how, *technically,* such a mass murder could have taken place. It was technically possible because it did occur. That is the obligatory starting point for any historical investigation of the subject. Our only option is simply to recall this truth: there is not, there cannot be, a debate over the existence of the gas chambers.[44]

In substance this statement captures the historians' reflex reaction that no argument is possible about such a well-established fact, no mere detail but the most remarkable feature of the history of World War II. In form, though, it seems to treat this historical question, which, however sensitive, is a question like any other, as one that had been definitively answered. This proved not to be the case: conferences organized subsequently by the Ecole des Hautes Etudes en Sciences Sociales and, later, the IHTP and attended by many petition signers showed that the subject was open to further exploration and could still be an object of controversy.[45]

This tentative response was perhaps disturbing to some and, worse still, may have cast doubt on the assurances given by specialists in the field. There were several reasons for it, however. In the first place, the historians initially had no way of judging the effect of Faurisson's allegations on public opinion, and many feared, with good reason, that any public response would only strengthen the negationists' hand. Vidal-Naquet was one of the first to sense the danger of spreading false assertions:

> The day that Robert Faurisson, a man with full academic credentials and employed as a teacher at a major university, was allowed to express his views in *Le Monde,* even though those views were im-

mediately refuted, was the day when the question ceased to be marginal and became central, and those who had no direct knowledge of the events in question, particularly the young, were entitled to ask whether anyone had anything to hide.[46]

It was, moreover, probably easier to eradicate six million people from memory than to reconstruct the complex mechanisms of the Final Solution. But the crucial point here is that the work of reconstruction had already been done; most of the facts had been established. Hence the challenge was not historiographical but ideological and pedagogical, and historians found themselves in the same boat as journalists and eyewitnesses. Countless books on the subject were available to everyone. The problem now was to *reread* them in such a way as to respond to the negationists' provocation. The negationist phenomenon certainly stimulated the publication in France of works on the Holocaust, French historians in this respect having lagged far behind American, German, and Israeli scholars. Philippe Burrin's *Hitler et les juifs* (1989), a book dealing with Hitler's role in the origins of the genocide, is a powerful and brilliant example.

At this point the media again entered the picture. In a society apt to believe the slightest rumor, and where the opportune disclosure of some "secret diary" can undermine forty years of historiography (for a few days at any rate), Faurisson's pseudo-scientific approach itself made news. Journalists were no more responsible for this than were their readers. But note that the negationist arguments always received more press (if only to condemn them) than did the imposing historians' conferences and books, which were reported but only after the negationists' falsehoods had filtered down to the general public.

One final aspect of the phenomenon is more directly related to the structure of collective memory: the negationist approach took advantage of the flaws that existed in a mode of historical representation. The negationists benefited, in the first place, from the revisionism of what I have called the broken-mirror period. The same benefit of the doubt, the same sense of revealed truth, which helped to shatter the mirror that had impeded vision of wartime events in the 1950s and 1960s and which had drawn so much attention to *The Sorrow and the Pity,* the historical and other works published during the forties revival, and the televised *Holocaust* also served Faurisson, even if all he offered was lies. That was what was so perverse about the nega-tionist message: it immersed itself in the reinterpretation, the revision, of the history of the 1940s that had been under way for a decade. A young and uncritical public was not always quick to perceive the fun-damental difference between a *reinterpretation,* based on new sources and open to critical assessment, even to resistance from society, but never contemptuous of established truth, and the simple *negation* of an overwhelming fact on purely mechanistic grounds ("it is impossi-ble"). From this point of view, what does it matter that Faurisson, Roques, and their associates were ideologues? After all, a large part of the history of the twentieth century (that of the Stalinist era, it just so happens) has been subject to repeated, and agonizing, revision. On what basis can good revision be distinguished from bad?

> Tell me, good people: How long will it go on—this dignity-cloaked uproar over the Chomsky-Faurisson encounter? How long will we continue to hear Faurisson dismissed out of hand with peremptory assertions? . . . Who will finally have the courage and consistency to explain, and therefore to vulgarize—a fine word for a fine deed— the concept of "historical method," and who will explain to millions of listeners and readers who were not at Buchenwald or Birkenau or the Hotel Lutétia in 1945 why they must believe that there were millions of victims in the Nazi camps? Who will explain why Faurisson is a liar, and explain it calmly and methodically . . . I am forty-nine years old; I was at the Hotel Lutétia when the deportees arrived . . . I am not the one you have to convince.[47]

No matter that what Faurisson said was a lie—he had to be answered, not out of duty but out of necessity. Pierre Vidal-Naquet, Georges Wellers, François Furet, Raymond Aron, the CDJC, the IHTP, and many others felt the need.[48] The public was entitled to a full-scale response, even if, to specialists who felt that once the facts were es-tablished it was up to others to give them publicity, there seemed to be no need for any such thing.

A second important point is that negationism burst onto the scene at a time when Jewish remembrance of the war was undergoing a profound mutation. Survivors, eyewitnesses, organized groups, and much of the Jewish community suddenly felt the need to "talk about it," to lift some but not all of the old taboos, to end their silence.

Faurisson and his followers knowingly poured gasoline on this rekindled fire. Just as victims of the genocide were beginning to reemerge from the recesses of collective memory, here they were threatened once more with extermination, just when it seemed that repression might finally be laid to rest. It is understandable that some reacted with panic, almost with fear of the void, as they felt themselves drawn into a many-sided controversy. It begins to be clear why Faurisson succeeded where Rassinier failed: it was now or never.

The four affairs described here are thus closely related: the Darquier interview served as a trigger, which hastened the broadcast of *Holocaust* and made it a dramatic event, led to the actual or potential indictment of former Vichy officials, and provided the French negationists with the opening they needed to gain the public eye. One affair followed closely on the heels of another, plunging the country into lasting and bitter turmoil, as if the national memory had suddenly come down with a fever. There was a sense that France had entered an obsessional phase, whose major symptom, apart from the violence of the crises, took the form of repetition.

Each of these affairs, with its parcel of revelations, polemics, historical articles and books, seemed an incomplete response to expectation or desire. Even the way in which they unfolded is significant: what was initially a relatively minor event was amplified by the media (an important but not definitive sign) and extended through a series of related affairs, which kept the scandal in the public eye and helped to install the past in the consciousness of the present. These scandals were not mere "veterans' quarrels" but events in themselves, to such a degree that their historical or mnemonic content was sometimes obscured by other issues: freedom of the press, freedom of intellectual inquiry, the nature of academic discourse, and so on. In other words, there was in each case both a supply and a demand. Although individuals (Ganier Raymond of *L'Express*, the Klarsfelds, Marek Halter) played a key role in initiating some of these scandals, they were able to do so only because the message they were putting out found receptive ears. Neither the recurrence nor the vehemence of these episodes can be understood without taking this public expectation into account. The forties revival had only grazed the surface of this desire; the Darquier affair showed its full depth. It should therefore come as no surprise that these several affairs exhibit common features.

Antisemitism and Banalization

The first of these common features is antisemitism, in the past and in the present: from Darquier to Faurisson, the same refrain—a "Jewish conspiracy"—served first to justify the death camps and then to deny their existence. Yet there are signs of erosion. We live in a world in which torture, dictatorship, and, closer to home, racism are familiar phenomena. We are treated to photographs and televised images of terrible oppression around the globe. The antisemitism and genocide of the war years must now take their place among other horrors. Survivors and eyewitnesses have spoken critically of what they regard as a *banalization* of extraordinary evil (the allusion, of course, is to Hannah Arendt's "banality of evil").

Yet the term "banalization" has been applied to very different phenomena. It refers, first of all, to a denial of the uniqueness of the Shoah, to a tendency to compare it with other massacres in ways that make no historical sense, all questions of morality and ideology aside. And it is certainly correct to denounce the pernicious effects of anachronistic comparison. "Banalization" has also been used to describe the familiarity with which certain memories are treated, to the casual way in which references to the past are repeatedly used for present purposes. People do talk about the past—sometimes too much, often badly, but always with the inherent risk of tiring their audience. Despite persistent ignorance, therefore, the subject may often seem old hat, and from this comes a thirst for novelty that, we are told, accounts for the unhealthy interest in negationist views. Banalization is an inevitable consequence of historicization: the Final Solution, having become a historical subject like any other, should, it is argued, be studied with the same rigor as any other—neither more nor less. Hence it loses its status as a unique and—let us be candid—a sacred event. Finally, banalization is essential if the genocide is to be used as an example: it is hard to invoke Nazi antisemitism as grounds for denouncing other forms of racism if one insists exclusively that Nazi racism was unique.

This series of scandals enables us to measure the distance traveled since the 1960s. Vichy's responsibility in the genocide of the Jews, which at one time seemed such an astonishing revelation, is now taken for granted, even by the law. In itself Vichy's role no longer makes news. Only the indictment of some notorious personality makes page one: a fascist like Touvier on the run and protected by the Catholic hierarchy or a former minister like Papon. Of course the last word on the subject has yet to be said; for that we must await the outcome of the Touvier trial, which in a sense will be Vichy's day in court, fifty years after the fall of the regime.

The change that began in 1979 has been considerable. Here we have an investigating magistrate announcing a series of indictments. Only eight years earlier, the mere mention in a film of French antisemitism aroused a storm of protest, even though it was presented as an inevitable consequence of the Occupation and not as the result of deliberate French policy.

Historiographic representations of the Vichy regime have undergone a similar evolution (see Chapter 6). On the one hand, the myth that there was a good and a bad Vichy has collapsed. It has become difficult to invoke the legacy of Pétain without also accepting responsibility for the policy of collaboration and for Vichy's antisemitism. To be sure, that has not prevented the political resurrection of certain aspects of the National Revolution, most notably in the National Front, but it has put an end to misleading and one-sided interpretations of the Vichy regime. In the 1980s the historiography of Vichy entered a relatively calm and objective phase. In some cases Vichy policies were reevaluated, and the regime was no longer charged with crimes it did not commit. But for now, at least, no one has attempted to write a negationist or revisionist history of Vichy of the sort loyal Pétainists have always hoped for.

On the other hand, the notion of "crimes against humanity" has given systematic emphasis to the antisemitic aspect of Vichy policy, even though antisemitism was not a central theme of the National Revolution. Vichy was an exclusionary regime, but its worldview, unlike that of Nazism, did not place hatred of Jews at its center. In this respect the Touvier affair offers a case in point. In order to bring Touvier to trial fifty years after the fact, he had to be shown to have committed crimes against humanity, in particular against Jews. This led to neglecting the fact that, whatever Touvier's personal responsibility may have been, the primary role of the Milice in *l'Etat français* was the battle against the Resistance. Because of the way the law is written, this aspect of Touvier's activities has been relegated to the second rank. But progress has been made in the Touvier investigation owing to the expanded definition of crimes against humanity given by the court of appeals in its decision of 20 December 1985 in connection with the Barbie case (see Chapter 5).

The Courts

Another common—and novel—feature of all these cases is the role of the courts. Now judges and lawyers joined the men and women who had witnessed the past, the politicians who exploited it, the filmmakers who drew on it for images, and the historians who plumbed its depths. The involvement of the courts, which became almost routine (with the indictments of Touvier, Leguay, Faurisson, Papon, and Barbie, to say nothing of the countless—and traditional—suits for libel), marked an important change in the formation of France's collective memory. The amnesty of 1951–1953 had reflected the nation's willingness to forgive. Whatever its defenders may say, the amnesty inaugurated a long period of neglect, occasionally interrupted by long-delayed trials, few of which had major consequences. But when Jean Leguay was indicted in 1979 under a law passed fifteen years earlier suspending the statute of limitations for crimes against humanity, a very different process was set in motion. Memories, which now enjoyed the symbolic support of the law, began to crystallize; the involvement of the courts gave such memories a legitimate reason for existing in the present. The suspension of the statute of limitations, like the operation of memory itself, abolished time. There was, however, one crucial difference: memory is by definition selective, unfaithful, and changeable. Justice is not.

These developments may have been a victory against repression, but they also had unintended side effects. Judges found themselves forced to write history and pronounce historical judgment in the historian's place. In this role they were profoundly uncomfortable, as a glance at the records of the Faurisson, Touvier, and Barbie cases makes clear. The memories of witnesses proved insufficient either to convict or to exonerate, and historians maintained a healthy caution. Prosecution involved an enormous mass of documents, many of them difficult to interpret. Writing history is one thing; judging an individual according to the rules of law is another.[49] The courts in many cases were forced to rely on shaky interpretations of events, and thus the trials unintentionally exacerbated the existing tension between memory, history, and truth. As of 1986, there had been no final verdict in any of the four cases of crimes against humanity (Leguay, Touvier, Papon, and Barbie), although prosecution had begun eight years earlier. Barbie, the German, has been judged and found guilty; Touvier, the Frenchman, may soon be convicted. But it has taken a long time to overcome the doubts and difficulties that stood in the way of judgment for all those years.

How To Talk About It?

Ultimately all the scandals point to a single question: how is the past to be transmitted? If the question were rephrased as a Jewish joke, it would have three parts: Must we talk about it? How should we talk about it? Why did we talk about it? From the foregoing it might seem that the adversaries in the debate were well chosen: antisemites of the past and present, those who would censor or shun any and all references to an unsavory past, as against former victims and those whose vocation it was to oppose collective amnesia. As the scandals developed, however, it became clear that the controversy was more often over how to talk about the past. How to respond to Faurisson, for example: should one try to organize an academic colloquium on the subject or a television series? Should the matter be taken to court? Should the Darquier interview have been published? Should a film about the Final Solution be broadcast? Determination to speak out, particularly in response to the negationists, vied with determination to remain silent for fear of not doing justice to the subject. Such ambivalence was particularly evident among survivors, the preeminent repositories of memories of the genocide. Among them, the fear of forgetting was rivaled only by the conviction that it is impossible to speak about the unspeakable. Survivors demanded to speak out, indeed were forced to speak out sooner than they might have wished, because they had not foreseen either the attention that would be given to Faurisson or the unfolding of the various scandals, which seemed to proceed according to a diabolical logic of their own. Their memories, seemingly unified by a common experience of horror, turned out to be various and even divergent. In a remarkable essay on the Faurisson affair, Alain Finkielkraut called attention to this phenomenon:

> We will never know. In that experience there was something incommunicable, a nocturnal portion, which ceaselessly spurs our desire to know but which must be protected against the always arrogant, always mystified belief that, once illumination has come, nothing incommunicable remains. As prolific and detailed as the deportees' accounts may be, their words remain in a sense shrouded in silence . . . Memory wants both to know the genocide and to recognize it as unknown; it wants to guarantee its presence so that it may not be forgotten, yet hold it at a distance so as to prevent reductive explanations; it wants to make the event contemporary and yet maintain it beyond our grasp; it wants to welcome it without assimilating it—and in this respect, no doubt, the mnemonic faculty might even be termed religious. It is the antithesis of obscurantism.[50]

In other words, the tension between the desire to remember and the tendency to repress is supplanted (at least for a minority concerned with public opinion) by a second contradiction, between the desire to speak out, agitate, protest, and punish and the desire to remain, deliberately, silent so as to preserve the authenticity of memory. To be sure, this more inward, more directly individual, tension had long been present: "The desire to bear witness that was felt by people in detention (or in the camps) yielded only a relatively small number of actual accounts," according to Nathalie Heinich and Michael Pollak.[51] During the period in question, however, the desire to speak out reached something like crisis proportions, because the memory of the genocide, now a matter of topical interest, was simultaneously jeopardized by radical denial. Here, I think, we touch on the outermost limits of the process by which collective memory is formed.

In all the episodes I have discussed so far, Jewish memory was, broadly speaking, attacked from outside. There was also considerable debate within the Jewish community concerning the memory of the Shoah and the attitude of certain Jews during the Occupation. The earliest controversies erupted in 1966, just a year before the outbreak of the Six-Day War and the ensuing crisis of Jewish identity.

In 1966 a young writer of Jewish descent, Jean-François Steiner, published a book about the Treblinka death camp that focused on the August 1943 revolt of camp inmates. Such inmate uprisings were quite rare. Obsessed with the past, Steiner hoped to resolve a burning question, posed in no uncertain terms by Simone de Beauvoir in a preface that condensed, yet also qualified, Steiner's concerns: "Why did the Jews allow themselves to be led to the slaughter like lambs?" Beauvoir of course rejected any notion that the Jews were "passive." She pointed out that those who would become victims of the Shoah were peaceloving civilians, as were most citizens of the countries occupied by the Reich. There was nothing in their background to prepare them for armed uprising. But she does make one gross distinction: "The fact that the prominent Jews who made up the Judenräte [Jewish councils] colluded with the Germans is well known and easily understood. In all times and places, with few exceptions, the prominent [among the vanquished] have collaborated with their conquerors: a matter of class."[52]

Wittingly or unwittingly, Steiner did raise two issues that had previously remained hidden or unexplored: the existence and extent of Jewish resistance and the role of the Jewish councils in carrying out Nazi orders in the ghettos. These were sensitive issues, however, and Steiner's work not only lacked rigor but also failed to guard against possible extremist misinterpretations of his findings. His book was soon taken up by the antisemitic extreme right. By May *Rivarol* was trumpeting the notion of "Jewish collaborators," as the MRAP had warned.[53] Worse still, Steiner granted an exclusive interview to *Candide* that was published in a special issue of the magazine distributed free of charge to nonsubscribers:

> Steiner: The way things were presented to us . . . was sometimes rather simplistic and crude. Watch out! The villainous torturers . . . were always villainous torturers. The Germans were bastards, sadists, and the Jews were poor victims, mistreated innocents, martyrs. A whole language was created, adjectives reserved for just that purpose . . .
>
> *Candide:* But still, you didn't write this book to rehabilitate the torturers, to show that the Germans were not the monsters they've been accused of being and the Jews were not the martyrs over whom tears have been shed?

> Steiner: Of course not. I wrote this book because what I felt, more than the outrage and emotion I was taught to feel, was shame at being the son of a people six million of whom ultimately allowed themselves to be led to slaughter like sheep.[54]

It is not difficult to imagine the furor unleashed by these words (even more than by the book). Léon Poliakov accused Steiner of giving new life to old antisemitic stereotypes, such as the accusation of Jewish cowardice. He asked himself whether Steiner's book and other scandalous works (*Le Vicaire* or *The Last of the Just*) did not express a "need for diversion or even 'projection' in the face of the atrocious truth of the Holocaust."[55] Poliakov, together with Henri Bulawko and Vladimir Jankélévitch, organized a Committee of Vigilance for the Respect of the Deportation and Resistance.[56] Ironically, Steiner's book won the Grand Prix de la Résistance in that same year. The paradox, however, is more apparent than real. The résistants were honoring a book that spoke of *one* form of resistance, while the representatives of the Jewish community were rejecting the portrayal of Jews as consenting victims. Beyond that, they felt embarrassed and divided over the idea of a Jewish resistance and a Jewish collaboration.

Ultimately two things explain the scandal. First, it raised anew issues first broached during the Eichmann trial in Israel four years earlier. The agonizing question of passivity had first been raised by young Israelis, brought up on a new military tradition and startled to learn, through Eichmann's testimony, of the incredible machinery of the Final Solution. The role of the Judenräte had also been exposed by this trial. Simone de Beauvoir had merely transcribed whole passages from Hannah Arendt, whose book on the Eichmann trial had just been translated into French and would be published at the end of the year: "Wherever there were Jews, there were Jewish officials, recognized as such, and with very few exceptions those officials collaborated in one way or another, for one reason or another, with the Nazis."[57]

Second, Steiner served to revive a traditional debate about the *uniqueness* of Jewish history, a debate that was only complicated by World War II. On the one hand it is hard to deny that the Nazis attacked the Jews specifically as a distinct (and inferior) group, but on the other hand it is not so easy to argue that resistance as well as cooperation on the part of Jews was specifically "Jewish" in form. For example, the Union Générale des Israélites de France (UGIF), established in 1941, was shaped in part by the nature of the French Jewish community (and may in that respect be considered a form of Judenrat), but it was also shaped by the nature of the Vichy regime, which was a legal, national government that enforced antisemitism.

It was in fact over that very issue, the UGIF, that controversy erupted again in 1980, in the midst of the Darquier affair, with the publication of a book by another son of Jews deported in 1942, Maurice Rajsfus, and entitled *Des Juifs dans la collaboration. L'UGIF, 1941–1944*.[58] Rajsfus' book included a preface by Pierre Vidal-Naquet who, as he had done in the case of the Steiner book, praised the author for courageously attacking a taboo subject (but, again like Steiner, not with consummate skill). Once again publication triggered polemics. Some critics tried to dismiss the work as an incendiary ideological pamphlet, since the publisher was known as the distributor of Trotskyite tracts. (In an article on ultraleft support for the Faurissonians, Annie Kriegel went so far as to charge that Rajsfus was a pseudonym used by the publishing house—a house with which, incidentally, she herself had once published.[59]) A member of the council of the Central Consistory of the Jewish community denounced the book as divisive: "In the wake of attempts to sow discord between Ashkenazys and Sephardics, here is an attempt to sow discord between the community and its leaders." Significantly, this same critic attempted to defend the UGIF by arguing that it had served as a shield, an argument reminiscent of the Pétainist characterization of Vichy as a shield, and he called for the Jewish community to unite against the concert of antisemitic attacks.[60] A few years later, in 1985, the so-called Manouchian affair would revive the debate initiated by Steiner's book over the notion of Jewish resistance.[61] I mention both episodes only to point out that the by no means monolithic Jewish community was affected not only by the various affairs stemming directly from the so-called Vichy syndrome but also by other, more internal matters. It was not just how *others* talked about the Shoah or the Occupation that caused controversy, but how Jews themselves went about discussing a complex historical reality that was more than an "unspeakable horror."

* * *

On the evening of Friday, 3 October 1980, as if to punctuate the series of scandals coming after the Darquier interview, a bomb exploded in front of a synagogue on the rue Copernic in Paris. Four people died and more than twenty were injured. To this day the French police are in the dark about the origins of this crime, which followed attacks and threats against other synagogues and Jewish cemeteries. An obscure neo-Nazi group, the Fédération d'Action Nationaliste Européenne (FANE), was suspected of involvement in the earlier crimes and was officially banned on 3 September. After the rue Copernic incident, Marc Fredriksen, FANE's leader, was indicted and found guilty of being the author of racist texts.

The rue Copernic attack was in no sense a product of the Vichy syndrome. It belongs, rather, to the history of anti-Jewish and anti-Zionist terrorism that has marked the final decades of the twentieth century. Yet the earliest reactions to the event give some idea of what people were thinking. The right wing, then in power in France, seemed for the most part caught short by the attack. Prime Minister Raymond Barre, questioned shortly after the explosion (but not before he had prepared an official statement), deplored "this odious attack, which was intended for Jews on their way to the synagogue and which struck innocent French people [read: non-Jews] crossing the street."[62] Of all the ministers of government, only Simone Veil visited the scene of the attack on Saturday morning. President Giscard d'Estaing issued a brief communiqué but did not interrupt his hunting weekend. As for Christian Bonnet, minister of the interior at a time when the police were under suspicion after the discovery that certain police officials were affiliated with FANE, he too appeared on TF1 on Friday night and reacted "as a young Jew might react." The government seemed incapable of understanding this lethal manifestation of antisemitism, the first overt attempt in France since 1944 to strike out blindly and randomly at Jews. Part of the reason for the gaffes, embarrassments, and slips of the tongue no doubt had to do with fear of being suspected of racism at a time when, for tactical reasons, the right-wing majority was showing indulgence toward the extremist right.

Now Jewish groups, left-wing parties, and trade unions joined in voicing their anger on a wide scale. Over the next few days there were countless demonstrations against the revival of the absolute evil: fascism. On few occasions since the end of the Algerian War had the "antifascist struggle" brought so many people into the streets. But was fascism really the enemy? Significantly, in the wake of the rue Copernic attack, the Jewish community did not direct its wrath against Palestinian groups, including the Palestine Liberation Organization (which had maintained an office in Paris for several years), although Palestinian groups were usually blamed for anti-Jewish violence.

To be sure, following the revival of "black terrorism" in 1977, there had been a series of spectacular attacks over the previous few weeks that signaled the presence of active neo-Nazi groups on French soil. Yet some commentators who were normally apt to see the hand of the PLO everywhere for once remained oddly silent about its possible involvement. On 18 October, fifteen days after the attack, *L'Express* reported that investigators were on the trail of a pro-Arab group, but the news caused no particular stir. Four years later, the Israeli secret service identified those responsible for the crime as a dissident faction within George Habbash's FPLP (Popular Front for the Liberation of Palestine).

Of course no one knew this at the time. Why would the French Jewish community and the left think to blame a Palestinian group? To French minds in the 1980s it seemed perfectly logical to assume that the assassins were fascists, heirs of Nazism, ghosts of the past. Hence it was possible to organize huge demonstrations against an undeniable, universally despised enemy. And the government, fearful that it might be accused of collaboration with an extreme right somehow implicated in the crime, could only stammer its good will, since it too was caught up in the same logic. In this sense, the aftermath of the rue Copernic attack marked the climactic crisis in a relentless fever that had gripped the country from 1978 to 1981. In these events we detect the same desire for remembrance, the same need to dramatize the past, that we have encountered before, this time in the form of a fantasy that went far beyond the facts of the case.

5

OBSESSION (AFTER 1974):
THE WORLD OF POLITICS

The obsession with Vichy in the 1970s and 1980s was also a consequence of changes in the French political landscape. The election of Valéry Giscard d'Estaing to the presidency in 1974 ended Gaullism's domination of the right. Then, in 1977, the Socialists and Communists reached an agreement on a "common program" that temporarily (but crucially) reunified the left and led to François Mitterrand's election to the presidency in 1981. Ideological debate was subsequently rekindled when the extreme right began to gain ground on several fronts. The critical economic situation, coupled with international tensions, helped to create a climate in which the obsession with Vichy could flourish.

Stinging accusations, many of them couched in the rhetoric of the 1940s, emanated from all parts of the political spectrum. Meanwhile, however, the Occupation was receding into the past and a new generation was entering public life. References to the past became increasingly erratic. Several questions arise. Why were these still burning issues? For a decade and a half, hardly a year had passed without some sort of polemic related to the war. Why the 1940s? Who was most likely to refer to that period, and in what terms?

It is impossible to examine all the barbed remarks and polemical comments that kept the political microcosm in a state of turmoil. Interested readers will find in Appendix 1 a chronology that is as comprehensive as I was able to make it. For a time I considered trying my hand at a typology. But it seemed to me that, while the history of the Vichy syndrome has a logic of its own, it has largely been shaped by long-term changes in the French view of the world. Hence it makes more sense to continue with the chronological approach of earlier chapters. Nevertheless, the extreme right calls for an analysis of its own, which may be found in a separate section of this chapter.

"Giscardo-Vichyism"

Valéry Giscard d'Estaing's seven-year term as president coincided with, and in some ways suffered the effects of, the forties revival. Giscard was affected not only personally (as were most other politicians of national prominence) but also politically; even his "image" was not exempt.

Born in 1926, Giscard was not yet twenty years old when the war ended. Initially, therefore, criticism was directed not at the president himself but at his family. Both his father Edmond and his uncle René had been close to Marshal Pétain and had received the *francisque* (awarded for service to Vichy); his grandfather Jacques Bardoux, a prominent figure in the Third Republic, had served as a member of Vichy's National Council. Furthermore, after Giscard's election as deputy from Puy-de-Dôme in Auvergne in January 1956, he received staunch support from local ex-Pétainists, including Georges Lamirand, the mayor of La Bourboule and former secretary of state for youth in the first Vichy governments. In all this there was nothing too damning, since the local Independents and Peasants Party drew much of its support from people who supported the Marshal.

As fate would have it, however, the Auvergne was precisely the region of France featured in *The Sorrow and the Pity*. Lamirand's presence in the film was widely noted, and, worse yet, Pierre Mendès France revealed that a Giscard d'Estaing had promised his attorney, Rochat, that he would intervene with the Marshal on Mendès' behalf in order to secure his release from prison but had failed to follow through.[1] Mendès' recollection of this anecdote was not totally without guile, and the association of the name Giscard with the idea of collaboration was subsequently blown out of all proportion, so easy is it to blur the distinctions between Marshalism (support for Pétain as leader), Pétainism (support for the ideas of the National Revolution), and collaboration (approval of an alliance with the Third Reich, which was not incompatible with the other two).

Although Valéry Giscard d'Estaing was in no way responsible for his relatives' actions, he did raise questions about his own behavior by trying to establish a role for himself in the Resistance. His biographer, Olivier Todd, is blunt: "Giscard as résistant is a delicate subject."[2] Delicate, perhaps, but not mysterious. On several occasions (most notably in 1975) Giscard hinted that he had belonged to the

Défense de la France movement led by Philippe Viannay and that his assignment had been to distribute the group's newspaper (one of the most important of all underground publications) to the students of the Lycée Louis-le-Grand in Paris. Marie Granet, the historian of the movement, listed Giscard's name among those she interviewed, although he does not figure anywhere else in the book and does not appear to have been the source of any crucial information.[3] The satirical newspaper *Canard enchaîné,* which pursued the matter with considerable zeal, went so far as to assert that Giscard had himself volunteered to be interviewed, as if by so doing he would bolster his claim of participating in the Resistance.[4] In 1974 and 1975 Génia Gemahling, the movement's archivist, sent Giscard several letters questioning him about his contacts and activities; all went unanswered. It appears that Giscard did seek and obtain an unofficial endorsement, rather hastily granted, in order to qualify for certain educational benefits available to students who had participated in the Resistance; or perhaps his reason for seeking the endorsement was to help his father, who was somewhat compromised by his relations with Vichy.[5] The only incontestable fact is that Giscard enlisted in the French First Army in December 1944 and subsequently saw combat with a tank unit in Germany.

For my purposes it makes little difference whether or not Giscard actually participated in the Resistance: he was neither the first nor the last to make questionable claims about resistance activity. In March 1977, for example, Françoise Giroud became caught up in an affair revolving around the validity of her claim to a Resistance Medal. But the ambiguities surrounding Giscard's role and the inevitable political use that was made of the situation did raise doubts, and ultimately the damage was greater than it would have been if Giscard had simply accepted the consequences of his family's "Marshalism." The injury was further exacerbated by the new climate created by *The Sorrow and the Pity.*

To make matters even worse, however, the president, like his predecessor, went out of his way to draw attention to his ambivalence about commemoration of the Resistance. In 1975 he decided that 8 May (V-E Day) would no longer be celebrated as a national holiday, continuing the downgrading of that occasion that had begun in 1969 (see Chapter 6). France was just then going through a phase of bitter recollection. Was the country ready, and even more important, were certain segments of the population ready, to accept this official banishment of memory on the pretext that it was necessary to build a new Europe? Giscard's error (like Pompidou's in the Touvier affair) was to underestimate the degree to which the past was once again on people's minds, or at any rate to overestimate his own power to cope with such difficulties by executive order.

Another presidential action that led to misunderstanding was an order to the prefect of the Vendée to place flowers on the grave of Marshal Pétain on the Isle of Yeu in commemoration of the sixtieth anniversary of the Armistice (11 November 1978). Ten years earlier, General de Gaulle had done the same thing, and President Mitterrand would repeat the gesture on 22 September 1984, a day on which he also shook hands with Chancellor Helmut Kohl. De Gaulle's complex relation to the memory of Pétain has already been discussed at length. As for Mitterrand, whatever he may have felt personally about Pétain, it was difficult to claim that France had finally been reconciled with her hereditary enemy, Germany, without making some gesture of this sort toward the man who had been Germany's objective ally from 1940 to 1944. In any case, the man who was honored on this occasion was of course the military hero of World War I, not the man of 17 June.

By contrast, Giscard's wreath did not go unnoticed. *Le Monde* mischievously gave as much space to the story as to its report on the president's speech, while in the middle of the page devoted to Armistice Day Jean Planchais commented on an article, not obviously related to the day's events, on "European hero worship" by Alain de Benoist.[6] On three occasions (5 and 15 December 1978 and 2 February 1979) opposition deputies questioned the government, which invariably replied that its purpose had been "to pay official homage to all the marshals of France in the 1914–1918 and 1939–1945 wars."[7] The amalgamation of the two wars cut two ways. In Rethondes, two weeks after publication of the Darquier interview, the president spoke of his desire to "protect France from that true perversion of the spirit, racism in all its forms, overt or covert."[8] Giscard's attitude was therefore paradoxical, because to treat Pétain as one of "the marshals of the two wars" was tantamount to denying the uniqueness of World War II, in particular its fratricidal aspect—

something that all governments since 1945 had tried to do in commemorating the war. But to denounce racism while celebrating the end of World War I was to commit a grave historical anachronism. What it showed, in the end, was that it was the remembrance of World War II that raised the more burning issues.

Even worse, the progress of the "new right" and the "end-of-an-era" climate that prevailed during the final years of Giscard's term were signs that misled many people into comparing this period with the 1940s. Philippe de Saint-Robert described Giscardism as "fascism with a liberal face."[9] Jean Bothorel saw Giscard's policies as yet another plot by technocrats to take over the government, a revival of the alleged "Synarchy conspiracy" by technocrats under Vichy (recounted by the American historian Robert Paxton in a book that appeared a few years earlier). Such comparisons were frequently made. The surprising thing is that the conditions that made the Synarchy plot plausible in the 1940s were the same as those that made rumors of conspiracy plausible now: a small group of men, a "technocratic elite," wielded great power, some said for their own ends. To minds disposed to see conspiracy, no further proof was needed.[10]

The most serious charge of all would come from Jacques Chirac. From the Cochin Hospital (in lieu of the BBC) the former prime minister launched an appeal to the people of France on 6 December 1978. He made dark allegations about President Giscard's pro-European policy, questioning not only the financing but also the proposed expansion of the European Economic Community (Common Market):

> In the history of a people there come moments of serious crisis . . . The votes of 81 French representatives will count for very little against the 389 votes of countries subject to undue pressure from across the Atlantic . . . The groundwork is being laid for the vassalization of France; assent is being given to her subjugation . . . As always when France's humiliation is at stake, the foreign party has gone to work with its calm and reassuring voice.[11]

For those who may have missed the allusion, Chirac made it clear that he was speaking of the "party of national renunciation," operating on the right as well as the left "for the benefit of Germano-American interests."[12] Later Yves Guéna did not hesitate to elaborate the metaphor still further:

We saw the same thing, for example, in 1940. Within each party there was a "foreign party." On the right, of course, with Maurras. In the Radical Party it was the "Munich-ites." In the Socialist Party there were socialists who joined Pétain's government, and in the Communist Party there was Doriot.[13]

Finally, Paris deputy Pierre Bas, even more erudite than Guéna, raised the specter not of Vichy but of the counterrevolution, "the army of the princes . . . those of Koblenz or of 1815, still present."[14]

This was a remarkable history lesson for a right wing in power to administer. Was it really necessary to cast Doriot as a member of the Communist Party in 1940, when he had quit the party in 1934? Why not allude instead to the German-Soviet pact? Because to have done so would have been more incisive, perhaps, but it would also have proved more embarrassing to the Communist Party, which as it happens was also opposed to Giscard's European policy. Was it really necessary to overlook the fact that there were Munich-ites in all parts of the political spectrum? And what of the tone of the attack, more reminiscent of the highly Pétainized RPF than of Free France?

As it turned out, Chirac's weapon proved to be a double-edged sword. A few weeks later, Gilbert Comte published a full-page article in *Le Monde* under the title "And What If Chirac Were Vichy?"[15] In it he drew a parallel between Vichy's conception of the state and that of Chirac's party, the RPR. Perhaps the oddest aspect of the whole affair is that the "Cochin appeal" was reportedly the brainchild of two of Chirac's advisers, Garaud and Juillet, who probably stood closer to Pétainist authoritarianism than did either Chirac or Giscard.

To be fair, no one party had a monopoly on fuzzy thinking or overheated polemic. In November 1978, in the midst of the Darquier affair, a furor erupted among the Socialists. It appeared that Michel Rocard would challenge François Mitterrand for the leadership at the next party congress. In response to this news, Gaston Defferre spoke contemptuously of Rocard's proposed platform: "This policy is strangely reminiscent of Pierre Laval's."[16] The ambiguity was diabolical: was Defferre referring to Laval's deflationist policy in 1935 or to his collaboration in 1942? The clear implication was that Rocard, who obviously had nothing whatsoever to do with Laval, was somehow also a traitor.

French Ideologies

The ghost of Pétainism, having haunted the presidency of Giscard, continued to hover over the 1981 presidential election campaign. In January of that year, while the candidates' headquarters were busy sharpening their knives, a new book caused a sensation. Its title had the pithy certitude of an advertising slogan: *The French Ideology*.

Intrepidly ferreting out totalitarianism wherever it lurked, the author, Bernard-Henri Lévy, explained to the good people of France not only that Vichy and collaborationism were nothing less than "fascism in French colors" but also that Pétainism was the very essence of French political culture. It was not, as was sometimes naively believed, just backward-looking conservatives and new-right intellectuals who counted among the Marshal's remaining adepts. Many others lurked within the French Communist Party and even on the staffs of the journal *Esprit* and the newspaper *Le Monde*, venerable institutions generally considered to lean to the left. Georges Marchais, Hubert Beuve-Méry (*Le Monde*'s founder), Emmanuel Mounier (*Esprit*'s founder), the *planistes* of the 1930s, and even Charles Péguy and the "neosocialists of the CERES" all had been, were, or would be fascists.

Lévy has been amply criticized for his scholarly incompetence, blurring of distinctions, and crude logic, and there is no need to demolish his argument again here.[17] To be fair, he never denied that the book was written for a polemical purpose. More interesting than the book itself, however, are the reactions it provoked, which can be interpreted as symptoms of the Vichy syndrome. Although the argument of the book was torn to shreds by several critics, it received extraordinary attention from the media. *L'Express* paid Lévy the signal honor of disclosing that his book had caused dissension among the magazine's editors, as a result of which it published two diametrically opposed reviews. In a highly academic piece Raymond Aron angrily attacked Lévy for "relying so heavily on largely fanciful interpretations of serious scholarly works." The philosopher attacked the "young" colleague whose earlier works he had championed not long before, accusing Lévy of hysteria and, worse yet, of "fomenting [hysteria] in a segment of the Jewish community [that is] already disposed to unreasonable words and actions."[18] In the other review, Jean-François Revel, speaking more as a political activist than as an academic, praised the book, absolved its author of responsibility for "minor, inadvert mistakes," and flatly declared that historical truth (and the historian's idea of truth) mattered less than political struggle here and now:

> *L'Idéologie française* . . . reveals that moment in the crisis of western consciousness when all attempts to distinguish between totalitarianism of the right and totalitarianism of the left had to be, and were, abandoned. That moment is still very recent. Scarcely five years ago, any attempt to compare the Soviet regime to the Hitlerian regime drew protests; now such a comparison draws only blasé shrugs . . . More important than the history of antisemitism, which is only one component of the raw stuff out of which totalitarianism is concocted—and by the way, a component shared, as is well known, by Nazi Germany and Soviet Russia—more important even than that, it seems to me, is Lévy's effort to locate within France itself the roots of a certain totalitarian, "communitarist," antiliberal, antidemocratic sensibility at a stage when such thinking, still inchoate, had yet to differentiate itself into two opposing forms, black fascism and red fascism.[19]

Les Nouvelles littéraires did a feature article on the book in which editor Jean-François Kahn, while expressing some doubts about Lévy's tendency to blur distinctions, generally had favorable things to say about the work of the "Inspector Maigret of anti-Pétainism," who was only too happy to find in books written by other people what he himself deeply believed: that France had been the scene of a civil war between a "Stalinism of the right" and a "Stalinism of the left."[20] Meanwhile, *Le Monde,* even though its founder Beuve-Méry was one of Lévy's targets, published no fewer than three long articles on the book: a hostile review by Bertrand Poirot-Delpech; a response by Lévy (a privilege rarely granted to writers criticized in the book section); and a second, milder review by André Fontaine.[21] And *Le Nouvel Observateur,* for all that it championed some of the values denigrated by Lévy, published an enthusiastic two-page review, as if giving in to a masochistic impulse to kiss the hand that punishes.[22]

As Revel was quick to perceive, the heart of the controversy was political. Leaving aside Lévy's talent for self-promotion, his point was to attack totalitarian tendencies, particularly within the French left. But in order to get this point across to an intelligentsia that he, along with many others of his generation, believed to be blinded by Marxism, he was forced to take a roundabout approach. He had to show, first, that Stalinism, fascism, and Nazism shared the same historical foundations. He had already written a study of Stalinism, and he knew that fascism and Nazism automatically elicited a negative judgment without the need for further research, so his task was to show that France had not been spared by fascism, indeed that it had been the source of some of its essential ideas. For that he drew heavily on the work of Zeev Sternhell.[23] Having done that, what could be simpler than to focus his book on Vichy, a bestselling subject and one likely to upset people on the left? And of course Lévy was not the only one to notice that the topic was of considerable current interest.

Even this was not enough, however. Lévy still had to show that Vichy and the collaboration were not exceptions but were rooted in French political tradition. In this he was not entirely wrong, but to make his case he not only drew extensively on but seriously distorted the work of Robert Paxton. Out of these diverse elements Lévy pieced together a spider's web and placed the 1940s at the center. There must, he argued, be a link between Vichy and anything that in his eyes remotely resembled a totalitarian ideology (or simply an ideology that he did not like). Sometimes these links were real enough, even if Lévy exaggerates their importance: the Vichy officials trained at the Uriage "leadership academy" were indeed Marshalists but not necessarily fascists. At other times he simply reads history backwards, as in his account of Doriot's alleged orchestration of fascist mobs on 6 February 1934, when in fact Doriot participated as a Communist and opposed both parliamentary democracy *and* fascism. And in some cases his interpretation of history is just fantastic, as when he characterizes the PCF of 1940 as "the first Pétainist party in France."[24]

If communists are simply red fascists, why aren't Franco supporters black communists or, as Jean-François Kahn might put it, Stalinists of the right? Answer: such a formulation would be absurd, since it would leave out a common feature of all fascist movements, namely, anticommunism. And anyway the magical, incantatory power of the conjunction would not be as great as in the formula "red fascist."

Read with detachment, *L'Idéologie française* is a piece of crude agitprop, whose peremptory, inquisitorial tone cannot obscure the fact that Lévy was one of the so-called *nouveaux philosophes*, former Marxists whose divorce from the old ideology was celebrated as noisily as their earlier marriage. The book is a flagrant illustration of the limitations of totalitarianism as a concept, particularly when used polemically to demonize an adversary: Nazism is absolute evil; between Stalinism and Nazism there is not a dime's worth of difference, hence Stalinism is also absolute evil. Such reasoning obscures the radical differences between the two systems: the central role of antisemitism in Nazism and the uniqueness of the Jewish genocide. Nor does it do justice to the highly controversial theory most fully elaborated by Hannah Arendt in the 1960s, a theory that emphasizes not the destructiveness of the two systems but their structural similarities: single mass party, charismatic leader, total regimentation of the people, destruction of "civil society," and so on. In the writing of Lévy and others, such parallels, invoked without proper precautions, fall to the level of pure invective: it becomes a tactic of denunciation to identify one's target, whether fascist or communist, with Auschwitz, thus magnifying the emotional force of the accusation. When Lévy calls Péguy and Mounier fascists, he relegates them to the category of those who shipped victims to the death camps. How could anyone defend them after that? How could anyone argue with Revel's opinion that such charges contain an element of truth, that "somewhere there is a skeleton in the closet"? All thinking is rendered useless. Let the historians labor to restore the truth and eliminate the anachronisms. Who cares? In this sense Lévy's "revisionism" is scarcely different in its effects from that of the negationists. What difference do the complex realities of history make? All that matters is the ideological objective. The negationists deny the existence of the Final Solution. Lévy finds so many people guilty of the crime that he makes it completely unintelligible. The worst of it is that his work has attracted many disciples.[25]

All such considerations aside, *L'Idéologie française* provoked such an emotional response that it must be interpreted as yet another florid symptom of the Vichy syndrome. Lévy's originality lies in the premeditated, calculated way in which he sought to derive maximum profit from his polemical outburst. Taking advantage of his reputation as one of the leading *nouveaux philosophes,* he produced a work that is actually a spontaneous interpretation of the syndrome by a sufferer. His book bears all the earmarks of the affliction. It incorporates a certain number of repressed or merely forgotten truths. It is couched in the form of an apostrophe addressed to French society as a whole (witness the title of the work). Ultimately, however, it reflects only the author's obsessions—which are close enough to the obsessions of many others to be passed off as an analysis of events. (In Lévy's case, his concerns reflected the new sensitivities of many French Jews, for whom he claimed to be a spokesman.)

The Marchais Affair

Was Lévy trying to steer debate in a particular direction at the beginning of the presidential campaign season? Possibly. In any case, the book appeared at an opportune moment, applying to Giscard the same method that had brought its author so much success in dealing with men of the left. Without a moment's pause, Lévy wrote that the "relaxation of tensions" (*décrispation*) effected by Giscard was "at the heart of the problem of Pétainism," an unrelaxed ideology if ever there was one.

Lévy's media success was amplified by subsequent events. On 23 February 1981 the weekly magazine *Le Point* revived the dormant Marchais affair. It had long been alleged that Georges Marchais, the secretary-general of the French Communist Party, had, as a young metalworker not yet enrolled in the PCF, signed up in late 1942 to work as a laborer in Germany under the Service de Travail Obligatoire (STO, or Compulsory Labor Service). The magazine published seemingly definitive proof that Marchais had not, as he claimed, been drafted by the STO in late 1942 and escaped in 1943, but rather that he had volunteered on 12 December 1942 to work in a plant in Leipheim, Bavaria, where the Messerschmitt-109 fighter plane was produced, having been employed previously (since November 1940) at a French plant in Bièvres that had been commandeered to do work for the Luftwaffe.[26]

These charges had first been raised in the 1970s, when Georges Marchais replaced Waldeck Rochet as the head of the Communist

Party, and they resurfaced periodically since then. In 1977–78 the courts dismissed Marchais' libel suit against Auguste Lecoeur, former head of the party's clandestine apparatus during the Occupation. In 1980 *L'Express* published a document from the Augsburg archives which suggested that Marchais had in fact been in Germany in May 1944. And finally, in 1981, *Le Point,* the historian Philippe Robrieux, and others uncovered the chief facts still missing from the story.

In this affair it appears likely that the charges against Marchais were well founded. A case like this was sufficiently rare that it was worth noting. What is remarkable about the charges was that they affected the leader of the Communist Party, which based its claim to legitimacy entirely on its struggle against the occupying power. The central question for analysts of French communism was this: how could a man who falsely claimed to have been a *déporté du travail* (as Marchais, who often posed as self-appointed spokesman for men forcibly enrolled in the STO, frequently referred to himself) have become head of the "first party of the Resistance"? How could a party so keenly attuned to the values of that time, so protective of the memory of those who had been shot by the Germans, and so quick to brand others (rightly or wrongly) as *collabos* have succumbed to the leadership of a man who at best had not resisted working for the Germans and who at worst had volunteered to go to Germany? Was this the logical culmination of the party's practice in the 1950s of removing from its leadership all those who had served as officials in the underground?

The Presidential Campaign

An attack on the right, an attack on the left: the striking thing about the obsession with the Occupation that gripped France in the 1970s and 1980s is that it affected all parties across the political spectrum. Never was this more apparent than in the final days of the 1981 presidential campaign.

The 1981 election, in which the major issues were the economic crisis and unemployment, was particularly important because it promised to determine the country's political future for some time to come. The electorate was younger than ever, since for the first time young people between the ages of eighteen and twenty-one were being allowed to vote in a presidential election. Many of the day's political leaders had not been adults during the war. Of the ten major candidates, six had not reached the age of fifteen by 1945: Michel Crépeau (born in 1930), Jacques Chirac (1932), Marie-France Garaud (1934), Huguette Bouchardeau (1935), Arlette Laguiller (1940), and Brice Lalonde (1946). Giscard, born in 1926, was nineteen in 1945. Only three candidates had been over twenty-five at the war's end: Michel Debré (1912) and François Mitterrand (1916), both former résistants, and Georges Marchais (1920).

Yet once again memories of the Occupation were a central feature of a sometimes heated and occasionally fantastic political debate. On 30 April, after the first round of the election, Colonel Passy, former head of special services for Free France, called upon voters to elect Mitterrand, a partisan declaration that General Massu declared to be "treason" to the memory of the "officers, comrades, and subordinates killed on the battlefield [in colonial wars]."[27] This appeal was followed several days later by a statement issued by eminent members of the resistance establishment (including Pierre Emmanuel, Paul Milliez, Claude Bourdet, Generals Buis and Binoche, and Gilberte Pierre-Brossolette): "On 26 April we did not all vote for the same candidate. Today we call upon the people of France to vote on 10 May for François Mitterrand ... the only candidate interested in pursuing the broad program of the Conseil National de la Résistance." Thus initially those who remembered the Resistance seemed to lean toward the left. Hoping to drive in the final nail, Le Canard enchaîné accused the incumbent budget minister, Maurice Papon, of having allowed 1,690 Jews to be deported when he was secretary-general of the prefecture of the Gironde. This affair contained all the usual ingredients: it involved a high political official, it revealed a carefully hidden past, it shattered the accused's alibi that he had been working for the Resistance, and above all it offended Jews already outraged by previous disclosures.[28]

A counterthrust soon followed. Of 419 surviving members of the Compagnons de la Libération, 198 issued a statement calling on voters to reject Mitterrand. Over the protests of some of their comrades, they invoked the Gaullian legacy of 1958.[29] On Thursday, 7 May, two days after the televised debate between the two remaining candidates, Giscard and Mitterrand, General Alain de Boissieu, grand chancellor of the National Order of the Legion of Honor and son-in-law of Charles de Gaulle, faced reporters in Orléans:

Some people are attempting to use the Resistance and to pass off M. François Mitterrand as a great resistance fighter. Well, I can tell you how General de Gaulle judged this period in François Mitterrand's career. He told me this in the presence of witnesses: "After having worked for Vichy and earned the *francisque,* he made contact first with the Resistance, then with Allied intelligence, and finally with our Free French intelligence before placing himself in British hands." He took from anyone who would give, and he behaved throughout this period of his career like a calculating man on the make (*un arriviste et un intrigant*).[30]

What is more, de Boissieu threatened to resign if the candidate of the left was elected. After the election he did resign, not before pointing out that he had acted with the "authorization of the president of the Republic [Giscard]," a claim that was never denied.[31]

The charge was immense, and Mitterrand wasted no time launching a counterattack—on 8 May, of all dates, one day after Boissieu's statement. The candidate pointed out that his past in the Resistance had never been challenged by de Gaulle. For that, "one naturally had to wait for the collaborationist breed (*la race des collaborateurs*) to take a hand in the matter."[32] As usual, the implications of the statement were spelled out by someone else, in this case Gaston Defferre: "While François Mitterrand and I were being chased by the Gestapo, Giscard d'Estaing and his family were collaborators. He [Giscard] was too young, but his family was full of collaborators."[33]

Analyzing this dispute is a good way to understand the mechanics of invective and its specific role in the development of the Vichy syndrome. It also provides an opportunity to make useful comparisons with other signs and symptoms of memory disorders. To begin with, the controversy erupted at a time of particularly intense political discord. More perhaps than in other presidential elections, the 1981 campaign was a clash between two intransigent camps, standing on either side of a rift in French politics that could be traced back for nearly two centuries. The battle involved not just the two standard bearers but the historic right versus the historic left. So it should come as no surprise that the old dispute between résistants and collaborators resurfaced now: the symbolism of that dispute made possible an effective and dramatic compression of contemporary issues. Effective, because the word "Vichy" retained all its connotations of evil power, especially since the French had just endured a serious crisis in their evolving remembrance of the war. Dramatic, because the symbolic compression of contemporary issues heightened and focused the obsession with the past and gave it political meaning. Voters who made up their minds on the basis of such denunciations could feel that they had somehow taken a position in an enduring controversy. Thus one could cast a "Jewish" vote or a "resistance" vote or a "Pétainist" vote and protest against collabos in the government, against the implications of the phrase "innocent victims" in the response to the rue Copernic attack, or against the neglect of the Marshal's remains, honored only with ambiguous wreaths.

Now political scientists have long argued that there is no Jewish vote in France, and no doubt they could prove that memories of the war played no part in the 1981 election. Still both sides wooed this supposedly nonexistent vote, at times deliberately, which shows that the politicians at least did believe in its importance. Neither Giscard nor Mitterrand sought to calm passions in the final days of the campaign, and both were willing to allow discussion to center on the 1940s. Perhaps blundering and opportunism were partly to blame, but it is clear that both sides thought there were some votes to be gained. Of course there is no denying that their thinking was shaped in part by stereotypes, not to say myths.

For many men and women of the left, the right had to be on the side of Vichy, not in a historical but in a structural sense. This belief manifested itself, for example, in May 1984, when a group called La Mémoire Courte (Short Memory) triggered a battle of advertisements in Le Monde by placing this notice: "Our capital, today as yesterday, in 1789 as in 1871, is not Versailles. And it never was Vichy."[34] Mitterrand's jibe about the "collaborationist breed" can be placed within this tradition, according to which the seeds of fascism are inherent in the politics of the right, quite apart from the actual experience of the men involved (in this case de Boissieu and Giscard). It was for this reason that one of the major concerns of right-wing polemicists over the next few years would be to shift the burden to the left, by accusing it (as Lévy did) of having fathered the beast.

Similarly, for a segment of the right, domestic political resistance by parties and movements, and armed resistance by the Communist FTP or by the FFI, has always been suspect. When a man like General Massu raised charges of treason, he too was invoking a certain conception of the Resistance, one involving uniformed heroes and regular combat, not the guerrilla warfare of the partisans of 1944, a form of combat with which French troops would have to contend after World War II in Indochina and Algeria. General de Boissieu's attack was based on the same kind of reasoning. If only Free France was the legitimate government, and if only those who supported de Gaulle *after* the war were entitled to invoke the spirit of 18 June, then in order to defeat the enemy one had no alternative but to discredit other tendencies within the Resistance. Anything else would be tantamount to betraying de Gaulle's ideas. In itself the fact that François Mitterrand was awarded the Pétainist *francisque* in the autumn of 1943 was not a solid argument. Mitterrand had not asked for the award, which was given to him for his work with the Centre d'Entraide, an agency that assisted prisoners of war, but by then he had already left for London and later Algiers, where he met with de Gaulle. The future president himself has repeatedly offered these facts in evidence, and so far neither his enemies nor scholars have been able to discover anything further on the subject, although some have speculated that the young man was vaguely sympathetic to Marshalism.[35] The only option, then, was to make the dead speak, or if need be to make them lie. In his *Memoirs* de Gaulle mentions Mitterrand only once, in the list of those sent on missions inside occupied France. He makes no other comment, though he was by no means reluctant to discuss other personalities when the spirit moved him.[36]

Furthermore, this kind of controversy served as a substitute for other debates. In a prosaic sense it diverted attention from the absence of any official commemoration of 8 May. Embarrassed when called upon to explain this unpopular measure, Maurice Plantier, secretary of state for veterans' affairs, chose instead to attack Colonel Passy ("an authentic résistant whose career ended badly") and François Mitterrand ("he took from anyone who would give").[37] In a deeper sense the dispute was a way of transcending the traditional rift between right and left, as if in 1981 the prize suddenly took on historical weight and rose to the level of the century's most important contests:

the most vociferous spokesmen for the right-wing fringe hinted that a vote for Mitterrand was a vote for both the Gulag (Communists in government) and fascism (the Vichyite *francisque*).

The government's approach was fraught with contradictions. The 1975 abolition of 8 May as a national holiday was intended to draw an official veil over "the fratricidal war for Europe," as Giscard put it in his letter to the members of the European Council. A side benefit, and one well within the tradition inaugurated by de Gaulle, was that a veil would simultaneously be drawn over France's internal conflicts. Six years later, the same leaders, embarrassed by the unpopularity of their decision, did not hesitate to stir up memories of the civil war within France, thus revealing what they had sought to hide: the ideological nature of World War II and the absence of a national consensus as to the nature of that conflict or the manner in which it should be represented.

This inscription in history dramatized the final days of the confrontation: theatrical staging filled the void when political argument petered out. Foreign-trade statistics and figures on inflation gave way to exciting, mysterious discussions of secret combat; millions of victims upstaged millions of unemployed. Routine political struggle, complicated by rumors of unsavory scandal, proved too trivial to sustain the imagination; memories of past combat offered release. Was this not the meaning of the various statements made by former resistance fighters, statements that went beyond mere polemic? What was the point of the allusion to the CNR but to revive memories of a France fighting to maintain not its standard of living but its freedom? Of similar import was Mitterrand's real response to the attacks on his reputation: to go—alone—to the Pantheon to pay homage to Jaurès, Schoelcher, and Jean Moulin. To be sure, he was representing the nation, but he was also paying his respects as a member of the Resistance under attack and even more as a member of the left reclaiming a legacy that the post-Gaullist right had been ready to sell off rather too cheaply.

Parliamentary Invective

In the years after the election of Mitterrand, the right several times attempted to reverse the trend, not by reviving a now useless resistancialism but by attacking the authenticity of the left's commitment to the Resistance. It was in the National Assembly, that scene of so many titanic debates, that invective most often found its natural home.

On 15 September 1981, when Prime Minister Pierre Mauroy proposed a plan to use unemployed youths to restore the natural beauty of France's forests, Robert-André Vivien, an RPR deputy and a master in the tactics of parliamentary debate, stood and shouted the old Vichyite pledge, "Maréchal, nous voilà!" (Marshal, here we are!), an allusion to the Chantiers de Jeunesse [a sort of Vichyite Civilian Conservation Corps]. A shaken Pierre Mauroy gave a solemn reply in which he accused "a certain bourgeoisie" of having followed Vichy for vengeful purposes. This allegation was a commonplace, found in all the history textbooks, but it provoked a flurry of oratory in the Assembly. Once again the reference to the past was simply a theatrical substitute for present concerns, but this time the performance was pure comic opera.

Even more significant was the outpouring of passion that gripped the National Assembly during debate over proposed amendments to 1944 legislation regulating the press. The reforms proposed by the left were intended chiefly to curtail the press empire of Robert Hersant, who had abandoned the moderate left for the reactionary right. What is disconcerting in reading the minutes of these sessions is the violence of reactions to seemingly minor provocations. Once again the mechanism of invective worked to perfection. It all began with an unfortunate allusion by a Communist deputy:

> Edmond Garcin (PCF): Admittedly, this is not 1944. Let me point out, however, that I stand with those who fought during the Occupation.
> François d'Aubert (UDF): With Monsieur Marchais?
> Alain Madelin (UDF): With the Communists?
> François d'Aubert: Did Monsieur Marchais come home from [the] Messerschmitt [plant]?
> Alain Madelin: Have you ever heard of the Nazi-Soviet pact?
> Edmond Garcin: I wasn't the only one to fight, and anyway it wasn't only Communists, there were others. I will not allow anyone to insult me.
> Jacques Toubon (RPR): And what were the Communists up to before 1941?
> Edmond Garcin: Monsieur Toubon, you weren't even born!
> Jacques Toubon: But I've read books!

Edmond Garcin: 75,000 of us were killed! What you are saying is outrageous! If I were you I'd be ashamed.

Jacques Toubon: Who asked the Kommandantur to allow *L'Humanité* to recommence publication?

The chair: Calm down, gentlemen.

Jacques Toubon: And before 1941?

Edmond Garcin: Stop insulting the French workers who fought alone against the *grande bourgeoisie* that formed a fifth column against France! Enough of this subject!

Jacques Toubon: Who asked that *l'Humanité* be allowed to publish legally? The Communist Party!

Edmond Garcin: It's not up to you to teach us lessons, and as for what went on back then, I will answer you without qualms. In the concentration camps there were none of your friends but many of mine!

Jacques Toubon: What? What does that mean? This is too much!

Alain Madelin: That old saw won't do any more!

Edmond Garcin: Where was Monsieur Hersant? Maybe we ought to talk about him, since this law affects his interests! (*Applause from the Communist benches.*)

Jacques Toubon: And Mitterrand?

Raymond Forni (PS, chairman of the legislative committee): Where was Monsieur Hersant, your employer, Monsieur Madelin?

Alain Madelin: And Mitterrand?

Edmond Garcin: Enough of your innuendoes, gentlemen. Our amendment, I repeat, is intended to inhibit any attacks on pluralism of the press from outside.

Jacques Toubon: And Mitterrand?

Raymond Forni: And Monsieur Hersant? . . .

Raymond Forni: Monsieur Madelin, Monsieur Toubon, if you continue in this direction, you may well run into certain contradictions. You may well find yourselves asked what Monsieur Hersant was doing during World War II.

Alain Madelin: Go on, ask! What was Monsieur Mitterrand doing just after the war? . . .

Georges Filioud (secretary of state for communication): I have twice heard the name of the president of the republic mentioned in this chamber—

Jacques Toubon: Yes, indeed!

François d'Aubert: Monsieur Mitterrand has a past!

Georges Filioud: —in connection with innuendoes against which I protest.[38]

The session resumed the next day. The Socialists had decided to heighten the tension by having Pierre Joxe, the leader of their parliamentary delegation, raise the prospect of invoking article 75 of the Assembly rules, under which any deputy guilty of insulting the president of the republic was subject to censure. Several hours of legalistic wrangling followed, at the end of which Alain Madelin, who was so far guilty only of having "alluded to the name of the president," was finally allowed to explain his insinuation about Mitterrand's activities at the time of the Liberation: he "was the managing editor of a review called *Votre beauté* [whose] ownership I would urge historians to look into."[39]

So much for the insult to the president. After this the RPR deputy Pierre de Bénouville made a moving speech defending his friend Mitterrand and his role in the Resistance, and after more wrangling too tedious to recount the Assembly voted to censure deputies Toubon, Madelin, and Aubert, the first such vote since 1950.

The whole affair was very odd. The two sides shadow-boxed without landing a blow. The brawl began with a Communist deputy, Garcin, making a clumsy allusion to his resistance past. Three deputies of the opposition then responded provocatively by raising standard arguments against the Communists: Marchais' questionable activities and the party's behavior in the period 1939–1941. For the right, the real objective of the polemic was to create a diversion so as to avoid a potential debate over the past activities of Robert Hersant. To that end vague charges were leveled at Mitterrand. At this point the Assembly became incensed. Mere mention of the president's name (in connection with *postwar* activities) not only provoked an uproar but broke the camel's back: an opposition deputy spoke out in defense of Mitterrand, alluding not to what he actually did after the war but to what he did during the war, a subject no one had even mentioned until then. In other words, the majority of the Assembly and the president's defenders anticipated that the issue of the president's *francisque* and supposed Pétainist past would be raised—a striking illustration of the power of the unstated in politics.

In some respects this episode is a caricature of the Vichy syndrome's effects on political debate. Dramatization and substitution here reached unprecedented heights. The Assembly was occupied for two full days with a debate that saw a record number of amendments and adjournments. We see the perverse effects of the "taboo," here raised to almost hysterical proportions. What shameful things about François Mitterrand's past were the Socialist deputies attempting to hide? None. What sacrilegious acts had the right committed? None, or at any rate very few. Yet caught up in the logic of charge and countercharge, the Socialists reacted by conditioned reflex and refused to admit that the Communist deputy's collabos were no more real than the opposition's abundant innuendoes. Meanwhile, Hersant was forgotten. That was the whole point of the trap that had been set.

But the trap proved to be only a delaying tactic, because the Hersant affair erupted once more only a few weeks later, when a group led by former résistants lodged a protest with Simone Veil, leader of the opposition candidates for election to the European parliament, concerning the presence on the list of Hersant, who was eventually elected.

After the right was returned to power in the March 1986 elections, the idea that collaboration and fascism were somehow born on the left, an idea that had first taken shape while the left was in control of the government, ceased to be mere insulting rhetoric and became a "historical concept" approved by various authorities. Encouraged by this shift in opinion, by this new revisionism, Charles Pasqua, rightist minister of the interior, calmly charged that certain friends of the Socialists had "prostrated themselves before the occupying power." This charge was launched on 20 May 1986 during debate over whether to replace proportional representation with winner-take-all balloting. Again we see all the elements of the syndrome: retroactive blurring of boundaries, calculated provocation, uncontrolled reaction, and ultimately diversion.

It would be easy to minimize the impact of these polemical attacks. But we have seen that they had a specific function, an intrinsic role in the French political debate, and one that was rooted in tradition. A clear sign of the perpetuation of this tradition is that politicians born during or after the war, and thus not personally implicated in the events, resorted to the same kinds of attack. This enduring turmoil has had profound consequences on memories of the war.

Generally these attacks followed a standard pattern, involving what Evelyne Largueche calls "allusive insult."[40] In most of the instances described above, four parties were involved: the insultor, who launches the attack; the insultee, or object of the attack; the insulted, mentioned in the attack (Vichy, collaboration, non-Resistance); and, finally, the witness to the insult. All the classical devices of rhetoric are employed, from metonymy ("X . . . is Vichy!") to allusion ("And Mitterrand? And Hersant?") and amalgamation (Giscard and the collaboration, Rocard's policy and Laval's).

Accusations charging a specific person with a specific crime are rare. Exceptions include the Hersant, Marchais, and Papon cases, all of which came before the courts either because libel was alleged or because potentially solid charges existed. More often a double or triple language was used so as to avoid libel: it was alleged, for example, that "friends" of the Socialists "prostrated themselves before the occupying power," or that X or Y "worked with Vichy" without further elaboration (when of course thousands of people, including many authentic résistants, fit that description), or that X or Y belongs to the "collaborationist breed," without actually stating that X or Y personally collaborated.

In attacks of this kind, what counts is the general effect on public opinion and not direct damage to the ostensible adversary, and for this witnesses are required—the media first of all and through them "public opinion." It is the media and the public who, *on their own,* draw the conclusion that so-and-so is a collaborator and therefore a traitor or criminal. A typical example of this was the debate on regulation of the press, when it was the Socialists who first raised the question of Mitterrand's past, not after the war, as the opposition urged, but during the war, thus (unwittingly) leaving it to the media and the public to ask what was being covered up.

In other words, the fraudulent "truths" of polemical attack are framed not only by those directly involved but also by spectators who, in spite of themselves, maintain the climate of suspicion. This systematic practice of appealing to the public is a crucial factor in the history of the syndrome. In many respects, the appeal seems to have been out of step with the actual state of opinion: as we shall see later, the public appears to have been less preoccupied with these quarrels than many people, especially politicians, believed at the time. What the turmoil did do, however, was to force people to ask questions about the past.

The use of veiled language and the fact that politicians of every stripe used similar kinds of invective tended to confuse the image of the past. The political truth of the moment periodically supplanted the truth of history. Words like "collaborator" lost all real meaning. Worse still, they suggested that everyone involved had something to hide or to be ashamed of, since insult is by definition a mechanism of defense. Thus the polemics often had unintended consequences, and often it was those who initiated them, on both right and left, who suffered the worst damage.

It is rather surprising how little is added to our understanding of the past by this kind of political rhetoric. The attacks, far from routing the enemy, served only as periodic reminders that no party and no individual, no matter how reputable, emerged from the Occupation unscathed. In a sense, this banal judgment signifies the ultimate failure of the resistance heritage: forty years later, the heroism and lucidity of a few cannot make up for the real or alleged faults of others.

The Extreme Right and the Ghost of the Father

The obsession with the past that gripped France in the 1970s and 1980s was sustained in part by the rebirth of the extreme right. In disrepute after the Liberation, the failure of the OAS and *Algérie française,* the political ascendancy of Gaullism on the right and the cultural ascendancy of Marxism and its successors on the left, the old extreme right—"nationalist," "authoritarian," not to say "profascist"—had apparently fallen silent, its ranks reduced to a few old men nostalgic for the brown-shirted rallies of another era and to a few young firebrands with shaved heads.

Within the space of a decade, however, extremists had reasserted their presence in the political landscape, particularly after 1981. Their progress can be charted in parallel with the evolution of wartime memories. In the summer of 1979 the media, and therefore the public, "discovered" the new right. Tranquil vacationers were suddenly deluged with articles attacking the resurgence of what was described as nothing less than "intellectual neofascism," to which the darkest designs were attributed. First *Le Monde* and then *Le Nouvel Observateur, Libération, L'Express,* and even *Le Figaro* published surveys, reports, and commentaries on the Groupement de Recherche et d'Etudes pour la Civilisation Occidentale (Western Civilization Research and Study Group, known as GRECE) and its journal *Eléments;*

Pétain on the cover of *Figaro Magazine*, 17 May 1980

the Nouvelle Ecole; and the Club de l'Horloge. Within a few weeks more than 350 articles had appeared on the subject in the French and foreign press.[41]

Yet none of these groups was really new. The GRECE had been founded in 1967 by former members of the neofascist group Europe Action, including Alain de Benoist, a former member of the Fédération des Etudiants Nationalistes (FEN), who in 1979 was described as one of the leaders of the new right. The Club de l'Horloge, which aspired to become a "Club Jean Moulin of the right," had been in existence since 1974 and drew most of its members from the prestigious school for state administrators, the Ecole Nationale d'Administration. The papers had several times reported that various members of this new right favored eugenics, opposed egalitarianism, or called for the defense of western values, without arousing the furor that suddenly erupted (with considerable help from certain newspapers) in the summer of 1979. All the fuss did focus attention on the "Gramscian" strategy of the new right, that is, on its initially discreet but now openly avowed determination to join in a war of ideas on the cultural battlefield. In 1978 the Académie Française awarded its essay prize to Alain de Benoist for his book *Vu de droite* (View from the Right),[42] and in the same year Robert Hersant transformed his *Figaro Dimanche* into *Figaro Magazine,* which for a few years after 1981 became the official organ of the new right.

The crucial point is that suddenly people discovered a body of thought that identified itself as right-wing and that invoked a tradition, a system of values, and a vision of the world which rightly or wrongly recalled the accursed decade 1934–1944. In the following year, fears of black terrorism reached fever pitch. In the fall of 1980 it was disclosed that some twenty members of the French police had been found to be members of the neo-Nazi FANE, headed by Marc Fredriksen. On 26 September, in Paris, the synagogue of the Consistory, the Jewish memorial, and a Jewish school were struck by machine-gun fire from a moving car that vanished without a trace. When the bomb exploded on the rue Copernic on 3 October, people understandably began to speak of a resurgence of neo-Nazi violence. The paranoia analyzed earlier was not entirely without factual basis: between 1977 and 1981 some 290 acts of violence had been attributed to the extreme right (counting the rue Copernic attack, which, as we have seen, was actually launched from another source). Included in this total were the murders of the Algerian Laid Sebai (2 December 1977), Henri Curiel (4 May 1978), and Pierre Goldman (20 September 1979), and the attempted murder of Henri Noguères, president of the Human Rights League (21 September 1980).[43]

What was initially believed to be a "new" right, however, turned out to be as traditional as could be, at least in its leadership if not also in its electorate. The real resurgence of the extreme right was the work not of modernist intellectuals (who ultimately lent support to the traditional parties) but rather of a heterogeneous movement led by Jean-Marie Le Pen, a veteran of the old Poujadist movement and of *Algérie française* and a survivor of the internecine struggles among various extreme "nationalist" groups. Within three years, Le Pen's National Front succeeded in electing representatives in various municipalities, most notably Dreux, where in September 1983 the Front concluded an alliance with the parliamentary opposition to elect one of its members mayor. The National Front went on to win seats in the European Parliament in June 1984; in the National Assembly in March 1986, where it claimed thirty-five seats, as many—astonishingly—as the Communist Party; and finally in the 1988 presidential elections, in which Le Pen received nearly 14.5 percent of the votes in the first round. The party is now a firmly established fixture in the French political landscape.

We may therefore identify three phases in the resurgence of the extreme right as well as three distinct elements (intellectuals, perpetrators of violent acts, and political activists). Although the various families that make up this component of the French political spectrum are connected, it would be a mistake to blur the important differences among them. Yet that has frequently been done, largely because of the fortuitous conjunction of certain events, the proximity of certain issues, and above all the spontaneous references to the "dark years" that crop up here and there in the statements of both the extremists and their opponents.

What the new right accomplished was to liberate certain men and ideas from the isolation into which they had been cast by the failure of the struggle to keep Algeria French. The new right not only let its hair grow long and hid its tire irons in the attic, but also attempted to rehabilitate the very term "right" by giving it intellectual luster and by denying, in reaction against what the rhetoric of the traditional parties seemed to suggest, that the word carried shameful connotations. In 1976 Alain de Benoist wrote:

> Today the right seems to have disappeared. It would be more accurate to say that no one wants to hear it mentioned any more. One wonders whether it ever existed. It is as though the word "right" today connotes all the baggage of emotions formerly attached to the term "extreme right" . . . The left is on the left, and so is the extreme left. The Giscardians and the Gaullists are vying to see which can outflank the other on the left.[44]

Benoist's irony captured a feeling that was shared not only by other young Turks but also by men of more traditional, not to say Maurrassian, outlook, such as Gilbert Comte:

> The right, which for more than a century enjoyed the support of political parties, notable newspapers, and eminent theorists, no longer offers any official, candid, and acknowledged image of itself . . . The reluctance of the present-day right to fly its own colors certainly deceives no one. It reflects not just opportunism and trimming in certain individuals but a deep and persistent malaise, a kind of moral division, in contemporary France.[45]

There were many reasons for the reluctance to accept the appellation if not the thing itself. The Giscardian brand of liberalism defined itself in terms of its wish to strike a balance between conflicting goods such as "order and progress" and "security and freedom," and to do this it was necessary to occupy a position in the center, at the fulcrum of this imaginary balance. The Gaullists, for their part, rejected the very idea of political duality and therefore dismissed both the labels "right" and "left."[46] Furthermore, the heirs of the man of 18 June were reluctant to link the heritage of the Resistance to the right, precisely because the Occupation had discredited the right more than any of France's other political groupings. Everyone was jostling to occupy the center—a geometrical impossibility—because the right still gave off faint whiffs of sulfur. The new right, preoccupied with its intellectual explorations, therefore could not avoid a direct confrontation with the diffuse and confused memory of "Vichy."

This confrontation was executed with considerable skill, all the more so since ideological affinities were not lacking: the new rightists, like their forebears, rejected the liberal economy, admired an authoritarian and antiegalitarian state, and resurrected the social eugenics of Alexis Carrel.[47] And they did so without false modesty. Their writings reflect three new attitudes: rejection of nostalgia, exoneration of collaboration, and revision of what it meant to collaborate.

Alain de Benoist, for example, had nothing but contempt for those nostalgic for the past: "Some want to go back to 1789, others to 1933 or 1945 . . . This kind of attitude has always proved sterile."[48] The same note was sounded by Henri de Lesquen of the Club de l'Horloge: "The Nazis? They were brutish and stupid."[49] Others took upon themselves the legacy of Vichy and the war but attempted to place Nazi crimes in context, for example by applying the term "genocide" to the French Revolution's war in the Vendée.[50] A third group turned the accusation back against the left. Using the work of Zeev Sternhell and the incendiary book of Bernard-Henri Lévy, they sought to prove that collaboration was chiefly a left-wing affair, since there were Socialists and Communists at Vichy and among the ranks of the collaborators, and, further, that the essence of fascism is socialism.[51] These misreadings of history found immediate application in parliamentary debate, as we have seen. This line of argument appears to constitute one of the most effective rebuttals at the present time to the charges that the left first raised against the right in 1945.

The attitude of the traditional extreme right, the group that has gravitated toward the National Front, is less ambiguous. Not all of these people look at the 1940s as a bad memory. A few were active Pétainists or collaborators. Among the backers of the daily newspaper *Présent,* launched in 1981 on behalf of the "real France, the France of the Christian virtues of work, family, and fatherland," we find the names of Admiral Auphan, Maurice Bardèche, Serge Jeanneret (a staff assistant to Abel Bonnard, minister of national education from 1942 to 1944) alongside those of Pierre Chaunu, R. P. Bruckberger, and Pierre Debray-Ritzen.

Rivarol, four decades after the war's end, steadfastly continues to side with the vanquished of 1945. To take just one example, the magazine published a letter from a disgruntled reader in its 19 November 1982 issue. The letter writer, after stating his hostility to former collaborators, criticized the pilgrimage that several friends of the journal had made to the grave of Jean Hérold-Paquis, a former member of the PPF who was executed after the Liberation and who had been well known for his program on Radio Paris, which always ended with the line, "For like Carthage, England will be destroyed." The editors replied:

> We remind our correspondent that *Rivarol* is a meeting place for those who were "Pétainists but not collaborators," those who were "collaborators but not Pétainists," and those who were neither but who were a little slow to understand that the Allies had killed "the wrong pig."[52]

Other, even more marginal journals kept alive this nostalgia for the 1940s. One such was *Militant,* supported by the likes of Saint-Loup, a former journalist with the LVF. Although obsessed with the immigration issue, *Militant* did not eschew the occasional foray into subtle political analysis:

> In France, you have to admit that changes of regime are almost always carried out by force. The First Republic came from a revolution, the First Empire from a coup d'état, the Restoration from a foreign invasion, the July Monarchy from a revolution, the Second Republic from a revolution, the Second Empire from a coup d'état, the Third Republic from a coup de force, the Fourth Republic from the Resistance and the Allied victory, and finally the Fifth from 13 May. Only the *Etat Français* [of 1940–1944] stemmed from a vote of Parliament entrusting full powers to Marshal Pétain in July 1940.[53]

Stranger than fiction, this reading of history.

As another example of the filiation between the new right and the 1940s, consider French Friendship Day, 16 October 1983, an occasion that brought together nearly all the elements of the nascent extreme right: Jean-Marie Le Pen of the National Front, Philippe Malaud and Pierre Sergent of the Centre National des Indépendants et Paysans (which had become the respectable political springboard for extreme right-wing politicians), Yves Durand of the Union Nationale Interuniversitaire, François Brigneau of *Minute* and *Présent,*

Romain Marie of the Christian Solidarity Association, André Figuéras, and Jo Ortiz. From the podium, in an auditorium filled with people who had come to vent the animosities, fears, and fantasies of another age, particularly in regard to immigration, one speaker, Arnaud de Lassus, denounced "the four superpowers [that are] colonizing France: the Marxist, the Masonic, the Jew, and the Protestant, symbolized by ministers Fiterman, Hernu, Badinter, and Rocard," while another, Jacques Ploncard, drew applause when he stated that Marshal Pétain "in August 1940 dissolved the secret societies."[54] Apart from the style, reminiscent of rallies in occupied Paris or during the Algerian War, these speeches are notable for their reliance on Maurrassian themes, the same ideas that shaped Vichy and its exclusionary principles (hostile to Jews, Freemasons, Communists, Socialists, and foreigners).

Since then, Le Pen has strikingly, and deliberately, demonstrated that he is obsessed with the 1940s. Although he staunchly denies any connection with the antisemitism of that era, Vichy and the war are much on his mind: in 1987 he referred to the gas chambers as a "minor point in the history of World War II"; in 1988 he made an atrocious pun on the name of the Jewish government minister Michel Durafour, referring to him as "Durafour crématoire" (*four crématoire* means "crematory oven"); and in the same year he alluded to the "dual nationality" of another Jewish minister, Lionel Stoléru.

The connection with the 1940s was also made outside the new right, which was thus immediately cast in a diabolical role, all the more so since the phenomenon appeared to have begun just as Darquier resurfaced and neo-Nazi bombs began to go off. Although each of these episodes was distinct, they reinforced one another. When *Le Nouvel Observateur* published a special issue on the new right in the summer of 1979, it included an article by Henri Guillemin on Pétain, in which it is argued that the Marshal had hatched the idea of a conspiracy against the republic even before the outbreak of the war. The editors gave no reason for publishing this article in the issue on the new right, but the clear implication was that the new right was not only the heir to Pétain but yet another conspiracy against democracy—a feeble critique, made even more feeble by the fact that historians had long since refuted the charge of a Pétainist conspiracy.[55]

We saw earlier that the attack on the rue Copernic had first been blamed on the extreme right and that both the Jewish community and the left had mobilized not for the defense of Israel but around the issue of antifascism. Examples abound of this kind of systematic assimilation of the entire contemporary extreme right to the Pétainists and collaborators of the forties. During the municipal election campaign in Dreux, which became the symbol of the resurgence of a racist extreme right (possibly in collusion with the traditional parties), left-wing activists spontaneously began singing "Le Chant des Partisans."

The blurring of distinctions, which in this case was more emotional than calculated (unlike the deliberate use of political insults we saw earlier), initially made it impossible to grasp the true nature of the phenomenon. It took a while for political observers to overcome the notion that deathless collabos were somehow returning to haunt the present and to recognize what was new in the National Front's rhetoric and success at the polls. Was it the extreme right that characteristically balked at discarding some of these relics, or was it the left of the 1980s that found it difficult to jettison its reductionist notion of the extreme right?

Be that as it may, the revival of the extreme right was also aided by the cultural divisions of the late 1960s. The challenge to de Gaulle's ecumenical vision of occupied France and the battering of the resistance myth encouraged all who were nostalgic for the past, from all parts of the political spectrum. Devastated and demoralized by the Algerian failure, the extreme right set out to patch its image. In this it received inadvertent assistance from those who had helped to destroy the myth, first and foremost Georges Pompidou and Valéry Giscard d'Estaing. First in the 1968 legislative elections and then in the 1969 presidential elections, anti-Gaullists who had favored keeping Algeria French moved closer first to the parliamentary majority and then to the new president (Giscard). In 1974 Giscard entrusted responsibility for maintaining order at his political rallies to men who were well known as rightist activists, men who in that very year founded, with Giscard's blessing, the party of the new movement.

Many of these extreme rightists were apparently unable to quell their nostalgia for and fascination with the 1940s. Despite the modernist rhetoric of the new right, it seemed utterly incapable of renouncing this legacy. And why should it? That was the only period during which the men, ideas, and symbolism of the movement had enjoyed the slightest authority. Can any political group turn its back on its own history or prevent the formation of a rudimentary tradition of power? To be sure, neither the National Front nor the new right can be reduced to neo-Pétainist ideology or dismissed as a mere resurgence of "French fascism," which is still a matter of heated controversy. Yet it remains true that the "father" was never really killed, and that a vague nostalgia for "work, family, and fatherland" lingers on, and not only on the extreme right. Even Raymond Barre broke the taboo in December 1985: "Yes to *work,* yes to the *family,* yes to the *fatherland,* but in a *France free* because free men will have wanted it that way."[56] This was no innocent allusion, as the former prime minister and presidential candidate himself confirmed in a television interview on 12 January 1986; it was a deliberate attempt to get to the essence of Marshalism, to the slogan that was its credo and yet also the symbol of the insuperable obstacle in the way of the National Revolution. How could that revolution be effected in a France no longer occupied by any foreign power, yet without being seen as the offspring of collaboration?

Obsession with the past could thus take forms other than insult and invective. The durability of the legacy played its role, all the more so in that many politicians, on the left as well as the right, still believed in the redemptive virtues of the Marshal's name, which could be invoked as an emblem of either courage or evil.

Barbie: A Cathartic Trial?

On Saturday, 5 February 1983, at a military base in Orange, France, a man of seventy, tired and drawn, arrived on a DC-8 from Guiana and was immediately transferred to the prison at Montluc. There Christian Riss, an investigating magistrate born after the war, notified the prisoner of his indictment for crimes against humanity, handed down the year before. The criminal, it seemed, was returning to the scene of his crimes forty years after the fact: SS Captain Klaus Barbie, head of the Fourth Section of the Lyons security police from 1942 to 1944, was now in the hands of the children of people he had tortured and put to death.

From the first the Barbie affair was treated, in accordance with the express wishes of Robert Badinter, the minister of justice, as a symbolic event. The momentousness of the occasion was underscored by a ban on the media. No pictures were allowed of the Bolivian citizen who called himself Klaus Altman; the authorities felt that maintaining an air of mystery would ensure the intended emotional impact of the trial.

Sought by the police since 1945, the fugitive Barbie had been found guilty of war crimes in 1952 and 1954.[57] Yet he had received protection from American intelligence (as the United States officially conceded on 16 August 1983) and managed to make his way to Bolivia, where in 1971 he was located by Beate Klarsfeld. Later Beate's husband Serge revealed that French military intelligence had been aware of Barbie's whereabouts since 1963.[58] Thus it was only after considerable pressure had been brought to bear that French authorities finally, in 1972, asked for Barbie's extradition for the first time; over the next ten years repeated requests for extradition proved fruitless. When the left came to power in France in 1981, the pace accelerated. Extradition was facilitated by the election of Silès Zuazo, the chief of a left-wing coalition, as president of Bolivia on 10 October 1982.

With the election of François Mitterrand in France, the resistance tradition had regained some of its former prominence, particularly during postelection ceremonies at the Pantheon. Jean Moulin was believed to have died in July 1943, and with the fortieth anniversary of his death coming up, what better commemoration could there be than to bring to justice the man held responsible? Perhaps the Socialist-led government decided that it would be better to do without an official ceremony, which would have to include representatives from all parts of the political spectrum. In the political climate of the time, with left-right "cohabitation" and dialogue still some way in the future, it would be difficult to bring all elements of the Resistance, Gaullists as well as Communists, together for the purpose.

With the help of Régis Debray, Serge Klarsfeld was able to take advantage of the situation to persuade the government to reopen the Barbie case in 1982. Several ministers were directly concerned as former members of the Resistance: Claude Cheysson, Charles Hernu, Gaston Defferre, and of course President Mitterrand himself, who may have met Serge Klarsfeld's father in the course of clandestine operations.[59] Robert Badinter, the justice minister whose father had died in Auschwitz after being deported from Lyons and who had personally attended the Eichmann trial in 1961, also had a direct interest in the case.[60] As the symbol of the Jewish deportees, Badinter at this stage of the proceedings could still act in perfect harmony with those who invoked the memory of the Resistance.

Barbie's arrival in France therefore reflected the deeply felt wishes of the government, despite opposition charges that it was merely a political ploy for the municipal elections of March 1983. But the Barbie case was not just one more eddy in the turbulent currents of postwar memory, nor was it just another manifestation of the Vichy syndrome. With the trial the government hoped to shape collective memory. To that end it presented Barbie as a symbol of Nazi barbarism: the man who tortured Jean Moulin would be judged in the name of the law and of the impossibility of forgetting the past. This was to be a "historic" trial, yet another in a long line.

Evidence of this can be seen in Minister of Communication Georges Filioud's proposal that the trial be broadcast on live television, the first such broadcast in French history. Despite initial support from Badinter, the idea was subsequently dropped (though not before paving the way for passage of a law allowing important trials to be recorded for historical purposes). Still the French people were invited to take part in what was envisioned as a celebration of unity joining victims and heroes. Because justice was to play the leading role, there would presumably be no hint of partisan politics or state self-glorification. In Martinique on 6 February 1983, shortly after Barbie's arrival in France, Prime Minister Pierre Mauroy declared:

> In taking the decision to try Klaus Barbie, the French government was not acting out of a spirit of vengeance. Its concerns were two: first, to enable French justice to do its work, and second, to honor the memory of that time of grieving and struggle by which France preserved her honor. French men and women must not forget this history, which is theirs. Members of the younger generation must know what was then endured so that they will always be ready to defend the dignity of their fatherland and, still more, the dignity of man.

Obviously the government was not unaware of the complexities of the Barbie case. In the event, however, not even the government could control the consequences of the trial, demonstrating once again how difficult it is to contain memories of World War II within predefined and structured categories even with the support of the government and the active involvement of private groups.

At first, things seemed to proceed smoothly enough. A poll conducted as the news was still breaking showed that the public was nearly unanimous: 80 percent of those interviewed felt that France was right to ask Bolivia for Barbie's extradition (only 15 percent were opposed); 54 percent approved of bringing him to trial in a French court (compared with 33 percent in favor of an international tribunal, 3 percent a German court, and 10 percent who felt that "France should steer clear of the whole affair"); 71 percent said that they would follow the trial "with interest," 18 percent "with passion," and only 10 percent "with indifference."[61] But these results are only a momentary reflection of the reality, since few people were in a position, particularly at this stage of the affair, to grasp what was at stake and what difficulties lay ahead.

The ambiguities started. Prominent personalities differed over the timing of Barbie's expulsion and the significance of the coming trial. While Jacques Chirac said he was pleased that justice could now take its course, Simone Veil, whose opinions were widely sought, expressed the hope that there might be not a trial but "a contribution to history," because no matter what happened "human justice will not be satisfied."[62] Many former résistants and deportees shared this view and called for an educational trial.

On the extreme right there were, as might be expected, some (though ultimately a minority) who would have preferred to forget the whole business. Among them were Jean-Marie Le Pen and the magazines *Minute* and *Aspects de la France,* the latter responsible for the characterization of Barbie as only a "clumsy torturer."[63] Among opposition deputies, Raymond Barre confessed his discomfort and quoted the archbishop of Lyons, Monsignor Decourtray: "This is one of those events that call for silence rather than words," a precept that Barre himself occasionally forgets.[64] François Léotard, secretary-general of the Parti Républicain, openly expressed his fears that the trial would be "coopted." As a member of a younger generation, he even tried to capitalize on his political virginity: "It is not necessarily in the interest of certain of today's politicians to look too closely into this

past." But despite a forest of microphones eagerly awaiting some revelation, he refused to elaborate on his delphic remark.[65] Innuendo was
again on the agenda. Old affairs were dredged up by both the right
and the left. Under the headline "Those Who Tremble" *Le Matin* published an article about former collaborators who might have something to fear from revelations at the trial. Thus the first danger was
that the Barbie affair would rekindle the *guerre franco-française* and
thereby lose its symbolic significance. But this fear proved groundless
because the trial, which was directed at evil incarnate, the Nazi Barbie, initially had the effect of calming passions in the country and
served as both a reminder of the trauma of the war and a focal point
for the obsession with the past.

The second immediate danger was that public attention would be
diverted from the main event by numerous side issues. There was, for
example, the tragicomic role played by Jean Moulin's former wife,
Marguerite Storck Cerruty, who briefly occupied page one of all the
papers even though the couple had divorced in 1928, one year after
their marriage.[66] And there were the revelations, worthy of a spy
novel, of the role played by American and French intelligence agents
in protecting Barbie after the war. Later, in 1985, new information
came to light about the involvement of certain neo-Nazi organizations and of the Swiss financier François Genoud.[67]

The danger that was hardest to gauge, however, and most significant in its potential effects on memory, was intimately bound up with
the event itself. On 23 February 1983 the Lyons prosecutor, Jean Berthier, released the text of the indictment to the public. There were
eight counts, all involving the arrest, torture, and deportation of civilians, particularly Jews. In this Berthier was faithfully following the
broad guidelines laid down by the minister of justice, who insisted
throughout that the law be strictly observed:

> Not included under the head of crimes against humanity are acts
> alleged to have been committed by Klaus Barbie against the person
> of members of the Resistance . . . These acts were war crimes for
> which the statute of limitations is now in effect, and they do not
> appear to constitute crimes against humanity, that is, massacres,
> murders, and deportations inflicted on civilian populations during
> the Occupation, including acts of genocide and hostage taking . . .

Because resistance fighters fought against the Vichy regime and the army of occupation, they are considered to have been volunteer combatants, as they themselves have always forcefully insisted and as the law has recognized . . . Legally, therefore, they cannot be confused with the civilian population that endured the kinds of treatment described in the charter of the International Tribunal of Nuremberg.

These are crucial distinctions, and it was at this stage of the proceedings that the contradictions between justice, memory, and history began to make themselves felt.

The first problem was to prove the alleged crimes. As a suspect, Barbie was entitled to all the usual legal guarantees. The historical facts were not in dispute: Barbie had belonged to the SS and the Nazi Party; his activities in Lyons and the scope of his responsibilities were well known. But courts require concrete, material proofs to establish the guilt of an *individual*, not a cog in a machine considered part of a criminal system. Therein lay a first source of friction. Forty years after the fact, the witnesses—Barbie's victims—could not be expected to provide conclusive proof. As for documents, only originals could be admitted as evidence. In December 1983 a defense objection alleging that a photocopy of a telegram from Barbie ordering the deportation of forty-three Jewish children from Izieu on 6 June 1944 was a forgery was sustained by the court. This small symbolic victory for the defense proved inconsequential, however. Thanks to the arduous efforts of Serge Klarsfeld at the Centre de Documentation Juive Contemporaine, the original of this telegram was located, and in December 1984 it became prosecution exhibit A.[68] No historian would ever have thought to question the validity of the copy, which had been made by the tribunal at Nuremberg. But the court had no choice but to insist on the original once the defense raised the issue. Because of technical issues like this, only a few of Barbie's many crimes were ultimately judged—so it is legitimate to ask what "educational" value such a trial might have.

A second problem had to do with conflicting memories of the events. A few days after Barbie's indictment was handed down, several victims and their families, along with some twenty-two organizations (including the Ligue des Droits de l'Homme, the Amicale des

Anciens de Dachau, the Union Départementale du Rhône des Combattants Volontaires de la Résistance, and the FNDIRP), joined the
case as civil parties. But the court, obedient to the law, would insist
on the fundamental distinction between "war crimes" committed
against soldiers *or the equivalent,* such as resistance fighters, subject
to a twenty-year statute of limitations, and "crimes against humanity"
committed against civilians, especially in connection with the Final
Solution, for which there was no statute of limitations. Therefore the
court considered the death of Jean Moulin and Barbie's merciless pursuit of guerrilla fighters in Lyons, the capital of the Resistance in the
Southern Zone, as matters outside its jurisdiction, "forgotten" in the
legal sense of the term, even though Barbie had been brought to justice specifically in order to counter the lapse of memory.

The contradiction was glaring: ultimately the man responsible for
the death of France's national martyr would be convicted of crimes
against a few hundred civilians, mainly Jews. In court the Resistance
found itself reduced to silence. Some whispered that "it was only
right." The memory of the Holocaust, so long in manifesting itself, at
last received the attention it was due, having been overshadowed as
late as 1970 by official celebration of the Resistance. After Eichmann
in Jerusalem, Barbie in Lyons would make it possible to condemn the
antisemitism that was the essence of Nazism.

But this possibility was bought at the expense of former résistants,
particularly those who had been close to Jean Moulin. Was respect
for the law to be allowed to eclipse the national hero, to remove the
emblematic figure from the proceedings? Perhaps that figure was too
emblematic, and perhaps his heroic status had been too suddenly
achieved, not to conceal certain misgivings and opportune omissions
that would be revealed in controversies to come. Within their own
frame of reference the résistants' concerns were justified, to judge by
a poll carried out in April 1987, a few weeks before the beginning of
the trial, and published in *Le Monde* on 2 May: 40 percent of those
surveyed spontaneously characterized Barbie as a Nazi and member
of the SS, 37 percent called him a murderer or torturer, and only 2
percent saw him as "the man who tortured and murdered Jean Moulin." Nevertheless, this contradiction between justice and history
might have remained latent, since respect for the rules of law was the
very essence of a trial whose purpose was to demonstrate the superi-

ority of the democratic system over Nazism, the ultimate negation of the rule of law. To say this, however, is not to reckon with one unforeseen element in the case: Barbie's attorney Jacques Vergès.

Vergès, who had joined the FFL at age seventeen and became a Communist after the war, who had served as an attorney for the Algerian National Liberation Front and had close ties to various Palestinian organizations, chose, for personal political reasons and out of hatred of "bourgeois democracy," to become involved in the case, whose political and legal complications he quickly mastered. It is worth pausing a moment to consider his role in greater detail because, had it not been for the omissions, paradoxes, and ambiguities inherent in the Barbie case, Vergès probably would have found another cause to champion.

"It was Vergès who chose Barbie and not the other way around."[69] Until 15 June Barbie was defended, in theory at least, by Alain de la Servette, the public defender of Lyons. He secured the services of Robert Boyer, a lawyer-priest, and of Jacques Vergès, possibly on the recommendation of François Genoud, a Swiss financier with neo-Nazi connections. On 14 June 1983, however, Monsignor Decourtray, the archbishop of Lyons, publicly criticized the participation of a member of the clergy in the case, invoking the need to fight against the "banalisation du nazisme" (the routinization of Nazism). The next day Alain de la Servette also declined to defend Barbie, thus leaving the task solely in the hands of Vergès.[70]

Only a few days later, Vergès made what appeared to be a well-prepared address to a conference organized by the Committee for Prison Justice in which he set forth the manner in which he intended to defend the former Nazi. Vergès, the leftist radical, proposed a "strategy of rupture" with the bourgeois state. After reminding his listeners that Barbie "became part of the history of our country after arresting Jean Moulin," he protested against the exclusion from the trial of the Moulin affair on technical grounds. The definition of crimes against humanity, he argued, could easily be extended to apply to this situation. According to Vergès, the real reason for avoiding the issue lay elsewhere:

> If this [the murder of Moulin] were counted as a crime against humanity, it would become necessary to discuss the conditions under which Jean Moulin was handed over to the Germans. Because Mou-

lin was not arrested by accident in a random roundup; he was turned over to the Germans by other members of the French Resistance, and there are politicians today who invoke the name of the Resistance and who wish to appear in the eyes of the public and perhaps—if they are megalomaniac enough, and they are—in the eyes of history as pure heroes, latter-day Vercingetorixes, and who, if such a debate were to take place, would be seen for what they are: men who were playing a double game, who were feeding at two troughs, and who, whether they were anti-Gaullists or anti-Communists, forgot their duty to the Resistance because of partisan political passions.[71]

Vergès then charged that the reason why crimes against humanity were not exempted from the statute of limitations before December 1964 was to prevent lawyers like himself, committed supporters of the FLN, from inundating the courts with charges. France, he said, must air its own dirty linen first.[72] In public this was his most common argument.

On this occasion Vergès' audience consisted of extreme left-wing militants, many of whom were distressed by his remarks. One, as it happens a German, declared that for him Barbie was a "monster." Vergès answered: "A trial is an event. It provokes, it creates a drama, a spectacle designed by others, and it is up to us to rewrite the script to our own liking. And by rewriting the script, I mean not manipulation but simply giving a meaning to facts in our possession."[73] Later he added: "We are in the position of not having power, and we can only provoke a debate by seizing the opportunities that those in power, through their blindness and incompetence, offer us."[74]

Vergès thus revealed his plan in a few succinct sentences to a supportive audience, and he would follow it to the letter. From the first he understood how difficult it was for any government, even democratic, to judge another political system, however criminal, retroactively: it was the same as the debate over the Nuremberg trials, only forty years later. To remember a crime, to maintain a vigil out of respect for the dead, is one thing; to condemn that crime in different circumstances, in a climate wholly unlike the one surrounding the Allies' discovery of the death camps and according to the laws of a democratic system of justice, is something else—necessary perhaps, but a very ticklish business.

Vergès also sought to turn the educational intent of the trial to his own advantage, thereby illustrating the naiveté of those who hoped to use the case as an object lesson. The Eichmann trial of 1961–62 had pointed up the dangers. That case revealed the banality of evil and hence the possibility of its occurrence anywhere. It demonstrated the hypocrisy involved in judging a man as the representative of a defeated system in a world where other totalitarian systems and other forms of genocide still existed. The Eichmann trial also called attention to certain hidden aspects of the Final Solution, such as the attitude of the Judenräte and the passivity of the victims.[75] So what had begun as a simple (if farfetched) plan ended in confusion. The aim had been to judge, in Israel, a state that owed its very existence to the magnitude of the Nazis' crimes, one of the principal officials responsible for the genocide. Still the Eichmann trial had such ideological and emotional significance, and was so important to consolidating the identity of the young Jewish state, that the game was probably worth the candle.

Vergès found the Achilles' heel of the French plan to try Barbie: the memory of the Resistance. Members of the Resistance were excluded from the arguments in court and obliged to stifle their rage. Even worse, they were upstaged by Vergès, who not only shamelessly exploited what he knew to be a sensitive issue but did so in such a way as to stir up old controversies. The battle proved all the more painful in that it pitted résistant against résistant by distorting the harsh human and political realities of the clandestine struggle. Vergès' tactics were similar to those used by Faurisson in exploiting Jewish memories.

The circumstances of Moulin's arrest became a matter of discussion soon after Barbie's return to France. What exactly had taken place on 21 June 1943 was reconsidered, as was the role of René Hardy, the man whom many résistants considered to be the traitor even though charges against him had been dismissed by the courts. In short, the Moulin affair, excluded from the courtroom, inevitably found its way into the press. With the groundwork thus laid, Vergès aroused a furor in November 1983 by publishing a twelve-page pamphlet entitled "Enough of Pontius Pilate."[76] Rehashing old books without adding a single new fact, he set forth his case for Moulin's "betrayal," strictly following the tactical plan he had announced at the June colloquium.

It was not the word "betrayal" that caused a stir: it had been known for forty years that Moulin was betrayed. Rather it was Vergès' allegation that "secret documents" existed to prove his charges. Now, historians working at various institutes devoted to the history of World War II spotted detectives employed by Vergès searching for the decisive letter or document—proof that Vergès had less up his sleeve than he intimated.

But what evidence he did or did not have is of no importance. The provocation worked, and former résistants broke their silence. Statements, corrections, eyewitness accounts, and pamphlets poured forth in an avalanche that seemed perhaps too defensive.[77] More was yet to come. At the behest of the FNDIRP, the ANACR, the Ligue des Droits de l'Homme, the MRAP, and other groups, a counterattack was launched. The Cour de Cassation examined the prosecution files in the Barbie case, which had been closed by court order on 5 October 1985. On 20 December the appeals court, in a historic decision, gave a new interpretation of crimes against humanity that allowed certain acts against résistants to be included in the indictment. The whole prosecution case had to be rebuilt, a task that was not completed until 9 July 1986. On that day a Paris court handed down an indictment that included, in addition to the charges already mentioned, three of the six crimes against résistants of which he had been accused. The text of the indictment is instructive: one of the counts was "deportation of persons . . . because of actual or alleged resistance activities." By contrast, the 1943 murder under torture of a policeman who had allowed résistants in his custody to escape was omitted. "The author of a crime against humanity," the indictment read, "must have acted out of adherence to a policy of ideological hegemony such as the national-socialist ideology of the Third Reich. This motive must be special, whereas a war crime requires only culpable intent."[78] It is a fine distinction indeed that can discriminate between the hegemonic intent of Nazism and ordinary military and police operations under Nazi rule. Was not the ultimate objective of the war begun by the Nazis one of permanent hegemony over Europe?

It is hard to resist the conclusion that Vergès did score a number of points. Had he not foreseen this outcome as early as 15 June 1983? Had he not grasped the rivalries that existed among people with different memories of the event? Who but he could have enjoyed the unfortunate dispute that erupted between Serge Klarsfeld, Henri No-guères, and Vercors, Jewish memory on one side, resistance memory on the other?[79] What educational benefit was there in a dispute among victims?

Even before the trial began, the Barbie case raised questions about the nature of memory. The trial was heralded as a cathartic event: a few days after Barbie's arrival, the historian Emmanuel Le Roy Ladurie predicted that the trial would be "an enormous national psychodrama, psychotherapy on a nationwide scale."[80] There were also questions about future collective representations. Should the uniqueness of the Final Solution be emphasized, and with it antisemitism as the essential and novel perversion of Nazism? Or should the nature of the Nazi political system as a whole, along with all who became its victims, be the focus of attention?

To make the fate of the Jews the central issue was in a sense to do what the Nazis had done when they took the Jews for their principal, although neither their first nor their only, target. International law chose this course by distinguishing between war crimes and crimes against humanity, the latter meaning primarily crimes committed in connection with the Final Solution. The alternative was to take a more "political" approach and to emphasize the unity (real or alleged) of the Resistance. Instead of focusing on any one aspect of Nazism, even one as crucial as antisemitism, this approach emphasized the universal need to struggle against oppressive systems everywhere, no matter who their victims might be. And what about the case, mentioned earlier, of the résistant who was also a Jew: which mattered more, his resistance or his Jewishness? It was this argument that the appeals court found persuasive in 1985. What characterizes a crime, the court ruled, is not the identity of the victim but the nature of the act and the ideology of its perpetrator.

This judgment, however, still does not dispel all ambiguity. If the legal distinction between war crimes and crimes against humanity were reduced, might it not mean that résistants would lose one of the things for which they had fought hard ever since the Liberation—the recognition that they had indeed been combatants? In any case, is it up to the courts to determine the meaning of history? The restrictive interpretation of "crimes against humanity" accorded with the law as it was understood before 1985. Not that the law was necessarily wrong. But attitudes had undoubtedly changed. The court was interpreting not only the law but collective memory. But the courts, as has been evident on countless occasions since the end of the purge, do not always offer the most faithful reflection of the public mind.

Impact of the Trial

In hindsight, the Barbie trial, which lasted from 11 May to 4 July 1987, can be seen in a different light. Did it really serve a cathartic purpose? Did memory of the war rise to a new level from which no regression is possible? Surely not, even though the trial undeniably marked an important turning point.

In keeping with the 1985 appellate court ruling, the charges against Barbie were not limited to crimes related to the Final Solution. There were five counts to the final indictment: the liquidation of the UGIF's Lyons committee and the deportation of 84 individuals following a 9 February 1943 raid on the rue Sainte-Catherine in Lyons; the deportation of 43 children and 5 adults arrested in Izieu on 6 April 1944; the fatal torture inflicted on Professor Marcel Gompel; the deportation of certain individuals in 1943 and 1944; and the deportation of the Lesèvre family, whose only survivor, Lise Lesèvre, testified at the trial. The last three counts involved crimes against individuals who were Jews as well as members of the Resistance, and no attempt was made to say whether the act was directed primarily against the résistant or the Jew. Thus Barbie was sentenced to life imprisonment because of the nature of his crimes, not the identity of his victims. Subsequent debate has focused on the wisdom of this decision, which undeniably undermined the principle of the uniqueness of the Final Solution and genocide of the Jews.

At the same time, however, the decision had important implications for the future, because it separated the concept of crimes against humanity from the contingent criminals, Nazism and the Nazis actually brought to justice. Although the decision is open to challenge from several points of view, it did facilitate the subsequent indictment of Touvier, whose anti-Jewish activities were secondary to his battle against the Resistance. The trial thus crystallized a new attitude toward the law, already evident in the December 1985 appellate court decision. It was no accident that the prosecution of Leguay and Tou-

vier now began to move more rapidly. After the crime had been re-
defined and the new law applied to a German defendant, there was
no excuse for not using the same law against French defendants accused of similar crimes.

Note too that Vergès' strategy at first sight seems to have fizzled.
There were no startling revelations, nor did Vergès become the hero
of the courtroom drama despite the calculated absence of the defendant. In his closing statement Paul Vuillard, one of the attorneys representing the civil parties in the case, had this to say about Vergès'
threat of revelations: "It was all pure bluff."

And bluff it surely was. Still the contradictions between Jewish
memory and resistance memory were real, even if they were soft-
pedaled during the trial. Vergès successfully exploited this one issue,
taking advantage of long-standing differences between two socially
and historically distinct forms of memory, differences that had already
come out in the debate over the definition of crimes against humanity.
During a hearing on 1 July, for example, Michel Zaoui, representing
the Federation of Jewish Societies, interrupted the closing statement
of Nabil Bouaïta, an Algerian attorney who was attempting to draw
a parallel between Nazi and Israeli policies. Zaoui denounced this line
of argument as intolerable and announced that he intended to offer a
rebuttal. He was then challenged by Eric La Phuong, attorney for a
resistance group known as Ceux de la Libération, another civil party
in the case: "The defense is free. You, ladies and gentlemen of the
jury, are its only possible censors."[81] But earlier, in another hearing
on 23 June, Henri Noguères, attorney for the Ligue des Droits de
l'Homme, historian, and spokesman for the resistance groups, had
issued a warning to Vergès: "If Barbie's attorney attempts in his closing statement to reiterate or elaborate the grave allegations for which
he has been condemned [specifically, unsubstantiated charges against
former résistants and having to do with Moulin's arrest], if he attempts to raise this issue yet again by availing himself of the latitude
allowed the defense attorney, I shall feel compelled to ask the court
for permission to rectify his allegations as I deem necessary."[82] Alain
Finkielkraut asks: "Why was it legitimate for Noguères to interrupt
on behalf of the résistants if it was a sacrilege for Zaoui to avail himself of the same right on behalf of the Jews? How is this double standard to be explained?"[83] The surprising tactical alliances between

some resistance lawyers and the attorney for the defense probably had less to do with anti-Zionist attitudes than with the actual situation in which they found themselves: for diametrically opposed reasons, both Vergès and the resistance lawyers wanted the Resistance to figure in the debate, and to that end the Moulin affair served as a useful instrument. In a similar way, the same attorneys hailed the decision of the appellate court. Vergès was engaged in a diversionary maneuver, a tactic that proved not altogether successful. Meanwhile the Resistance (and not just those of Barbie's victims who happened to be résistants) regained a central role in the trial, a place many believed it deserved on historical grounds and regardless of subtle legal distinctions between crimes.

In this respect, then, the Barbie trial marked a turning point in the memory of the Resistance. It showed how crucial that memory had become to representations of World War II. In the years leading up to the trial, moreover, the memory of the Resistance had been the target of systematic attacks, not always well founded or high-minded and often distorted by ideology. Vergès' attacks, for example, had drawn heavily on Claude Bal's television film *Que la vérité est amère*, which accused certain members of the Resistance of having betrayed Moulin, thus following the lead of René Hardy, the man long suspected of having fingered Moulin for Barbie. There had been attacks on the Communist Party for its role in the Resistance in another film, *Des terroristes à la retraite*, in June 1985. There had been attacks by Alexandre de Marenches, who in September 1986 claimed to have found "unpublished Gestapo archives" documenting the treachery of "certain illustrious resistance fighters."[84] And many others. Clearly it was as if someone during this period had been trying to blow the lid off the "secrets of the Resistance." As a result, former résistants found themselves in the same situation as survivors of the genocide. About to become a part of history, they were faced with a need to put things in perspective and restore reality to what had become a myth.

The uproar that greeted the publication of Daniel Cordier's book on Jean Moulin in 1989 (after the Barbie trial, fortunately) is a case in point. But Cordier, unlike others who had written on the subject, was an insider, secretary to Moulin himself, and had authentic documents in his possession. He urged historians to forget about firsthand accounts and turn their attention instead to the files he had assembled. His purpose was not to attack or libel anyone but to re-establish a truth that had long been obscured by the absence of solid documentation. Nevertheless, leading Resistance spokesmen reacted as if they were in a bunker under siege. How dare anyone question the belief that the Resistance had been united behind Moulin and de Gaulle? How dare anyone suggest that some résistants, such as Henri Frenay, had been uncertain about what attitude to take toward Pétain? Yet the facts of the matter had long been fairly well known, despite the absence of documentary evidence.[85]

In his closing statement at the Barbie trial on 18 June, Paul Vuillard, an attorney, former résistant, and onetime public defender of Lyons, resorted to prophecy: "No schism in the French Resistance will take place here; it is an indissoluble monolith (*bloc*), which nothing can destroy."[86] Neither the date, 18 June, nor the choice of words was fortuitous: for had not Clemenceau used the same word, *bloc*, to describe the French Revolution? [In saying "la Révolution est un bloc," Clemenceau meant that the positive achievements of the Revolution could not be separated from such negative aspects as the September massacres and the Terror.] Ironically, contemporary historiography has left what had been the monolith of the Revolution fissured with cracks; no doubt it was this danger that the guardians of the sacred flame were seeking to avoid.

Beyond the polemics and courtroom tactics, however, the Barbie trial was above all an occasion for witnesses to come forward and tell their stories: résistants, survivors of the genocide, people with many different experiences to relate. Surprisingly, and despite the fears voiced prior to the trial, their testimony proved to be the major event. Truche, the prosecutor, preferred to rely on documentary evidence, so the testimony of Barbie's victims had little to do with the conviction, although it gave the trial a dimension all its own. The victims spoke in a place that was not simply a memorial site but a seat of justice, with all the corresponding solemnity. Pent-up feelings were vented as those who had suffered took revenge on history. The witnesses— André Frossard, Lise Lesèvre, Raymond Aubrac, Marie-Claude Vaillant-Couturier, and many others—were the heroes of the trial because they gave, symbolically, faces to the dead, who were on everyone's mind. Alain Finkielkraut remarked: "The Barbie trial delayed that moment, that stroke of midnight, when the victims of Nazism will have ceased to be real and become historical."[87] The observation is apt, even if it makes little sense to deplore, as Finkielkraut does, what is in any case inevitable. Just because the Barbie trial took place at a moment when survivors of the tragedy felt threatened by this process of historicization, the courtroom drama, more than being a "history lesson" or an opportunity to "raise consciousness," served the immediate and down-to-earth purpose of doing justice to the victims. Teaching history and raising consciousness are praiseworthy goals, but other institutions could achieve them as well as the courts. Nothing but a trial could satisfy the victims' need for justice, however. And their statements after the trial made it clear that this was what they felt too, far more than they cared about participating in any educational process.

Thus the Barbie trial confirmed the role of the courts, which had gained prominence in the 1980s. Throughout the decade the courts served as the primary forum for the expression of historical memories—not without ambiguities, as has already been pointed out by many. "What counts," according to Claude Lanzmann, "is not education, which is the teaching of lifeless knowledge. It is transmission, resurrection, abolition of the distance between the past and the present. Trials are not memorials."[88] Furthermore, "if what is at stake is transmission, in the sense of transmitting what actually happened, it was more important to make *Shoah* than to have a trial forty years after the fact."[89] This forthright statement illustrates what became the central issue in the 1980s. The problem could no longer be reduced to a simple incantation: "memory or oblivion." Now that the return of the past was a tangible, readily observable reality as well as a moral necessity, the question became how best to transmit memory: film, trial, or essay? But is it accurate to speak of a competition? *Shoah* was broadcast on French television during the Barbie trial. True, the showing was late at night, whether because of the innate nervousness of television executives or concerns about low ratings, but even the unfortunate choice of hour did not stop millions of people from tuning in. In the statement quoted above, Lanzmann, a filmmaker, is clearly championing his own medium, but he does touch on an important point: his film probably had a far greater impact than the Barbie trial. An image may crystallize representations of the past, but it does so in a specific historical context, one that may be more or less receptive to what the image contains. Furthermore, films do not freeze representations forever. Their presentation of the past is less constraining than that of the courts, which must interpret history in solemn decisions. In the Barbie case, the courts were obliged to give a strict definition of National Socialism, whereas historical truth (and not just the truth of historians) is in its essence relative, changeable, and subject to constant reinterpretation.

Part II

Transmission of the Syndrome

6

VECTORS OF MEMORY

In the previous part I by no means described every resurgence of the past, every scandal or controversy. But the degree to which memories of the Occupation were of concern in France after Vichy can be roughly measured. A glance at the temperature chart (overleaf) is enough to show when the syndrome was at its most severe and when it was in relative remission.

The graph reflects the frequency of crisis situations in which the presence of the past cannot be denied. It measures the intensity of symptoms without attaching more importance to one kind than to another. I have treated literary fashions and films on the same level as political crises, the only criterion for selection being whether or not the Occupation was involved. My aim was to capture the full diversity of "collective memory" by recording all its visible signs.

The purpose of this chapter is to relate the developments charted above to the existence of certain carriers of memory. A nation's memory, part of its common heritage, is shaped by signals emanating from many sources. By "carrier" I mean any source that proposes a deliberate reconstruction of an event for a social purpose. The collective memory of an event is shaped by all representations of that event, whether conscious or unconscious, explicit or implicit. Between individual or family memories and local memory there is a series of mediations; the same is true of group memories in relation to the national memory. At any given time, some of these mediators are more important than others.

Official carriers of memory include ceremonies, monuments, and regular or irregular celebrations organized by national or local governments. Generally these offer a comprehensive, unitary representation of the event, usually the result of compromise among various

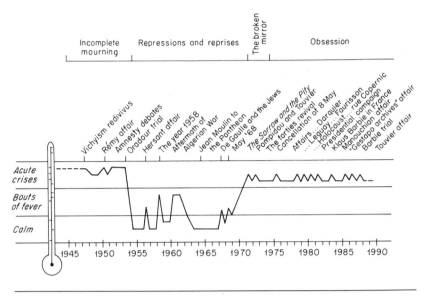

Temperature curve of the syndrome

contending forces. Among these official carriers we should also include the courts, whose central role in shaping the image of the war and the Occupation has been evident throughout.

Organizational carriers of memory include groups of deportees, resistance members, soldiers, STO workers, and others who join organizations for the purpose of preserving and unifying the personal memories of group members. Groups sometimes become attached to a rather static image of the past, which they then promote actively as well as passively.

Cultural carriers of memory operate on a very different level. They express what appear to be highly individualistic views of the past in a variety of media, including literature, film, and television. Usually their message is implicit rather than explicit.

Scholarly carriers of memory reconstruct the facts and propose ways of interpreting them. Looked at in this way, a work of history is a carrier of memory like any other and subject to the same changing influences. Critical detachment is limited. Scholarly works in turn influence textbooks and school curricula, the primary social means by which memory is transmitted from generation to generation.

All these carriers propose and at the same time reflect a given state of the national memory and a particular representation of the event. It is not always possible to determine where the impetus for a given representation originates. At best one can compare how different representations evolve.

I do not propose to examine here all the different memory carriers, each of which has its own history and rules. Instead I shall focus on three representative examples: official commemorations, film, and scholarly research. I shall omit aspects of the story that deserve chapters of their own: literary remembrances of Vichy, for example, or a study of groups other than the ADMP, at which we looked briefly in Chapter 1. Official commemorations have the merit of illustrating otherwise hard-to-grasp aspects of the syndrome, whereas film and scholarship serve to illustrate two very different means of transmitting historical memories.

In studying each of these carriers, I have tried not to lose sight of the overall picture embodied in the "temperature chart." The method may at times seem rather circular, since the chart was itself based on an assessment of the importance of some of the same carriers on which I focus here. The comparison is intended only as a heuristic tool. Nevertheless, it seems fair to say that no one mode of representation has predominated since 1945. Indeed, one of the characteristic features of memories of Vichy is their habit of popping up where least expected.

The Silences of Commemoration

On 24 October 1922 the eleventh of November was made a national holiday. Previously, in 1921, legislators had decided that Armistice Day ought to be celebrated on the Sunday following the eleventh, on the grounds that there were already too many nonworking holidays. Under pressure from veterans, however, the government capitulated. As Antoine Prost has skillfully demonstrated, the holiday of the *poilus* thus became a national holiday.[1] To this day it has remained a national holiday, almost as important as the Fourteenth of July (Bastille Day).

Evolution of the commemoration of V-E Day (8 May)

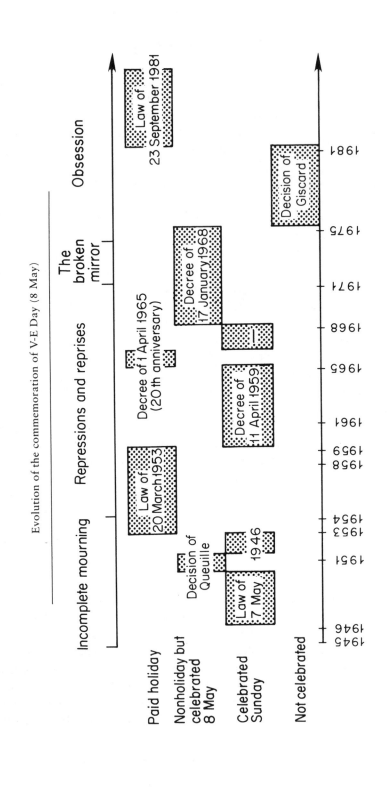

If even a war fought under the banner of *union sacrée* could pose problems of commemoration, it was inevitable that the commemoration of World War II would run into even greater obstacles. Robert Frank has given a good account of the many forms this elusive commemoration has taken,[2] and I summarize it in the accompanying chart.

The law of 7 May 1946 established the day for "commemoration of the victory won by the French and Allied armies" (note the hierarchy of victors) as the eighth of May if it should happen to fall on a Sunday, otherwise on the following Sunday.[3] In other words, no additional nonworking holiday was to be added to the calendar, an addition that would of course have given the celebration greater impact. This law was fairly faithfully observed until 1953, although in 1951 Henri Queuille, minister of the interior, gave in to pressure from veterans' and resistance groups and agreed to hold ceremonies on the eighth even though it fell on a Tuesday.[4]

The law of 20 March 1953 marked a first change in the holiday's status. This law, which remained in force until 1959, stated that "the French Republic celebrates the armistice annually" and that the eighth of May would be an official holiday.[5] The use of the term "armistice" rather than "surrender" is a revealing slip; it suggests either the armistice of 11 November and thus the uncontroversial victory of 1918 or else the "armistice" of June 1940. The confusion was not uncommon: an armistice is a suspension of hostility between two states and is signed by governments; an unconditional surrender is a military capitulation signed by field commanders. The surrender of the German army took place in Eisenhower's headquarters at Rheims on 7 May. It was ratified in Berlin on the night of 8–9 May. Oddly enough, the choice of 8 May as V-E Day did not coincide precisely with either event. It was the result of a decision by the western Allies and contrary to the wishes of Stalin, who preferred 9 May.[6]

In 1959 Charles de Gaulle canceled the holiday, and until 1968 the end of the war was commemorated on the second Sunday in May (except for the twentieth anniversary, which was celebrated on 8 May 1965). After 1968, pressure from veterans' groups again secured government approval for a celebration on 8 May at the end of the day, an arrangement that lasted until 1975. De Gaulle acted as he did in part because of his misgivings about veterans' organizations, which also led him to cancel veterans' pensions for a brief period (see Chapter 2), and in part because he did not want to increase the number of holidays to the detriment of business activity.[7]

It is important to note that commemoration ceremonies did not become more elaborate during the period of Gaullist "resistancialism." Maintaining the myth went hand in hand with a certain silence about the events of 1939–1945. After 1968, however, the status of the commemoration was clearly at odds with the revival of interest in the war and the many questions that arose about the wartime years. The younger generation, more interested in learning about the past than in celebrating it, was largely indifferent to the absence of pomp. After May '68, however, new questions came to the fore at a time when Jewish memories of the deportation were reawakening, a phenomenon that was soon followed by a marked upturn in commemorations of the Resistance.

As a result, Valéry Giscard d'Estaing's blunt decision simply to cancel all commemoration of the war's end was perceived as an outright attack. The decision was made in 1975, just as the Vichy syndrome was entering its obsessional phase, and its effect was precisely the opposite of what was intended: it revived old controversies. Yet it was consistent with the way in which V-E Day had been treated from the beginning, namely, with neglect.

Finally, with the passage of a new law on 23 September 1981, the government of Pierre Mauroy reinstated 8 May as a national holiday. This decision met with widespread approval, and it was not rescinded by the right when it returned to power from 1986 to 1988.

Except for this final period, the status of V-E Day seems for the most part to have been out of phase with the mood of the public. Each time public interest in the dark years revived (in the late 1940s, between 1958 and 1962, and after 1974), the government tried to limit commemoration of the war's end. By contrast, V-E Day was an official holiday in the period 1953–1959, when interest in the wartime years stood at a relatively low level. I do not say that there was any causal relationship, but it is tempting to view the status of V-E Day as a sign: when old memories were reawakened, there was a desire to counterbalance them by playing down the commemoration ceremonies.

Official ceremonies were never able to dispel the ambiguities inherent in the commemoration of V-E Day or, for that matter, of other aspects of the war. When an event is so heterogeneous, can any single, ecumenical, national date obscure that fact? What would it mean to celebrate V-E Day in ceremonies based on the remembrance of Armistice Day? What dead would be honored in the minute of silence? The martyrs of the Resistance and soldiers killed on the field of battle? Of course, as banners and medals attest. The victims of the concentration camps? Obviously, as the participation of survivors' organizations would indicate, although the victims being honored included all who were deported, not those specifically designated by the Final Solution. And what about all the others? The civilians killed in bombing raids (by both the Allies and the Germans)? The hostages who had not participated in the Resistance themselves but who had been executed in reprisal? Those who had been denounced by their neighbors, rounded up by the Vichy police, and tortured by the Milice? And then of course there were the French men and women who had joined the other side, the 10,000 collaborators and others who were "summarily purged" (executed) at the end of the Occupation.

Individuals always remembered their loved ones, regardless of which uniform they wore and no matter how they died. But the celebration of V-E Day was of no help in forgetting acts committed by people still alive, any more than it was capable of rendering martyrs equal in death. Two facts attest to this incapacity. First, the celebration of the end of World War II was often obscured by other celebrations: the feast day of Joan of Arc falls around the same time, and celebration of victory in World War II was often combined with celebration of the end of World War I, as in the great Gaullist fête of 11 November 1945.[8] Second, V-E Day was often neglected in favor of other occasions: 18 June, the liberation of Paris, or the anniversary of some major resistance battle or of the death of a local martyr.

Robert Frank puts it aptly: "What is sadly memorable is not easily commemorable."[9] The silences of 8 May are too oppressive, too present, to be covered up by a symbolic ritual, especially one whose status has changed so frequently. Unlike the Great War, World War II as historical entity cannot by its very nature be an object of commemoration in France. This impossibility is part of the reason why the past has "spontaneously" come back to life outside the official institutional settings. The persistence of the Vichy syndrome is the most striking sign of the failure of official memory.

The Dark Years and the Silver Screen

Film has played a particularly important role in the transmission of memory. Mass entertainment since the 1930s, the movies are a significant indicator of contemporary attitudes. During the war itself, moreover, film exerted a powerful influence on people's minds. Newsreels and propaganda films were an important source of information. Drama and other nondocumentary films enjoyed immense popularity during the Occupation as a form of escape. In June 1940, while German tanks were rolling over France, more than 800,000 people found time to go to the movies.[10] It is hardly surprising, then, that

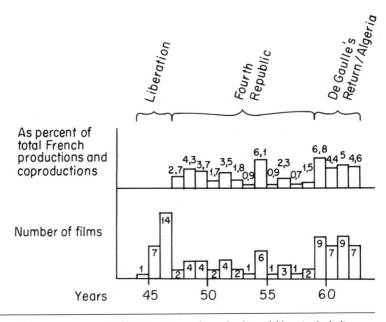

World War II in French film (see Appendix 2 for list of films included)

people who lived through the events should have sought to recapture the experience in movie theaters after the war. Furthermore, film sometimes proved better than other media at capturing the repressed and the ineffable, owing in part to the immediate impact of archival footage, in part to film's power, however imperfect, to reconstruct an era. Two striking examples of that power are of course *The Sorrow and the Pity* and *Shoah*.

Still World War II inspired few films and even fewer filmmakers. Between 1944 and 1986 only two hundred French-produced or co-produced films took the Occupation, the war, or the Resistance as their central theme or used the period as a dramatic setting. Even in periods when wartime films were at a peak, they never accounted for more than 7 percent of total French production, at most a dozen films per year. In forty years France has produced fewer films about the war than were made during the four years of the Occupation. More than twice as many foreign (mostly English and American) films on

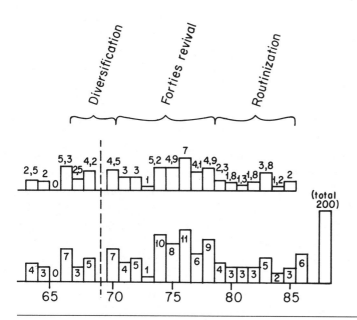

(1944–1969 figures are for calendar year; 1969–1986 figures are for film season, August–August)

the subject have been distributed in France. The figure shows the variation in French film output over time.[11] When we look at the content of these films, it becomes clear that the production of films about the wartime years evolved through several phases.

The Liberation

The period from the Liberation to the end of 1946 is exceptional in every respect. Twenty-two films were produced in a little over two years. Nearly half were documentary montages produced with the aid of the army (*Fils de France* by Pierre Blondy and *Caravane blindée* by the Army Film Service, 1946), the Resistance (*La Bataille du rail* by René Clément, 1946), or the Allied governments (*Présence au combat* by M. Cravenne, 1946). Of this total, fourteen films focused primarily on the Resistance, the remainder on the war. *Le Père tranquille* by René Clément (one of the period's most inspired directors) was probably the most notable film of the moment. Although it honors the achievements of resistance fighters, it does not embrace the resistancialist mythology. The guerrilla war is portrayed as a difficult feat, more a daily struggle than an epic conquest. The hero is no misfit but a good family man whose commitment to the struggle disrupts his family life. And when obliged to execute an informer he seems less a vigilante than a citizen, tormented by an act he is forced to commit.

The Discretion of the Fourth Republic

Not only were fewer films produced in the period from 1947 to 1958, but those that were made had none of the historical realism of the earlier phase. In eleven years barely thirty films were produced. War films such as Georges Péclet's *Le Grand Cirque* (1950) and resistance films such as Titus Vibe-Muller's *La Bataille de l'eau lourde* (1949) still predominated. Austere, lyrical works such as Jean-Pierre Melville's *Le Silence de la mer* (1949) were relatively rare. According to Jean-Pierre Jeancolas, films made during the Fourth Republic were notable primarily for their treatment of everyday life, for showing how the majority of French people lived during the dark times. The masterpiece in this genre was Claude Autant-Lara's *La Traversée de Paris* (1956), which created what has since become the hackneyed (if often accurate) image of a nation preoccupied with its own survival and more intent on killing hogs than Germans. In its own way the film tossed the first brickbats at the nascent myth of the Resistance. As Jacques Siclier noted, "Autant-Lara 'bit the bullet' at a time when Robert Bresson was striking a proud and tragic pose in *Un Condamné à mort s'est échappé*, a 1956 film that turns the escape of a partisan into a spiritual adventure."[12]

Significantly, however, the first allusions to more delicate subjects began to appear. Although collaboration, Vichy, and fascism still have no political status and are rarely mentioned except by allusion, the collabo has become a familiar, even commonplace, figure in such films as Clément's *Les Maudits* (1947), Henri-Georges Clouzot's *Manon* (1948), André Cayatte's *Les Amants de Vérone* (1949), and Autant-Lara's *Le Bon Dieu sans confession* (1954).

Only one film, André Berthomieu's *Le Bal des pompiers* (1948), chose to show directly a family divided by the Occupation. For some critics this was an "ignoble" film, but Siclier called it "emptyheaded and edifying."

Although the deportation was largely a taboo subject during this period, it did inspire a few filmmakers, such as Dréville, Clouzot, Cayatte, and Lampin in *Retour à la vie* (1949) and above all Alain Resnais, who shot his very famous *Nuit et brouillard* (Night and Fog) in 1956. This short subject was based on a script by Jean Cayrol and produced with the cooperation of the Comité d'Histoire de la Deuxième Guerre Mondiale. Unlike *Shoah*, Lanzmann's film of thirty years later, Resnais focused more on the deportation of resistance fighters and political prisoners than on deportation for racial reasons. François Truffaut's reaction is interesting:

> *Night and Fog* is a sublime film about which it is difficult to speak. Any adjective, any aesthetic judgment would be out of place in speaking of this work, which is not an "indictment" or a "poem" but a "meditation" on the deportation. The film's impact lies entirely in the tone adopted by the filmmakers: a terrifying mildness. You leave the theater feeling "devastated" and not very happy with yourself.[13]

Perhaps the film was too sublime, too isolated, and surely too far ahead of its time. Selected for the Cannes Film Festival in 1956, the film ran afoul of the censors. Resnais was forced to remove an of-fending gendarme's *képi*, which appeared in a shot of the transit camp at Pithiviers, a camp set up by the Germans but administered by the French. The censors thus obliterated not the filmmaker's words or images but an actual historical detail, an incontestable fact. The fact that an official historical agency was involved in the production of the film made no difference. Ultimately the film was shown outside the festival in the wake of diplomatic pressure from the West German embassy and the French foreign ministry.

The Reawakening: 1958–1962

De Gaulle's return to power served as a stimulus to the imagination. More than thirty films were made between 1958 and 1962, as many as over the previous eleven years; these accounted for 4 to 7 percent of total French film output, compared to around 1 percent for the previous period. Unsurprisingly, the Resistance was portrayed in more "Gaullist" and military colors: in addition to Christian-Jaque's *Babette s'en va-t-en guerre* (1959), which combined the period's two living myths, Brigitte Bardot and General de Gaulle, other notable films included Dréville's *Normandie-Niémen* (1960) and Denys de la Patellière's *Un Taxi pour Tobrouk* (1961).

This same period also witnessed the emergence of the antihero, the countermodel who was reassuring because he stood in closer prox-imity to the public than did the august figure of de Gaulle. Compared with Reggiani, Frankeur, Blier, and Ventura, the somber heroes of Julien Duvivier's *Marie Octobre* (1959), Fernandel rather stands out in Henri Verneuil's *La Vache et le prisonnier* (also 1959). The prisoner of war, that most un-Gaullist figure, figured in any number of films: André Cayatte's *Le Passage du Rhin* (1959), Jean Renoir's *Le Caporal épinglé* (1962), and Alex Joffé's *Les Culottes rouges* (1962). A few films attempted to explore other shadowy subjects: J. Kerchbron's *Vacances en enfer* (1961) dealt with a milicien who deserts in the company of a young woman, much as in Modiano and Malle's *Lacombe Lucien,* while Jean Dewewer's *Les Honneurs de la guerre* (1962) bucked the tide (and flopped at the box office) by stressing the hazard of circumstance rather than opportune heroism. Armand Gatti's *Enclos* (1961) was perhaps the only film set in a concentration camp. Finally, Jacques Doniol-Valcroze's *La Dénonciation* (1962) and Alain Resnais' *Muriel* (1963) were among the few films of this period to draw an explicit parallel between the struggles of the Occupation and those connected with the Algerian War.

Perhaps another film, seemingly unrelated to the 1940s, ought to be added to the list: Yves Robert's *La Guerre des boutons,* which came out in 1961. Based on a novel by Louis Pergaud first published in 1912, the story is more a child's fable than an account of the *guerre franco-française.* And yet even in Pergaud's original book, politics was not entirely absent from the rivalry between the two villages: "For the people of Velrans were churchgoers, while those of Longeverne were reds."[14] Transposed into postwar France, the story is redolent of the atmosphere of the troubled years. In Robert's film, the general, Lebrac, resembles a partisan chief. The traitor, Bacaillé, the only character in the film who wears a cape and Basque beret, is the very image of a man who would denounce his neighbors. To top it off, he is the victim, in the film's harshest scene, of a rather brutal purge. The Aztec—the enemy—arrives one day in a terrifying "armored vehicle" (a brand new tractor), a veritable deluge of iron that surprises the people of Longeverne as they celebrate victory. The more naive villagers, having made a heroic cavalry charge against the enemy (in the finest traditions of the French military academy at Saint Cyr), believe that they are safe in their entrenched camp. There is, moreover, an extraordinary rapport between generations: the sons go off to war as their fathers did before them and as their children will do after them, to fight the hereditary enemy. All of this takes place in a rural world that has not quite entered the technological era or abandoned the Pétainist harrow. If Pergaud's novel is an archetype of internal struggle in France, set against the background of the Commune, the struggle between church and state over education, and the birth of the Republic, Robert's film embodies perhaps the only possible screen treatment of that novel fifty years after it was written, and after Vichy.

Diversification in the Sixties

Interest in World War II continued in the period 1963–1970, although no clear trend can be discerned. It might seem almost as if a balance had been struck among various possible ways of dealing with the past. To be sure, René Clément's *Is Paris Burning?* (1966) struck a pompous and false note. The film's opening in Paris on 24 October was the occasion for a street demonstration, military parades, and, despite the heavy rain that fell on the capital that night, a sound-and-light show.

A purer, more faithful portrayal of a Free French resistance network could be seen, however, in Jean-Pierre Melville's *L'Armée des ombres* (1969). Oddly enough, the film contains no trace of May '68 or of de Gaulle's departure from office. It treats the careers of a few exceptional but easily comprehensible individuals and with its excellent screenplay and discreet (but already anachronistic) Gaullism might well have crystallized a certain view of the era. But, beyond arriving on the scene too late, the film showed too much of the actual diversity of temperaments and types and was therefore incompatible with the abstract and timeless idea of "Resistance" honored by de Gaulle and Malraux. Too much concerned with individual fates, the film lacked political punch.

For that very reason, Melville's masterpiece, which appeared five years after the Pantheonization of Jean Moulin, marked a turning point. It ended all possibility that a film would ever be made that might serve as foundation for the myth of the Resistance. Soon Ophuls' *The Sorrow and the Pity*, which was shot at about the same time, would make it pointless even to think of such a thing. For different reasons neither Clément nor Melville had the makings of a great "official filmmaker" on the model of Eisenstein.

A significant fact about this period is that the Occupation and the war lost their special status and became suitable backgrounds for ever more numerous light comedies, such as Jean-Paul Rappeneau's *La Vie de château* (1966) and above all the smash hit *La Grande Vadrouille* by Gérard Oury (1966), probably the only film to have made the children of parents who survived the short rations of the 1940s regret that they had not been born before the end of the war.

Thus in the late 1960s the French cinema presented a variety of reassuring images of the war years, images from which the occasional dark memory was not excluded. It is misleading to say that Gaullism offered a monolithic image of the period. Film in the Gaullist years drew on many different sources of inspiration, although the government, with its own preferences, encouraged some and discouraged others.

The Forties Revival

The release of *The Sorrow and the Pity* in April 1971 marked the beginning of a new phase, which took two more years to build up steam. Between 1974 and 1978 the number of films devoted to or inspired by World War II increased sharply. Some forty-five films were shot in this period, more than during the entire previous decade. The eleven films made in 1976 alone accounted for 7 percent of France's total film output that year, as high a proportion as in 1946. No doubt about it: the "breaking of the mirror" had an impact on French cinema. Many of these films dealt directly with the Occupation as subject, moreover, and not merely as background.

Still we must be careful not to overstate the importance of the forties revival. Although the vogue for the past did plunge French movie-goers into the thick of the Occupation, it also conveyed a variety of messages in a range of genres. (In Chapter 3 we saw that the same held true in literature.)

Apart from *The Sorrow and the Pity,* which stands in a category all its own because it directly or indirectly inspired so many subsequent films, four genres may be singled out:

Prosecutors. There were not many of these, but they caused a considerable stir. Following the lead of *The Sorrow and the Pity,* they sought to discredit Vichy, collaboration, and Nazism generally. Some of the films in this category were documentaries: Harris and Sédouy's *Français si vous saviez* (1973), Jérôme Kanapa's *La République est morte à Dien Bien Phu* (1974), which was only partially concerned with the Occupation, Marc Hillel's *Au nom de la race* (1975), and André Halimi's *Chantons sous l'Occupation* (1976). Others were historical reconstructions: Costa-Gavras' *Section spéciale* (1975) and Frank Cassenti's *L'Affiche rouge* (released in November 1976). Another film in this vein was Jean Yanne's *Les Chinois à Paris* (1973), whose message, though simplistic, was of the same order. However zealous or moderate, all these prosecutorial films called attention to virtually unknown aspects of the period, from Vichy's special tribunals, presided over by genuine magistrates, to resistance groups composed of immigrants. All partook of a certain self-flagellatory mood in the country, with the French generally portrayed as cowards if not outright fascists. Yet all gave prominence—in some cases systematic prominence—to previously neglected historical realities.

Chroniclers. These filmmakers attempted to capture the atmosphere of the Occupation in a realist vein shot through with personal memories. Examples of the genre include Pierre Granier-Defferre's *Le Train* (1973), Michel Drach's *Les Violons du bal* (1974), Edouard Molinaro's *L'Ironie du sort*, Michel Mitrani's *Les Guichets du Louvre* (1974), André Téchiné's *Souvenirs d'en France*, Jacques Doillon's *Un Sac de billes* (1975), René Féret's *La Communion solennelle* (1977), and many others. The Occupation is not the only subject of all these films, but all do touch on it, more with nostalgia than with revulsion. In most cases Jewish memories and commemoration of the genocide play a central, almost obsessive, and again rather systematic role.

Aesthetes. Some filmmakers distinguished themselves by flirting with scandal. Perhaps the most notorious of the group was Louis Malle, whose 1974 film *Lacombe Lucien,* based on a screenplay by Patrick Modiano, was considered heretical at the time. In hindsight it is not difficult to see what seemed so shocking. What was problematic about the film was its philosophy: whereas previous films had portrayed the period as a conflict between good and evil, Malle created a murky, ambiguous atmosphere by following the uncertain fortunes of a young French aide to the Gestapo, a character who, of all the types of French collaborationists, is the most difficult to understand and the hardest to excuse because it is unmotivated by ideological misconception. He flirts for a while with joining the Resistance only to sign up ultimately with the Gestapo, not out of political conviction but because he likes to fight, thirsts for action, and is drawn to the violence in the air. The film came out at a time when the French public was just beginning to rediscover the fact that France had produced its own ideologically committed fascists. Hence at least some moviegoers probably expected the film to contain analysis or indictment and were surprised to find it silent on the political aspect of Lucien's engagement while implying that commitment to the Resistance stemmed from similar motives. Caught up in the logic of Modiano's story, Malle turned his back on history, as he had every right to do, even if he sometimes played with rather too heavy a hand on sensitivities of which he was perfectly well aware. His film is therefore more provocative than thought-provoking. With the benefit of hindsight, however, it is clear that this film altered the simplistic image of the 1940s as much as, and perhaps more subtly than, *The Sorrow and the Pity*.

Under this same head one can also place several other films of varying quality but similar in their fascination with Nazism and the Occupation: Liliana Cavanni's *Portier de nuit* (1974), Claude Lelouch's *Les Bons et les méchants* (1976), Christian Gion's *One two two* (1978), a harbinger of the genre's exhaustion. On an altogether higher plane, Joseph Losey's *Monsieur Klein* (1976) is probably the strongest allegorical treatment of the Occupation's destructive effects on body and spirit.

Opportunists. Generally mediocre, these films use the Occupation setting in pat and formulaic ways. Included in this category is an endless succession of war films such as Robert Lamoureux's *Mais où est donc passée la 7e compagnie?* (1973), *Opération Lady Marlène* and *On a retrouvé la 7e compagnie* (1975); Jacques Besnard's *Le Jour de gloire* (1976); and Philippe Clair's *La 7e compagnie au clair de lune* (1977)—a film a year until interest shifted from World War II to peacetime maneuvers. There was also a series of pornographic films, inaugurated (unwittingly) by Lilianna Cavanni's *Portier de Nuit*: Guy Pérol's *Le Commando des chauds lapins* (1975), James Gartner's *Train spécial pour SS* (1977), Mark Stern's *Elsa Fraulein SS* (1977), and José Benazéraf's *Bordel SS* (1978). The picture of the Occupation in these films is perforce limited, but it shows that interest in the subject cut across all genres: this breadth was part of what sustained the forties revival.

Endlessly scrutinized, reworked, and even eroticized, the Occupation became familiar to people of all generations in the France of the 1970s. It was a frequent object of reference and a constant presence.

The 1980s: Normalization?

From 1978 to 1987 the tide seemed to be ebbing, but after the Barbie trial in May 1987 the subject of World War II came back in vogue. It is now a "classic" subject, a regular fixture of the cinema. Fourteen films about the wartime years were released between August 1987 and December 1989. The stark opposition between resistance and collaboration gave way to a more complex view; it was now possible to show a more complete image of the past, without the political manichaeanism and mythologizing of past years. As a result, the cinema ceased to be the great violator of taboos (with a few notable exceptions). What matters during this period is not so much the quantity as the importance of certain films (as judged by a historian, not a film critic), in particular those films that indicate a significant evolution in popular ideas and attitudes.

François Truffaut's *Le Dernier Métro* (1980) gives an accurate, balanced picture of the time, a sort of consensus view, and as such it was acclaimed by the critics. Significantly, the film's reputation rests not so much on its subject—a theater in occupied Paris and the people associated with it—as on its inherent qualities as film. What interested the critics was a new film by a noted director, not a new film about the Occupation, a sign that scandal was no longer in vogue. Contrast this situation with that of a decade earlier, when the qualities of a film like *Lacombe Lucien* were all but overshadowed by the choice of subject.

Jean-Marie Poiré's *Papy fait de la Résistance* (1982) suggested a different sort of evolution. Though hardly a masterpiece, the film was as iconoclastic as anyone could wish: a very French family steadfastly resists the invader. A German who happens to be a poet (a caricature of the officer in *Silence de la mer*), a collaborationist concierge, a pontificating Gaullist, and a reluctant résistant disport themselves in this unpretentious farce, whose target is not so much the Resistance as its sacred images, particularly those so often seen in French films over the previous forty years. The film respectfully thumbs its nose at Melville, Clément, Oury, and others. Willy Holt, the film's designer, was a man of much experience in the genre, having worked previously on such films as *Is Paris Burning?* More important, *Papy* was probably the first film about the Occupation that never once touched on the period's tragic dimension, that made no concession to the "context," that showed no respect for anybody or anything. The comic masterpiece *La Grande Vadrouille,* on which *Papy* was modeled, adopted an attitude of instinctive humility whenever it touched on a hero or martyr. *Papy* did no such thing. Significantly, this irritating bit of fluff aroused no protest. In 1973 Jean Yanne's heavily allegorical *Les Chinois à Paris* had unleashed passions and drawn howls of protest from former résistants outraged by its portrayal of the French as cowardly and ridiculous. Ten years later, no criticism of this sort was heard, unless it was from the Communists, who rather clumsily denounced the film's "irresponsibility," or *Le Matin de Paris*, which saw nothing but "imbecility."[15]

It is striking, moreover, to measure the distance traveled by Louis Malle between *Lacombe Lucien* and *Au Revoir les enfants* (1987). Acclaimed by all the critics, the latter film won seven Caesars in 1988 and appealed to a wide audience. Suddenly Malle had ceased to be the provocative director who had made *Lacombe Lucien* and *Murmur of the Heart*. He was now the director of a film that spoke to the concerns raised by the Barbie trial and the fate of the children of Izieu, whose disappearance was related, however remotely, to the incident that inspired the film. In any case, the quality of the film derives less from its moving depiction of the fate of a Jewish child as seen through the eyes of an "Aryan" classmate than from its unblinking and unsentimental depiction of adolescence. Here again, as in the Truffaut film, the setting lends substance to the story without overwhelming it. Of course the subject lent itself to such treatment, but the film can also be seen as yet another sign of the "normalization" of the Occupation as a theme, which made it possible to view works of art as art rather than as didactic lessons in history. Privately, however, Malle apparently prefers *Lacombe Lucien,* a film that was ahead of its time, whereas *Au Revoir les enfants* reflected the prevailing atmosphere.[16]

In broad terms, then, the films of the 1980s abandoned the militancy, didacticism, and criticism of the forties revival. The Occupation had become a subject of adult films for an adult public. Even documentary films evolved along similar lines. Although documentary by definition is historical and educational, newer films in the genre were less schematic than earlier ones.

Claude Lanzmann's *Shoah* (1985) and, to a lesser degree, Marcel Ophuls' *Hôtel Terminus* (1988) illustrate the point. *Shoah* is undeniably a great work, and though hardly without faults it has become something of a sacred cow for critics: "This is a work that insists on introspection . . . It belongs not to the realm of entertainment but to that of ritual."[17] Highly original, the film uses no archival footage and is based entirely on eyewitness accounts. What is so striking is the choice of subject: the genocide not as historical phenomenon but as survival in the present, as a density of images in the minds of survivors and spectators alike. *Shoah* is thus a fine illustration of the conflicts that may arise between history and memory, between a scientific reconstruction of the past, which erects the facts into a hierarchy, stands aloof, and risks losing sight of individuals and hardening into an abstraction, and a "re-creation" with a moral purpose: to bring back the dead, to whom survivors lend their voices and their presence, thus abolishing the apparently irreducible distance between past and present. To be sure, *Shoah* offers a subjective view of history, in ways that are not always made explicit. Why attach such importance to Polish antisemitism rather than to the antisemitism of other countries, such as France, that participated more or less voluntarily in the Final Solution? What historical link is there between the undeniable antisemitism of the Poles and the location of Nazi death camps in Poland (occupied and partly annexed by the Third Reich)? Is there any reason to think that, if the Poles had not been antisemitic, they could have done any more than anyone else to stop the slaughter? These judgments are implicit in the editing and structure of the film. It makes no difference that all the words are spoken by actual participants in the drama: victims, torturers, and "others." Yet the force of the film lies precisely in its subjectivity, in the filmmaker's avowed partiality. The significance of the film would have been lost if it had tried to be "historical," which is to say didactic and impartial. But this is why it is so absurd to insist that this is the only way in which the genocide should be represented. True, Lanzmann did succeed, as he claimed often enough, in doing what few professional historians had done. He demonstrated that the unnameable was not necessarily ineffable. He showed that one could touch the conscience of a generation too young to have lived through the war. And he proved that it was by no means impossible to think about Auschwitz, indeed that to do so would be among the most important tasks of the late twentieth century. The film was powerful because it gave voice to people who, rightly or wrongly, felt they were being excluded from history.

Survivors, beleaguered by the negationists, were also troubled in a different way by the proliferation of scholarly works on the genocide. In this respect Simone Veil's attitude is typical. On numerous occasions, for example during a conference organized by the Institut d'Histoire du Temps Présent in December 1987, she stated that the historian's point of view was in almost every way incompatible with the survivor's point of view. (Since then she has moderated her position somewhat.) In addition, *Shoah* was well attuned to the reawakening of Jewish memory and to the obsessional phase of the syndrome (1970–1980). The film played something of the same role that *The Sorrow and the Pity* had played with respect to the Occupation, although its manner and tone were of course quite different. Hence *Shoah* remains an essential key to understanding the representations of the 1980s.

Marcel Ophuls' *Hôtel Terminus* (1988), a film about the career of Klaus Barbie, his work for U.S. intelligence, and the early stages of his trial, had less of an impact than *Shoah* despite Ophuls' talent as a director. The film failed to find an audience. The work was probably less well attuned than *Shoah* to what the audience of the eighties was looking for, and its style was familiar from Ophuls' earlier work. Furthermore, the film was inevitably overshadowed by the trial itself. Yet it is one of the few recent works to continue along lines first laid down in the 1970s, at a time when most others have taken a "deconstructive" stance for political and didactic ends.

Earlier François Garçon wrote: "The 1980s are no longer the time for inner conflict or for rummaging in the recent and nauseating past."[18] One question remains, however: what connection is there, finally, between cinematic representation and collective memory? How is the syndrome related to the developments described above?

During the Fourth Republic, few films dealing with the Occupation were made, but this lack of interest in the subject hardly reflects what was going on in the world of politics, nor does it correspond to the turmoil evident in public opinion through 1954. To judge solely by the movies, moreover, it would be hard to identify the end of the Fourth Republic as a turning point. Filmmakers seem to have hung back, remaining silent and avoiding the subject. Film thus made little contribution to the creation of myths about the war and instead was content with ratifying the status quo.

The shift that occurred between 1958 and 1962 came about in a period of turmoil stemming primarily from the Algerian conflict. The intention of the movies, however, seems to have been to put a damper on the passions born of civil war: the majority of films, whatever reservations they may have expressed, celebrated an ecumenical and benevolent version of Gaullism. Over the next few years the cinema reflected the dearth of events likely to bring up memories of the past and celebrated the Gaullist myth of the Resistance; the first signs of a trivialization of the subject can also be seen.

May '68 did little to change this state of affairs, although it had a kind of delayed action in the work of Ophuls. Earlier in this book I counted Ophuls among the factors contributing to the upheavals of the 1970s, but as a strictly cinematic phenomenon his work should be viewed as a product of the 1960s. For the first time, some film-makers broke with the conformism of their peers to anticipate, and even to help bring about, a change in people's attitudes. But only a few films may be credited with such prescience. Thereafter it became fashionable to take a critical view of the past, and many people followed the lead of the pioneers, so that by the 1970s film was playing a fundamental role in stirring up old memories.

In sum, film in the 1980s evolved in two directions. In the first place, the Occupation shed its sulfurous aura. Most films dealing with the period reflected the popular view. The last taboos evaporated, and the wartime years ceased to be a subject of scandal. It became easier for filmmakers to produce individual statements about the period without fear that wartime memories would overwhelm artistic intent. Second, film no longer played the role of harbinger of the future. The obsessions of the 1980s were first expressed elsewhere, primarily in the courts, and only later transferred to the screen. It should come as no surprise that memories of the Jewish genocide were a dominant and recurring theme, not only in *Shoah* and *Au Revoir les enfants* but also in Frank Cassenti's *Le Testament d'un poète juif assassiné* (1988) and Bernard Cohn's *Natalia* (1989).

Film in the whole period only rarely anticipated changes in people's attitudes. The movies were, however, the clearest and most influential expression of broader changes; they were able, unlike most works of history or even novels, to make events remote in time seem suddenly close. Film revived the past and stirred memory using the same instrument that we use today to experience history in the making: the image. But of course the use of images entails risks of distortion and therefore anachronism.

Scholarly Memory

If few films were made about the period, thousands of books, papers, and articles were written, reflecting a variety of genres, styles, and shades of opinion. From this enormous volume of material I have attempted to pick out scholarly works, that is, works based on careful research and substantiated by various kinds of documentary evidence—"history books," in short. Instead of attempting an exhaustive selection, I have chosen works representative of certain lines or tendencies of thought concerning the history of the Occupation.

It would, however, be naive of a historian to suppose that scholarly views of history are somehow autonomous or clearly delineated. In this case it was difficult to confine attention strictly to texts written by historians, academics, and journalists because important light has been shed on the period not only by such secondary works but also by eyewitness accounts—even if some eyewitness testimony has only added to the confusion. The historiography of the Occupation (where historiography is broadly understood to include not only works of history per se but also memoirs and autobiographies) evolved along with the Vichy syndrome. This parallel is all the more interesting since the influence of scholarly work has thus far not figured in my analysis.

The Foundations

From the Liberation until 1954 the leading figures of the Franco-French civil war dominated the publishing scene with their cacophonous voices. Although top leaders rarely spoke out, slightly less prominent personalities were quick to take up their pens. On the Resistance side, for example, we have Pierre Guillain de Bénouville's *Le Sacrifice du matin* (1946) and Yves Farge's *Rebelles, soldats et citoyens* (1946), to name only two titles from a long list (many of which were mentioned in Chapter 1).

On the Vichy side we find works such as Louis Rougier's *Mission secrète à Londres* (1946), Henri du Moulin de Labarthète's *Le Temps des illusions* (1946), and Louis-Dominique Girard's *Montoire, Verdun diplomatique* (1948), all three written by men close to Marshal Pétain. Representing the collaboration were primarily the posthumous publications of Fernand de Brinon, Pierre Pucheu, Jean Hérold-Paquis, and others, along with trial records and the writings of various less well-known figures.

This first generation of memoirs reflected contemporary political battles, the elimination from political life of vestiges of the resistance movement, and the revival of Vichyite and extreme right-wing sentiment. All these works appeared during what I have called the "mourning phase" of the syndrome.

Sidestepping these struggles, historians lost no time commencing their investigations. In October 1944 the Commission d'Histoire de l'Occupation et de la Libération de la France (CHOLF) was established, under the ministry of national education. Members of the commission's board of directors in 1949 included the historians Georges Lefebvre, Henri Michel, and Edouard Perroy; Pierre Caron, the honorary director of the Archives of France; and various political figures such as the minister of national education and Gilberte Brossolette, vice-president of the Council of the Republic. The commission immediately directed its work toward the study of the Resistance, while another group, the Comité d'Histoire de la Guerre, also established in 1945, was made responsible for collecting documents from the various ministries and administrations of the government. This second committee was headed by Lucien Febvre, Pierre Caron, Pierre Renouvin, and Henri Michel. In 1951 the two groups merged to form the Comité d'Histoire de la Deuxième Guerre Mondiale (CHGM).

The joint efforts of these two groups paved the way for the publication, before the end of the 1940s, of the first historical articles on the war, which appeared in the first journal devoted to the subject, *Cahiers d'histoire de la guerre*. After four issues this was renamed *Revue d'histoire de la deuxième guerre mondiale*, and it has remained one of the leading specialist journals in the field. Thanks to assiduous work by many archivists, numerous document collections have been inventoried and catalogued, and some have been published: for example, the papers of the armistice delegation, edited by Pierre Caron and Pierre Cézard. In 1950 Henri Michel published the first book on the war to appear in the famous "Que sais-je?" series, devoted to the Resistance in France.

In addition to these official institutions, there was also the Centre de Documentation Juive Contemporaine (Center for Contemporary

Jewish Documentation, or CDJC), established in secret in 1943. After the war it amassed one of the most comprehensive archives for materials of all kinds pertaining to the Final Solution. A museum and research institution, the center has also been a memorial since the monument to the unknown Jewish martyr was built there in 1957.[19]

In 1955 Joseph Billig, an official of the center, published the first volume of a comprehensive study of the Commissariat for Jewish Affairs. Twenty-three years before the Darquier affair, the scope of French participation in the Final Solution was revealed to the world, but the book was read by few and there was little reaction. Officials of the CDJC, such as Georges Wellers, Serge Klarsfeld, and others, tirelessly continued to publish studies of the gas chambers, Nazi criminals, and concentration camps, even though their work elicited little response until the 1970s. The first major scholarly treatise on the deportation was published in 1968: Olga Wormser-Migot's *Le Système concentrationnaire nazi, 1933–1945*. This book stressed the distinction between concentration camps and extermination camps and gave precise locations of the gas chambers. It drew polemical fire from certain quarters.

De Gaulle's Vichy and Aron's Vichy

In 1954 two literary events marked a first milestone: Charles de Gaulle came out with the first volume of his *Mémoires de guerre: L'Appel, 1940–1942*, and Fayard published the first comprehensive work on the Vichy regime, Robert Aron's and Georgette Elgey's *Histoire de Vichy*. Oddly enough, the two books inaugurated two parallel series: in 1959 de Gaulle published the third volume of his memoirs (*Le Salut, 1944–1946*), while Aron published his *Histoire de la libération de la France* on the same period. Beyond this coincidence of timing, however, the general and the historian had little in common, except that each contributed, in these waning years of the Fourth Republic, to the crystallization of a particular view of the 1940s.

De Gaulle's memoirs, written between 1952 and 1958, reflect the disappointment he suffered in 1946. Yet, though the General turned his acerbic pen against the "republic of the parties," his memoirs are also imbued with the same grandiose conception that had convinced the writer of his special destiny. An eminently political work, de

Gaulle's memoirs are profoundly original in that they attach a positive significance to the events of 1940–1944. Pétain exploited the defeat, but de Gaulle hoped to profit from the victory. The Marshal had capitalized on chaos, but the General called upon France, ten years after the fact, to recapture the glory of the days of combat, of a war waged by "France in its entirety": "The flame of national ambition, smoldering beneath the ashes, was revived by the storm's blast. How can it be kept hot after the wind subsides?"[20] In other words, having won the war, how could France win the peace and, even more important, recover its grandeur?

De Gaulle's history lesson was intended to drive home several fundamental truths. First, the French owed their salvation and redemption to "de Gaulle," a double of whom the author speaks in the third person. Without him and the burst of energy he administered, "the soul of France would have died a little more."[21] To read him, you might think that the man of June Eighteenth had fought a solitary battle. Without denying that many people played a role in the Resistance, he is critical of their flaws. At the height of the cold war, he carefully separates the wheat from the chaff. The men of the Secret Army or the FFL are beyond reproach. By contrast, the "politicians" did not always grasp de Gaulle's message. As for the Communists, the honeymoon was definitely over. The General even went so far as to blame them (in veiled words) for the shootings that took place outside Notre Dame in Paris on 26 August 1944: this was an act of provocation, according to de Gaulle, which certain unnamed people hoped would convince the public that resistance organizations and liberation committees should remain armed.

Last but not least, he spoke of the other side with a certain moderation of tone. Collaborators are rarely mentioned, but "if they were guilty, many of them were not cowards."[22] He also admitted (as had long been suspected) that Pétain's obstinate insistence on appearing before the jury of the Haute Cour had embarrassed him, de Gaulle, politically and perhaps also personally: "I did not want anyone to have to see him."[23] Harking back to an argument he had used in his 1947 speeches, he alluded to Pétain's "old age, which the chill of years [had] deprived of the necessary strength."[24]

The General's memoirs provide an important first-hand account of events, but they also encourage an ambiguous interpretation of the Occupation. Naturally the emphasis is on the Resistance and Free

France, and there is no reason why it should have been otherwise. But history has been transformed. What is really at issue is the history of *France,* whereas in de Gaulle's account it is reduced to the saga of a handful of individuals. The country's center of gravity has shifted from Paris and Vichy to London and Algiers. The "de facto authority" of Vichy, whose acts were officially nullified in 1944, is simply bracketed out. Political will takes precedence over objective reality, and history is confounded with morality.

Yet the view put forth in the memoirs is not simplistically "resistancialist." It was not the French people who uniformly resisted so much as it was the "soul of France," that quintessential Gaullian abstraction. If France is to merit, in retrospect, the glory of having defeated the occupying power, then he who embodies the essence of France must once again preside over the country's highest destiny. France has capital to invest but waits for the right opportunity to use it.

From his lonely retreat the General could not singlehandedly make the history of Vichy disappear and take under his wing the forty million French men and women who had no choice but to remain in France. Hence Robert Aron's book was of great historiographical significance.

In the 1930s Robert Aron was an impassioned essayist associated with a group of intellectuals known as "nonconformists," a catch-all term for a noisy generation of maverick, prolific writers, many of whom were drawn to certain aspects of fascism or "economic planning." The war, however, cooled him down. A fugitive Jew, he escaped the antisemitic laws of the government thanks to the good offices of Jean Jardin, the director of Laval's cabinet, and managed to reach haven in North Africa. He made a brief, semiclandestine visit to Vichy, from which he took away memories of the men and atmosphere of the Marshal's court, memories not untinged by a kind of gratitude. In his memoirs Aron speaks of his disappointment with the CFLN and de Gaulle, who he charges tried "to eliminate the influence of his adversaries [Pétainists and Giraudists] and erase from history periods of which he disapproved."[25]

Aron's *Histoire de Vichy,* written in collaboration with Georgette Elgey, relies heavily on eyewitness testimony and on trial records of the Haute Cour, at that time unavailable to most other historians. In all his works, moreover, Aron makes abundant use of unpublished sources provided by leading figures from the worlds of politics and business with whom he has remained on excellent terms. His files are thus full of documents and testimony not to be found in more official archives.[26] But with that advantage goes a serious drawback: being unpublished, many of Aron's sources have been hard to check. His books are barely annotated, and even where the sources are identified, they often have been inaccessible to other researchers.

The *Histoire de Vichy* is an enormous tome of more than seven hundred pages describing the evolution of *l'Etat français* almost day by day. For more than fifteen years, it served as a standard work of reference. The book was written in a period that did not encourage a scholarly distance from the subject. It flew in the face of the prevalent hostility to the Vichy regime and was deeply indebted to the views of former ministers and others close to the government. What Aron proposed was a "minimalist" interpretation of the regime and its policies.

The argument is simply summarized: there were two Vichys, Pétain's and Laval's. Take, for example, one crucial point: the discussions between French and German officials at Montoire on 22–24 October 1940. Most historians today agree, and Vichy archives confirm, that these discussions initiated official collaboration between Vichy and the Germans. But Aron draws a sharp distinction between the head of state and the head of government:

> For the Marshal, the armistice was not and could not be anything more than a pause, allowing France to subsist temporarily while awaiting the outcome of the war between England and the Axis. Montoire, which for him figured in this same vision, was therefore a minor episode that introduced nothing new in his policy toward Germany. By contrast, for Laval, the armistice was supposed to have paved the way for a reversal of alliances, of which Montoire was to mark the definitive beginning. (pp. 308–309)

Seen this way, collaboration was nothing more than a misunderstanding. The regime's official declarations were more equivocal than its actions, "but the French people could not know this." Aron lays great stress on the "secret negotiations" with the Allies to support his contention that Vichy was playing a double game. Still he does acknowledge that the government made errors of judgment, particularly concerning the timing of its efforts to restructure French society. So he underestimates the impact of the National Revolution and its determination to survive within the framework of a German Europe.

Pursuing his quest in the subsequent *Histoire de la Libération,* Aron showed himself to be far less cautious in attacking the "crimes" of the Resistance. For many years his authority was cited to justify claims that "thirty to forty thousand people" had been summarily executed by resistance units, but in reality this figure was obtained by striking a middle ground between the exaggerated estimate of 100,000 and the low figure of around 10,000, the latter being close to the truth. General de Gaulle in person wrote Aron to express his doubts about Aron's statistical methods:

> In all sincerity I write to express my warmest compliments for this magisterial work. Certain details and various figures that you cite are somewhat at odds with what I saw or know to be the case. For example, the number of executions carried out by the Resistance is known from detailed and verified reports prepared by the prefects. I cited the exact number [roughly 10,000] in *Le Salut,* and it is smaller than the number you indicate.[27]

Elsewhere in the same work Aron exaggerates the revolutionary threat that France faced in the summer of 1944. It would take years, however, for a different view of the period to emerge.

The Spirit of the Resistance

Charles de Gaulle and Robert Aron thus contributed, each in his own way, to quieting the many controversies stemming from the war, de Gaulle by inventing a retrospective honor and offering it to France, Aron by minimizing Vichy's evil role and spattering the resistance escutcheon, particularly that of the Communists and their allies.

With the General's return to public life and in the aftermath of the Algerian crisis, historians turned in earnest to the task of exploring the dense world of clandestine combat. In the 1960s the field was dominated by the Comité d'Histoire de la Deuxième Guerre Mondiale under the leadership of Henri Michel, who was assisted by a team of skilled researchers who contributed in no small part to the establishment of Michel's international reputation.[28] Michel wrote a thesis on "currents of thought in the Resistance" that gave full weight to their variety, not to say conflicts. The work was published in 1962 by Presses Universitaires de France in the collection "Spirit of the Resistance," edited by Michel himself and Boris Mirkine-Guetzevitch.

Meanwhile, the CHGM pursued several avenues of investigation with the aid of research assistants in France's various *départements*. Among its studies was one of the first to investigate the statistics of the deportation, even though the general public at the time (the 1950s) was still little concerned with the subject. Other committee projects included chronological and geographical surveys of resistance activity (begun in the early 1960s), punishment for acts of collaboration (1968), and the wartime economy (1970s).

These studies may be taken as representative of historiography in the period, particularly since the CHGM, owing to its contacts with the government, the army, the archives, and resistance groups, acted as a central clearing house for wartime research. Rather than list all of the many works the committee produced, it makes more sense to pause a moment to consider the best and the worst. The CHGM was responsible for producing a chronology of the Resistance, that is, a catalogue, department by department, of all "acts of resistance" of any kind, from sabotage to intelligence, from parachute drops to propaganda. Recorded on cards, these thousands of items were to be gathered at a central location for use in constructing a comprehensive portrait of the struggle against the occupying forces.[29] The project, begun before computers were widely available, envisioned processing about 200,000 items recorded on ordinary index cards; some 150,000 cards were actually prepared, yet by the admission of some of the very people who organized the project, they are all but unusable. To be sure, one might argue that serial and quantitative history were all the rage at the time, but what is interesting in hindsight is the notion that the "whole" Resistance could somehow be captured in a box (actually, a specially prepared file cabinet). Verified, indexed, sorted, and categorized, the leaders of the clandestine struggle saw themselves reduced to a part of the national heritage. Historians, working in a righteous cause, became memorialists.

By contrast, the study of the purge—the best of the CHGM's works—dispelled doubts about the number of "summary executions."[30] Conducted with a more rigorous and critical spirit than the chronology, this project yielded concrete results, establishing a figure of roughly 10,000 as the most plausible estimate. Of these liquidations, half were carried out before D-Day, or while the hold of the occupying forces was still strong. The results of this study have been widely used by historians and should have put an end to the recurring polemics about the number of executions, which, as we have seen, were one symptom of the syndrome.

Although Henri Michel himself was a Socialist, his work lent historical support to the Gaullist vision of the Resistance. At the same time, Communist historiography was making marked advances, as Stéphane Courtois has shown. After fifteen years during which the wartime years were a forbidden subject owing to internal conflicts within the party, in which veterans of the armed struggle and the FTP ultimately lost out, the Resistance once again became a political prize of major importance. In 1964 the party published what became a bible to its grassroots organizers, a textbook entitled *Histoire du parti communiste français*. In 1967 *Histoire du PCF dans la Résistance* was published under the direction of Jacques Duclos, and in 1969 *Cahiers de l'Institut Maurice-Thorez* began publishing numerous articles on the subject.[31]

The explanation for this reversal lies in the party's internal history and in the unifying role of Duclos, who had been a leader of the underground party, after the death of Maurice Thorez in 1964; from 1969 on, the rise of the Union of the Left, an alliance of the Socialist and Communist parties, also played a part. According to Courtois, the change in the attitude of the Communists was even a kind of response to its Maoist rivals on the extreme left, who attempted to take over the Resistance heritage by declaring themselves the "new resistance." In substance, however, the Communists' picture of the war years remained unchanged: they still defended the Nazi-Soviet pact without mentioning its secret protocol, and they still maintained that the party had committed itself to the Resistance in July 1940 and become its mainspring after June 1941.

The implicit alliance of the 1960s between Gaullist and Communist memories, which we encountered earlier in the discussion of the ceremonies surrounding the transfer of Jean Moulin's ashes to the Pantheon, thus appears to have found historiographic expression, with the terrain occupied by the Communists on one side and the CHGM on the other.

By contrast, little research was done on collaboration or Vichy. Significantly, Robert Aron opened no new avenue of research and produced no real disciples, although his ideas were widely accepted. In 1964 Michèle Cotta published a brief but densely written work on the collaborationist press: *La Collaboration, 1940–1944.* But she carefully (and prudently) refrained from analyzing tendencies of similar inspiration within the Vichy government prior to 1943. Despite this precaution she was not spared the angry reactions of certain people mentioned in the book (or of their families). Between the time of the first edition published in 1964 and the second in 1965, she eliminated biographical details concerning the fate, at the time of the Liberation, of various individuals: Claude Jeantet, Jean Loustau, Claude Maubourguet, Ralph Soupault, and Lucien Rebatet (who was no longer described as "currently a journalist for *Rivarol*"). Most of them had received heavy sentences, and a few even the death sentence, but under the terms of the 1953 amnesty it was illegal to mention their names. In theory, incidentally, this law is still on the books.

Meanwhile Henri Michel also branched out into new areas of research. In 1966 he published *Vichy année 40,* a study of the early days of the Vichy regime. Oddly enough, although Michel is renowned primarily as a specialist on the Resistance, this is one of his best books. It was one of the first to demonstrate the intimate connections between the National Revolution (domestic policy) and state collaboration (foreign policy). Also in 1966 Jacques Duquesne published the first comprehensive work on a complex and controversial subject, which he handled with great care: *Les Catholiques français sous l'occupation.* Jacques Delarue summarized his meticulous archival work in *Trafics et crimes sous l'occupation* (1968), and Jacques Delperrié de Bayac traced the history of the Milice (*Histoire de la milice,* 1969).

Of even greater importance, the publishing house Fayard (far ahead of other houses in this area) showed courage in publishing a translation of the German historian Eberhard Jäckel's *France in Hitler's Europe.* This work, the first to reveal, through the use of German archives, the mechanisms of state collaboration, offered a dramatically different picture from that painted by Aron and should have marked a major turning point in historical studies of the period. According to Jäckel, it was in 1942, *prior to* Laval's return to power on 18 April, that French efforts to reach an understanding with the Reich and to enter into state-to-state negotiations despite the Occupation reached a climax. Thus Pétain, far from having been subjected to Laval's "bad influence," was the prime mover behind the Montoire policy, which was unambiguously formulated by the Darlan government (1941–42). Furthermore, it was the Germans who, because they were engaged in a total war, rejected any notion of cooperating with the French, thereby encouraging the French to outdo themselves with ever greater offers of support, to the point of expressing hope that the occupying power would win the war.

Nevertheless, Jäckel's work, innocent of the passions that aroused the French, was ahead of its time, although it did inspire a number of historians in France and other countries to reverse de Gaulle's shift of focus from London to Vichy and from Algiers to Paris. In France Jäckel's book attracted little attention and went largely unread (see Chapter 7).

An American in Vichy

In 1970 the historical picture of the period was subjected to a thoroughgoing revision. In March of that year René Rémond and Janine Bourdin organized a colloquium on the early years of the Vichy government at the Fondation Nationale des Sciences Politiques. Scholars met with men who made no bones about their role at Vichy, such as René Belin, François Lehideux, and Jean Borotra, in a setting that encouraged open discussion. The shroud of silence seemed to lift of its own accord, and former officials explained their policies with considerable candor. True, the distinction between Pétain's Vichy and Laval's Vichy, patterned on Aron's, had been given official sanction by one of the leading lights of the foundation, André Siegfried, in an article published in *Revue française des sciences politiques* in 1956, and it was frequently invoked at the colloquium. And true, the subjects discussed (the labor charter, youth, the constitution) were mainly institutional and ideological in nature, and in this tranquil setting these topics were unlikely to trigger even a mock reprise of the *guerre franco-française*. True, too, neither the policy of collaboration nor the

period 1942–1944 nor the antisemitic laws figured on the colloquium's agenda.

René Rémond was quite candid about all this in questioning the
usefulness of walling off domestic from foreign policy, a distinction
that had definitely been a crucial element in the history of Vichy:
"Montoire determined social policy as well as youth policy."[32] Still,
even with the omissions that are inevitable in any scholarly conference, and despite the cautious choice of topic and avoidance of certain
issues, the collective work of the FNSP at least pointed a way forward
even if it did not step boldly into the breach.

In the following year, 1972, Yves Durand published a brief book
(176 pages) soberly entitled *Vichy, 1940–1944*, a broad-brushed portrait of the regime whose perceptiveness and intuition (given the state
of research at the time) deserve great credit and still have much to
teach us. But it was from across the Atlantic that a powerful blast was
unleashed at Pompidou's "tranquil France." In a series of articles published in French between 1956 and 1972, Stanley Hoffmann, the
Franco-American specialist in French politics at Harvard University,
broke down the impregnable walls that Aron, Siegfried, and many
others had erected between the Pétainists in Vichy and the fascists in
Paris: "Collaborationism, whether servile or ideological, could not
have developed so readily in a country that remained fundamentally
deaf to its appeal had there been no state collaboration," he wrote in
1969.[33]

In January 1973 Editions du Seuil brought out a work first published a year earlier in the United States, *Vichy France: Old Guard
and New Order, 1940–1944*. Translated by Claude Bertrand, the
mother of historian Jean-Pierre Azéma, and prefaced by Stanley Hoffmann, the new book was entitled in French *La France de Vichy,
1940–1944*, and from the outset it dispensed with all traditional
views of the subject.[34] Previously Vichy had referred to a government,
a regime, a particular period. At the time, however, it was highly unusual to associate all of France with the government that grew out of
the defeat and governed only a small fraction of French territory.

To some, the author of this new work, Robert Paxton, had several
counts against him: he was young (forty-one), an American, had not
experienced the events about which he wrote, and dared to write
about issues that even French specialists approached only with the

greatest circumspection. His work, moreover, exploded several myths. First, Vichy never engaged in any kind of double game, and still less did it offer any resistance to the occupying power. Indeed, Vichy had begged the Germans to accept its collaboration, and had done so since the summer of 1940. Paxton thus corroborated and extended the argument of Eberhard Jäckel. Then Paxton, like Henri Michel, maintained that collaboration and the National Revolution were two aspects of a single policy. Still Paxton differed radically with Michel over the legacy of Vichy. Far from diminishing the regime's accomplishments, as Aron and Michel did, Paxton devoted several dense chapters to the subject of domestic reform. The reforms, he argued, revealed the extent of Vichy's ambition to transform both state and society. Championed by a small number of technocrats and shaped by a spirit of revenge against the Popular Front, the reforms prefigured the transformation of France in the 1950s and 1960s (a subject also broached by the FNSP colloquium). Finally, Paxton emphasized the specificity of the Vichy regime, whose policy, particularly in regard to the war against the Jews, was only partly dictated by the occupier and partly the result of its own initiatives.

In the heat of intellectual passion, Paxton at times pushed the logic of his case so far that he appeared to give too little weight to the undeniable constraints imposed by the Germans and the situation. The power of the argument and the occasional excess were truly shocking and caused something of a scandal.

Marc Ferro was quick to sense the political consequences of this new interpretation of Vichy. It would disturb the left because it demolished the reassuring notion that only the elites had betrayed France in 1940, "whereas in reality heroic resistance to the last man from Bayonne to Africa made no sense for anyone." It would disturb the Gaullists because they were cast as "heirs of the regime they fought against." And it would disturb "all who leaned toward Pétain, who believed, who wanted to believe, and who tried to make others believe that the Marshal was playing a double game."[35] In the event, however, the book was defended primarily by the left.

The Communists applauded what they regarded as a corroboration of their assertion that Vichy had been a creation of "state monopoly capitalism." Jewish groups commended the book warmly, clearly satisfied that an American scholar had lent authoritative support to their relentless criticism of Vichy. The reaction of resistance groups was more mixed. Some said that this was a book that "all résistants ought to read dispassionately, without hatred, but with open eyes."[36] Others, however, were disturbed by Paxton's brief remarks, in the introduction, about early resistance fighters: "They reveal no serious problems of dissent for the regime until well into 1941."[37] In countless seminars and conferences Paxton has had to endure the diatribes of courteous but irritated keepers of the flame.

Unsurprisingly, the most hostile reactions came from the right. Writing in *L'Aurore* Dominique Jamet questioned the American historian's competence: "Apparently Mr. Robert Paxton is currently teaching at Columbia University. It is hard to believe."[38] *La France catholique* lashed out at the "ivory-tower intellectual" afflicted with "para-Marxism" and expressed its preference for the memoirs of Admiral Auphan, which had been published a few months earlier.[39] The admiral himself, president of the Pétain association, proved the most virulent of all the critics. Leaving it to his colleague Jean Borotra to argue for the existence of the so-called secret telegrams, the heart of the Pétainist gospel, Auphan shamelessly wrote in a letter to *Le Monde* that the whole business was one better "dealt with *entre Français.*"[40] Elsewhere he published a review that makes it clear just how much of a bombshell the book had been for the small band of Pétainists:

> The secret of Mr. Paxton's exposé is not revealed until the final sentence. Here it is: "The deeds of occupier and occupied alike suggest that there come cruel times when to save a nation's deepest values one must disobey the state. France after 1940 was one of those times." This American, who was eight years old at the time and quietly playing ball on the other side of the Atlantic when his country's leaders helped push us into war while hiding behind the "cash and carry" law to keep out of it themselves, today claims to have proved that the only solution for bloodied, humiliated France in 1940 was revolution, a war of subversion. The only reason for the book is to lend substance to this opinion.[41]

A reader also objected that Paxton had failed to grasp the horrors of civil war. He answered that, coming from the American south, he could understand those horrors as well as anyone. On one occasion

Paxton debated directly with Auphan, who again charged that he was too young to understand.[42]

What was especially revealing about the whole episode was that on several occasions Admiral Auphan invoked the authority of Robert Aron, whom he had denounced in 1955 as "partial" but whom he now considered, in 1973, a "moderate."[43] Here is a sure sign that Paxton's book made obsolete the work of Aron, which had so admirably fulfilled the needs of many people, particularly on the right.

The scholarly reactions to the book were no less interesting, for they tell us a great deal about the strengths and blind spots of earlier historiography. Henri Michel was full of praise for Paxton's "masterpiece." Yet while he rejoiced, in the name of the Resistance with which he identified himself, at this "implacable indictment of the Vichy regime," he could not refrain from expressing regret that the American historian "did not also praise [Vichy's] adversaries," detecting in this failure a "tinge of hostility to France."[44] In *Revue française de science politique* Janine Bourdin confessed to "a certain discomfort" with the book, which she criticized for its factual errors, its exclusive use of German sources, and its failure to take account of recent French research. Clearly she was reluctant to accept all of Paxton's findings, for example, on the subject of "Vichy's willful antisemitism."[45]

The most virulent attack came from Alain-Gérald Slama: "I find the refutation of his arguments in his own book."[46] It was a bold exercise, but in retrospect what it illustrates most clearly is how little French historians had to offer. Those who agreed with Paxton properly expressed regret that the book had not been written by a Frenchman. Those who disagreed were seldom able to refute him by pointing to other sources, since French archives were for the most part closed. Some French scholars hailed his work, others assailed it as a gross exaggeration, but no one can deny that Paxton powerfully (if unintentionally) drove French scholars out of their ivory tower.

It is in no way to detract from the merits of Paxton's book to point out that *Vichy France* profited immensely from the "Ophuls effect" and from the new climate in France in the period 1971–1974. Although other works of similar intent were published at the time, Paxton's, perhaps more than all the rest, was deemed to lend scholarly authority to the return of what had been repressed. Published two years after the turbulent release of *The Sorrow and the Pity,* the book was believed to provide dispassionate, objective proof of the points made with great passion in the film. Like Ophuls, moreover, but for different reasons, Paxton was not afraid of controversy.

Fire at Will on German France

In Paxton's wake, numerous studies of the dark years began to appear. In 1971, of 90 advanced dissertations on World War II, 15 dealt with the Resistance and only 6 with Vichy. By 1978, some 130 dissertations were submitted, 16 of which dealt with the Resistance or the Liberation, along with 13 on Vichy and the Occupation, 18 on the economy and society, and 10 on popular attitudes and culture.

The Resistance remains a popular topic to this day, but now the attitude is less celebratory, despite the fact that the subject does not easily lend itself to probing critique. There has been interest in the sociology of resistance movements (Dominique Veillon, *Le Franc-Tireur,* 1977) as well as in spiritual aspects of the Resistance (Renée Bédarida, *Témoignage chrétien, 1941–1944,* 1977).

Collaboration has also been the subject of careful research: important works on the subject include Claude Lévy, *Les Nouveaux Temps et l'idéologie de la collaboration* (1974), Jean-Pierre Azéma, *La Collaboration, 1940–1944* (1975), Fred Kupferman, *Pierre Laval* (1976), Pascal Ory, *Les Collaborateurs, 1940–1945* (1976), and, by the same author, *La France allemande* (1977).

This new wave of scholarly research was not exempt from revivalist tendencies of its own, particularly when inquisitorial instincts manifested themselves. Individuals whose not-so-spotless backgrounds were brought to light found themselves placed on the index, as it were, or at any rate listed in the index at the back of the volume. Some writers chose a favorite adversary, whose past they then pilloried. Any number of newspaper and magazine articles dredged up unsavory acts of collaboration, thereby encouraging further polemics.[47]

As new works continued to pour from the academy, books for nonspecialist readers began to flood the market: Jean Mabire on the French SS, Christian Bernadac on the camps, Philippe Aziz on collaborationist criminals, and above all the works of Henri Amouroux.

At the rate of one volume every year or two, Amouroux published his *Grande Histoire des Français sous l'Occupation* during the syndrome's most obsessional phase. Aided by considerable publicity, provided free of charge by fellow journalists (many of whom resented the competition of historians on what they considered their turf, contemporary history), Amouroux accomplished the considerable feat of making himself, in the eyes of the average French citizen, the uncontested expert on the period. He deserves credit for his talent, his success at turning up countless unpublished documents, and his prodigious capacity to digest the work of others. But the secret of his success lies elsewhere.

In style and tone Amouroux offered the French an antidote to the Vichy syndrome. As the country experienced scandal after scandal and revelation after revelation, Amouroux went about his business with the tranquillity of a great sage, offering a seamless, inoffensive picture of history as it impinged on ordinary men and women. He had no ax to grind. Relying on down-to-earth common sense, he had no use for sophisticated analyses: there were good and bad in every camp. First the French were Pétainists, then they were Gaullists. As for what Amouroux in 1983 called the "merciless civil war," it did not begin until 1943: both sides are dismissed with the observation that "terror answered terror." In short, the tragedies of the Occupation could be blamed on the inevitable pressures of war.

Met with reserve by many former résistants (those whose political commitments did not allay their doubts), hailed by the media, accepted by the public, Amouroux was granted the status of supreme authority by certain segments of the right, including some former Pétainists. In 1978, for instance, the secretary of the Pétain Association wrote to Amouroux: "If the French are one day to be reconciled, your involvement and your historical work will have contributed in no small way to bringing it about."[48] The sixth volume of Amouroux's work, on the civil war, is dedicated to Robert Aron, a "man of peace," whose work has "freed itself from Manichaeanism." Like Aron's work, Amouroux's fulfilled the expectations of certain readers not only by virtue of its accessible style but even more by its reassuring tone.

While this literary revival was under way, a second generation of memoirs began to appear. Former collaborators and Vichyites as well as former résistants took up their pens, and this time many of those who chose to write had been leaders in the forties. Among the former, the more committed they had been in the past, the more aloof they pretended to be in the present. Many were only now choosing to break long silences. Among this group were ex-Waffen SS officer Christian de la Mazière, who figured so prominently in *The Sorrow and the Pity* and who in 1972 published *Le Rêveur casqué;* and Victor Barthélemy, a former leader of the PPF, who in 1978 published *Du communisme au fascisme.* Those who had been close to Vichy were now eager for rehabilitation and apt to stress the idea that Pétain had been playing a double game and that Vichy had resisted the Germans. Among these were Admiral Auphan (*Histoire élémentaire de Vichy,* 1971), former labor minister René Belin (*Du secrétariat de la CGT au gouvernement de Vichy,* 1978), and Raymond Abellio (*Sol invictus, 1939–1947,* 1980).

As for the resistance leaders, also long silent, two now published memoirs of particular significance: Henri Frenay, head of the Combat movement, brought out *La Nuit finira* in 1973, and Claude Bourdet wrote *L'Aventure incertaine* in 1975. In addition, Henri Noguères published the first volume of his five-volume *Histoire de la résistance en France* in 1967 (and the last in 1981). Participant become historian, Noguères attempted what the CHGM failed to do: to provide a day-by-day description of resistance activities. These veterans were not interested in assailing collaborators or filling pages with red, white, and blue ink: that day was past. As old memories resurfaced and new revisionisms loomed on the horizon, their purpose instead was to leave a trace.

Toward the Future

A new phase began in the late 1970s. The CHGM was supplanted by the Institut d'Histoire du Temps Présent. Scholars associated with this new institute tended to see World War II as part of a larger context, a "history of the late twentieth century" extending from 1939 to the present. In 1979 Jean-Pierre Azéma published *De Munich à la libération,* a work unmarred by either misguided omissions or obligatory obeisances, which quickly became the standard reference on the subject.

The study of World War II soon developed into a flourishing discipline. In 1985 some 240 scholars were working in or around the field.[49] They have extended research into a variety of new areas: the economy, the Catholic and Protestant churches, propaganda, and public opinion, to name a few. Pierre Laborie's *Résistants, Vichyssois et autres* (1980) and *L'Opinion française sous Vichy* (1990) explore public attitudes. Jean-Baptiste Duroselle's *L'Abîme, 1939–1945* (1982) draws extensively on diplomatic sources to demolish the notion of Vichy resistance. Duroselle describes the scope of state collaboration as seen from the French, and no longer exclusively the German, side. Michèle Cointet was one of the first scholars to earn a *doctorat d'Etat* (France's highest academic degree) for a study of the Vichy regime (devoted to the Conseil National). Little-known figures began to emerge from the shadows. Pierre Assouline's *Une Eminence grise* (1986) shed new light on Jean Jardin, the director of Laval's cabinet. Denis Peschanski edited the papers of Angelo Tasca, a former Communist who worked for the Vichy information service. Philippe Burrin's *La Dérive fasciste: Doriot, Déat, Bergery* (1986) began to explore "left-wing" tendencies within Vichy, a subject that, as we saw earlier, the right also exploited for polemical purposes.

There was also a marked increase of interest in culture, scholarship, and science during the Occupation. Cultural life under Vichy is explored in "Politiques et pratiques culturelles dans la France de Vichy," published in *Les Cahiers de l'IHTP* in June 1988. Research is continuing into the exact role played by Vichy in various areas: the question is whether activity continued in spite of the regime or with its assistance. Major advances have also been made in the understanding of French antisemitism with the publication of Robert Paxton's and Michael Marrus' *Vichy France and the Jews* (1981) and Serge Klarsfeld's *Vichy–Auschwitz* (1983, 1985).

Finally, as we saw earlier, the Barbie-Vergès affair yielded a third crop of memoirs caught up in the polemic surrounding the tragic end of Jean Moulin (from such figures as René Hardy, Henri Noguères, and Lucie Aubrac, to say nothing of Daniel Cordier's bombshell). These writings mark an important turning point toward a critical study of the Resistance, where by "critical" I mean a study devoid of prejudice, whether favorable or unfavorable. The Resistance has at last come down from its pedestal and can now be subjected to rigorous, and inevitably indiscreet, examination. To date we have only an inkling of discoveries to come, reported by François Bédarida, for example, and often instigated by former participants such as Daniel Cordier, who worked closely with Jean Moulin.[50]

Can the job be done? The Resistance poses unprecedented problems for historical research, and at first the whole area was abandoned to uncritical hagiography and prudent discretion. Once the mirror cracked, Vichy became the first focus of new research and revisionist interpretations; attention has now turned to antisemitism and the genocide. Slowly and not without difficulty it has become possible to do scholarly, dispassionate research in both areas. Given the role played by the Resistance before and after the Barbie trial, has its turn now come? Time will tell.

Historians and the Public

Historians play the role of intermediaries in shaping collective memory. They rely on available sources of information and respond in large part to what the public—including other scholars—expects of them. Once they have written their works, they in turn exert an influence on people's attitudes, not least because courses on the subject are largely shaped by the findings of scholars. This chain of transmission plays a key role in shaping representations of the past. Let us examine some of the crucial links.

Factors influencing historical scholarship. Historians interested in the 1940s have always faced great difficulty in gaining access to source materials. Some documents have been lost, others destroyed. In some areas there is too much material, in others too little. And the controversial nature of the topic has in itself influenced the survival and availability of sources.

This is particularly true in the case of public archives, toward which the government has always taken an ambivalent attitude. Because it was essential to measure the disastrous dimensions of the Occupation, the magnitude of the nation's sacrifice, and the costliness of er-

convertie au catholicisme et avait été baptisée fût regardée comme juive parce qu'elle avait trois grands-parents juifs. La loi de l'Église était explicite : « *Un juif qui a reçu valablement le baptême cesse d'être juif pour se confondre dans le troupeau du Christ.* » C'était là « *le point unique où la loi du 2 juin 1941* [le second statut des juifs] *se trouve en opposition avec un principe professé par l'Église romaine* ».

Même ainsi, Vichy s'en tirait à bon compte. « *Il ne s'ensuit point du tout de cette divergence doctrinale que l'État français soit menacé [...] d'une censure ou d'une désapprobation.* »

En conclusion, Bérard rassurait Pétain : la papauté ne ferait aucune difficulté sur cette question. « *Comme quelqu'un d'autorisé me l'a dit au Vatican, il ne nous sera intenté nulle querelle pour le statut des juifs.* »

Mais Vichy devait veiller à ce que ses lois fussent appliquées en tenant compte comme il se devait « *de la justice et de la charité* ».

Pétain utilisa aussitôt ce message. Quelques jours après l'avoir reçu, il se trouva à un dîner de diplomates auquel participait Mgr Valerio Valeri, nonce en France. En présence des ambassadeurs du Brésil et d'Espagne, le Maréchal fit allusion à la lettre de Bérard, leur disant que la papauté n'avait pas d'objection sérieuse à la législation antijuive. Le nonce, qui était opposé au statut des juifs, fut dans l'embarras. Il déclara que le Maréchal devait avoir mal compris les intentions du Saint-Siège. Pétain répliqua avec bonne humeur que c'était le nonce qui n'était pas en accord avec le Saint-Siège, et lui offrit de lui montrer le texte de la lettre. Son interlocuteur le prit au mot, et il semble qu'il ne pût rien trouver à répondre.

Dans une lettre au cardinal Maglione, alors secrétaire d'État, le nonce s'éleva contre les lois antisémites, disant qu'elles contenaient de « *graves erreurs* » du point de vue religieux. Il se demandait qui avait donné cette information à Bérard. Maglione jugea que l'affaire méritait d'être tirée au clair. Il résultat de ces recherches que les sources de Bérard étaient haut placées au secrétariat d'État, et comprenaient Mgr Tardini et Mgr Montini, le futur pape Paul VI. A la fin d'octobre, Mgr Maglione répondit au nonce, confirmant la substance du rapport de Bérard, mais marquant son désaccord avec les « *déductions excessives* » que, selon lui, Pétain en avait tirées. Le sentiment du Vatican était que le statut des juifs était une « *loi malencontreuse* » qui devait être limitée dans son interprétation et son application.

Quelle que fût l'importance de ce curieux échange, Vichy supposa qu'il avait l'appui du Vatican, et agit en conséquence.

* *
*

A l'instar des SS, qui comptaient méthodiquement les juifs envoyés à l'Est, nous pouvons calculer le résultat de la « solution finale » en France. A la fin de l'année 1944, un peu plus de 75 000 juifs avaient été déportés de France vers les centres d'extermination situés sur l'ancien territoire de la Pologne. A leur arrivée, la plupart d'entre eux furent immédiatement envoyés dans les chambres à gaz, tandis que les autres étaient mis au travail dans des conditions qui signifiaient une mort presque certaine au bout de quelques semaines ou de quelques mois. Environ 2 500 de ceux-ci, soit près de 3 %, ont survécu. Auschwitz fut la destination d'environ 70 000 déportés de France.

Vichy, une des 1ères stations thermales d'Europe.

Un équipement thermal de 1er ordre orienté vers les affections digestives et métaboliques, la migraine et certaines séquelles rhumatismales, mais aussi capable de rendre leur tonus aux surmenés de la vie moderne.

Demandez notre documentation gratuite, en particulier celle des forfaits "santé", "pleine forme", "passeport sportif", "golf tennis".

Vichy, ville de vacances.

Lac d'Allier, un plan d'eau de 120 ha, plus de 100 ha de parcs et promenades fleuries. Un équipement sportif des plus complets. Vichy, ville artistique et de culture.
Venez vous remettre en forme.

Nom
Adresse
Office de Tourisme : 19, rue du Parc - B.P. 113 - 03204 VICHY CEDEX

vichy

A failed act?

An excerpt from the French edition of Marrus and Paxton's Vichy and the Jews, *along with some timely advertisements* (Le Point, *18 April 1981*).

ror, many archives were quickly opened to investigators. Scholars learned about the mechanics of Nazi exploitation and began writing the military history of the war and the Resistance. The government's attitude was reflected in the status of the CHGM, which was attached not to a ministry but directly to the office of the *président du Conseil* and, later, of the prime minister. This alliance of government, archives, and historians proved quite fruitful, despite the ever-present temptation to write a kind of authorized history.

In other respects, however, the government saw itself as a kind of Cerberus at the gate, protecting its treasure trove of information from scholars (and ordinary citizens) in order to prevent any revival of internal hostilities. This argument has been raised many times, even quite recently.

The first postwar legislation concerning archival documents was passed on 19 November 1970. It states that all public documents prior to 10 July 1940 are to be freely accessible. Thus the date of the Vichy regime's inception stands as a symbolic barrier. The scholar who wishes to venture beyond this fatal date must come brandishing multiple authorizations, granted at the discretion of the ministry in charge. When Hervé Villeré applied for authorization to consult the judicial archives for a work on Vichy's *sections spéciales* (special courts set up in 1941), Justice Minister René Pléven flatly refused on the following grounds: "It is indeed quite important to avoid any prejudice to private interests and any reawakening of public passions."[51]

The same reasoning that prevented the showing of *The Sorrow and the Pity* was thus partly responsible for determining the direction of historical research. In the end, however, such obstructionism proved of no avail. Once the dam was broken in the late 1960s, memory could no longer be controlled by decree.

In 1979, in response to an initiative taken seven years earlier by the National Archives, the government adopted a far more liberal statute concerning the storage, consultation, and use of both public and private records. All documents were now to be made available after thirty years, except for medical records (150 years), personnel records (120 years after the birthdate of the individual concerned), court documents and statistical records containing "personal information" (100 years), and documents "bearing on personal behavior or affecting state security" (60 years). The new law made a broad range of documents public but still left many aspects of social life in the shadows.[52]

It was the legislature that restricted freedom of access in the name of individual rights and upon advice from the Conseil d'Etat. At no point in senate or assembly debate, however, much less in the proposal of the government, was anything said openly about fears of releasing controversial information, particularly concerning the Occupation. During the debate, one senator who was also a historian, Henri Fréville, calmly discussed technical reasons why the archives of the Comités Départementaux de Libération (the only legal power during the first weeks of the Liberation) ought to be opened to the public.[53]

The new law thus marked a sharp departure from the old rule of silence. Remarkably, the law was passed at a time when France was being subjected to a series of scandals with legal ramifications (Darquier, Leguay, Bousquet, and others), in which the antagonists battled one another with documents and revelations. The law of 1979 granted considerable autonomy to the National Archives and enhanced freedom of access to historical information, but France still has a long way to go compared with other western countries. Nevertheless, thanks to the efforts of certain curators, many document collections are now available for scholarly use.[54]

For thirty years the rule of silence roused passions because it suggested, not without reason, that the skeleton in the closet was of immense proportions. Without doubt this rule of silence was one of the chief causes of the Vichy syndrome; in other words, the effect of silence was the exact opposite of what was intended. By the time accurate information became available, some obsessions had grown too powerful to eliminate overnight.

The difficulty of gaining access to written documents meant that great weight was attached to the oral testimony of eyewitnesses and participants. Historian and witness frequently formed an indissoluble pair in the reconstruction of the past. I think it fair to say that the study of World War II in France and other countries has given rise to a new kind of relationship between scholarly reconstruction and individual and group memories.

It is remarkable, for example, that the study of the Resistance preceded that of Vichy, even though the latter, as the legal authority in charge of the machinery of government, left an incomparably greater volume of documents, records, and other objective sources (not counting German archives, which fill miles of shelves in both France and Germany). Historiography itself was subject to the influence of the "dominant memory."

Firsthand testimony was treated as direct evidence rather than as the product of numerous influences reflecting not only the past but also the present. This practice was occasionally attacked on the grounds that it all too often yielded fanciful reconstructions of events. Daniel Cordier, for example, waited nearly forty years before writing his vast tome on the activities of Jean Moulin. As Cordier tells it, he tired of hearing the same accounts repeated over and over, accounts that contradicted one another and contradicted documents in his possession. He therefore wrote his book as an antidote to all forms of "oral history."[55] Although this is the reaction of one individual, it illustrates how private memories may conflict with the exigencies of historical writing. Of course there is something paradoxical about an author who was himself a participant in events before becoming a historian claiming that the eyewitness accounts of resistance veterans are without scholarly interest. No professional historian who was not also an eyewitness would presume to go that far.

In the final analysis, the changing expectations of the audience can account for the changes in French historiography of the period. In the 1950s and 1960s interest in the wartime years was primarily official. Little was said about Vichy (beyond the minimalist interpretations of Aron), and the Resistance was singled out as the primary focus of historical investigation. During these two decades the Vichy syndrome was in its quiescent phase, and the social demand for historical works was primarily of an official nature.

In the 1970s that social demand shifted to reflect the expectations of a new generation, the generation of Ophuls and the skeptics of '68. Historians lagged slightly behind filmmakers and writers. But the change that occurred around 1971 was in part the product of purely intellectual curiosity. Marcel Ophuls and Robert Paxton did not share the same motives—the coincidence of their findings was fortuitous. Ophuls, along with Sédouy and Harris, was pursuing a political agenda defined by a reaction against the prevailing image of the wartime years and by political conflicts within France. Paxton, like most foreign specialists on Vichy France and unlike their French counter-parts, was relatively impervious to these internal political considerations. Yet both Ophuls and Paxton were interested in French fascism, whose least ambiguous manifestations were Vichy and collaboration (however subtly one might choose to draw the line between the two). American historians may also have been influenced by the fact that the views of Hannah Arendt, who classed Vichy as a totalitarian regime, gained influence there earlier than in France, where the expectations of the new generation and intellectual curiosity about fascism developed simultaneously.

Educating future generations. How is historical knowledge transmitted to future generations? The question actually conflates two other questions: how are teachers trained, and how do they convey what they have learned to their students?

In France aspiring teachers take an examination known as the CAPES (Certificat d'aptitude au professorat de l'enseignement secondaire); access to lycée and university teaching positions is determined by a competitive examination known as the *agrégation*. It is interesting to observe the way in which World War II has been dealt with in these two examinations.

In 1971 (the same crucial year that saw the release of Ophuls' film and the publication of Paxton's book), the 1940s figured for the first time in the syllabus for the agrégation and CAPES, included as part of a broader but no less explosive topic: "France from February 1934 to May 1958," a period spanning the main Franco-French conflicts of the twentieth century. This substantial change in the curriculum marked an incontestable triumph for historians working on contemporary history—*le temps présent,* as it is known in France. Jean-Baptiste Duroselle remarked "how satisfying [it is] to see the agrégation venture boldly into areas that are contemporary in the strict sense of the word."[56]

The change in these two key examinations was an important event for French society. From 1971 to 1973 thousands of students immersed themselves in the period. For the six relevant competitive exams (agrégation in history, agrégation in geography, and CAPES in history/geography, each given separately to men and women), 13,000 students registered in 1972 and 13,250 in 1973. Countless courses were given, research papers assigned, and lecture notes reproduced; history departments did everything to provide instruction on the topics in the syllabus, and this teaching inspired some students to embark on advanced research in the field. Last but not least, books on the subject (including works by both academics and nonacademics) found a much-expanded audience, and this encouraged the publication of still more books.

There remained no shortage of difficulties for both students and teachers. These were recent events about which passions still ran high, and interpretations were inevitably controversial. The wartime years were generally speaking even more controversial than the rest, and no comprehensive, objective text was available. Of the forty books listed by Jean-Baptiste Duroselle, nearly half were firsthand accounts or collections of primary sources, and there were fewer than a dozen scholars with any real authority in the area.[57]

Contemporary questions actually appeared on three of the examinations given in 1972 and 1973, and two of these included the Occupation: the geography agrégation in 1972 dealt with the topic "legislature and government in France from 1934 to 1958," and the same agrégation in 1973 dealt with "France versus Germany from the German rearmament (March 1935) to the treaties of Rome (March 1957)." In the oral examinations due attention was paid to contemporary topics along with other questions on ancient, medieval, and modern history; none of the juries attempted to avoid the subject of the 1940s. In the 1972 history agrégation, for example, 49 of 200 candidates drew a contemporary history question on their orals, and a dozen of these dealt specifically with the Resistance or Vichy. Juries for the agrégation did, however, tend to avoid questions dealing with collaboration or collaborationists. Neither term appears in the index of documents to be commented on. By contrast, the CAPES juries did address these topics, particularly in 1973.

The initiative was bold, but there were plenty of traps lying in store for unwary candidates. The average grade on the written exam in geography was quite low: 50 percent of the men's exams in 1972 and 62 percent in 1973 earned grades of less than 5.5 (out of 20); for women, 40 percent of the 1972 exams and 29 percent of the 1973 exams achieved scores of 1 or under (out of 20).[58] The jury reports contained perhaps even more than the usual number of caustic or incredulous remarks. Consider these observations on the women's geography agrégation oral for 1972:

> Answers to questions concerning the period 1940–1944 were particularly poor (average 5.31, down from 7.14), regardless of whether the subject was the Resistance, the Occupation, or Vichy. It appears that some candidates know absolutely nothing about works dealing with this period . . . that they have never seen certain films and have heard nothing about literary works of the time. One candidate had never heard of Vercors or *Le Silence de la mer*.[59]

Or this, on the women's CAPES oral for 1972:

> The question on contemporary history raised fears that [examiners would hear] impassioned statements concerning Pétain, de Gaulle, the Resistance, or collaborators . . . Don't worry! This period of our history seems to have about as much personal meaning to many candidates as the Median Wars or the English Revolution.[60]

On the men's geography agrégation for 1973:

> As for the collaboration, it is regrettable that most of the candidates seem unaware of the American R. O. Paxton's recent book, even though the publication in this country of *Vichy France* gave rise to a considerable debate, which was reported in the press in the months prior to the examination. Do our candidates read the newspapers?[61]

And on the women's geography agrégation for 1973:

> We are not particularly fond of enumerating student howlers, but . . . we cannot refrain from mentioning, without further comment, a few of the errors found: the armistice signed at Montoire, the Maginot line mistaken for the demarcation line . . . North Africa as a center of resistance before 1942, the French declaration of war provoked by the invasion of Belgium, Pétain as president of the Republic . . . the LVF transformed into a resistance movement, Weygand in favor of continuing the war in June 1940.[62]

Thus 1971 was a crucial year for historians and for scholarly work on the war: it was then that the Occupation became a field of study like any other, with a regular place in the examination syllabus. These early examinations revealed, moreover, a generation gap between the teachers, whose interest in the subject was not merely professional, and the aspiring teachers, most of whom had been born in the late 1940s and for whom the period was nothing more than a difficult part of the exam, apparently remote from their everyday concerns. It is remarkable, for example, that the examiners seem unhappy about the lack of passion and personal investment they find in the students, when initially they feared just the opposite. Was the generation of '68 burned out just three years after the events, or was the spirit of '68 by this point confined to a few marginal groups?

These remarks need to be qualified. Some students were no doubt reluctant or afraid to show any passion, lest they choose the wrong side and thereby risk the wrath of an ideologically hostile jury. Such fears only compounded the students' difficulties and resulted in low grades.[63]

The poor performance of this crop of students is indeed surprising, but, the examiners' comments to the contrary, the students were not to blame. They were still the cream of the crop, and their lackluster performance gives an idea of how World War II (and indeed all of contemporary history) used to be taught in France's secondary schools.

Secondary-school teaching deserves a closer look. As a result of decisions taken in 1959, World War II was included in the history curriculum for the final year of the lycée in 1962. The course was revamped in 1983. The subject did not appear in the freshman history curriculum in 1969. Thus it was not until quite late, and in conjunction with the advent of the Fifth Republic, that French students were exposed to an objective, systematic, and uniform treatment of the wartime years.

Consider next the texts used for teaching students about World War II. The textbooks of the 1960s and those of the 1980s are quite different, at least with respect to their treatment of the Occupation (military matters are dealt with fairly extensively in both generations of texts). In the textbooks of the 1960s, World War II is presented as the culmination of a period that runs from 1914 to 1945. The latter year is portrayed as a watershed: afterwards a new world begins. The dark years are confined to two or three pages, with a careful balance struck between collaboration on the one hand and resistance on the other. The "Aronian" view of Vichy, with its questionable distinction between Pétain's reactionary and Laval's collaborationist regime, is uniformly favored. Although little emphasis is placed on the Montoire talks, most writers were already pointing out that collaboration intensified in 1941 under Admiral Darlan.

Although most of the texts are careful not to understate the complexity of the Resistance, they generally respect a similar hierarchy, always giving priority to the appeal of 18 June and the organization of Free France. It is as if resistance activities within France only discovered their true identity through the person of General de Gaulle. Last but not least, the specific nature of French antisemitism and French initiatives in enacting anti-Jewish laws are generally ignored.[64]

The textbooks of the 1980s are dramatically different. The senior-year course now begins with 1939, so that the war stands at the dawn of an era that ends with the present. The Occupation gets a chapter of its own, more than ten pages long. As for Vichy, Paxton has dethroned Aron, although Aron still has some supporters: some writers treat Montoire as the origin of the Vichy system of collaboration,[65] while others view it as a token of France's "well-intentioned neutrality" toward the Third Reich.[66]

The old hierarchy of the Resistance has disappeared. The early résistants rejected the New Order "without waiting for orders from anyone."[67] The new textbooks devote considerable attention to French antisemitic laws as well as to everyday life (not only rationing and shortages but also new directions in literature and art). The Communists probably come in for the worst treatment, but they published a textbook of their own.[68] A new reform in 1988 again placed the period 1939–1945 at the end of the first cycle, which was "just plain common sense" because it lightened the load of students in their final year and "made it possible to give a clearer account of the long-term cycle of war followed by depression followed by war."[69]

Almost all the texts adopted an objective approach. All sides are presented, often in the form of reproductions of original documents. As a result, they have sometimes been criticized for being overly detached and uncommitted, no doubt in reaction against the previous generation of texts.[70]

Those first-generation textbooks had reflected the spirit of the times, offering a carefully controlled and rather fleeting glimpse of the period. What is interesting, though, is the length of time it took for advances in historical research between 1971 and 1974 to find their way into teaching texts: nearly ten years elapsed before textbooks began to reflect changes in scholarly thinking. Admittedly, the history curriculum changed as part of a general overhaul of the secondary-school curriculum, and that took time. Furthermore, many teachers did not wait for directives from the ministry in 1983 to begin teaching their students about the Final Solution or the existence of French fascism. Still the lag suggests, as do the results of the agrégation, that it was some time before the breaking of the mirror that occurred in the early 1970s had any real impact on the minds of the young.

Knowledge of the past was also transmitted in other ways. World War II was honored with "educational commemorations" reminiscent of the republican celebrations of the early twentieth century. Deportation Day, first observed in 1954, was aimed primarily at students. An interesting anecdote in this regard concerns a 1959 memo, probably written by the minister of education and sent to all teachers, which manages the remarkable feat of describing all the horrors of the deportation in less than a page without once using the word "Jew." Admittedly, for this worthy Gaullist, the deportation was significant only because it struck at people who resisted (a subject that merits a paragraph to itself).[71]

In addition, a competition for the Resistance and Deportation Prize has been held every year since 1964, attracting the attention of teachers, students, and parents. It is questionable whether this event, sponsored by the ministry of education and by various resistance and deportee groups, has been able to avoid cooptation for official purposes. But it has been received enthusiastically by students and for a long time served to compensate for some of the deficiencies of the curriculum.

Memory of the past has thus been transmitted by one set of carriers, while the Vichy syndrome has been transmitted by another. The two have not always evolved at the same pace, and the resulting image of the war has been a composite, further complicated by differences between generations. The collective memory is therefore diverse. To whom has that memory been transmitted? No memory can exist in a void. The officials, writers, artists, filmmakers, scholars, and teachers who have helped to shape France's national memory had to have an audience. It is to the nature of that audience that I want to turn next.

7

⟨◆⟩

DIFFUSE MEMORY

Most of the manifestations of the Vichy syndrome considered so far were the result either of society's difficulty in dealing with the Occupation (witness the amnesty, trials, and recurrent outbursts of hatred) or of ideological and political conflicts that gave rise to competing representations of history. They directly affected political, intellectual, and cultural life and revealed contradictions between views of the past promoted by the government, political parties, and other organized groups.

It is in the nature of some groups to formulate views of the past, to interpret history and invest it with meaning, sometimes deliberately and explicitly, at other times inadvertently and at random. The analysis is still incomplete, however. To finish the job we must now ask about those who received the message: the public, with its diffuse memory. The messages emitted by organized groups are modified by the individuals who receive them, individuals with many different histories and sensibilities. It is impossible to state precisely what the collective memory of an event is, because there is always a zone of obscurity, of individual difference, which no model can reduce and no sociology can penetrate. People were obsessed with the memory of Vichy and the Occupation: that much is a fact. But overt, identifiable manifestations of a collective obsession are one thing; individual feelings are another. How do we measure the difference between the two? The history of the Vichy syndrome is a history of misunderstood words and actions, missed opportunities, malleable myths. But a larger question remains unanswered: how deep were the roots of the syndrome in French society?

Part of the answer can be gleaned from the various ways in which memory was shaped and controlled. Although political debate may at times appear to be superficial, politics is never totally divorced from the concerns of citizens. Vichy, collaboration, and the Resistance became major issues in French politics because they were issues of concern to most French men and women. Since 1945 many individuals have joined or contributed to organizations and groups with some connection to World War II. Furthermore, writers and filmmakers chose the Occupation as a subject or setting because people were interested in it, or so they assumed.

When all is said and done, though, much is still left to the imagination. One can look at quantitative evidence: book sales and film attendance figures. An interesting, if not necessarily representative, sample of public opinion can be obtained from letters sent to newspapers, television stations, and writers. Opinion polls can measure the degree to which particular representations of the past or of historical figures are accepted at a given point in time. Unfortunately, such polls are rare and tell us only about the recent past. But the very frequency of this type of polling in recent years (partly in connection with historical research) does confirm that World War II is a topic of widespread current interest. Between 1971 and 1985 numerous surveys dealt with World War II issues. (In just one fourteen-month period, October 1979 to December 1980, there were four different polls.) Before 1971, however, polling on these issues was practically nonexistent. Since polling data are essential for what I want to do here, I have focused in what follows on the 1970s and 1980s.

A Moderate Interest

Moviegoers

Not many filmmakers chose the Occupation as a subject for their films, and moviegoers do not appear to have gone out of their way to see those films. A really successful move in the Paris region is normally seen by 800,000 to a million people in the first year after release.[1] Before 1969 few films achieved this level of success. One of them was *La Grande Vadrouille*, which was seen by 17 million people, breaking all previous box-office records in France. But it was as much accident as symbol that this smash hit happened to be set against the background of the Occupation.

For the period between 1969 and 1986, I have examined box-office figures for 89 films dealing with the wartime years, four of which may be termed truly successful: *Le Dernier Métro* (1,100,000 attendance in 69 weeks), *Les Uns et les autres* (850,000 in 51 weeks), *L'As des as* (1,223,000 in more than 35 weeks), and, the most astonishing success of all, *Papy fait de la résistance* (927,000 in just 13 weeks). Nationwide, *Papy* and the Truffaut film (*Le Dernier Métro*) rank among the 120 most successful films of the past fifteen years, seen respectively by 4 million and 3,379,000 people as of 1985.[2]

Three of these four hit films came out between 1979 and 1983 and were the work of big-name directors (Truffaut, Lelouch, and Oury). *Papy,* the biggest hit of all and in many ways the most significant, marked a turning point and was perceived as such by the public.

Some dozen films reached a respectable audience (400–800,000 viewers). Leaving aside the war films, these include: *Lacombe Lucien* (528,373 in 23 weeks), *Les Violons du bal* (415,644 in 33 weeks), and *Le Vieux Fusil* (773,978 in 25 weeks). The first two came out in the 1973–74 season, which was one of the most prolific in films about the Occupation: ten in all with a total of 2,580,000 viewers and an average first-run showing of 13 weeks.

Some 30 percent of the films were seen by fewer than 400,000 people, even though some of them marked a new departure or innovation in the representation of the period. Included in this group were *L'Armée des ombres* (258,327 in 15 weeks), which was subsequently broadcast several times on television; *The Sorrow and the Pity* (232,091 in 87 weeks); and *Les Guichets du Louvre* (132,660 in 12 weeks).

These figures are cited solely as indications. Who can say why people go to see a particular film or gauge the film's historical impact on those who see it? Still the figures do confirm the public's enthusiasm for the forties revival from the 1973–74 to the 1975–76 season. While the vogue of a certain style probably played an important role, the revisionism that permeated most of these films very likely had something to do with their popularity as well. The fact that after 1980 the subject lost some of its emotional charge and became routine is also reflected in the popularity in this later period of inoffensive and frivolous films about the war, while relatively few films offered an original or personal vision: only 20,000 people saw Ophuls' *Hôtel*

Terminus about the Barbie case. As a general rule, moreover, the truly outsanding films (the choice is inevitably subjective) did not draw the largest crowds upon release; their influence was indirect, slowly making its way through the fabric of the culture.

Readers

Fortunately, the importance of a historical work is not determined by commercial success. But sales figures are interesting for gauging the influence of a book beyond the audience of specialist readers.

To keep things in perspective, the enormous sales of certain novels should be borne in mind. Régine Deforges' *La Bicyclette bleue*, a recent novel about the Occupation with overtones of *Gone with the Wind*, enjoyed sales in the hundreds of thousands. Such figures dwarf those achieved by the books I shall examine here.

The works of Robert Aron have sold very well indeed. *Histoire de Vichy*, *Histoire de la libération*, and *Histoire de l'épuration* (the purge), published originally by Fayard, have since been brought out in a number of bound and paperback editions.

The figures here reflect sales of the original edition only.[3]

Title	Sales	Period	1st year	Average per year
Vichy	53,000	1954–81	?	1,892
Libération	41,000	1959–82	37,000	1,708
Epuration				
vol. 1	24,700	1966–82	19,500	1,453
vol. 2	18,700	1970–82	13,500	1,438
vol. 3				
part 1	7,600	1974–82	6,000	844
part 2	6,400	1975–82	5,700	800

These figures indicate the immediate impact of each book, not the more enduring influence through paperback sales (which generally number in the tens of thousands). What emerges from the table is a clear set of priorities: the public enthusiastically welcomed the books on Vichy and the Liberation but showed little interest in the history of the purge. Sales of the latter decreased steadily with each new volume, and this poor performance no doubt accounts for the absence of a paperback edition.

Robert Aron died in April 1975. His popularity seems to have peaked in the 1950s and 1960s, during the phase of repression, while his star was in sharp decline throughout the 1970s, the decade during which the new historiography made its mark.

Consider now the following figures for several works published over roughly the same period (1973–1985) by Seuil.[4]

Title	Sales	Period	1st year	Average per year
La France de Vichy (Paxton)				
hardcover	13,382	1973–85	11,845	1,030
paperback	45,072	1974–85	7,844	3,756
Les Pousse-au-jouir du maréchal Pétain (Miller)	6,107	1975–85	4,554	555
Les Collaborateurs (Ory)				
hardcover	8,296	1977–85	6,894	921
paperback	14,213	1980–85	6,653	2,368
De Munich à la libération (Azéma) paperback	45,863	1979–85	13,887	6,551
Ni droite ni gauche (Sternhell)	7,443	1983–85	6,848	2,481
Pétain (Lottman)	17,597	1984–85	16,921	8,798

Ils partiront dans l'ivresse (Aubrac)	29,374	1984–85	24,164	14,687

Generally speaking, these books sold reasonably well, neither better nor worse than other books dealing with less controversial periods. Looking only at first editions of historical works, the Pétain biography is the clear winner, despite its relatively recent publication. The most likely reason for this is that biographies in general have been quite popular of late, since the work itself is rather mediocre. Jean-Pierre Azéma's history, first published in paperback, comes in second, thanks to its adoption as a standard reference text.

The really surprising figures are for Paxton's *La France de Vichy*. Despite the importance of the book and the controversy it triggered, its sales have remained fairly modest, only slightly higher overall than the more recent works of Ory and Miller, which owe a great deal to Paxton's pioneering effort. Similarly, Sternhell's book on French fascism in the 1930s, which stirred up even more violent controversies than Paxton's, derived few sales from the savor of scandal.

All the books mentioned so far, moreover, were easily outstripped by *Ils partiront dans l'ivresse*, Lucie Aubrac's resistance memoir of her work with Jean Moulin. Admittedly, Aubrac appeared as a guest on "Apostrophes," a popular television show where authors discuss their books, where her faceoff with Jacques Isorni produced sparks. Still it seems fair to conclude that the public prefers firsthand accounts to scholarly reconstructions.

Another point to notice is that none of the books has taken off over time. First-year sales generally account for 75–80 percent of the total. Hence the fact that a subject is of topical interest over a considerable period does not ensure the success of historical works on that subject, any more than the historical importance of a book guarantees that it will have an impact on the public. The most flagrant example is Eberhard Jäckel's *France in Hitler's Europe*, which Fayard published in French translation in 1968. Fewer than 3,000 copies have been sold over ten years, even though the book marked a real advance in historical understanding.

Yet there can be no doubt that the reading public is interested in

World War II. A glance at any newspaper stand in France will show that periodicals on the war abound. In October 1979, when Atlas was preparing to market an encyclopedia of the Resistance (*Le colonel Rémy raconte une épopée de la Résistance*), the publisher commissioned a survey, which found that, while 59 percent of those questioned considered World War II to be a remote event, 62 percent discussed it often.[5]

Another example: in 1983, when Hachette brought out a weekly series of facsimile editions of wartime newspapers, the publisher's marketing department predicted a "coefficient of penetration" of 0.67 percent, or 263,000 potential buyers (in a population of 39 million French citizens over the age of fifteen). In fact, around 410,000 copies of the first issue were sold in metropolitan France alone. The war did better than knitting, art, and fishing. The marketing survey predicted that the most interested readers would be "historians," eager to understand the facts, and people in search of their roots, namely, "young people interested in discovering the past and older people interested in reliving it," particularly in regard to daily life in the wartime period.[6]

In other words, history is not of interest only to historians—nothing surprising about that, since history is a shared heritage and historians are in no sense its official guardians. As a result, teachers, journalists, and other popularizers play a much more important role in shaping historical memory than is generally realized. We saw earlier how long it takes for the results of historical research to find their way into textbooks. That leaves writers like Henri Amouroux, whose sales, possibly in the millions, far exceed those of the historians mentioned above, to say nothing of television personalities like Alain Decaux, who are in a position to relay the findings of scholars to a vast audience. But do they always use that position to best advantage?

The Image of Contemporaries

Interest is one thing, opinion is another.[7] But what about simple knowledge of the facts? In 1976, 53 percent of French men and women did not know who had been chief of state from 1940 to 1944, and 61 percent did not know that the man in question had been the commander of French troops at Verdun in 1916 (*Sondages*). In 1980,

50 percent of the French believed that Germany had declared war on France in 1939, and only 19 percent knew the number (90–100,000) killed in the fighting of May and June 1940 (*Figaro Magazine*).

These figures will not surprise anyone who has taught students. If the Vichy syndrome was in part the result of official silence, it was also in large measure the fruit of ignorance. With this in mind, let us now survey public opinion in the 1970s and 1980s. The results are sometimes surprising.

The War and the Armistice

The French are no longer divided about the defeat of 1940. When asked about the causes of the debacle, 56 percent blame the Third Republic for leaving France militarily unprepared; 31 percent cite the incompetence of the generals; 20 percent mention a "defeatist spirit"; and 16 percent blame a "fifth column." In a crude way these reactions reflect the reality. Only 6 percent still explicitly blamed the Popular Front (*Figaro Magazine*, 1980).

Forty-one percent believed that France in 1939 should have "sought an arrangement to avoid war." Only Communists (at the rate of 50 percent) would have favored an alliance with the Soviet Union (*Les Nouvelles littéraires*, 1980).

In hindsight the majority also seems pleased with the armistice: 53 percent approved the statement that "the government was right to sign [the armistice] and to remain on French soil." (Among supporters of the UDF, 62 percent approved.) On the whole, 10 percent rated the armistice a "very good thing" and 53 percent called it a "good thing" (*Figaro Magazine*, 1980).

Collaborators and Partisans

Apparently there has been little change in the public perception of collaborators (Pétain excepted). In 1980, 43 percent of those surveyed considered them to be "inexcusable traitors" and 27 percent, "cowards." Only 8 percent appeared to excuse their behavior, and 5 percent characterized them as "honorable." Pierre Laval was the focus of everyone's hatred: 33 percent would have him executed again, 19 percent would have him sentenced to life in prison, and 2 percent would have him granted a pardon, with 27 percent undecided (*Les Nouvelles littéraires,* 1980). Political affiliations did not affect these attitudes. No doubt the formulation of the questions influenced the results. The pollsters did not attempt to ascertain the effect of the collaborators' political affiliations (except, indirectly, by asking whether collaborators were "fascists prepared to do anything to secure the victory of their ideas," to which 11 percent answered yes). Purely moral judgments took precedence over political ones. But it seems clear that collaborators, and Laval first and foremost, have few admirers in today's France.

Attitudes toward the Resistance and résistants are just as traditional on both the left and the right. The only interesting finding to emerge from the 1980 survey was that 58 percent (mainly older people) regarded partisans as "patriots" compared with 26 percent (mainly the young) who regarded them as "heroes." Only 8 percent judged that resistance fighters were "revolutionaries." Why did contemporaries of the résistants hesitate to call them heroes? Was it some old psychological predisposition that made them prefer "patriot" as a less ambiguous, less problematic term?

In December 1983 a poll taken by *L'Histoire* prior to the fortieth anniversary of the Liberation raised a different issue: "The Liberation of France was due to the combined efforts of several forces struggling against Nazism. Which seems to you to have been most important?" Unsurprisingly, 40 percent answered "the Americans," 6 percent "the Soviets" (19 percent among Communist sympathizers), and 4 percent "the British." But 34 percent said "the French" (15 percent for the French of London and 19 percent for the maquisards). This is an incredible response, nine times greater than the number who mentioned the British, despite the fact that hundreds of thousands of British troops landed on the beaches of Normandy. Here again the responses varied with age and political affiliation, as the accompanying graph shows.

Consider, first, the distribution of responses crediting either of the two main components of the resistance (London or partisans in France). There is a clear difference between generations. Those over fifty, who lived through the war, greatly overestimate the role of the French (45 percent of the eldest group give them primary credit), while younger people, still in or only recently graduated from school, appear to be rejecting the resistancialist myth (51 percent of the eigh-

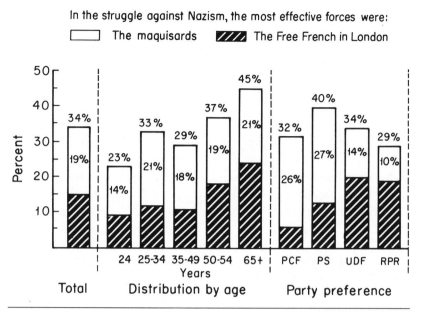

The struggle against Nazism
(Robert Frank and Henry Rousso, *L'Histoire*, May 1984)

teen-to-twenty-four age group gave primary credit to the Americans).
The graph of political distribution shows that the myth had more of
an impact on the left than on the right.

The graph also shows that the young tend to give more credit to
partisans fighting in France, whereas their elders favored the Free
French. This difference is accentuated by political factors: on the left
an overwhelming majority gave primary credit to résistants fighting
inside France, whereas most people on the right gave credit to the FFL
(UDF sympathizers more so than the supposed Gaullists of the RPR).

The Man of June Eighteenth

Positive as the partisan's image may be, it is nothing compared with
that of General de Gaulle:

Question: Of the following images, which most closely approxi-
mates your idea or memory of the Liberation of France in 1944?

An American soldier greeted by a crowd: 16.
A partisan wearing an armband: 15.
General de Gaulle marching down the Champs-Elysées: 47.
A woman with a shaved head: 8.
Other: 3.
Don't know: 11.

Overwhelmingly favored by those over sixty-five (68 percent) or on the right politically (63 percent of the UDF and 60 percent of the RPR), de Gaulle was relegated to second place (after the American soldier) by young people aged eighteen to twenty-four (28 percent) or on the left (43 percent of Socialists and 32 percent of Communists).

All the polls reflect de Gaulle's drawing power. It is interesting to compare the results of a 1983 survey with those of other polls conducted since de Gaulle's death in 1970. Consider the accompanying graph, which shows respondents' choices of various possible descriptions of the General. Of all the appellations, the one that remains most popular, albeit with a steadily diminishing proportion of the populace, is the man of 18 June (see graph).

Responses to questions concerning the consequences of 18 June also demonstrate that it was de Gaulle who gave substance to the resistancialist myth: 79 percent believe that the appeal of 18 June "saved France's honor" (compared with 6 percent who hold that it "divided the French for no purpose"), while 57 percent consider that the appeal enabled France to "take her place among the victors," compared with only 22 percent for whom "it did nothing to alter France's position" (*Histoire Magazine*, 1980).

Finally, when the General is made to bear responsibility for the purge, memory of that time becomes less painful: for 24 percent it was a "settling of scores" and an injustice; for 26 percent it was "necessary," even if "excesses" occurred; for 11 percent it was necessary and there were no excesses; and for another 11 percent it was insufficient.

By contrast, the notion that France needed two strings in her bow, Pétain and de Gaulle, has not held up well, although there has been some tendency to confuse historical reality with obscure retrospective desires. In response to a poll conducted by *Figaro Magazine* in May 1980, and despite the rather Manichaean phrasing of the questions, those surveyed clearly distinguished the two principal antagonists in

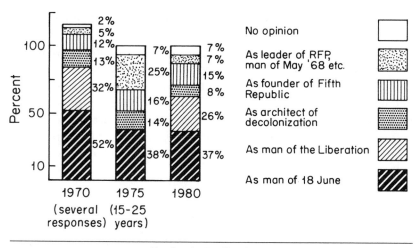

Charles de Gaulle, the man
(*L'Histoire Magazine* and *L'Express*, November 1975)

the Franco-French war: 42 percent felt that "their roles were opposed, since Marshal Pétain collaborated with Germany and fought the Resistance, while General de Gaulle fought against Germany and organized the Resistance." On the other hand, 31 percent approved of the statement that "their roles were complementary, because Marshal Pétain protected France's interests as best he could in Vichy, while General de Gaulle prepared for the Liberation in London." When faced with this alternative, 27 percent declined to answer. Nevertheless, 59 percent "would have liked" to have seen the two men come to an understanding between 1940 and 1944 (including 72 percent of the UDF, 68 percent of the RPR, and—astonishingly—42 percent of Communists).

The Myth of the Pétain Myth

In the first chapter I tried to analyze how the Pétain myth was forged after the Marshal's death in 1951. But there I was concentrating exclusively on the factors that shaped the myth, such as the role of the Pétain Association and the influence of Pétainist ideas in politics. Now I want to consider Pétain as perceived by the public. From this standpoint it is clear that Pétain's memory is still alive and still controversial.

The media are well aware of the power of Pétain's memory. Whenever the subject of the Marshal is broached, a flood of mail pours in from readers, listeners, or viewers. It would be tedious to explore in detail the thousands of letters and the many different points of view expressed. Still, since polling is such an imprecise art and since the picture of public opinion recorded by polls is necessarily fleeting, it is worth pausing a moment to plumb the depths of what is sometimes called *la France profonde*.

On 15 August 1985 Jean-François Kahn overcame the doubts of editor-in-chief Albert du Roy and published, in *L'Evénement du jeudi*, a brief resumé of Pétain's career on the fortieth anniversary of his trial. The article was a success, and sales of the magazine rose, as did the number of letters to the editor. Although the article appeared at the height of summer, normally a slow season for reader mail, dozens of letters, some more than five pages long, others continuing sagas spread over several episodes, arrived at the offices of the magazine, which published a number of them.[8]

Most of the writers were supporters of Pétain who gave the impression that they thought of themselves as history's castoffs. The subjects most frequently touched on were "Vichy as shield," Pétain's supposed double game, and his "resistance to German demands." The Marshal was rarely cast as the leader of the National Revolution but always portrayed as France's savior and father-protector (even of his enemies). A reader from Metz wrote:

> The necessity of the armistice and the uncertain outcome of the war were the two issues that really concerned Pétain personally. The rest—the rather childish and ridiculous "National Revolution"—was not really Pétain's doing but the work of men who wished to exploit for their own benefit the extraordinary discredit that attached to the leaders of the Third Republic. The government's chief concern was to protect them from popular wrath. That was the reason for certain administrative internments.

Henri Amouroux was frequently invoked as an authority lending credence to these arguments. Incidentally, Amouroux himself made extensive use of mail he received as a "source" of information. A reader from Saint-Quentin wrote:

Amouroux captures the reality of the situation quite well. We had had the daylights beat out of us. The officers were the first to run. A way had to be found to stop a defeat that was about to turn into a disaster. After that, Pétain shilly-shallied. He played a double game.

On the other hand, some of the views made popular by this authority outraged certain readers, such as this one from the Nord:

No doubt Henri Amouroux and his friends were Pétainists—trees hiding in the forest—but I call upon him to subtract from his "40 million" [alluding to the forty million Frenchmen whom Amouroux claimed had supported Pétain]:

(1) My parents, who were floored by the announcement of the armistice;

(2) Myself, who did not wait until 18 June to resist in spirit and who did what I could while waiting for the chance to join a [resistance] cell . . . as a result of which I was ultimately deported;

(3) My sister and her friends from the lycée who passed around photographs of de Gaulle;

(4) My friend X, whose brother was a sailor in England and whose boyfriend was an aviator, and my friend Y, whose father and younger brothers went over to Free France.

The most sensitive issue was unquestionably that of the Jews, a subject that occasioned many revealing slips of the tongue, silences, and naive confessions. Sometimes the tone was friendly, as in this letter from a "Pétainist" reader, aged seventy-nine, to Jean-François Kahn: "Since I assume from your name that you are Jewish, permit me to say that this is the first time I have ever heard a person of your religion speak with the impartiality you have demonstrated." Other times it was curious, as in this letter, from the same Saint-Quentin reader, to Pierre Enckell, the author of a highly polemical article on Pétain: "I think that the author of the article ought to tell us his age and background. If he is Jewish, it is not surprising that he feels resentment toward Pétain and especially his government." Many letters share this inquisitorial tone, typical of the extreme right. A reader from Caluire is obsessed with the question of identity: "Who is this Mr. Pierre Enckell? Who is this guy who writes that Marshal Pétain, 'quite stubborn but not very smart,' was a coward? We know that Mr. Henry Rousso is a researcher at the CNRS, but who is this Mr. Pierre Enckell?"[9]

To restore a proper perspective, I should also mention the many letter writers who recalled the handshake at Montoire, the Riom trials, the belated denunciation of the Milice, and the criminal role of the French police. Some of their arguments were no sounder than those on the other side (including charges of an alleged prewar conspiracy and allegations that Pétain took refuge in Sigmaringen, when in fact he was taken there as a prisoner by the Germans). But most of the hostile letters expressed irritation that the whole business was being dredged up once again, as in this one from a reader in Paris: "'Pétain, traitor or victim?'!!! Oh, no! Not you! Since everyone, including you, knows the answer, leave the question to the dyed-in-the-wool Vichyites, who every so often like to challenge established facts."[10]

And then there are the letters from readers who must be placed in rather bizarre categories, proof of the complexity of the issue: the "Pétaino-Gaullists" and the "anti-Gaullist Pétainist résistants," to say nothing of anticommunists of various persuasions. Consider this diatribe from a reader in Bayonne:

> The Marshal, the first person in France to resist . . . did not surrender one square inch of French territory to the Nazis and did all he could to limit the damage to a France that had been soundly beaten. Colonel de Gaulle, for he was nothing but a colonel in a general's uniform who never saw a German helmet up close, never saw combat and did nothing but give away the French departments of our colonial empire . . . A veteran of World War II, I helped more than twenty escaped prisoners and aviators make their way to Spain, but not for de Gaulle's cause.[11]

Hatred from the remote past merges with hatred from more recent times, confusing the issue and reminding us once again that divisions during the Occupation were not so clearly delineated as the passage of time has made it possible to believe.

The Pétain issue has always interested pollsters, who as early as 1944 sensed that reactions to the Marshal's fate were a useful tool for gauging the state of French public opinion. The question most often asked has to do with the appropriateness of the sentence. The Haute Cour sentenced Pétain to death in 1945, but that sentence was commuted to imprisonment for life on the Isle of Yeu. What else could

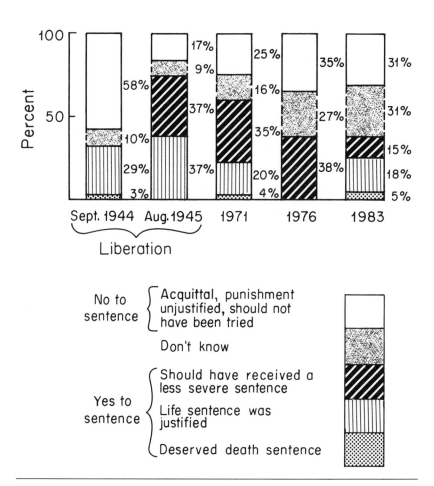

Pétain (for sources see Chapter 7, n. 12)

the court have done? Consider the results of five polls shown here, taken in 1944, 1945, and between 1971 and 1983.[12]

The dramatic change in opinion that occurred between September 1944 and August 1945, the date of Pétain's trial, was due to the public's shock at the condition of returning deportees and fatigue with a war that was taking a long time to end. Pétain bore the brunt of the public wrath that followed the brief outburst of joy in the summer of the Liberation. The Marshal, in any case, had always claimed the role for himself: "It is I alone whom history will judge."[13]

Polls concerning this aspect of public opinion are lacking for the 1960s. Nevertheless, the results of an IFOP poll (published in *Sondages*, 9 June 1966) comparing Pétain and de Gaulle in regard to how well each man protected the interests of France are worth noting:

	Did some good	Did some harm	Don't know
Pétain	51	17	32
de Gaulle	80	5	15

These results would seem to contradict public opinion (both before and after 1966) concerning the Marshal's sentence, unless a segment of the population deemed that Pétain's actions had been useful in protecting French interests but still felt that he should be punished.

Between 1971 and 1983 opinion remained fairly stable and may be broken down into three broad categories: the undecided, whose number increased steadily; a second group favoring leniency, whose numbers declined to under one-third of those surveyed; and a third group of intransigents, who insisted on at least a symbolic penalty. The number calling for the death penalty declined to a small minority, however.

The fact that public opinion remained fairly static over a period of nearly fifteen years suggests that the debate over Pétain's role was passed on from one generation to the next. This hypothesis is confirmed by a comparison of responses to the 1971 and 1983 surveys grouped according to age (see graph).

The two polls reveal certain structural similarities. The closer people surveyed were to the event, the less likely they were to decline to answer: the number of undecided is far higher in the lower age groups

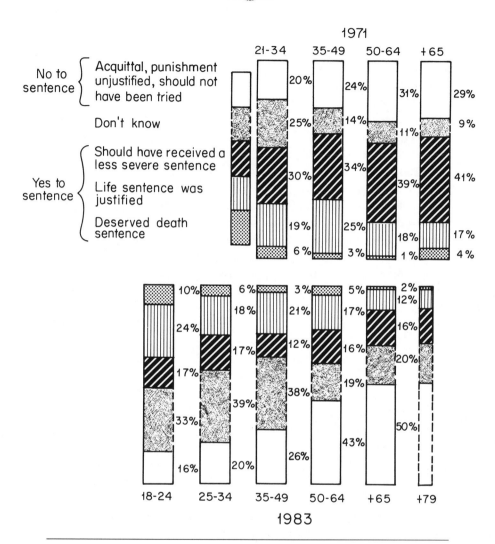

The Pétain sentence: Evolution of opinion by age distribution, 1971 and 1983
(*Sud-Ouest*/SOFRES, November 1971; Louis Harris-France/*L'Histoire*,
December 1983)

*Note: Participants in the survey who were between 21 and 34 in November 1971 were
between 33 and 46 in December 1983, and those who were between 50 and 65 in 1971
were between 62 and 77 in 1983. Thus the age group in the two polls
are roughly comparable.*

(under thirty-four in 1971, under fifty in 1983). Not surprisingly, Pétain was more likely to cause dissension among those who had direct memories of the Occupation.

In 1971 a clear majority felt that Pétain ought to have been punished in one way or another: totals ranged from 55 percent in the youngest group to 62 percent in the oldest group. In 1983 the corresponding range was from 51 percent to 30 percent. Not only were hostile opinions less common, but, even more remarkable, the young now took a harsher attitude toward Pétain than did their elders. Older people had become far more likely to show leniency.

If we follow the shifting opinions of particular age cohorts as they grow older, we find a systematic increase in leniency: in 1971 the twenty-one to thirty-four age group was 55 percent hostile to Pétain and the thirty-five to forty-nine age group was 62 percent hostile; by 1983, the former group (now thirty-five to forty-nine) was only 36 percent hostile, and the latter (now fifty to sixty-four) was 38 percent hostile. Those who had been between fifty and sixty-four in 1971 and who were over sixty-five in 1983 had changed their opinion radically: the rate of hostility decreased from 58 to 24 percent.

These figures suggest the following hypothesis: opinion for and against Pétain has not been permanent; rather, there have been cycles of hostility and leniency, with the proportion of each varying according to age. Those who lived through the events were mostly against Pétain as long as the events were still relatively fresh in their minds. With the passage of time, their hostility decreased, while a younger generation that had not endured the Occupation discovered anti-Pétain reflexes of its own. Will this generation also change its opinion once it passes forty?

In other words, the older generation has lost its animosity, but that sentiment has been passed on to the younger generation. This observation is an important key to understanding the ups and downs of the Vichy syndrome. The 1983 poll included a question about the way in which memories (of the Liberation, to be precise) were passed on: 40 percent of those responding credited television, while another 40 percent gave priority to stories told within the family. These two possibilities far outpaced official ceremonies, which came in third, and books or classroom teaching, which came in fourth (except for the lowest age group, including children still in school, which ranked this category second). But television and family discussions are the forms of transmission most likely to capture the conflicts of memory inherent in the case, certainly more likely than official ceremonies, which are designed to do just the opposite, or the classroom. Old newsreel footage on television has had a tremendous impact. Beyond that, television has been drawn to every controversy, even the most insignificant. Have not the networks by their very nature magnified the political, cultural, and intellectual turmoil swirling around Vichy? As for the role of the family, it may be that the situation is in some ways comparable to that surrounding the Dreyfus Affair, which was once the hot topic at every family table.

It is also clear that the power of the Pétain myth has probably been overstated. Those favoring leniency have always been in the minority. Furthermore, indulgence toward Pétain has not been any more permanent than animosity. To judge from the available figures, only a very small percentage of the population has not changed its opinion. Pétain became an abstraction, a common denominator, so that it is plausible to say that reactions to him are only remotely related to the internal battles of 1940 and are significantly influenced by today's political struggles. The following table, which shows attitudes toward Pétain grouped by party affiliation, corroborates this hypothesis.

	1971 (Sud-Ouest/SOFRES)			1983 (L'Histoire/Louis Harris)		
	Punish	Acquit	Don't know	Punish	Acquit	Don't know
Communists	68	17	15	49	18	33
Socialists	69	20	11	47	27	26
UDR/RPR	57	26	17	37	26	27
"Center"/ UDF	(55)	(31)	(14)	28	50	22

Pétain thus divided the left from the right, but less in 1983 than in 1971. Meanwhile the percentage favoring leniency and, above all, the undecided increased sharply: 33 percent of Communists answered "don't know" in 1983, which makes one wonder how much the Communist electorate really cared about representations of the war, even though this formed one of the pillars of the Communist Party.

These results are far more illuminating than the misleading cover published by *Figaro Magazine,* which in May 1980 proclaimed that "66 percent of the French do not condemn Pétain," a figure obtained by adding the 59 percent who felt that the Marshal was "sincerely convinced of the national interest but was overtaken by events" (a logical choice, since the description could equally well apply to most collaborators, including avowed fascists) and the 7 percent who considered Pétain to be a "hero [who was] unjustly condemned." Perhaps it is in the nature of myths to mystify everything, even their own existence.

The Politics of Memory

When the French public is asked about actual or possible political decisions bearing on wartime memories, the results are diverse. The public is even less capable than the politicians of dealing rationally with symbols stemming from the 1940s.

In a survey of opinion regarding the transfer of Pétain's ashes to Douaumont in 1971, 72 percent said they would approve: 26 percent in order to "do justice to the man"; 21 percent because "after twenty-five years the time has come to forget and forgive"; and 25 percent "because [the transfer] does not pose any problems." Only 11 percent declared themselves to be adamantly opposed, and 17 percent had no opinion.

Now the *very same poll* that produced this result also showed that a clear majority believed that Pétain should have been punished in one way or another. There can be no doubt that many of the people who participated in the poll did not understand (or refused to admit) the significance of a decision to transfer Pétain's ashes. Like the authentic Pétainists (but for different reasons), they apparently believed that the transfer ceremony would help to bring about "national reconciliation." How else can one explain why 56 percent of those polled who were classified as belonging to the extreme left (including Communists) approved of the transfer, and did so three years after May '68?

Perhaps the way the questions were phrased played a part. Still, at a time when received images of the past were being subjected to searching criticism, it is astonishing that so many people could believe that it was right to condemn Vichy's head of state but that the victor of Verdun should be buried on the site where he had won his laurels. Certainly their intention was not to glorify the National Revolution but to consign it to oblivion.

Remember that this happened in 1971, a critical year in the evolution of the Vichy syndrome. Yet only a small minority had yet felt the impact of revisionist thinking about the past. Most French people still basked in the "invented honor" that had been bestowed upon them in order to facilitate forgiveness and forgetfulness. They never gave a thought to the possibility that the transfer of Pétain's ashes to Douaumont might reopen old wounds. (This is why all the presidential candidates did nothing to dampen rumors that the transfer might occur if they were elected, and it is also why the president, once elected, quickly moved to stifle any hint that he might actually make good on such a promise.)

Similarly, when *L'Express* polled the French in May 1975 about Giscard's cancellation of the official commemoration of 8 May, opinion was fairly evenly divided: 48 percent were opposed (especially the left and the elderly, where opposition ran as high as 60 percent), and 43 percent were in favor (65 percent on the right). This time the ostensible reason for the decision was the need to foster Franco-German cooperation: 51 percent felt that the cancellation might help in that regard, while 41 percent disagreed. The results may well have been distorted by contemporary political controversy, however. The poll did not distinguish between liberals and Gaullists on the majority side, and so it may have reflected party divisions more than clear-cut opinions concerning the ceremony in question.

Support for this comes from two polls conducted four years later: in 1979, 74 percent felt that young people ought to know about what had gone on between 1939 and 1945 "in order to prevent such things from happening again," while 75 percent favored the broadcast of *Holocaust,* which for a time was threatened, as *The Sorrow and the Pity* had been, with censorship through inaction. After viewing the program, however, 67 percent did not feel any "more sensitive to the problem of racism" than they had before.

One other finding is worth reporting: the first of the two polls mentioned in the preceding paragraph also found that 25 percent of those questioned ranked the defeat of 1940 and the Occupation first among factors that helped to determine their political opinions; 19 percent ranked the Liberation first (for a total of 44 percent citing factors related to the war); 32 percent singled out May '68; 18 percent, the Algerian War; and 16 percent, the Popular Front.

The polling data are disparate, it is true, but no better information is available. Taken as a whole, the results confirm that the public has been highly attuned to World War II memories over the past fifteen years, although less than one might assume from all the political and intellectual debate on the subject. Most important, the public's interest has been focused on issues different from those of concern to politicians and intellectuals.

Opinion is no longer divided over the timing of the armistice or the causes of the defeat in 1940. Furthermore, none of the polls really reflects understanding of the connection between the cessation of hostilities with the Germans and the beginning of a fratricidal war of ideologies that had been in the cards since Munich. According to the polls, the French now agree that the military struggle had to be ended, but they do not agree about the alleged need to establish a new order.

Everyone now disapproves of collaborators, but opinions about the résistants vary. When considered on their own merits, they receive a grade of "satisfactory": they were "patriots." When compared with other anti-German forces, such as the Allied armies, their score improves markedly as nationalist reflexes come into play. But when compared with General de Gaulle, the resistance fighters are completely blotted out by the towering image of the man of June Eighteenth. On the whole, however, there is little controversy about the Resistance.

The only issue that really divides the French is Pétain (not Vichy). Thus the notion that his ashes can somehow effect a national reconciliation is even more absurd than it would be otherwise. Pétain survives as a disembodied abstraction, an object of fantasies and tenacious enmity. If we judge by public opinion, his memory is the quintessence of the syndrome, which in this connection might better be called the Pétain syndrome instead of the Vichy syndrome.

Unsurprisingly, it is ideology that prevents the French from agreeing about the nature of the war. The typical right-wing voter is more likely to have a positive attitude toward Pétain or toward those resistance fighters who wore uniforms and carried flags (the FFL), whereas the typical left-wing voter is more likely, even today, to repudiate the Marshal (though less than one might think) and to admire the partisans who fought a clandestine guerrilla war against the Germans.

Generational differences tell us more. Marked differences of attitude separate those who lived through the war from members of the baby-boom generation born after it. These differences influence views of prominent wartime figures as well as postwar myths. Younger people reject the resistancialist myth in particular, and it therefore seems fair to say that their thinking was changed forever by the new works that appeared between 1971 and 1974. They also reject the myth of the man with the steely blue gaze, although attitudes toward Pétain generally moderate with increasing age. Only de Gaulle still commands widespread allegiance.

Nevertheless, the baby-boomers, like their parents and grandparents before them, are still affected by the *guerre franco-française*. A not insignificant portion of the under-thirty-five age group still insists that Pétain should have been put to death in 1945. Generally speaking, moreover, there are few issues about which any age cohort holds a close-to-unanimous view. Although differences of opinion may diminish or change over time, it seems unlikely that they will disappear altogether.

CONCLUSION

We now know how the Vichy syndrome has worked, but much remains to be done before we can claim to understand why it exists. I will explore two possibilities by way of conclusion. One has to do with the nature of the original event, the other with the specific way in which memories of that event have evolved.

The New Dreyfus Affair

The depth of the crisis into which France was plunged between 1940 and 1944 is obviously one reason why memories of that period have periodically resurfaced ever since. But note that my initial hypothesis—that internal quarrels left deeper scars than either the defeat or the German occupation—seems to have been largely confirmed. The crux of the matter, from the amnesty debates to the scandals of the seventies and eighties, has been the existence of Vichy and the consequent emergence of a political resistance, which was organized to fight not only the Nazis but also the collaborators and the regime born of defeat. The same structural factors that make this crisis an archetype of Franco-French conflict have also shaped the way it has been remembered since the end of the war.

Three of those structural factors deserve special mention here. All have deep roots in French cultural and political tradition. First, the culture of traditional Catholicism played a crucial part in shaping and sustaining a Pétainist view of history. This was particularly true after 1951, when the original hard core of Pétain supporters was joined by others from various parts of the political spectrum, including former members of the Resistance. The Association pour Défendre la Mémoire du Maréchal Pétain openly proclaimed its adherence to traditional Catholic values, although it is true that these values were not the only thing that its members and sympathizers shared. Furthermore, the ADMP functioned like a religious sect and developed a veritable catechism of *maréchalisme*. This common trait helps us to understand the behavior of certain individuals and groups: we comprehend the actions of Abbé Desgranges during the purge; the support of the Christian-Democratic MRP for amnesty; the behavior of Colonel Rémy, whose conversion to Pétainism coincided with a spiritual crisis; and the staunch support of the philosopher Gabriel Marcel, Monsignor Duquaire, and a part of the Catholic hierarchy for milicien Paul Touvier (perhaps because of his history in Catholic youth groups), support that contributed to the scandals of 1972 and 1989.

Most of these individuals and groups shared a set of values, even if those values did not necessarily constitute a coherent body of doctrine. They included reconciliation and pardon, an apolitical interpretation of history, a mystique of the Savior who would take upon himself the sins of others, a visceral rejection of social disorder, which some (Rémy, for instance) identified with the Resistance at the time of the Liberation, and the impossibility of accepting a nonreligious society, all of which encouraged nostalgia for the National Revolution or at any rate for an idealized version of it.

In other words, Pétainism, in this interpretation, was a kind of ideal for those who in one way or another remained loyal to some form of a counterrevolutionary Catholic tradition. This group accounted for the more or less steady support for Pétain revealed by all the polls: the one-third who consistently favored leniency.

Michel Winock recently offered an updated version of a standard explanation of political crisis in France: "The nostalgic yearnings of intransigent Catholicism perpetuated a source of counterrevolutionary sentiment that played a part in every political crisis up to 1940."[1] But what about after 1940? It might also be objected that support for the Marshal stemmed from political as well as religious sources and that some of the individuals and groups who embraced Pétainism had no discernible traditionalist Catholic affiliation.

We thus come to the second of the structural factors mentioned above. Of an ideological order, this factor has to do with the nature of traditional political divisions in France. To a large extent Vichy and collaboration stemmed from right-wing and extreme right-wing political traditions: the counterrevolutionary right and the technocratic right with its "fascistoid" (to borrow Philippe Burrin's term) and totalitarian tendencies. The fact that some figures from the left embraced these ideologies does not alter their basic nature. After the war, both ideologies were explicitly excommunicated from the "right," but this did not prevent them from influencing political thinking, usually in ways that were covert because of reluctance to admit to associations with what was considered a shameful past. From Algérie Française to the Front National of the 1980s, the extreme right has been unwilling to reject out of hand the one experience of power it has known. It has had to tread a careful path between the Pétainist tradition and the memory of outright collaboration. Similar tendencies exist in some quarters of the authoritarian right as well, from the RPF of the late 1940s to certain of today's "liberals," who are quick to declare their allegiance not to the values of fascism but to those of Work, Family, and Fatherland, the watchwords of the National Revolution.

Nevertheless, after the RPF had flirted with Gaullo-Pétainism for a time, it became clear that this was not a viable option. When de Gaulle returned to power in 1958, he based his legitimacy in large part on memories of Free France and wartime Gaullism. It was this move that enabled the right, long discredited by its association with Vichy, to rehabilitate itself.

Meanwhile, the left drew upon resistance thinking to reshape its agenda. Although the attempt to create a party of the Resistance in 1944–45 ended in failure, the Fourth Republic, justifiably or not, invoked the resistance heritage as an ideal standing above all parties. The Communists, for their part, attempted to restore their political virginity by emphasizing the importance of their role in the clandestine struggle (and quantitatively they did provide the largest number of resistance fighters). At the same time, the noncommunist left attempted to refurbish its vision of society by heaping praise on the democratic ideals of the résistants. Although allegiances under the Occupation reshaped the French political landscape, the main divisions remained largely unaltered.

The third structural factor affecting the Vichy syndrome was antisemitism. The reawakening of Jewish memory in the late 1960s made the past a potent political issue in the present. Afraid that the old demons were about to reemerge, a part of the Jewish community and a number of prominent Jewish individuals (Beate and Serge Klarsfeld, Marcel Ophuls, Bernard-Henri Lévy, Claude Lanzmann) set out to throw new light on a previously neglected aspect of the Vichy regime. What followed was a series of scandals and criminal trials, which reached a climax in the period 1978–1981. The Darquier affair led to the first use in France of the law suspending the statute of limitations for crimes against humanity, even though that law dated from 1964. Bear in mind that, since the law has been applied, all the indictments handed down and all the cases still under investigation, with the exception of Klaus Barbie, involved former Vichy functionaries: Leguay, Touvier, Papon, Bousquet, and Sabatier.

To be sure, France was not the only country that found the unthinkable crimes of the Shoah difficult to comprehend, explain, or rationalize. But this sudden resurgence of the past reveals what has been a constant in French history since the Dreyfus Affair: the existence of a political, nonreligious, antisemitic tradition, which at intervals has surfaced to create a division within French society.

An enduring Catholic tradition, a left-right cleavage heightened and transformed by allegiances during the Occupation, and antisemitism: three factors that, along with others, have created the deeply divided identity of today's France. The memory of Vichy, the conflicting representations of the regime, have been shaped by the same antagonistic values that led to the Vichy crisis itself. Whenever any party refers to the Occupation, it invariably touches on the century's central issues: society or nation, equality or hierarchy, state or individual, morality or efficiency, segregation or integration of alien cultures and ethnicities. Whenever any of these issues has cropped up in postwar France, memories of Vichy have bubbled to the surface, as though Vichy has taken the place of the Dreyfus Affair as a central political symbol.

Another aspect of the case lends substance to this idea. The French have been relatively indifferent to other countries' memories of the war, whereas people abroad, particularly in the United States and West Germany, have shown considerable interest in France's feverish domestic battles. In 1962, the year in which Adolf Eichmann was hanged in Jerusalem after a spectacular and unprecedented trial, Karl Oberg, who headed the SS in occupied France, and his assistant Helmut Knochen were released from French prisons. At the time the French view of the past was almost invariably filtered through the prism of the Algerian War, then nearing its end. On 8 May 1985, when Ronald Reagan went to the Bitburg cemetery in West Germany to pay his respects to fallen German soldiers, including members of the Waffen SS, some of whom were assumed at the time to have participated in the massacre at Oradour-sur-Glane, neither French politicians nor the population at large demonstrated any real anger, except for the Communists, delighted at this propaganda windfall, and a few groups of young Jews supported by the antiracist organization SOS-Racisme. No official protests were lodged, and there was no debate in the National Assembly—in short, the event caused no scandal in France. A few weeks later, the media, politicians, and intellectuals were in an uproar the likes of which had not been seen in France since the Darquier affair. What caused it? A televised documentary about the Manouchian affair.[2] And in 1986, when the Nazi past of the former secretary-general of the United Nations and future president of Austria, Kurt Waldheim, was revealed, the only attempt to mobilize public opinion in France came from a few Jewish organizations and met with little success. By contrast, Alexandre de Marenches and his ton of secret archives created a furor a few months later.

Admittedly, these examples are limited in scope, but they strongly suggest that the memory of World War II has been experienced primarily in national terms. Since 1945, however, most of the other countries involved in the war have witnessed similar phenomena, sometimes more acute than the Vichy syndrome in France. West Germany, for example, has had its *Historikerstreit,* or historians' controversy, over the interpretation of World War II, and there have been persistent questions about German identity and its implications for the understanding of Nazism. This national dimension is no doubt a direct legacy of the war, in that the transnational ideological conflict engendered (or in some cases was a consequence of) grave national identity crises. France is a case in point, but not an isolated one.

A Necessary Evil?

Does this mean that the Vichy syndrome is useful primarily as a concept for interpreting French politics? Certainly not. The history of the syndrome, its high and low points, and its main carriers indicates that it is the result of disparities, tensions, and contradictions between different ways of structuring memory, a function performed in various ways by communities and groups, scholars, the media, and others. Supply and demand are almost always out of phase, and the Vichy syndrome is a symptom of that discrepancy.

Initially, the memory of Vichy was couched in the form of rival myths. These myths reproduced the original antagonisms of the time. Worse, they proved incapable of establishing a generally acceptable representation of the event that could stand the test of time.

This criticism applies first of all to the Pétainist myth, which eliminated from the memory of the Occupation all but the image of the Marshal, around which an attempt was made to develop an anachronistic cult of personality. The political character of the National Revolution was repeatedly denied, and history was rewritten to eliminate all unassimilable facts: state collaboration, the French origins of Vichyite antisemitism, and the deeply partisan, anti–Popular Front character of the regime, which was the source of deep and lasting divisions in French politics. As a result, the Pétainist myth soon found itself in an impasse. It was based on an idea of reconciliation, presumably to be effected symbolically through a revision of the verdict of Pétain's trial or a transfer of the Marshal's ashes to Douaumont. Yet, according to all surveys of public opinion, the Pétain case remained one of the most divisive issues in France. The myth could not sustain a political doctrine capable of attracting support in contemporary France, although it was certainly part of a long political tradition that occasionally created a demand for what the myth had to offer. All too often the consequences were embarrassing: Pétainists were obliged to lie. The myth gained real influence, moreover, only during periods of crisis: the cold war, the Algerian War, and, more recently, the years of high political tension in the 1980s, when debate became so heated that it was possible to overlook certain historical inaccuracies.

The fate of the resistancialist myth was quite different. Although it garnered the support of both the Communists and the Gaullists, and although it reflected a real and profound popular desire, the myth succeeded for only a short period of time. It first took shape at the time of the Liberation and served as the foundation of the Fourth Republic but did not gain official status until after de Gaulle's return to power, reaching its apogee between the end of the Algerian War and May '68. Like the Pétainist myth, the resistancialist myth also sought to disguise the realities of the Occupation. Gaullists and Communists found a common interest in exaggerating the scope of French resistance; the Gaullists identified the Resistance with a certain *idea* of France, taken as a whole and embodied in the person of the General, while the Communists depicted the Resistance as a vast popular movement, a national insurrection against the Nazis. Furthermore, both sides had a common interest in minimizing the role of Vichy, a regime that the Gaullists characterized as a handful of traitors and the Communists as the representatives of the bourgeoisie. As a result, the resistancialist myth played down the importance of struggles within France, just as the Pétainist myth did and despite the fact that the very existence of these two competing myths was the most obvious sign that those struggles were still going on.

Alfred Mornet, the prosecutor-general who called for the death penalty against Pétain and who was neither a Gaullist nor a résistant, much less a Communist, has given a strikingly naive illustration of the resistancialist myth in action. In 1949 Mornet entitled his memoirs *Quatre ans à rayer de notre histoire* (Four Years To Erase from Our History) but quickly qualified his choice: "This title cries out for a response, a response that has been given by the résistants who, from London to Chad, from Bir-Hakeim to the maquis of France, made those four years *four years to remember in our history*."[3] Ultimately it is the intrinsically ideological nature of the resistancialist myth that accounts for its weaknesses. It was unable to accommodate experiences of the Occupation that had nothing to do with resistance. The memories of prisoners of war, for example, had no place in the myth: more than a million Frenchmen never experienced the Occupation at all, and many of them remained devoted to the Pétain of World War I, so that their perception of events was radically different from that of their countrymen. The workers of the STO felt ashamed of what they had done, particularly after those who had evaded service in the labor battalions were glorified after the war and even confounded with the maquisards. And deportees, especially Jewish deportees, had no place in the idyllic saga of the Resistance. It was the reawakening of their memories in the 1970s that made it necessary to revise the widely accepted picture of the wartime years. Finally, many résistants themselves felt deprived of their own history by the resistancialist myth, which they found unacceptable because of doubts they harbored about Gaullism, Communism, or both.

For all these reasons, the resistancialist myth went into rapid decline after the death of de Gaulle. And when the Socialists attempted to revive it for their own benefit in 1981, ideologues and politicians attacked the leftist resistance tradition for similar reasons. The misrepresentation of history has not been the monopoly of either the right or the left; polemic, insult, and innuendo have been plentiful on both sides, a sure sign of the defects in post-Vichy mythologies.

Still the mythological nature of these representations of the past cannot explain the whole of the Vichy syndrome. Throughout this book we have seen countless politicians blunder; we have seen attempts to celebrate World War II as if it were some other war; we have seen men put on trial for the wrong reasons; and we have noted innumerable perverse effects of the syndrome. All these things are the result of disparities between different levels of collective memory, which is subject to many kinds of tension, not all of them ideological.

There is, for instance, a never-ending conflict between the desire to forget and the desire to remember, between the need for repression and the unpredictable return of the repressed, between the inexorability of ignorance and the aspiration to truth. There have been conflicts between official memory, which celebrates, selects, and censures in the name of the state, and other organized forms of memory: regional (as in the Bordeaux trials), religious (Jewish memory from the Finaly to the Darquier affair), associative, and so on. There have also been conflicts between generations, which probably are the key to understanding the various turning points in the evolution of the Vichy syndrome.

In 1954 the French people began to see the first real effects of economic growth as postwar shortages came to an end. The amnesty seemed to have closed the book on the war once and for all. Those who had lived through the Occupation as adults wanted to forget the past. Some preferred ignorance to knowledge. Others—men as different as Sartre and Pompidou—may have felt an obscure sense of shame at not having been present when crucial decisions were made. The older generation chose silence; the polemics quieted down, and filmmakers and historians avoided certain subjects, apparently with the tacit approval of the public. At any rate, there is little evidence to the contrary. Paradoxically, even former résistants and deportees contributed to this state of mind (which they later criticized, but in an entirely different context): résistants, particularly those who had been most committed, maintained a discreet silence, while deportees found it impossible to describe what they had endured.

In 1971 the mirror was finally broken by a generation born during or after the war. May '68 had opened the way for filmmakers, writers, and historians of varying motivation. Some, like Modiano, were fascinated by the ambiguities of the period. Others, like the makers of *The Sorrow and the Pity,* were irritated by the resistancialist myth. Historians set out to penetrate the veils thrown over the past by Robert Aron, with foreign scholars leading the way but soon joined by reinvigorated French historians. French scholars not only braved the minefield of contemporary history but managed to revise important student examinations to include questions on these controversial issues, ensuring that they would be studied in the schools by future teachers and eventually passed on to subsequent generations. The break with the past was not so much political as cultural, and at times it exhibited the excesses common to all revisionist movements. In earlier periods of heightened interest in World War II, the turmoil had been concentrated in a relatively limited sphere: the legislature, the courts, the press, or the intelligentsia. By contrast, the new representations developed in the early 1970s meshed with genuine public demand.

What about tomorrow's generation, the children born while their parents were experiencing the forties revival? A few facts are clear. For one thing, obsession with the war is not yet a thing of the past: from the Barbie trial to the Touvier affair by way of argument over the Resistance, many events still have the potential to erupt into major controversies. For another, it is evident from the polls that, though the younger generation may be less interested than its elders in the history of the Occupation and the debate surrounding it, traditional differences of opinion about Pétain persist.

The purpose of this book was not to rewrite the history of France in light of the Occupation but to highlight certain neglected aspects of memory. But one historical finding does emerge: the deeper structures of French society did not disintegrate as a result of the Vichy crisis. After 1944, and despite all the postwar upheavals and divisions, what Stanley Hoffmann calls the "republican synthesis" was consolidated once more. For all that the resurgence of old memories may create an image of a country unable to pick up the thread of its own history, French society has little by little rediscovered areas of consensus. Was the Vichy syndrome the price to be paid for this progress? If memory was sick, perhaps it was because the body of society remained healthy. Or is the disease hereditary—and incurable?

APPENDIX I

Chronology of Events

23 Aug. 1939	Nazi-Soviet pact signed.
1 Sept. 1939	Germany invades Poland.
3 Sept. 1939	Britain, France, Australia, and New Zealand declare war on Germany.
20 Jan. 1940	French parliament bars Communist deputies.
22 March 1940	Paul Reynaud becomes président du Conseil.
10 May 1940	Germany attacks the Netherlands, Belgium, and Luxembourg.
19 May 1940	Weygand replaces Gamelin as commander of French armies.
28 May 1940	Belgian army surrenders.
10 June 1940	French government flees Paris.
14 June 1940	Paris surrenders.
16 June 1940	Reynaud resigns, Pétain becomes président du Conseil.
17 June 1940	Pétain announces armistice negotiations with Germany.
18 June 1940	de Gaulle, in London, broadcasts appeal to French nation to continue resistance.
22 June 1940	French-German armistice signed at Rethondes.
28 June 1940	Britain recognizes de Gaulle as leader of Free French.
29 June 1940	Government established in Vichy.
10 July 1940	Pétain granted "full powers" as head of Vichy.
24 Oct. 1940	Hitler and Pétain hold talks at Montoire.
2 June 1944	CFLN declares itself provisional government of French republic.
9 Aug. 1944	Provisional government assumes control of liberated territory.
25 Aug. 1944	Liberation of Paris; de Gaulle marches through city.
11 Nov. 1944	First postwar commemoration under auspices of PCF.
Jan. 1945	Dispute over additions to Pantheon.
10 Jan. 1945	First press reports on death camps.
12 Feb. 1945	Commemoration of 12 February 1934 by PCF.
2 April 1945	Flag Day in honor of French army.

1 May 1945	Commemoration of workers' movement.
8 May 1945	Official date of German surrender (V-E Day).
18 June 1945	Commemoration of de Gaulle's appeal.
14 July 1945	Bastille Day and commemoration of victory.
18 Aug. 1945	Beginning of commemoration of Liberation.
11 Nov. 1945	Ecumenical commemoration of two world wars.
20 Nov. 1945	Beginning of Nuremberg trials.
20 Jan. 1946	Resignation of de Gaulle.
10 Sept. 1946	First death sentence handed down in absentia to Paul Touvier, former head of Milice, by Rhône court.
1 Oct. 1946	Verdicts at Nuremberg trials.
13 Oct. 1946	Referendum on Fourth Republic constitution.
19 Dec. 1946	Beginning of war in Indochina.
Jan. 1947	First issue of *Ecrits de Paris*.
4 March 1947	Second death sentence handed down in absentia to Touvier by Savoy court.
4 May 1947	Dismissal of Communist ministers.
10 June 1947	First issue of *Aspects de la France*.
17 June 1947	France and Britain accept Marshall Plan aid.
13 April 1948	Creation of Honorary Committee for release of Pétain.
20 June 1948	In speech at Verdun, de Gaulle touches on fate of Pétain.
13 March 1949	Beginning of amnesty campaign under auspices of MRP and groups within RPF.
11 April 1950	Article by Rémy in *Carrefour* defending Pétain.
25 June 1950	Beginning of Korean War.
24 Oct. 1950	Beginning of amnesty debate in Chamber of Deputies.
9 Nov. 1950	Terrenoire amendment calls for release of Pétain.
5 Jan. 1951	First amnesty law on crimes of Occupation.
18 Jan. 1951	First issue of *Rivarol*.
15 Feb. 1951	Founding of CNIP.
17 June 1951	Election of Jacques Isorni, Paul Estèbe, and Roger de Saivre as deputies on list of UNIR, along with election of Jacques Le Roy Ladurie.
23 July 1951	Death of Pétain.
6 Nov. 1951	Creation of ADMP.
6 March 1952	Investiture of Antoine Pinay, with support from 27 RPF deputies.
7 March 1952	Charles Maurras pardoned for medical reasons; dies on 16 November.

27 May 1952	Pinay signs treaty on CED.
12 Jan. 1953	Beginning of Oradour trial before military tribunal of Bordeaux.
22 Jan. 1953	André François–Poncet assumes seat in Académie Française formerly held by Pétain.
3 Feb. 1953	Beginning of Finaly affair.
13 Feb. 1953	Severe sentences handed out to Alsatians in Oradour trial.
18 Feb. 1953	Vote on special amnesty law for those convicted in Oradour trial.
22 July 1953	Birth of Poujadist movement.
27 July 1953	Armistice in Korea.
6 Aug. 1953	Second amnesty for crimes committed during Occupation.
14 April 1954	Law establishing last Sunday in April as National Day for the Memory of Victims and Heroes of the Deportation.
7 May 1954	Fall of Dien Bien Phu.
18 June 1954	Mendès France becomes president of Council.
20 July 1954	Signing of Geneva accords.
30 Aug. 1954	Parliament rejects CED treaty.
9 Oct. 1954	Karl Oberg, former supreme commander of SS in France and under sentence of death in Germany but extradited to France on 10 October 1946, sentenced to death, along with aide Helmut Knochen, by military tribunal of Paris.
1 Nov. 1954	Beginning of insurrection in Algeria.
2 Jan. 1956	Pierre Poujade wins 11 percent of vote in legislative elections.
18 April 1956	Robert Hersant, elected deputy for Oise on radical-socialist ticket, declared ineligible by Assembly; reelected 18 June.
5 Nov. 1956	Anglo-French raid on Suez.
22 May 1958	Morand fails in first postwar attempt to gain election to Académie Française.
1 June 1958	de Gaulle becomes president of Council.
28 Sept. 1958	Adoption of Fifth Republic constitution.
11 April 1959	8 May ceases to be national holiday.
17 April 1959	de Gaulle says at Vichy that France is "a single nation."
5 June 1959	de Gaulle visits Mont-Mouchet, place honored by Resistance.

31 Oct. 1959	Granted reprieve year earlier by René Coty, Oberg and Knochen have death sentences commuted to life imprisonment.
6 Jan. 1960	Unit of Pétain Association established in Algeria.
22 March 1960	Return of Abel Bonnard, Vichy's secretary of education, from exile. Haute Cour commutes his death sentence to ten years' exile (time already served).
11 April 1961	Eichmann trial begins in Jerusalem.
22 April 1961	Putsch of generals in Algiers.
18 March 1962	Signing of Evian accords.
31 May 1962	Execution of Eichmann in Jerusalem.
28 Oct. 1962	Referendum on election of president of Republic by universal suffrage.
Dec. 1962	Oberg and Knochen released from prison and sent back to Germany.
2 Aug. 1964	Beginning of massive U.S. buildup in Vietnam.
17 Dec. 1964	Vote on first amnesty law for cases related to Algeria, 269 votes in favor and 210 abstentions.
17 Dec. 1964	Novak, Eichmann's aide, sentenced to eight years in West Germany.
18–19 Dec.	Transfer of Jean Moulin's ashes to Pantheon.
26 Dec. 1964	Parliament unanimously adopts law suspending statute of limitations for crimes against humanity.
30 Jan. 1965	de Gaulle refuses to allow funeral ceremonies for General Weygand, who died on 28 January, to be held in Invalides.
6 Nov. 1965	Jacques Vasseur, former collaborator arrested 20 November 1962, is sentenced to death; in February 1966 de Gaulle issues reprieve. Another collaborator, Jean Barbier, also sentenced to death, receives reprieve July 1966.
19 Dec. 1965	de Gaulle reelected president of Republic by universal suffrage.
21 June 1966	Joseph Cortial, another collaborator, sentenced to life imprisonment.
5 June 1967	Beginning of Six-Day War.
27 Nov. 1967	de Gaulle holds press conference on Israel, refers to Jews as "an elite people, sure of itself and domineering."
3 May 1968	Sorbonne evacuated by police; student protest grows.

24 Oct. 1968	Morand elected to Académie Française.
10 Nov. 1968	On eve of 50th anniversary of armistice, de Gaulle orders wreath placed on graves of Pétain, Galliéni, Joffre, and Clemenceau, "four great men not buried in the Invalides."
15 June 1969	Georges Pompidou elected president.
July 1970	Beginning of controversy over activities of Georges Marchais, assistant secretary-general of PCF, in Germany in 1942.
9 Nov. 1970	Death of de Gaulle.
April 1971	Release of *The Sorrow and the Pity*.
23 Nov. 1971	Pompidou reduces Touvier's sentence.
12 Feb. 1972	Incidents at Notre-Dame-des-Victoires during ceremony in memory of Xavier Vallat, Vichy commissioner of Jewish affairs, who died 6 January 1972.
1 July 1972	Law passed making it illegal to incite racial hatred.
18 July 1972	Demonstration at crypt of the deportees against reduction of Touvier's sentence.
21 Sept. 1972	Pompidou's speech on national reconciliation.
Feb. 1973	Pétain's coffin stolen from Isle of Yeu by right-wing militants.
19 March 1973	Beginning of polemic over Robert Paxton's *Vichy France*.
9 Nov. 1973	First charges of crimes against humanity filed against Touvier in Lyons, followed by additional charges in Chambéry, 27 March 1974.
2 April 1974	Death of Pompidou.
19 May 1974	Valéry Giscard d'Estaing elected president.
6 Feb. 1975	Appeals court overturns decisions of courts in Lyons and Chambéry, which had ruled they had no jurisdiction in Touvier case.
8 May 1975	Giscard declares end to official celebration of 8 May (V-E Day).
27 Oct. 1975	Paris court rules it has jurisdiction in Touvier case but statute of limitations is in effect.
13 June 1976	Giscard pays homage to Pétain at Douaumont.
30 June 1976	Another Paris court overrules decision that statute of limitations is in effect in Touvier case.
27 Jan. 1978	Robert Faurisson causes scandal at colloquium on French churches and Christians at Lyons.

17 May 1978	First issue of *Figaro Magazine*.
25 May 1978	Senate debates new law on archives; Assembly debates issue in December; law passed January 1979.
28 Oct. 1978	Interview with Darquier de Pellepoix published in *L'Express*.
1 Nov. 1978	Faurisson publishes article in *Le Matin de Paris;* on 29 December 1978 publishes another article in *Le Monde*.
11 Nov. 1978	For armistice celebration, Giscard orders flowers placed on grave of Pétain.
15 Nov. 1978	Attorney Serge Klarsfeld files complaint against Jean Leguay, former assistant to Vichy chief of police.
16 Nov. 1978	Academics in Lyons join criticism of Faurisson; historians begin to mobilize.
6 Dec. 1978	Jacques Chirac makes Cochin appeal, alluding to "foreign party."
27 Feb. 1979	Final episode of *Holocaust* broadcast on French television, followed by debate.
12 March 1979	Jean Leguay indicted for crimes against humanity.
7 June 1979	First elections to European Parliament.
19 June 1979	In response to query submitted 17 December 1976, foreign ministry states that Touvier case does not fall under statute of limitations.
22 June 1979	First article in *Le Monde* on "new right" and start of controversy.
11 Feb. 1980	In Cologne Herbert Hagen and Kurt Lischka found guilty and sent to prison.
8 March 1980	*L'Express* reopens Marchais affair.
11 April 1980	Poll in *Figaro Magazine* featured in cover headline: "66 percent of the French do not condemn Pétain."
23 Sept. 1980	Beginning of wave of antisemitic attacks and antiracist counterdemonstrations.
3 Oct. 1980	Attack on synagogue on rue Copernic kills 4 and injures 20.
4 Oct. 1980	Wave of demonstrations in France against antisemitism.
17 Oct. 1980	Indictment of Marc Fredriksen, head of neo-Nazi FANE.
13 Nov. 1980	Attack on headquarters of Pétain Association.

9 Dec. 1980	Law permitting groups to join prosecutions for crimes against humanity as civil parties.
20 Dec. 1980	Publication of *Mémoire en défense,* defense of Faurisson with preface by Noam Chomsky.
Jan. 1981	Publication of *L'Idéologie française* by Bernard-Henri Lévy.
6 May 1981	*Le Canard enchaîné* launches Papon affair by accusing former minister of having contributed to deportation of Jews from Bordeaux.
10 May 1981	François Mitterrand elected president.
21 May 1981	Mitterrand visits tombs of Jaurès, Schoelcher, and Moulin at Pantheon.
8 July 1981	Robert Faurisson sentenced to pay symbolic franc to MRAP, LICRA, and other groups.
28 Nov. 1981	Touvier, still a fugitive, indicted for crimes against humanity by Judge Martine Anzani, who issues international warrant for arrest.
5 Jan. 1982	First issue of *Présent.*
8 May 1982	8 May again celebrated as national holiday, pursuant to law of 23 September 1981.
19 Jan. 1983	Indictment of Maurice Papon for crimes against humanity.
5 Feb. 1983	Klaus Barbie indicted for crimes against humanity.
24 April 1983	*Der Stern* publishes Hitler's diaries; on 6 May Gerd Heidemann charged with their forgery.
16 Aug. 1983	American commission of inquiry admits Barbie used by American intelligence.
14 Nov. 1983	Jacques Vergès, Barbie's attorney, publishes *Pour en finir avec Ponce Pilate,* leveling charges at members of Resistance.
1 Feb. 1984	Incidents at Assembly concerning activities of Mitterrand and Hersant during war. Deputies Toubon, Madelin, and d'Aubert later censured.
12 Feb. 1984	Press reveals last three imprisoned collaborators, Vasseur, Cortial, and Barbier, released between late 1982 and August 1983.
13 Feb. 1984	Jean-Marie Le Pen appears for first time on major political broadcast.
17 June 1984	Robert Hersant elected to European Parliament on UDF list headed by Simone Veil.

22 Sept. 1984	Mitterrand and Helmut Kohl shake hands at Verdun; Mitterrand orders wreath for Pétain's tomb.
April 1985	Release of Claude Lanzmann's *Shoah*.
8 May 1985	President Reagan makes visit to cemetery at Bitburg, West Germany.
2 July 1985	After weeks of debate on Manouchian affair, Mosco's *Des terroristes à la retraite* shown on television.
5 Oct. 1985	Prosecution completes case against Barbie.
20 Dec. 1985	Cour de Cassation changes definition of crimes against humanity to include some crimes against resistance fighters.
16 March 1986	Right wins legislative elections; proportional representation gives National Front 35 seats. Beginning of "cohabitation" of left and right.
9 July 1986	Prosecution completes new case against Barbie.
Sept. 1986	Alexandre de Marenches, former head of French counterintelligence, causes scandal: unpublished Gestapo files indicate traitors in Resistance.
11 Feb. 1987	Appeals court dismisses charges against Papon, who is reindicted for crimes against humanity in July 1988.
22 Feb. 1987	Jewish and Christian delegations reach agreement in Geneva over departure from Auschwitz of Carmelite nuns there since August 1984.
11 May 1987	Barbie trial begins in Lyons.
4 July 1987	Barbie sentenced to life in prison.
13 Sept. 1987	Jean-Marie Le Pen: "The gas chambers . . . are a minor detail in the history of World War II."
8 May 1988	Mitterrand reelected president.
2 Sept. 1988	Le Pen attacks government minister Michel Durafour with allusion to "Durafour crématoire."
24 May 1989	Touvier arrested in Nice by gendarmerie and indicted by Judge Jean-Pierre Getti in Paris for crimes against humanity.
2 July 1989	Death of Jean Legauy just before case to come up in court; in break with precedent, court closes file with statement of Leguay's guilt for crimes against humanity.
3 July 1989	Cardinal Decourtray names commission of historians to look into archives of archbishopric of Lyons to

	determine if Touvier received help from church officials.
26 Aug. 1989	Monsignor Glemp, primate of Poland, rejects Geneva agreement and revives controversy over Carmelite convent at Auschwitz.
Oct. 1989	Controversy breaks out among former résistants over *Jean Moulin: L'Inconnu du Panthéon*, biography by Moulin's secretary, Daniel Cordier.
10 Nov. 1989	Berlin Wall comes down.
5 Dec. 1989	Le Pen asks secretary of state for planning Lionel Stoléru, a Jew, whether "it is correct that you have a dual nationality."
Summer 1990	Reopening of Bousquet affair. He will be killed in June 1993, just before the end of the inquiry.

APPENDIX 2

French Films and World War II

1944

La Libération de Paris (newsreel footage)

1945

Après Mein Kampf, *mes crimes* (A. Ryder)
Débarquement sud (SCA documentary)
Fausse Alerte (J. de Baroncelli)
Le Jugement dernier (R. Chanas)
Nuit d'alerte (L. Mathot)
Peloton d'exécution (A. Berthomieu)
Six juin à l'aube (J. Grémillon)

1946

Un ami viendra ce soir (R. Bernard)
La Bataille du rail (R. Clément)
Caravane blindée (SCA documentary)
Les Clandestins (A. Chotin)
Les Démons de l'aube (Y. Allégret)
Fils de France (P. Blondy)
La Grande Épreuve (SCA documentary)
Jéricho (H. Calef)
Mission spéciale (M. de Caronge)
Patrie (L. Daquin)
Le Père tranquille (R. Clément)

Présence au combat (M. Cravenne)
Tempête sur les Alpes (M. Ichac)
Vive la liberté (J. Musso)

1947

Le Bataillon du ciel (A. Esway)
Les Maudits (R. Clément)

1948

Le Bal des pompiers (A. Berthomieu)
La Bataille de l'eau lourde (T. Vibe-Muller)
Au coeur de l'orage (J.-P. Le Chanois)
Manon (H. G. Clouzot)

1949

Les Amants de Vérone (A. Cayatte)
Leclerc (Régnier and Lavergne)
Retour à la vie (Dréville, Cayatte, Clouzot, Lampin)
Le Silence de la mer (J.-P. Melville)

1950

Autant en emporte l'histoire (J. Marin)
Le Grand Cirque (G. Péclet)

1951

Casabianca (G. Péclet)
Les Mains sales (F. Rivers)
Les Miracles n'ont lieu qu'une fois
  (Y. Allégret)
La Tour de Babel (G. Rony)

1952

Éternel Espoir (M. Joly)
Jeux interdits (R. Clément)

1953

Deux de l'escadrille (M. Labro)

1954

Le Bon Dieu sans confession (C.
  Autant-Lara)
La Cage aux souris (J. Gourguet)
Le Défroqué (L. Joannon)
Double Destin (V. Vicas)
La Neige était sale (L. Saslavsky)
Tabor (G. Péclet)

1955

Les Évadés (J.-P. Le Chanois)

1956

*Un condamné à mort s'est
  échappé* (J.-J. Bresson)
Nuit et Brouillard (A. Resnais et J.
  Cayrol)
La Traversée de Paris (C. Autant-
  Lara)

1957

Les Louves (L. Saslavsky)

1958

La Chatte (H. Decoin)
Mission diabolique (P. May)

1959

Babette s'en va-t-en guerre (Chris-
  tian-Jaque)
Le Chemin des écoliers (Boisrond)
Hiroshima mon amour (A. Res-
  nais)
Marie-Octobre (J. Duvivier)
La Nuit des espions (R. Hossein)
Le Passage du Rhin (A. Cayatte)
La Sentence (J. Valère)
La Vache et le Prisonnier (H. Ver-
  neuil)
La Verte Moisson (F. Villiers)

1960

Le Bois des amants (C. Autant-
  Lara)
Candide (N. Carbonneaux)
La Chatte sort ses griffes (H. De-
  coin)
Fortunat (A. Joffé)
Une Gueule comme la mienne (F.
  Dard)
Normandie-Niémen (Dréville)
Le Septième Jour de Saint-Malo (P.
  Mesnier)

1961

Arrêtez les tambours (G. Lautner)
L'Enclos (A. Gatti)
Kamikaze (P. Wolf)
La Guerre inconnue (P. Wolf)
[*La Guerre des boutons* (Y. Robert)]
Léon Morin, prêtre (J.-P. Melville)
Qui êtes-vous, M. Sorge? (Y. Ciampi)
Un taxi pour Tobrouk (D. de la Patellière)
Le Temps du ghetto (F. Rossif)
Vacances en enfer (J. Kerchbron)

1962

Le Caporal épinglé (J. Renoir)
Carillons sans joie (J. Braibant)
Un Cheval pour deux (J.-M. Thibault)
Les Culottes rouges (A. Joffé)
La Dénonciation (J. Doniol-Valcroze)
Les Honneurs de la guerre (J. Dewewer)
La Traversée de la Loire (J. Gourguet)

1963

Le Jour et l'Heure (R. Clément)
La Mémoire courte (Torrent and Prémysler)
Muriel ou le temps d'un retour (A. Resnais)
Le Vice et la Vertu (R. Vadim)

1964

La Bataille de France (J. Aurel)
Le Repas des fauves (Christian-Jaque)
Week-end à Zuydcotte (H. Verneuil)

1966

Le Coup de grâce (J. Cayrol/ C. Durand)
La Grande Vadrouille (G. Oury)
La Ligne de démarcation (C. Chabrol)
La Longue Marche (A. Astruc)
Martin soldat (M. Deville)
Paris brûle-t-il? (R. Clément)
La Vie de château (J.-P. Rappeneau)

1967

Un Homme de trop (Costa-Gavras)
Le Temps des doryphores (D. Rémy)
Le Vieil Homme et l'enfant (C. Berri)

1968

Le Crime de David Levinstein (A. Charpak)
Drôle de jeu (P. Kast)
Le Franciscain de Bourges (C. Autant-Lara)
Le Mois le plus beau (G. Blanc)
Tu moissonneras la tempête (R. P. Bruckberger)

1969–70 (August–August)

L'Armée des ombres (J.-P. Melville)
La Grosse Pagaille (Steno)
Nous n'irons plus au bois (G. Dumoulin)
Les Patates (C. Autant-Lara)
Panzer Division (L. Mérino)
Pour un sourire (F. Dupont-Midy)
Sept Hommes pour Tobrouk (M. Loy)

1970–71

Le Chagrin et la pitié (M. Ophuls)
Le Mur de l'Atlantique (M. Camus)
Le Petit Matin (Albicocco)
Sous les ordres du Führer (E. Castellari)

1971–72

Pic et pic et colegram (R. Weinberg)
Les Portes du feu (C.-B. Aubert)
La Poudre d'escampette (Ph. de Broca)
Le Sauveur (M. Mardore)
Le Soldat Laforêt (G. Cavagnac)

1972–73

Français, si vous saviez (A. Harris and A. de Sédouy)
Une Larme dans l'océan (H. Glaeser)

1973–74

Les Chinois à Paris (J. Yanne)
Le Führer en folie (Ph. Clair)
Gross Paris (G. Grangier)
Lacombe Lucien (L. Malle)
Mais où est donc passée la 7e compagnie? (R. Lamoureux)
Portier de nuit (L. Cavanni)
Prêtres interdits (D. de La Patellière)
La République est morte à Diên Biên Phu (J. Kanapa)
Les Violons du bal (M. Drach)
Le Train (P. Granier-Deferre)

1974–75

Au nom de la race (M. Hillel and C. Henry)
La Brigade (R. Gilson)
L'Ironie du sort (E. Molinaro)
Les Guichets du Louvre (M. Mitrani)
Mariage (C. Lelouch)
Section spéciale (Costa-Gavras)
Soldat Duroc, ça va être ta fête (M. Gérard)
Vive la France (M. Audiard)

1975–76

Le Bon et les Méchants (C. Lelouch)
Chantons sous l'Occupation (A. Halimi)
Le Commando des chauds lapins (G. Pérol)
Jeu (R. Gray)

Les Mal Partis (J.-B. Rossi)
On a retrouvé la 7ᵉ compagnie (R. Lamoureux)
Opération Lady Marlène (R. Lamoureux)
Le Pont de singe (A. Harris and A. de Sédouy)
Un Sac de billes (J. Rouffio)
Souvenirs d'en-France (A. Téchiné)
Le Vieux Fusil (R. Enrico)

1976–77

L'Affiche rouge (F. Cassenti)
La Communion solennelle (R. Féret)
Monsieur Klein (J. Losey)
Le Jour de gloire (J. Besnard)
René la Canne (F. Girod)
Train spécial pour SS (J. Gartner)

1977–78

Bordel SS (J. Bénazéraf)
Elsa Fraulein SS (L. Stern)
Hitler, un film d'Allemagne (H. J. Syberberg)
Le Mille-pattes fait des claquettes (J. Girault)
Nathalie, rescapée de l'enfer (J. Gartner)
One, two, two: 122 rue de Provence (C. Gion)
Les Routes du sud (J. Losey)
La 7e compagnie au clair de lune (R. Lamoureux)
La Vie devant soi (M. Mitrani)

1978–79

Un Balcon en forêt (M. Mitrani)
De l'enfer à la victoire (H. Milestone)

Général . . . nous voilà! (J. Besnard)
Ya ya mon colonel (M. Guerrini)

1979–80

Le Dernier Métro (F. Truffaut)
La Prise de pouvoir de Philippe Pétain (J. Chérasse)
Les Turlupins (B. Revon)

1980–81

La Peau (L. Cavanni)
Les Surdoués de la 1ʳᵉ compagnie (J. Besnard)
Les Uns et les autres (C. Lelouch)

1981–82

L'As des As (G. Oury)
La Mémoire courte (Eduardo)
La Passante du Sans-souci (J. Rouffio)

1982–83

Un Amour en Allemagne (A. Wajda)
Au nom de tous les miens (R. Enrico)
Le Bal (E. Scola)
Papy fait de la Résistance (J.-M. Poiré)
Le Retour des bidasses en folie (Vocoret)

1983–84

Le Grand Carnaval (A. Arcady)
Le Sang des autres (C. Chabrol)

1984–85

Blanche et Marie (J. Renard)
Le Fou de guerre (D. Risi)
Partir, revenir (C. Lelouch)

1985–86

L'Aube (M. Jancso)
Berlin Affair (L. Cavanni)
Bras de fer (G. Vergez)
Douce France (F. Chardeaux)
Shoah (C. Lanzmann)
Le Temps détruit (lettres d'une guerre) (P. Beuchot)

1986–87

Dernier été à Tanger (A. Arcady)

1987–88

Au revoir les enfants (L. Malle)
Fucking Fernand (G. Mordillat)

De Guerre lasse (R. Enrico)
Le Testament d'un poète juif assassiné (F. Cassenti)
Les Années sandwich (P. Boutron)

1988–89

Ada dans la jungle (G. Zingg)
Hôtel Terminus (M. Ophuls)
Une Affaire de femmes (C. Chabrol)
Mon ami le traître (J. Giovanni)
Cinq jours en juin (M. Legrand)
Après la guerre (J.-L. Hubert)
Natalia (B. Cohn)
Baptême (R. Féret)

1989 (August–December)

L'Orchestre rouge (J. Rouffio)

BIBLIOGRAPHY

The bibliography was brought up to date for the second French edition. It does not include all the works cited in the notes, nor is it intended to provide an exhaustive reading list on the subject, which by its very nature touches on many different areas. Works on the period 1939–1945, for example, are not listed, nor are personal memoirs of the Occupation. The purpose here is simply to give an idea of the intellectual influences that went into the making of this book and to offer a representative sampling of French and English works connected with its major theme: the history of collective memory, of the representations and uses of the past, particularly in France, with special emphasis on the memory of World War II. Some of the books listed also deal with related issues, such as tradition, the concept of generation, and historiography.

1. Collective Memory, Representations, Uses of the Past

"Colloque histoire et mémoire, 9–10 mars 1985," *Psychanalystes. Revue du Collège de psychanalystes* 18 and 19 (January and April 1986).
"Documents de la mémoire," *L'Ecrit du temps* 10 (Autumn 1985).
"La Mémoire," *Bulletin de psychologie* 389 (January–April 1989).
"La Mémoire et l'oubli," *Communications* 49 (1989), special issue ed. Nicole Lapierre.
"Mémoires de femmes," *Pénelope. Pour l'histoire des femmes* 12 (Spring 1985).
"Memory and Counter-Memory," *Representations* 26 (Spring 1989), special issue ed. Natalie Zemon Davis and Randolph Starn.
"Politiques de l'oubli," *Le Genre humain*, Autumn 1988.

"Croire la mémoire? Approches critiques de la mémoire orale," Actes, 1988.
History and Memory. Studies in Representation of the Past. Athenaum/Tel Aviv University, I, 1 (1989), the first specialized journal, ed. Saul Friedländer.
Mémoire et histoire. Données et débats. Actes du XXVe colloque des intellectuels juifs de langue française. Paris, Denoël, 1986.
Le Moigne, Jean-Louis, and Daniel Pascot, eds. *Les Processus collectifs de mémorisation (mémoire et organisation).* Aix-en-Provence, Librairie de l'Université, 1979.

Usages de l'oubli. Contributions de Yosef H. Yerushalmi, Nicole Loraux, Hans Mommsen, Jean-Claude Milner, Gianni Vattimo au colloque de Royaumount. Paris, Editions du Seuil, 1988.

Binion, Rudolph. *Introduction à la psychohistoire.* Paris, Presses Universitaires de France, 1982.

Ferro, Marc. *Comment on raconte l'histoire aux enfants à travers le monde entier.* Paris, Payot, 1983.

Friedländer, Saul. *Histoire et psychanalyse. Essai sur les possibilités et les limites de la psychohistoire.* Paris, Editions du Seuil, 1975.

Girardet, Raoul. "Du concept de génération à la notion de contemporanéité," *Revue d'histoire moderne et contemporaine* 30 (April–June 1983).

Halbwachs, Maurice. *La Mémoire collective.* Paris, Presses Universitaires de France, 1968.

——— *Les Cadres sociaux de la mémoire.* Paris/The Hague, Mouton, 1976.

Hobsbawm, Eric, and Terence Ranger, eds. *The Invention of Tradition.* Cambridge, Cambridge University Press, 1983.

Jeudy, Henri-Pierre. *Mémoires du social.* Paris, Presses Universitaires de France, 1986.

Joutard, Philippe. *Ces voix qui viennent du passé.* Paris, Hachette, 1983.

Kriegel, Annie. "Le Concept politique de génération: apogée et déclin," *Commentaire* 7 (1979).

Le Goff, Jacques. *Mémoire et histoire.* Paris, Gallimard/Folio, 1988.

Lowenthal, David. *The Past Is a Foreign Country.* Cambridge, Cambridge University Press, 1985.

May, Ernest R. *Lessons of the Past: The Use and Misuse of History in American Foreign Policy.* New York, Oxford University Press, 1973.

McNeill, William H. *The Pursuit of Power: Technology, Armed Force, and Society since A.D. 1000.* Chicago, University of Chicago Press, 1982.

——— *Mythistory and Other Essays.* Chicago, University of Chicago Press, 1986.

Namer, Gérard. *Mémoire et société.* Paris, Méridiens Klincksieck, 1987.

Nora, Pierre. "Mémoire collective," in *La Nouvelle Histoire.* Paris, Retz, 1978.

Pomian, Krzysztof. "Les Avatars de l'identité historique," *Le Débat* 3 (July–August 1980).

———*L'Ordre du temps.* Paris, Gallimard, 1984.

Torres, Félix. *Déjà vu. Post et néo-modernisme: le retour du passé.* Paris, Ramsay, 1986.

Verret, Michel. "Mémoire ouvrière, mémoire communiste," *Revue française de science politique* 24 (June 1984).

Wachtel, Nathan. "Memory and History: Introduction," in "Between Memory and History," special issue of *History and Anthropology* 2 (October 1986).

Yates, Frances A. *The Art of Memory*. Chicago, University of Chicago Press, 1966.

Zonabend, Françoise. *La Mémoire longue. Temps et histoires au village*. Paris, Presses Universitaires de France, 1980.

2. Collective Memory, History, and French Identity

"Les Générations," *Vingtième Siècle. Revue d'histoire* 22 (April–June 1989), special issue ed. Jean-Pierre Azéma and Michel Winock.

"Les Guerres franco-françaises," *Vingtième Siècle. Revue d'histoire* 5 (January–March 1985), special issue ed. Jean-Pierre Azéma, Jean-Pierre Rioux, and Henry Rousso.

"Les Nostalgies des Français," *H-Histoire* 5 (June 1980).

"89: La commémoration," *Le Débat* 57 (November–December 1989).

"La Tradition politique," *Pouvoirs* 42 (1987).

Agulhon, Maurice. *Marianne au combat. L'Imagerie et la symbolique républicaines de 1789 à 1880*. Paris, Flammarion, 1979.

———*Marianne au pouvoir. L'Imagerie et la symbolique républicaines de 1880 à 1914*. Paris, Flammarion, 1989.

Amalvi, Christian. *De l'art et la manière d'accommoder les héros de l'histoire de France. Essais de mythologie nationale*. Paris, Albin Michel, 1988.

Belloin, Gérard. *Entendez-vous dans nos mémoires? Les Français et leur révolution*. Paris, La Découverte, 1988.

Bétourné, Oliver, and Aglaia I. Artig. *Penser l'histoire de la révolution. Deux siècles de passion française*. Paris, La Découverte, 1989.

Bonnet, Jean Claude, and Philippe Roger, eds. *La Légende de la révolution au XXe siècle. De Gance à Renoir, de Romain Rolland à Claude Simon*. Paris, Flammarion, 1988.

Canini, Gérard, ed. *Mémoire de la grande guerre*. Nancy, Presses Universitaires de Nancy, 1989.

Citron, Suzanne. *Le Mythe national. L'Histoire de France en question*. Paris, EDI/Editions Ouvrières, 1987.

Furet, François. "La Révolution dans l'imaginaire politique français," *Le Débat* 26 (September 1983).

Furet, François. *Penser la révolution française*. Paris, Gallimard, 1978.

Gérard, Alice. *La Révolution française. Mythes et interprétations (1789–1970)*. Paris, Flammarion, 1970.

Girardet, Raoul. *Mythes et mythologies politiques*. Paris, Editions du Seuil, 1986.

Joutard, Philippe. *La Légende des Camisards. Une Sensibilité au passé.* Paris, Gallimard, 1977.

Kimmel, Alain, and Jacques Poujol. *Certaines idées de la France.* Frankfurt, Diesterweg, 1982.

Lavabre, Marie-Claire. "Génération et mémoire," seminar on Generation and Politics, Congrès de l'Association française de science politique, October 1981, typescript.

———— "Mémoire et identité partisanes: le cas du PCF," Consortium européen de science politique, Salzburg, 13–18 April 1984, typescript.

Martin, Jean-Clément. *La Vendée de la mémoire, 1800–1980.* Paris, Editions du Seuil, 1989.

Nora, Pierre, ed. *Les Lieux de mémoire,* vol. 1: *La République;* vol. 2: *La Nation.* Paris, Gallimard, 1984 and 1986.

Ory, Pascal, and Jean-François Sirinelli. *Les Intellectuels en France. De l'affaire Dreyfus à nos jours.* Paris, Colin, 1986.

Ozouf, Mona. "Peut-on commémorer la révolution française?" *Le Débat* 26 (September 1983).

Prost, Antoine. *Les Anciens Combattants, 1914–1939.* Paris, Gallimard/Julliard, 1977.

———— *Les Anciens Combattants et la société française, 1914–1939.* 3 vols. Paris, Presses de la Fondation Nationales des Sciences Politique, 1977.

Rioux, Jean-Pierre, ed. *La Guerre d'Algérie et les Français.* Paris, Albin Michel, 1990.

Rudelle, Odile. "Lieux de mémoire révolutionnaire et communion républicaine," *Vingtième Siècle. Revue d'histoire* 24 (October–December 1989).

Sanson, Rosemonde. *Les Quatorze Juillet. Fête et conscience nationale, 1789–1975.* Paris, Flammarion, 1975.

Sirinelli, Jean-François. *Générations intellectuelles. Khâgneux et normaliens dans l'entre-deux-guerres.* Paris, Fayard, 1988.

Vovelle, Michel, ed. *L'Image de la révolution française. Actes du congrès mondial de la Sorbonne de juillet 1989.* Paris/London, Pergamon Press, 1989.

Winock, Michel. *La Fièvre hexagonale. Les Grandes crises politiques de 1871 à 1968.* Paris, Calmann-Lévy, 1986.

3. Memory and Aftermath of World War II

General

Azéma, Jean-Pierre. "La Guerre," in René Rémond, ed., *Pour une histoire politique.* Paris, Editions du Seuil, 1988.

Bédarida, François. "L'Histoire de la résistance: lectures d'hier, chantiers de demain," *Vingtième Siècle. Revue d'histoire* 11 (July–September 1986).

Borne, Dominique. "L'Histoire du 20e siècle au lycée: le nouveau programme de terminale," *Vingtième Siècle. Revue d'histoire* 21 (January–March 1989), and responses in 23 (July–September 1989).

Cornette, Joël, and Jean-Noël Luc. "'Bac-Génération' 84. L'Enseignement du temps présent en terminale," *Vingtième Siècle. Revue d'histoire* 6 (April–June 1985).

Courtois, Stéphane. "Luttes politiques et élaboration d'une histoire: le PCF historien du PCF dans la deuxième guerre mondiale," *Communisme* 4 (1983).

Faligot, Roger, and Rémi Kauffer. *Les Résistants. De la guerre de l'ombre aux allées du pouvoir (1944–1989)*. Paris, Fayard, 1989.

Frank, Robert, and Henry Rousso. "Quarante ans après: les Français et la libération," *L'Histoire* 67 (May 1984).

Haft, Cynthia. *The Theme of Nazi Concentration Camps in French Literature*. Paris/The Hague, Mouton, 1973.

Herberich-Marx, Geneviève, and Freddy Raphaël. "Les Incorporés de force alsaciens. Déni, convocation et provocation de la mémoire," *Vingtième Siècle. Revue d'histoire* 6 (April–June 1985).

Hoffmann, Stanley. *Decline or Renewal? France since the 1930s*. New York, Viking, 1974.

Institut d'Histoire du Temps Présent. *La Mémoire des Français. Quarante ans de commémorations de la seconde guerre mondiale*. Paris, Editions du Centre National de la Recherche Scientifique, 1986.

Laroche, Jacques M. "A Success Story in the French Popular Literature of the 1980s: *La Bicyclette bleue*," *French Review* 60 (March 1987).

Lévy, Bernard-Henri. *L'Idéologie française*. Paris, Grasset, 1981.

Namer, Gérard. *Batailles pour la mémoire. La Commémoration en France de 1945 à nos jours*. Paris, Papyrus, 1983.

Ory, Pascal. "Comme de l'an quarante. Dix années de 'rétro satanas,'" *Le Débat* 16 (November 1981).

Rioux, Jean-Pierre. *La France de la IVe république*. 2 vols. Paris, Editions du Seuil, 1980 and 1983.

——— "Le Procès d'Oradour," *L'Histoire* 64 (February 1984).

Rousso, Henry. "Vichy, le grand fossé," *Vingtième Siècle. Revue d'histoire* 5 (January–March 1985).

——— "Où en est l'histoire de la Résistance?" in *L'Histoire. Etudes sur la France de 1939 à nos jours*. Paris, Editions du Seuil, 1985.

Ruffin, Raymond. *Ces chefs de maquis qui gênaient*. Paris, Presses de la Cité, 1980.

Théolleyre, Jean-Marc. *Procès d'après-guerre*. Paris, La Découverte/*Le Monde*, 1985.

Thibaud, Paul. "Du sel sur nos plaies. A propos de *L'Idéologie française*," *Esprit* 5 (May 1981).

Veillon, Dominique. "La Seconde Guerre mondiale à travers les sources orales," *Questions à l'histoire orale, Cahiers de l'Institut d'histoire du temps présent* 4 (June 1987).

Wahl, Alfred, ed. *Mémoire de la seconde guerre mondiale. Actes du colloque de Metz, 6–8 octobre 1983*. Metz, Centre de Recherche Histoire et Civilisation de l'Université de Metz, 1984.

Wieviorka, Olivier. "La Génération de la résistance," *Vingtième Siècle. Revue d'histoire* 22 (April–June 1989).

Wilkinson, James D. "Remembering World War II: The Perspective of the Losers," *American Scholar*, Summer 1985.

Klaus Barbie

"Le Procès de Klaus Barbie," special issue of *Le Monde*, July 1987.

Astruc, Jean. "La Documentation sur le procès Barbie à l'IHTP," *Bulletin de l'Institut d'histoire du temps présent* 34 (December 1988).

Bower, Tom. *Klaus Barbie, the "Butcher of Lyons."* London, Corgi, 1984, rev. 1985.

Frossard, André. *Le Crime contre l'humanité*. Paris, Laffont, 1987.

Gauthier, Paul, ed. *Chronique du procès Barbie: pour servir la mémoire*. Paris, Cerf, 1988.

Givet, Jacques. *Le Cas Vergès*. Paris, Lieu Commun, 1986.

Hoyos, Ladislas de. *Barbie*. Paris, Laffont, 1987.

Lévy, Bernard-Henry, ed. *Archives d'un procès, Klaus Barbie*. *Globe*/Le Livre de Poche, 1986.

Mérindol, Pierre. *Barbie: le procès*. Lyons, La Manufacture, 1987.

Morel, Guy. *Barbie pour mémoire*. Paris, Editions de la FNDIRP, 1986.

Morgan, Ted. *The French, the Germans, the Jews, the Klaus Barbie Trial, and the City of Lyon, 1940–1945*. New York, Arbor House/William Morrow, 1989.

Paris, Erna. *L'Affaire Barbie. Analyse d'un mal français*. Paris, Ramsay, 1985.

Vergès, Jacques. *Je défends Barbie*. Paris, Picollec, 1988.

Vergès, Jacques, and Etienne Bloch. *La Face cachée du procès Barbie*. Paris, Samuel Tastet, 1983.

Touvier Affair

Flory, Claude. *Touvier m'a avoué*. Paris, Laffont, 1989.
Greilsamer, Laurent, and Daniel Schneidermann. *Un Certain Monsieur Paul. L'Affaire Touvier*. Paris, Fayard, 1989.
Moniquet, Claude. *Touvier, un milicien à l'ombre de l'Eglise*. Paris, Orban, 1989.

Extreme Right and Nostalgic Ideologies

"Droite, nouvelle droite, extrême droite. Discours et idéologie en France et en Italie," special issue of *Mots* 12 (March 1986), ed. Simone Bonnafous and Pierre-André Taguieff.
"Les Extrêmes Droites en France et en Europe," *Lignes* 4 (October 1988).
"Racisme et antiracisme. Frontières et recouvrements," special issue of *Mots* 18 (March 1989), ed. Simone Bonnafous and Pierre-André Taguieff.

Algazy, Joseph. *La Tentation fasciste en France de 1944 à 1965*. Paris, Fayard, 1985.
——*L'Extrême Droite en France de 1965 à 1984*. Paris, L'Harmattan, 1989.
Anderson, Malcolm. *Conservative Politics in France*. London, Allen and Unwin, 1974.
Benoist, Alain de. *Vu de droite. Anthologie critique des idées contemporaines*. Paris, Copernic, 1977.
—— *Les Idées à l'endroit*. Paris, Editions Libres/Hallier, 1979.
Chebel d'Appollonia, Ariane. *L'Extrême Droite en France. De Maurras à Le Pen*. Brussels, Complexe, 1988.
Chiroux, René. *L'Extrême Droite sous la Ve république*. Paris, Librairie Générale de Droit et de Jurisprudence, 1974.
Duprat, François. *Les Mouvements d'extrême droite en France depuis 1945*. Paris, Albatros, 1972.
Duranton-Crabol, Anne-Marie. *Visages de la nouvelle droite. La GRECE et son histoire*. Paris, Presses de la Fondation Nationale de Science Politique, 1988.
Girardet, Raoul. "L'Heritage de l'Action française," *Revue française de science politique* 7 (October–December 1957).
Mayer, Nonna, and Pascal Perrineau, eds. *Le Front national à découvert*. Paris, Presses de la Fondation Nationale de Science Politique, 1989.
Milza, Pierre. *Fascisme français. Passé et présent*. Paris, Flammarion, 1987.

Plenel, Edwy, and Alain Rollat. *L'Effet Le Pen.* Paris, La Découverte/*Le Monde,* 1984.

Rémond, René. *Les Droites en France.* Paris, Aubier-Montaigne, 1982.

Taguieff, Pierre-André. "Identité française et idéologie," in "Racines, derniers temps. Les Territoires de l'identité," special issue of *EspacesTemps* 42 (1989).

—— *La Force du préjugé. Essai sur le racisme et ses doubles.* Paris, La Découverte, 1988.

—— "Nationalisme et réactions fondamentalistes en France. Mythologies identitaires et ressentiment antimoderne." *Vingtième Siècle. Revue d'histoire* 25 (January–March 1990).

World War II in Film since 1944

Andrault, Jean-Michel, et al. "Le Cinéma français et la seconde guerre mondiale," *La Revue du cinéma* 378 (December 1982).

Azéma, Jean-Pierre, and Henry Rousso. "Les 'Années sombres' à la vidéothèque de Paris," *L'Histoire* 116 (November 1988).

Bazin, André. *Le Cinéma de l'occupation et de la résistance.* Paris, Union Générale de l'Edition, 1975.

Bertin-Maghit, Jean-Pierre. *Le Cinéma sous l'occupation. Le Monde du cinéma français de 1940 à 1946.* Paris, O. Orban, 1989.

Beuchot, Pierre, and Jean-Pierre Bertin Maghit. *Cinéma de l'ombre,* televised documentary, INA/A2, 1984.

Chirat, Raymond. *La IVe république et ses films.* Paris, 5 Continents/Hatier, 1985.

Daniel, Joseph. *Guerre et cinéma. Grandes illusions et petits soldats, 1895–1971.* Paris, Presses de la Fondation Nationale des Sciences Politiques, 1972.

Ferro, Marc. *Analyse de film analyse de sociétés. Une Source nouvelle pour l'histoire.* Paris, Hachette, 1975.

Ferro, Marc, ed. *Film et histoire.* Paris, Editions de l'Ecole des Hautes Etudes en Sciences Sociales, 1984.

Insdorf, Annette. *L'Holocauste à l'écran.* Paris, CinémAction/Editions du Cerf, 1985.

Jeancolas, Jean-Pierre. "Fonction du témoignage: les années 1939–1945 dans le cinéma d'après-guerre," *Positif* 170 (June 1975).

Siclier, Jacques. *La France de Pétain et son cinéma.* Paris, Henri Veyrier, 1981.

Works on specific films:

Bertin-Maghit, Jean-Pierre. "*La Bataille du rail*: de l'authenticité à la chanson de geste," *Revue d'histoire moderne et contemporaine* 33 (April–June 1986).

Garçon, François. "Le Retour d'une inquiétante imposture: *Lili Marleen* et *Le Dernier Métro*," *Les Temps modernes* 422 (September 1981).

Lanzmann, Claude. *Shoah*. Paris, Fayard, 1989.

Ménudier, Henri. "'Holocauste' en France," *Revue d'Allemagne* 13 (July–September 1981).

Ophuls, Marcel. *Le Chagrin et la pitié*. Paris, Alain Moreau, 1980.

Raphaël, Freddy. "'Holocauste' et la presse de gauche en France (1979–1980)," *Revue des sciences sociales de la France de l'est* 14 (1985).

Raskin, Richard, *"Nuit et Brouillard" by Alain Resnais. On the Making, Reception and Functions of a Major Documentary Film*. Aarhus, Denmark, Aarhus University Press, 1987.

"Spécial *Chagrin et la pitié*," *Téléciné* 171–172 (July 1971).

4. Jewish Memory, Memory of the Genocide, Memory of Nazism

"L'Allemagne, le nazisme et les juifs," special section, *Vingtième Siècle. Revue d'histoire* 16 (October–December 1987).

"La Mémoire d'Auschwitz," special section, *Esprit* 9 (September 1980).

"Mémoire du nazisme en RFA et RDA," special section, *Esprit* 10 (October 1987).

"Penser Auschwitz," *Pardès* 9–10 (1989), special issue ed. Shmuel Trigano.

"La Querelle des historiens allemands vue de l'est," special section, *La Nouvelle Alternative* 13 (March 1989).

Ecole des Hautes Etudes en Sciences Sociales. *L'Allemagne nazie et le génocide juif*. Paris, Hautes Etudes/Gallimard/Seuil, 1985.

Centre de Documentation Juive Contemporaine. *L'Enseignement de la Choa. Comment les manuels d'histoire présentent-ils l'extermination des juifs au cours de la seconde guerre mondiale*. Paris, Centre de Documentation Juive Contemporaine, 1982.

Devant l'histoire. Les Documents de la controverse sur la singularité de l'extermination des juifs par le régime nazi. Paris, *Passages*/Cerf, 1988.

Klarsfeld, Serge, ed. *Mémoire du génocide*. Paris, Centre de Documentation Juive Contemporaine/Association des Fils et Filles des Déportés Juifs de France, 1987.

Le Procès de Nuremberg. Conséquences et actualisation. Brussels, Editions Bruylant-Université Libre de Bruxelles, 1988.

Arendt, Hannah. *Eichmann in Jerusalem: A Report on the Banality of Evil.* New York, Viking, 1963.
———— *The Origins of Totalitarianism,* vol. 1: *Antisemitism.* New York, Harcourt, Brace, and World, 1951, rev. 1973.
Aron, Raymond. *De Gaulle, Israël et les juifs.* Paris, Plon, 1968.
Ayçoberry, Pierre. *La Question nazie. Essai sur les interprétations du national-socialisme (1922–1975).* Paris, Editions du Seuil, 1979.
Bédarida, François, ed. *La Politique nazie d'extermination.* Paris, IHTP/Albin Michel, 1989.
Birnbaum, Pierre. *Un Mythe politique. "La République juive." De Léon Blum à Pierre Mendès France.* Paris, Fayard, 1988.
Davidowicz, Lucy S. *The Holocaust and the Historians.* Cambridge, Harvard University Press, 1981.
Erler, Gernot, et al. *L'Histoire escamotée. Les Tentatives de liquidation du passé nazi en Allemagne.* Paris, La Découverte, 1988.
Finkielkraut, Alain. *L'Avenir d'une négation. Réflexion sur la question du génocide.* Paris, Editions du Seuil, 1982.
———— *La Mémoire vaine. Du crime contre l'humanité.* Paris, Gallimard, 1989.
Fresco, Nadine. "Les Redresseurs de morts," *Les Temps modernes* 407 (June 1980).
Friedländer, Saul. *Reflets du nazisme.* Paris, Editions du Seuil, 1982.
Grosser, Alfred. *Le Crime et la mémoire.* Paris, Flammarion, 1989.
Hartmann, Geoffrey, ed. *Bitburg in Moral and Political Perspective.* Bloomington, Indiana University Press, 1986.
Heinich, Nathalie, and Michael Pollak. "Le Témoignage," *Actes de la recherche en sciences sociales* 62/63 (1986).
Kaspi, André. "L'Affaire des enfants Finaly," *L'Histoire* 76 (March 1985).
Kriegel, Annie. *Réflexions sur les questions juives.* Paris, Hachette/Pluriel, 1984.
Lapierre, Nicole. *Le Silence de la mémoire. A la recherche des juifs de Plock.* Paris, Plon, 1989.
Lévy, Claude. "La Résistance juive en France. De l'enjeu de mémoire à l'histoire critique." *Vingtième Siècle. Revue d'histoire* 22 (April–June 1989).
Lewin, Roland. "Paul Rassinier ou la conjonction des extrêmes," *Silex* 26 (1984).
Maier, Charles S. *The Unmasterable Past: History, Holocaust, and German National Identity.* Cambridge, Harvard University Press, 1988.

Marrus, Michael R. *The Holocaust in History*. Hanover, N.H., University Presses of New England, 1987.

Müller, Klaus-Jürgen. "La Résistance allemande au régime nazi. L'Historiographie en république fédérale," *Vingtième Siècle. Revue d'histoire* 11 (July–September 1986).

Poliakov, Léon. *De Moscou à Beyrouth. Essai sur la désinformation*. Paris, Calmann-Lévy, 1983.

Pollak, Michael. "Des mots qui tuent," *Actes de la recherche en sciences sociales* 41 (1982).

———— "La Gestion de l'indicible," *Actes de la recherche en sciences sociales* 62/63 (1986).

———— *L'Expérience concentrationnaire. Essai sur le maintien de l'identité sociale*. Paris, Métailié, 1990.

Rousso, Henry. "La Négation du génocide juif," *L'Histoire* 106 (December 1987).

Rubinstein, Amnon. *Le Rêve et l'histoire. Le Sionisme, Israël et les juifs*. Paris, Calmann-Lévy, 1985.

Taguieff, Pierre-André. "La Nouvelle Judéophobie. Antisionisme, Anti-racisme et Anti-impérialisme," *Les Temps modernes* 520 (November 1989).

Vidal-Naquet, Pierre. *Les Juifs, la mémoire et le présent*. Paris, Maspero, 1981.

———— *Les Assassins de la mémoire. "Un Eichmann de papier" et autres essais sur le révisionnisme*. Paris, La Découverte, 1987.

———— "Le Défi de la shoah à l'histoire," *Les Temps modernes* 507 (October 1988).

Wieviorka, Annette. "Un Lieu de mémoire: le mémorial du martyr juif inconnu," *Pardès* 2 (1985).

———— *Le Procès Eichmann*. Brussels, Complexe, 1989.

————*Les Livres du souvenir. Mémoriaux juifs de Pologne*. Paris, Gallimard/Julliard, 1983.

Winock, Michel. *Edouard Drumont et cie. Antisémitisme et fascisme en France*. Paris, Editions du Seuil, 1982.

Yerushalmi, Yosef Hayim. *Zakhor. Histoire juive et mémoire juive*. Paris, La Découverte, 1984.

NOTES

Introduction: The Neurosis

1. Pierre Nora, ed., *Les Lieux de mémoire*, vol. 1: *La République;* vol. 2: *La Nation* (Paris: Gallimard, 1984 and 1986).

2. Ibid., vol. 1, p. xxv.

3. Philippe Joutard, *La Légende des Camisards. Une Sensibilité au passé* (Paris: Gallimard, 1977).

4. Antoine Prost, *Les Anciens Combattants et la société française, 1914–1939* (Paris: Presses de la Fondation Nationale des Sciences Politiques, 1977).

5. See, for example, Mona Ozouf, "Peut-on commémorer la Révolution française?", and François Furet, "La Révolution dans l'imaginaire politique français," *Le Débat* 26 (September 1983); cf. Maurice Agulhon, "Faut-il avoir peur de 1789?", *Le Débat* 30 (May 1984).

6. There was much debate surrounding Reynald Secher's *Le Génocide franco-français. La Vendée-Vengé* (Paris: Presses Universitaires de France, 1986). See also Jean-Clément Martin, *La Vendée et la France* (Paris: Seuil, 1987), and *La Vendée de la mémoire, 1800–1980* (Paris: Seuil, 1989).

7. See Alfred Wahl, ed., *Mémoire de la seconde guerre mondiale*, proceedings of a Metz colloquium, 6–8 October 1983 (Metz: Centre de Recherche Histoire et Civilisation de l'Université, 1984), and Institut d'Histoire du Temps Présent, *La Mémoire des français. Quarante ans de commémoration de la seconde guerre mondiale* (Paris: CNRS, 1986).

8. Related issues are explored in "Les Guerres franco-françaises," *Vingtième Siècle. Revue d'histoire* 5 (1985). For a comparison of crises, see Michel Winock, *La Fièvre hexagonale, les grandes crises politiques de 1871 à 1968* (Paris: Calmann-Lévy, 1986).

9. Krzysztof Pomian, "Les Avatars de l'identité historique," *Le Débat* 3 (July-August 1980). See also Pomian's *L'Ordre du temps* (Paris: Gallimard, 1984).

10. Figures cited by Pierre Guiral, in *Les Epurations administratives, XIXe–XXe siècles* (Geneva: Droz, 1977), p. 103.

11. Figures cited by Dominique Rossignol, *Vichy et les Francs-Maçons* (Paris: J.-C. Lattès, 1981), p. 214.

12. The most reliable figures on the purge may be found in Peter Novick, *Resistance versus Vichy: The Purge of Collaborators in Liberated France*

(New York: Columbia University Press, 1968), Jean-Pierre Rioux, *La France de la IVe république*, vol. 1: *L'Ardeur et la nécessité, 1944–1952* (Paris: Seuil, 1980); and in surveys conducted by the Comité d'Histoire de la Deuxième Guerre Mondiale and the Institut d'Histoire du Temps Présent. For a recent overview, see the many articles in *Bulletin du CHGM* and *Revue d'histoire de la deuxième guerre mondiale*, as well as Marcel Baudot, "L'Epuration, bilan chiffré," *Bulletin de l'IHTP* 25 (September 1986), 27–53. Herbert Lottman, *L'Epuration, 1944–1953* (Paris: Fayard, 1986), the most recent work on the subject, merely repeats these figures. On the purge of the professions, in addition to the works by Robert Aron discussed in Chapter 6, see Pierre Guiral, in *Les Epurations administratives*, and Henry Rousso, "Les Elites économiques dans les années quarante," *Italia contemporanea* 153 (1983), and *Mélanges de l'Ecole française de Rome (moyen age/temps modernes)*, vol. 95, 1983.

13. William H. McNeill, *The Pursuit of Power: Technology, Armed Force, and Society since A.D. 1000* (Chicago: University of Chicago Press, 1982).

14. The special case of the Association for the Defense of the Memory of Marshal Pétain is analyzed in Chapter 1. For other associations see Wahl, *Mémoire*, as well as studies under way by the IHTP. A case worthy of special attention is that of associations of former members of the Chantiers de Jeunesse, which propose a mixed message, an amalgam of Pétainism, resistance rhetoric, and in some cases experience of deportation.

1. Unfinished Mourning (1944–1954)

1. *L'Express*–Gallup Poll, 19 August 1983.

2. Charles de Gaulle, *Mémoires de guerre*, vol. 2: *L'Unité* (Paris: Plon, 1956), p. 308.

3. Georges Bidault, *D'une résistance à l'autre* (Paris: Les Presses du Siècle, 1965), pp. 359–360.

4. Speech delivered on 2 April 1945 at the Hôtel de Ville, Paris.

5. René Rémond, *Les Droites en France* (Paris: Aubier-Montaigne, 1982), p. 238.

6. Peter Novick, *L'Epuration française, 1944–1949* (Paris: Balland, 1985), p. 188; this is the French edition of Novick's *Resistance versus Vichy* (1968).

7. Maurice Agulhon, "Les Communistes et la libération de la France," *La Libération de la France* (Paris: CNRS, 1976), pp. 84–85. Not all of these conclusions were confirmed by work on "the powers at the time of the

Liberation" conducted by the IHTP: colloquium of 13–14 December 1989.

8. Jean Cassou, *La Mémoire courte* (Paris: Minuit, 1953), pp. 33–34.

9. Charles Rist, *Une Saison gâtée. Journal de la guerre et de l'Occupation* (Paris: Fayard, 1983), p. 40.

10. On the purge see Introduction, note 12.

11. On this point see "Le Midi toulousain. Occupation et libération," *Revue d'histoire de la deuxième guerre mondiale et des conflits contemporains* 131 (July 1983), especially the articles by M. Goubet and P. Laborie.

12. Antoine Prost, *Les Anciens Combattants, 1914–1940* (Paris: Gallimard/Julliard, 1977), p. 47.

13. On this point see Claude Cherrier, "Douleur et incertitude en Seine-et-Marne," *La Mémoire des français*, p. 147.

14. On commemorations and monuments, see ibid.

15. Quoted by Gérard Namer, *Batailles pour la mémoire. La Commémoration en France de 1945 à nos jours* (Paris: Papyrus, 1983), p. 20, a work that deals with the major commemorations of the Liberation.

16. On the Pantheon see Mona Ozouf, "Le Panthéon, l'Ecole normale des morts," in Nora, ed., *Les Lieux de la mémoire*, vol. 1.

17. See the comprehensive study by Jean-Pierre Rioux, "Cette immense joie pleine de larmes: les Français et le Jour V," in Maurice Vaïsse, ed., *8 mai 1945: la victoire en Europe* (Lyons: La Manufacture, 1985).

18. See FNDIRP, *Le Choc, 1945. La Presse révèle l'enfer des camps nazis* (Paris: FNDIRP, 1985).

19. Olga Wormser-Migot, "Le Rapatriement des déportés," *La Libération de la France*, p. 372.

20. *Esprit*, September 1945, quoted by Béatrice Philippe, *Etre juif dans la société française* (Paris: Montalba/Pluriel, 1979), p. 372.

21. Marguerite Duras, *La Douleur* (Paris: POL, 1985), p. 41. She is quoting from a speech delivered on Flag Day, 2 April.

22. Fred Kupferman, *Les Premiers Beaux Jours, 1944–1946* (Paris: Calmann-Lévy, 1985).

23. Figures cited by François Duprat, *Les Mouvements d'extrême droite en France depuis 1945* (Paris: Albatros, 1972), pp. 18–26. The author, himself a militant, was murdered in mysterious circumstances in March 1978.

24. Michel Dacier, "Le Résistantialisme," *Ecrits de Paris* 1 (January 1947).

25. Ibid.

26. Louis-Dominique Girard, *La Guerre franco-française* (Paris: Bonne, 1950).

27. *Aspects de la France*, 25 July 1947, in a review of Maurice Bardèche, *Lettre à François Mauriac* (Paris: La Pensée Libre, 1947). Although

united in hostility to the Resistance, the Maurrassians continued to oppose fascist tendencies, just as they had during the Occupation. This article is critical of Bardèche for conveniently forgetting about the presence of the Nazis in order to justify the positions taken by French fascists and thus also by collaborationists.

28. "Vingt ans en 1945," *La Table ronde* 20–21 (August-September 1949), quoted in Raoul Girardet, "L'Héritage de l'Action française," *Revue française de science politique* 7 (October-December 1957). On the extreme right see also René Chiroux, *L'Extrême Droite sous la Ve république* (Paris: Librairie Générale de Droit et de Jurisprudence, 1974). This is probably the most thorough of the many books on the extreme right in France.

29. Girardet, "L'Héritage."

30. *Rivarol* 1 (1951). The magazine was busy demonstrating that it had forgotten none of its old enmities and intended to emulate the foul-mouthed style of the Occupation's antisemitic newspapers. In the same issue Jacques Savin described Daniel Mayer as belonging to "the Jewish element of the SFIO, which luckily, thanks to the unleashing of Hitler's terror, was unable to make any headway."

31. Abbé Desgranges, *Les Crimes masqués du résistantialisme* (Paris: L'Elan, 1948), p. 10.

32. Ibid., pp. 44–50.

33. Abbé Desgranges, *Journal d'un prêtre député, 1936–1940* (Paris: Le Palatinat, 1960). See also Jean-Claude Delbreil, "Les Démocrates populaires, Vichy et la résistance, 1940–1942," in Xavier de Montclos et al., eds., *Eglises et chrétiens dans la deuxième guerre mondiale: La France,* proceedings of a Lyons colloquium, 27–30 January 1978 (Lyons: PUL, 1982), p. 118.

34. Desgranges, *Journal,* p. 183.

35. Speech by Paul Faure in Association des Représentants du peuple de la IIIe République, *Le Banquet des Mille,* brochure, 14 March 1948, Bibliothèque Nationale, 80 Lb (60) 37.

36. When the "affair" surfaced in the April-May 1985 issue of *Le Crapouillot,* Georges Guingouin reacted with outrage. On all these matters see Raymond Ruffin, *Ces Chefs de maquis qui gênaient* (Paris: Presses de la Cité, 1980).

37. The phrase is taken from Jean-Pierre Azéma, *De Munich à la libération* (Paris: Editions du Seuil, 1979), p. 169.

38. *Mes Grands Hommes et quelques autres* (Paris: Grasset, 1982), p. 130.

39. Besides the article in *Carrefour,* the phrase can be found in one variant or another in a number of Rémy's works, in particular the book on his

mystical conversion to Pétainism, *Dans l'ombre du Maréchal* (Paris: Presses de la Cité, 1971).

40. Letter from Rémy to the author, 13 August 1983.

41. Rémy, *Mémoires d'un agent secret de la France libre* (Paris: Solar, 1945), p. 455. The phrase was deleted from the abridged version, *On m'appelait Rémy,* which was published by France-Empire in 1951 (after the *Carrefour* article appeared), as well as from the 1959 edition.

42. On the telegram or telegrams allegedly sent by the Vichy government to Admiral Darlan in Algiers at the time of the Anglo-American landing, see the contradictory assessments of Jean-Baptiste Duroselle, *L'Abîme, 1939–1945* (Paris: Imprimerie Nationale, 1982), pp. 377ff, who did not find any telegrams; and Hervé Coutau-Bégarie and Claude Huan, *Darlan* (Paris: Fayard, 1989), who found at least one, dated 13 November 1942, informing Darlan of the Marshal's "tacit agreement"—this telegram was dictated by Admiral Auphan, who seems to have "interpreted Pétain's silences" (p. 618).

43. Speech of 20 June 1948 at Verdun, in *Discours et messages, 1946–1958* (Paris: Plon, 1970), p. 200.

44. Press conference of 29 March 1949, ibid.

45. Press conference of 16 March 1950, ibid.

46. See Jean Lacouture, *De Gaulle,* vol. 2: *Le Politique* (Paris: Seuil, 1985). Lacouture attributes little importance to the Rémy affair.

47. *Le Monde,* 14 April 1950.

48. Letter from de Gaulle to Rémy, 13 April 1950, made available to the author by Rémy. It has since been published in Charles de Gaulle, *Lettres, notes et carnets. 8 mai 1945–18 juin 1951* (Paris: Plon, 1984), p. 416.

49. Letter from de Gaulle to Colonel Fleuret, 10 May 1950, ibid., pp. 420–421.

50. Letter from de Gaulle to M. de la Bardonnie, 4 May 1950, ibid., p. 420; his italics. It should be noted that de Gaulle apparently did not hold this correspondent in very high esteem: see Georges Pompidou, *Pour rétablir une vérité* (Paris: Flammarion, 1982), p. 125.

51. Rémy, *De Gaulle, cet inconnu* (Paris: Solar, 1947), pp. 28–29.

52. According to the original manuscript, with handwritten corrections by de Gaulle, p. 13, from the files of Colonel Rémy, communicated to the author on 13 August 1983. Jean Charlot, *Le Gaullisme d'opposition, 1946–1958* (Paris: Fayard, 1983), comes to the same conclusions.

53. Pompidou, *Pour rétablir une vérité,* pp. 126–127.

54. *Journal officiel,* National Assembly debate of 9 November 1950.

55. Rémond, *Les Droites en France,* p. 249.

56. See the articles by Jean-Marc Théolleyre in *Le Monde,* 24–26 July 1951. See also the reports by Actualités françaises in the archives of the INA.

57. Article signed Sirius, *Le Monde*, 24 July 1951.

58. Account reported in *Le Monde*, 27 April 1948.

59. *Bulletin de l'ADMP* 1 (July 1952). The official organ of the association began as a quarterly newsletter printed on poor paper without illustrations but in March 1959 became a full-fledged journal, *Le Maréchal*, printed on high-quality paper in a large format with numerous photographs of Pétain and various pilgrimages. At first it was published bimonthly but later reverted to a quarterly.

60. For these figures see the *Bulletin* of January 1956 and *Le Maréchal* for May 1961, November 1971, and April 1976. The last figure was communicated to me by the attorney René Descubes during an interview on 22 June 1983, at which time he was secretary-general of the organization. The ADMP has refused to open its files to permit an accurate assessment of its membership.

61. Claude Michelet, *Mon père, Edmond Michelet* (Paris: Presses de la Cité, 1971), quoted by Rémy, *Mes Grands Hommes*, p. 285.

62. See Jacques Isorni, *Ainsi passent les républiques* (Paris: Flammarion, 1959). This affair led to the final break between Rémy and Isorni, who had already clashed as members of the ADMP.

63. Told to the author by Jacques Isorni, 5 November 1984. On Pompidou, see Chapter 3.

64. Congress of the ADMP, 1 May 1977, *Le Maréchal* 107 (July 1977).

65. *Le Maréchal* 81 (January 1971).

66. Jean Paulhan, *Lettre aux directeurs de la Résistance* (Paris: Minuit, 1951), reprinted by J.-J. Pauvert in 1968 with letters between Paulhan and angry members of the Resistance.

67. *Journal officiel*, laws and decrees, 6 January 1951.

68. Roger Duveau spoke in favor of the bill. *Journal officiel, Assemblée nationale, débats parlementaires*, 11 July 1952, p. 3899.

69. Ibid., 21 October 1952, pp. 4254–55.

70. Ibid.

71. *Journal officiel*, laws and decrees, 7 August 1953.

72. These are official figures from *Journal officiel, Débats parlementaires, Assemblée nationale*, sessions of 11 April 1950, 24 October 1952, 6 October 1956, and 15 May 1958. The latter two sessions are cited in Novick, *L'Epuration française*, pp. 297–298. Two preliminary laws were passed on 17 April 1946 and 17 August 1947, which concerned secondary offenses such as black marketeering or delinquency by minors under the age of twenty-one, crimes with insignificant penalties, and men who later distinguished themselves in combat in Indochina.

73. Cassou, *La Mémoire courte*, pp. 49–50.

74. André Kaspi, "L'Affaire des enfants Finaly," *L'Histoire* 76 (March 1985).

75. Jean-Pierre Rioux, "Le Procès d'Oradour," *L'Histoire* 64 (February 1984).
76. Jean Lefranc, speaking in favor of the bill. See *Journal officiel,* 18 February 1953, p. 1111.
77. Ibid., p. 1115.
78. Quoted by Pierre Barral, "L'Affaire d'Oradour, affrontement de deux mémoires," in *Mémoire de la seconde guerre mondiale,* pp. 243–252. This volume also contains several discussions of forcible conscription, particularly that of Alfred Wahl. See also Geneviève Herberich-Marx and Freddy Raphaël, "Les Incorporés de force alsaciens. Déni, convocation et provocation de la mémoire," *Vingtième Siècle* 6 (April-June 1985).
79. *Journal officiel,* 20 February 1953, p. 1255.
80. See Marc Sadoun, *Les Socialistes sous l'Occupation. Résistance et collaboration* (Paris: Presses de la Fondation Nationale des Sciences Politiques, 1982), p. 276.
81. Jean-Pierre Rioux, "L'Opinion publique française et la CED: querelle partisane ou bataille de la mémoire?" *Relations internationales* 37 (Spring 1984).

2. Repressions (1954–1971)

1. *Le Monde,* 2 October 1954. Cf. *Le Monde. Procès d'après-guerre,* a compendium of documents collected and introduced by Jean-Marc Théolleyre (Paris: La Découverte/*Le Monde,* 1985) p. 203.
2. Ibid., p. 205.
3. Notably in *L'Oeuvre,* 24 March 1941, which contains a photograph showing the opening of the Brévannes Center in which Hersant probably appears. In his statement of accusations, Jean Legendre incorrectly indicated an issue from March 1942. See *Journal officiel, Assemblée nationale, débats parlementaires,* 19 April 1956. See also the debate between Jean Balestre and "F. Montfort." Balestre accused Hersant of being the man who signed himself "Montfort" in *Au pilori,* 21 (September 1942 and 1 October 1942). Hersant denied it: see *Le Nouvel Observateur,* 2 May 1977.
4. On Hersant's career see especially Nicolas Brimo, *Le Dossier Hersant* (Paris: Maspero, 1977).
5. The LVF was created in July 1941.
6. Cf. Jean-Pierre Rioux, *La France de la IVe république,* vol. 2: *L'Expansion et l'impuissance, 1952–1958.* (Paris: Seuil, 1983), p. 61.
7. Report by Gerhard Heller, February 1941, cited by Gérard Loiseaux, *La Littérature de la défaite et de la collaboration* (Paris: Publications de la Sorbonne, 1984), pp. 88–90.

8. See Pascal Ory, *Les Collaborateurs* (Paris: Seuil, 1976), p. 251.

9. Institut de France, *Discours d'André François-Poncet, réception à l'Académie française,* 22 January 1953 (Paris: Institut de France, 1953). For de Gaulle's reaction ("He was good-looking, their shield!"), see Pompidou, *Pour rétablir une vérité,* p. 139.

10. Ibid.

11. Published by Fayard in 1954 (see Chapter 6). Aron had no shortage of praise for François-Poncet: "The Academy is indebted to its newly elected member for having made it the first institution in France to give voice to justice and truth," in *Histoire de l'épuration,* vol. 3, part 2: *Le Monde de la presse, des arts et des lettres, 1944–1953* (Paris: Fayard, 1975), p. 39. At the time Aron had rejoined his friends under the cupola of the academy.

12. "Les Elections à l'Académie française, analyse d'un scrutin significatif. L'Echec de M. Paul Morand," *Revue française de science politique* 8 (September 1958), 646–654. Despite the academic title, the article is by a well-informed and acerbic protagonist in the affair.

13. Letter of 20 April 1958, signed by François Mauriac, Jules Romains, Louis Pasteur Vallery-Radot, Robert d'Harcourt, André Siegfried, Georges Duhamel, Maurice Garçon, Fernand Gregh, Wladimir d'Ormesson, André Chamson, and Robert Kemp and published in *Le Monde,* 2 May 1958.

14. Cited in "Les Elections."

15. *Le Monde,* 13 May 1958.

16. Duc de Castries, *La Vieille Dame du Quai Conti. Une Histoire de l'Académie française* (Paris: Librairie Académique Perrin, 1978), p. 400.

17. According to a report in *Le Monde,* 6 July 1968, at the time of the final election. None of this prevented the head of state from thanking Jacques de Lacretelle for sending a copy of *Tiroir secret* in a letter that contained this observation: "What talent you have!" Letter of 24 October 1959, *Lettres, notes, et carnets, juin 1958-décembre 1960* (Paris: Plon, 1985), p. 274.

18. Quoted in Winock, *La Fièvre hexagonale,* pp. 299–300.

19. René Rémond, *1958: Le Retour de De Gaulle* (Brussels: Complexe, 1983), pp. 20–21.

20. François Mitterrand, *Le Coup d'état permanent* (Paris: Plon, 1964), p. 73.

21. The publication was *La Nef,* whose first issues were published in July 1944 in Algiers.

22. *Journal officiel,* second session of 2 June 1958, issue of 3 June 1958, pp. 2618–19. Prior to this debate, 360 deputies voted in favor of an amnesty covering acts of economic collaboration during the war committed by

foreigners from neutral countries. Many of those voting in favor were on the left (including Jules Moch, Gaston Deferre, and François Mitterrand); among the 189 voting against were the Communists and a deputy by the name of Robert Hersant.

23. Press conference of 10 November 1959.

24. Jean Touchard, *Le Gaullisme, 1940–1969* (Paris: Seuil, 1978), p. 271.

25. *Journal officiel,* 15 April 1959, p. 4763.

26. On commemoration ceremonies as carriers of memory, see Chapter 6.

27. *Le Monde,* 19 and 20 April 1959. This speech is not included in the Plon edition of *Discours et messages.*

28. Ibid.

29. Ibid.

30. Ibid., 7 and 8 June 1959.

31. This is the final scene of *The Sorrow and the Pity,* taken from the news-reel footage of Actualités françaises. We see a freeze frame when de Gaulle shakes Gaspar's hand (or at least we assume that he does, since the General, seen from behind, blocks our view); the frame gives the handshake more significance than it had at the time. Contrary to what Eugène Martres says in *La Mémoire des français,* pp. 284–285, de Gaulle does not appear to have been especially lavish in his greetings to Gaspar.

32. Pierre Vidal-Naquet, "Une Fidélité têtue. La Résistance française à la guerre d'Algérie," *Vingtième Siècle* 10 (April-June 1986).

33. Michel Winock, *La République se meurt, 1956–1958* (Paris: Gallimard/Folio, 1985), p. 127.

34. *Tribune socialiste,* 17 November 1962; quoted by Joseph Algazy, *La Tentation fasciste en France de 1944 à 1965* (Paris: Fayard, 1984), p. 240.

35. Winock, *La République se meurt,* p. 152.

36. Bernard Droz, "Le Cas très singulier de la guerre d'Algérie," in special issue on "les guerres franco-françaises" in *Vingtième Siècle* 5 (January–March 1985).

37. *La Nation française,* 17 July 1956. See Chiroux, *L'Extrême Droite,* pp. 45–46.

38. Charles Luca, at the first congress of the MPF, 20 and 21 December 1958, which caused quite a stir. *Fidélité,* February 1959. Luca had previously founded the Phalange Française, which was dissolved in May 1958; its secretary-general was Henri Jalin, alias Henri Roques.

39. Duprat, *Les Mouvements d'extrême droite,* p. 63.

40. *Le Maréchal,* January 1960.

41. *Mémoires d'espoir,* vol. 1: *Le Renouveau, 1958–1962* (Paris: Plon, 1970), p. 83.

42. Bidault, *D'une résistance à l'autre*, pp. 277–278.

43. *Le Maréchal*, January 1965.

44. Chiroux, *L'Extrême Droite*, p. 79.

45. Ozouf, "Peut-on commémorer la révolution française?"

46. From François Nourissier, "Le Cadavre dans le placard," *Le Point*, 11 March 1974.

47. *Journal officiel*, written question of 8 May 1963, response of 29 August 1964.

48. Letter of 23 April 1963 from the ministry of the interior to André Holleaux, Malraux's chief of staff. File on Jean Moulin at the Pantheon, preserved in archives of the Service des Palais Nationaux, unnumbered.

49. Decree of 11 December 1964, *Journal officiel*, 12 December 1964.

50. Note from military governor of Paris, 11 December 1964, ibid.

51. Note to Minister Malraux from Direction de l'Architecture concerning the interministerial meeting of 8 December, undated, ibid.

52. Note from military governor of Paris (see note 50). The description of the ceremony is based on the plans of the *direction de l'Architecture*, on the record of the interment prepared on 19 December 1964 by the conservator of monuments of Paris, and on published accounts in *Le Monde*. The INA archives contain a document from Actualités Françaises concerning the occasion.

53. Account and documents provided by Charles Fournier-Bocquet, former member of the FTP and secretary-general of the ANACR.

54. See Henry Rousso, "Cet Obscur Objet du souvenir," in *La Mémoire des français*, p. 53.

55. Editorial by André Wurmser, *L'Humanité*, 19 December 1964.

56. Mona Ozouf, "L'Ecole normale des morts," in Nora, ed., *Les Lieux de mémoire*, vol. 1, p. 162.

57. Ibid.

58. My italics. Oath of 22 October 1972, communicated to the author by Jean-Marie Guillon, correspondent of the IHTP in the Var. See his article in *La Mémoire des français*, p. 303.

59. Agulhon, "Réflexions," p. 43.

60. *Journal officiel*, 29 December 1964.

61. Ibid., session of 16 December 1964, issue of 17 December 1964.

62. André Siegfried, colleague of the deceased general in the Académie Française, in *L'Année politique*, 1965, p. 9.

63. Philippe Viannay, "Le Présent du passé," unpublished manuscript written in the 1970s and kindly made available to me. See also Viannay's memoirs, *Du bon usage de la France. Résistance, journalisme, Glénans* (Paris: Ramsay, 1988), especially pp. 159–169 on de Gaulle and the Resistance.

3. The Broken Mirror (1971–1974)

1. Pascal Ory, *L'Entre-deux-mai, histoire culturelle de la France, mai 1968–mai 1981* (Paris: Seuil, 1983), p. 13.

2. Nourissier, "Le Cadavre dans le placard."

3. Paul Thibaud, "Du sel sur nos plaies," *Esprit* 5 (May 1981), on *L'Idéologie française* by Bernard-Henri Lévy.

4. See covers of *Figaro Magazine,* 10 December 1983, and *L'Express,* 23 March 1984, both on the theme of "the good old days."

5. Films are analyzed in Chapter 6.

6. Marcel Ophuls, *Le Chagrin et la pitié* (Paris: Alain Moreau, 1980), p. 207. This is the screenplay with an introduction by the director alone after his quarrel with the producers, a symptom of a success that none of them had anticipated.

7. What Raphael Géminiani actually said was: "Uh . . . they were seen . . . No, no, we saw Germans because of the partisans . . . who came, but, you know, we weren't occupied." The next scene shows him on his bicycle with these words superimposed: "We never saw the Germans (Géminiani)," ibid., p. 118.

8. Michel Capdenac, *Les Lettres françaises,* 21 April 1971.

9. André Gisselbrecht, *L'Humanité,* 20 September 1971.

10. Jacques Langlois, *Rivarol,* 23 April 1971.

11. Alfred Fabre-Luce, *Le Monde,* 13 May 1971.

12. Germaine Tillion, *Le Monde,* 8 June 1971.

13. Claude Mauriac, *Le Figaro,* 23 April 1971.

14. Jean-Paul Sartre, *La Cause du peuple / J'accuse,* quoted in the press review *Téléciné* 171–172 (July 1971), 21, special issue on *The Sorrow and the Pity.*

15. Ibid., p. 31. On *Zoom* and *Munich,* see Jean-Noël Jeanneney and Monique Sauvage, eds., *Télévision, nouvelle mémoire. Les Magazines de grand reportage, 1959–1968* (Paris: Seuil/INA, 1982).

16. Ibid.

17. Jean-Jacques de Bresson's statement was widely reported at the time. On his career in the Resistance, see *Bulletin de liaison de l'ANMRF* 32 (January 1986).

18. Statistics published in *Le Film français;* see Chapter 7.

19. Ophuls, *Le Chagrin,* pp. 226–227.

20. See Chapter 4.

21. Simone Veil speaking on the radio station Europe 1 after the television broadcast; *Le Monde,* 30 October 1981.

22. See article by Danièle Heymann in *L'Express,* 28 August 1981.

23. See note 21.
24. André Harris in *Téléciné*, p. 38.
25. Stanley Hoffmann, "Chagrin et pitié?" *Contrepoint* 10 (1973), reprinted in *Decline or Renewal? France since the 1930s* (New York: Viking, 1974).
26. Ophuls, interviewed by Gilbert Salachas in *Téléciné*, p. 31.
27. Interview with Pierre Mendès France, *Téléciné*, pp. 42–52.
28. *New York Times Magazine*, 29 August 1971.
29. See *Le Monde*, 15 December 1971, which explains that according to Robert's *Dictionnaire* "hate" means *détester,* glossed as "to feel aversion from."
30. Letter to General Ginas, published in *Le Monde,* 3 February 1972.
31. Figures cited by Jacques Chambaz and Dominique Jamet, *Le Quotidien de Paris,* 22 August 1980 (confirmed impressionistically by a reading of press notices). The running interview was published between 21 August and 3 September 1980. According to Chambaz (interviewed by the author on 24 June 1985), the magazine was in search of a "strong subject" that would make news. There was in fact no justification for such an interview—"immense, immense, and too long"—at that time.
32. In 1972 Mazière published his memoirs: *Le Rêveur casqué* (Paris: Laffont, 1972). Despite the moderate image he offers of himself in *The Sorrow and the Pity* and in his memoirs, he appears to have reverted later to positions similar to those of his militant youth, as evidenced, for example, by his statements in the neofascist organ *Révolution européenne,* October 1989.
33. Pierre Mantello, "Le Mouvement populaire des familles en Savoie (1940–1945)," *Les Cahiers du Groupement pour la recherche sur les mouvements familiaux* 3 (1985), 318. These indications confirm Touvier's statements (to be treated with caution) in various brochures published by himself, his children, and his lawyers at their own expense: Chantal and Pierre Touvier, "Lettre ouverte aux représentants du peuple français suivie de 20 documents inédits," mimeographed, June 1976, and *Mes crimes contre l'humanité* (Imprimerie SPT, 1 November 1979).
34. Article by Nicolas Brimo, 23 March 1983.
35. Statement by chief of staff of the prefect of the Rhône to Jacques Derogy, *L'Express,* 5 June 1972, also mentioned in the Delarue Report, which was published by two journalists from *Le Monde:* Laurent Greilsamer and Daniel Schneidermann, *Un Certain Monsieur Paul. L'Affaire Touvier* (Paris: Fayard, 1989), pp. 237–254.
36. Ibid.
37. Interview with the author, 11 September 1984.

38. Document published in *Libération,* 30 October 1989, in the wake of questions raised by Greilsamer and Schneidermann in *Un Certain Monsieur Paul,* where it was claimed that Pierre Arpaillange had worked to secure a pardon. For their not very convincing response, see *Le Monde,* 31 October 1989. All will not be clear until the case is closed.

39. See in particular his statements to AFP, 19 August 1972.

40. Letter made public by *L'Express,* 19 June 1972.

41. "Lendemain de persécution," *Courier français du Témoignage chrétien,* 21 October 1944.

42. *L'Express,* 19 June 1972.

43. Interview with Jacques Delarue.

44. *Paris-Match,* 23 December 1972.

45. For example, see *L'Express,* 26 June 1972.

46. *L'Express,* 17 July 1972.

47. Bitterly reported by Louis-Martin Chauffier, *Le Figaro,* 17–18 June 1972.

48. *Combat,* 16 June 1972. Pierre Bourgeade's articles would shortly earn him an indictment for "offenses against the head of state." Portraying itself as one of the last publications surviving from the Resistance, the paper waged a vehement campaign against the pardon.

49. Georges Pompidou, *Entretiens et discours, 1968–1974* (Paris: Flammarion, 1984), pp. 157–158. *Le Monde* (23 September 1972) published the press conference in its entirety, and one can see that, immediately after this answer was given, the next question, about campaign issues, was asked by René Andrieu, editor-in-chief of *L'Humanité.* Clearly the Communist Party, apart from a few former résistants, had no interest in pursuing the Touvier issue, perhaps because it too was a victim of the syndrome. It was just two years earlier, in the summer of 1970, that the Marchais affair first came to public attention. Georges Marchais had been assistant secretary-general of the party since 8 February 1970 and was the designated successor of Waldeck Rochet. On 27 July 1970 *L'Express* described him simply as "a former conscript laborer who escaped in 1943," but doubts about his past soon began to appear in the bourgeois press. There is an odd symmetry in the positions of the leaders of the two groups in whom memory of the Resistance was primarily vested: the Gaullist heir had virtually nothing to do with Gaullism's founding myth, while the future leader of the Communist Party had done nothing to honor the memory of the "75,000 fusillés."

50. Pompidou, *Entretiens et discours,* p. 28.

51. Ibid., p. 29.

52. Ibid., p. 30.

53. The last collaborators remaining in prison were freed in the quietest possible way. Apart from Barbier and Vasseur, Joseph Cortial, also sentenced to death, had his sentence commuted by Pompidou. The length of time they spent in prison was because of the date of their trial: more than twenty years after the end of the war, they were judged between 1965 and 1970 and received no benefit from either the amnesty or the statute of limitations.

54. Cf. *Aspects de la France*, 23 December 1971, cited by Dominique Veillon, *La Collaboration, textes et débats* (Paris: Livre de Poche, 1984), p. 420.

55. Interview with Jacques Delarue.

56. "L'Occupation: pourquoi tout le monde en parle," *Le Point*, 11 March 1974.

57. Pierre Assouline, *Une Eminence grise, Jean Jardin (1904–1976)* (Paris: Balland, 1986), p. 338.

58. Pascal Jardin, *La Guerre à neuf ans* (Paris: Grasset, 1971), p. 136.

59. Ory, *L'Entre-deux-mai*, pp. 118ff.

4. Obsession (after 1974): Jewish Memory

1. Philippe, *Etre juif dans la société française*, pp. 389ff.

2. See Jean-Pierre Rioux, "L'Opinion publique ou le lion vieilli et le coq déplumé," in "Suez," *L'Histoire* 38 (October 1981).

3. Michel Winock, *Edouard Drumont et Cie. Antisémitisme et fascisme en France* (Paris: Seuil, 1982), p. 107.

4. Transcription from the newsreel. The text given in Charles de Gaulle, *Discours et messages*, vol. 5: *Vers le terme, 1966–1969* (Paris: Plon, 1970), p. 232, omits the final phrase: "Next year in Jerusalem."

5. Raymond Aron, "Le Temps du soupçon," reproduced in *De Gaulle, Israël et les juifs* (Paris: Plon, 1968), p. 20.

6. Ibid., p. 35.

7. Ibid., p. 18.

8. Xavier Vallat, *Aspects de la France*, 8 December 1967.

9. *Maariv*, 29 November 1967.

10. Letter of 19 April 1968, quoted in Raymond Aron, *Mémoires* (Paris: Julliard, 1983), p. 730.

11. Concerning the CRIF, the Jews, and the Communists during the war, see the impassioned memoirs of one of its founders, Adam Rayski, former member of the FTP (immigrant workers' section) and later one of the protagonists in the Manouchian affair: *Nos illusions perdues* (Paris:

Balland, 1985). See also Annie Kriegel, *Réflexions sur les questions juives* (Paris: Hachette/Pluriel, 1984), pp. 109ff.

12. Text reproduced in Kriegel, *Réflexions sur les questions juives*. After the war, the CRIF kept the same acronym but changed its name to Conseil Représentatif des Institutions Juives de France, a more modest and less expansive appellation, in which "Juif" replaced the more ambiguous "Israélite."

13. In particular the telegram of 6 July 1942 from Dannecker, in charge of Jewish affairs in France, to section IV B-4 (Eichmann) of the RSHA: "President Laval has proposed that, when Jewish families are deported from the unoccupied zone, children under sixteen should be deported with them. The problem of Jewish children in the occupied zone is not his concern." This document is now in the possession of the Centre de Documentation Juive Contemporaine.

14. *L'Express*, 8 May 1967, on Claude Lévy and Paul Tillard, *La Grande Rafle du Vél d'Hiv* (Paris: Laffont, 1967).

15. *L'Express*, 14 February 1972.

16. Quoted in *L'Express*, 4 November 1978.

17. Joseph Billig, *Le Commissariat général aux questions juives (1941–1944)*, 3 vols., Editions du Centre (CDJC), 1955–1960. In 1975 a student at the University of Paris submitted a master's thesis, under the supervision of Jacques Droz, on antisemitic propaganda, which made use of certain of Darquier's papers held by the CDJC. As a result of the Darquier affair, the thesis was published, a rare thing in France: Jean Laloum, *La France antisémite de Darquier de Pellepoix* (Paris: Syros, 1979), with a preface by Jacques Droz.

18. *Le Monde*, 4 November 1978. At the same session there was a bitter debate between the Communists and Louis de Guéringaud, the minister of foreign affairs. The minister denied that France's ambassador to Spain, Robert Barbara de Labelotterie, baron de Boisséson, had contacts with former collaborators or OAS members between 1964 and 1970.

19. Letter published on 3 November 1978, addressed to Jacqueline Baudrier (Radio France), Jean-Louis Guillaud (TF1), Maurice Ulrich (Antenne 2), and Claude Contamine (FR3).

20. *L'Express*, 4 November 1978.

21. Ibid., as well as following issue, 11 November 1978.

22. Ibid.

23. Philippe Ganier Raymond, *Une Certaine France. L'Antisémitisme 40–44* (Paris: Balland, 1975), pp. 11–12.

24. Ibid., pp. 29–30.

25. *L'Express*, 4 November 1978; *Le Monde*, 4 November 1978; etc.

26. In *Lettre de l'UDF,* 14 February 1979, and *L'Humanité,* 15 February 1979. See Henri Ménudier, "'Holocauste' en France," *Revue d'Allemagne* 12 (September 1981). See also Freddy Raphaël, "Bagatelles pour un génocide: 'Holocauste' et la presse de gauche en France (1979–1980)," *Revue des sciences sociales de la France de l'Est* 14 (1985).

27. *L'Express,* 17 February 1979.

28. Ibid., 27 January 1979.

29. Christian Beullac in *Le Monde,* 14 February 1979.

30. Charlotte Delbo, "Une Marque indélébile," *Le Monde,* 27 February 1979. A former deportee, Delbo is the author of several books about her painful experiences: *Aucun de nous ne reviendra* (Geneva: Gonthier, 1965), written in 1946; *Le Convoi du 24 janvier* (Paris: Minuit, 1965); and *La Mémoire et les jours* (Paris: Berg International, 1985).

31. *L'Express,* 27 January 1979.

32. On the debate see *Le Matin,* 7 March 1979; *Libération,* 8 March 1979; and *Le Monde,* 8 March 1979. On the Hersant case, the young "impertinent" read a part of the investigative report published in *Le Canard enchaîné* of 28 February 1979, which excerpted an article published in the Quebec newspaper *L'Action catholique* on 24 August 1940. The article mentioned an interview with Jeune Front leaders after demonstrations on the Champs-Elysées: "Its leader, Robert Hersant, stated during Tuesday's demonstration that this was only the beginning and that they were going to hunt down all the Jews and Freemasons 'because they are responsible for France's disarray.'" At this point Simone Veil did not defend Hersant, as she did later in 1984, when he was a prominent member of her list of candidates for election to the European parliament.

33. Guy Hocquenghem, "Une Simple Mention suffira. Mardi soir, aux débats des 'Dossiers' sur *Holocauste,* distribution des prix du martyre," *Libération,* 8 March 1979.

34. *L'Humanité,* 13 February 1979.

35. Interview with attorney Joe Nordmann, 4 October 1989.

36. See in particular his demonstration of Bousquet's personal role in Serge Klarsfeld, *Vichy-Auschwitz. Le Rôle de Vichy dans la solution finale de la question juive en France,* 2 vols. (Paris: Fayard, 1983 and 1985), especially vol. 1, pp. 93–104.

37. Writ of dismissal issued by Judge Jean-Pierre Getti, 11 September 1989, *Tribunal de grande instance de Paris,* p. 3.

38. "Réquisitoire définitif aux fins de constatation de l'extinction de l'action publique," *Tribunal de grande instance de Paris, Parquet du procureur de la République,* 26 July 1989.

39. *Le Matin de Paris,* 16 November 1978. According to Pierre Vidal-

Naquet, it was the appearance of another article by Faurisson in *Le Monde*, 29 December 1978, followed shortly by a response by Georges Wellers, which attracted so much media attention to the Faurisson affair. See his remarkable *Les Assassins de la mémoire. 'Un Eichmann de papier' et autres essais sur le révisionnisme* (Paris: La Découverte, 1987), p. 211, n. 71.

40. Robert Faurisson, *Mémoire en défense. Contre ceux qui m'accusent de falsifier l'histoire. La Question des chambres à gaz* (Paris: La Vieille Taupe, 1980). The book contains a preface by Noam Chomsky entitled "Some Elementary Observations on Freedom of Expression." Although Chomsky admitted that he "did not know [Faurisson's] works very well," he absolved the man of any hint of antisemitism and characterized him as "a fairly apolitical liberal" (pp. xiv–xv).

41. See Alain Finkielkraut, *L'Avenir d'une négation. Réflexion sur la question du génocide* (Paris: Seuil, 1982).

42. Paul Rassinier, *Passage de la ligne* (1948) and *Le Mensonge d'Ulysse* (1950), first published privately and then reissued by La Librairie Française (Henry Coston) and La Vieille Taupe (in 1979).

43. See Roland Lewin, "Paul Rassinier ou la conjonction des extrêmes," *Silex* 26 (1984), and Henry Rousso, "La Négation du génocide juif," *L'Histoire* 106 (December 1987).

44. *Le Monde*, 21 February 1979.

45. Ecole des Hautes Etudes en Sciences Sociales, *L'Allemagne nazie et le génocide juif* (Paris: Hautes Etudes/Gallimard/Seuil, 1985), and François Bédarida, ed., *La Politique nazie d'extermination* (Paris: IHTP/Albin Michel, 1989).

46. Pierre Vidal-Naquet, *Les Juifs, la mémoire et le présent* (Paris: Maspero, 1981), pp. 196–197, a reprint of his introduction to "Un Eichmann de papier," first published in *Esprit*, September 1980. This article is one of the best responses according to Faurisson's own supporters: "The most important attack on Faurisson. This article prevented the lightning-like diffusion of revisionist theses by convincing the French intelligentsia that the case was so odious and absurd that the argument was not even worthy of attention." See Jean-Gabriel Cohn-Bendit et al., *Intolérable intolérance* (Paris: La Différence, 1981), p. 196. Thus a few pages were enough to shoot down this "speeding missile."

47. Letter from André D. in the letters column of *Les Nouvelles littéraires*, 15 January 1981.

48. In addition to the colloquium proceedings (see note 45) and the article by Pierre Vidal-Naquet, Georges Wellers of the CDJC published *Les Chambres à gaz ont existé* (Paris: Gallimard, 1981) as well as numerous

articles in *Le Monde juif*. An important work by a group of German historians was published in French translation: Eugen Kogon, Hermann Langbein, and Adalbert Ruckerl, *Les Chambres à gaz, secret d'état* (Paris: Minuit, 1984). There were also numerous reactions to Henri Roques' so-called defense of his thesis on the "Confessions of Kurt Gerstein." Among others see the report on the round-table discussion organized by the IHTP in *Bulletin de l'IHTP* 25 (September 1986). One of the participants was the Dutch professor Harry Paape, coeditor with Gerrold van der Stroom and David Barnouw, of a scholarly edition of the various versions of the diary of Anne Frank: *Les Journaux d'Anne Frank* (Paris: Calmann-Lévy, 1950–1989), trans. Philippe Noble and Isabelle Rosselin-Bobulesco. There is a new English edition: Anne Frank, *Diary of a Young Girl* (New York: Random House, 1990). This book definitively refuted Faurisson's first revisionist thesis, that the diary was a postwar forgery.

49. On the relation between justice and history, see *Le Débat* 32 (November 1984). See also excerpts from the decision in the case of Laurent Wetzel and various survivors' groups versus Marcel Paul, in which the courts dismissed the suit against the historian on the grounds that he took a neutral position with respect to divergent interpretations: *Vingtième Siècle* 8 (October-December 1985), 117–121.

50. Finkielkraut, *L'Avenir d'une négation*, pp. 94–95.

51. Nathalie Heinich and Michael Pollak, "Le Témoignage," Mission recherche-expérimentation, Ministère des affaires sociales et de la solidarité nationale, 1985, published in *Actes de la recherche en sciences sociales* 62/63 (1986); see also other articles by Michael Pollak in the same journal: "Des mots qui tuent" 41 (February 1982), and "La Gestion de l'indicible," 62/63 (1986).

52. Simone de Beauvoir, preface to Jean-François Steiner, *Treblinka* (Paris: Fayard, 1966).

53. Review by Jean-Maurice Hermann, vice-president of the FNDIRP, in *Droit et liberté* 252 (15 April–15 May 1966).

54. "Les Juifs, ce qu'on n'a jamais osé dire," *Le Nouveau Candide* 255 (14–20 March 1966), special free issue. J.-F. Steiner was a reporter for *Candide*.

55. Léon Poliakov, "Treblinka: vérité et roman," *Preuves* 183 (May 1966).

56. Cf. *La Presse nouvelle*, 23–29 September 1966.

57. Hannah Arendt, *Eichmann in Jerusalem: A Report on the Banality of Evil* (New York: Viking, 1963).

58. Maurice Rajsfus, *Des juifs dans la collaboration. L'UGIF, 1941–1944* (Paris: Etudes et Documentation Internationales, 1980), preface by Pierre

Vidal-Naquet, and *Sois juif et tais-toi* (Paris: EDI, 1981), which triggered a new controversy over the role of André Baur, president of the UGIF, whose brother-in-law, Raymond Lindon, was a prosecutor in trials at the time of the Liberation and now came to his defense in "Hommage à André Baur," mimeographed, undated, available at the CDJC.

59. Cf. Annie Kriegel, "Vérité historique et mensonges politiques. Diversion et révisions sur l'antisémitisme," *Commentaire* 12 (Winter 1980–81), reprinted in *Réflexions sur les questions juives*, p. 87. Rajsfus was actually his mother's name.

60. Gérard Michel, *Tribune juive* 681–682 (17 July–10 August 1981).

61. On this point see *Les Juifs dans la résistance et la libération. Histoire, témoignages, débats* (Paris: Scribe, 1985), texts collected and introduced by RHICOJ; "La Résistance juive en France: où en est son histoire?" *Le Monde juif* 118 (April-June 1985); Lucien Lazare, *La Résistance juive en France* (Paris: Stock, 1987), and Claude Lévy, "La Résistance juive en France. De l'enjeu de mémoire à l'histoire critique," *Vingtième Siècle* 22 (April-June 1989).

62. This statement, made on the night of the attack, appeared in the press in a number of versions that differed, as reports of politicians' allusive utterances often do, in form if not content. The transcription given here is based on a videotape of the 11 o'clock news on TF1 for 3 October 1980. The statement was broadcast at 11:30, five hours after the attack, live from the steps of the Hôtel Matignon, as the prime minister was returning from Lyons. So this was not Barre's first reaction to the attack (he had been interviewed by telephone immediately afterward), nor was it an impromptu statement; he had plenty of time to prepare what he was going to say. (I wish to thank Yvan Charron of TF1 for allowing me to view this videotape.)

63. See the investigative report by Annette Lévy-Willard in *Libération*, 3 October 1984. It is possible, even probable, that the authors of the attack used the fear of a rebirth of fascism and perhaps even manipulated various small right-wing extremist groups.

5. Obsession (after 1974): The World of Politics

1. See Ophuls, *Le Chagrin*, p. 85. Contrary to what the note states, it was not Edmond, the father, but René, the uncle. Rochat, moreover, subsequently denied that such an undertaking was made, as reported in Christiane Rimbaud, *Le Procès Mendès France* (Paris: Librairie Académique Perrin, 1986), p. 170.

2. Olivier Todd, *La Marelle de Giscard, 1926–1974* (Paris: Robert Laffont, 1977), p. 53.

3. Marie Granet, *Défense de la France. Histoire d'un mouvement de résistance (1940–1944)* (Paris: Presses Universitaires de France, 1960), p. 200.

4. *Le Canard enchaîné*, 6 May 1981, between the two rounds of voting in the presidential elections.

5. Interview with Genia Gemahling, August 1986.

6. *Le Monde*, 14 November 1978.

7. Written questions from deputies Christian Laurissergues, Jacques Chaminade, and Hubert Ruffe of Lot-et-Garonne, and responses from the minister of defense, in *Journal officiel, Débats parlementaires, Assemblée nationale*, sessions of 10 February 1979 (p. 876) and 14 March 1979 (p. 1618). On 15 March, UDF deputy Emmanuel Hamel submitted another written question asking whether the anniversary of the German-Soviet pact would be the subject of television broadcasts. The minister of culture and communication answered that "television programming is the sole responsibility of the presidents and boards of directors of the broadcasting corporations [but that] the interest expressed by the honorable deputy ... has been communicated to the presidents in charge." Ibid., 14 July 1979.

8. Presidential speech at Rethondes, 11 November 1978, *Le Monde*, 14 November 1978.

9. *Le Monde*, 31 December 1980.

10. Jean Bothorel, *La République mondaine* (Paris: Grasset, 1979), pp. 101–105. "Synarchy" refers to a group of young technocrats who came to power with Admiral Darlan in February 1941. Apart from Paxton's book, there is a vast literature; see, for example, Richard F. Kuisel, "The Legend of Vichy Synarchy," *French Historical Studies* 6 (1970).

11. *L'Année politique*, 1978, pp. 161–162.

12. Ibid.

13. On the radio station France-Inter, 15 December 1978.

14. In a letter to the RPR group of deputies, 22 December 1978.

15. *Le Monde*, 6 February 1979.

16. Ibid., 24 November 1978.

17. See, for example, the vigorous reaction of Paul Thibaud, "Du sel sur nos plaies," *Esprit* 5 (May 1981), and the special section of *Le Débat* 13 (June 1981).

18. "Provocation," *L'Express*, 7 February 1981.

19. "L'Ambiguité française," ibid.

20. "Le Pétainisme constitue-t-il la vraie idéologie française?" *Les Nouvelles littéraires*, 15 January 1981. See also Jean-François Kahn, *La Guerre civile. Essais sur les stalinismes de droite et de gauche* (Paris: Seuil, 1982). *Les Nouvelles littéraires* opened its columns to letters from its readers,

which reveal that many readers supported Lévy out of a "generational solidarity" and a rejection of taboos still believed active. Lévy took in gullible readers with an argument that amounts to "where there's smoke, there's fire."

21. *Le Monde*, 16 January, 23 January, 31 January 1981.

22. Jean-Paul Enthoven, "Français, quand vous saurez," *Le Nouvel Observateur*, 26 January 1981.

23. Among the early works of Zeev Sternhell was *La Droite révolutionnaire, 1885–1914. Les origines françaises du fascisme* (Paris: Seuil, 1978), on which Lévy drew heavily. Sternhell's next book was *Ni droite, ni gauche. L'Idéologie fasciste en France* (Paris: Seuil, 1983), which stirred up a new storm with the allegation that French fascism "comes closest to the ideal type, to the 'idea' of fascism in the Platonic sense of the word" (pp. 41–42). Among the many refutations, see Philippe Burrin, *La Dérive fasciste. Doriot, Déat, Bergery, 1933–1945* (Paris: Seuil, 1986).

24. Bernard-Henri Lévy, *L'Idéologie française* (Paris: Grasset, 1981), pp. 18 and 86.

25. See the section on "French-style fascism" in *Globe* 21 (October 1987).

26. On these facts see Philippe Robrieux, *Histoire intérieure du parti communiste*, vol. 2: *1945–1972*, and vol. 4: *Biographies, chronologie, bibliographie* (Paris: Fayard, 1980–1984); and Auguste Lecoeur, *La Stratégie du mensonge, du Kremlin à Georges Marchais* (Paris: Ramsay, 1980).

27. *Le Monde*, 5 May 1981.

28. Compare Michel Slitinsky, *L'Affaire Papon* (Paris: Alain Moreau, 1983), with a preface by Gilles Pérault.

29. *Le Monde*, 9 May 1981.

30. Ibid.

31. Letter to the press following his resignation, *Le Monde*, 19 May 1981.

32. In a meeting at Mulhouse; see *Le Matin de Paris*, 9 May 1981.

33. Ibid. The paper also published numerous letters of protest from résistants of the left and right (Daniel Mayer, Joël Le Tac, Philippe Viannay, Claude Bourdet, and others).

34. "La Mémoire courte," advertisement in *Le Monde*, 16 March 1984. This battle of advertising continued from March to July. At one time or another, the Pétain association, groups of camp survivors, and others took part. Details may be found in "Les Guerres franco-françaises," *Vingtième Siècle* 5 (January-March 1985).

35. Catherine Nay, *Le Noir et le rouge ou l'histoire d'une ambition* (Paris: Grasset, 1984), illustrates these changes of line. Nay applied to Mitterrand a method already tried on others, most notably Giscard.

36. *Mémoires de guerre*, vol. 2: *L'Unité, 1942–1944* (Paris: Plon, 1956), p. 169.

37. On radio station France-Inter, morning of 8 May 1981.

38. Excerpt from stenographic record, *Journal officiel*, session of 1 February 1984, pp. 443–444.

39. Ibid., session of 2 February 1984, p. 447. For several months Mitterrand was associated with the publishers of *Votre beauté*, an affiliate of the firm L'Oréal, which was headed by Eugène Schueller, a former leader of the Social Revolutionary movement founded in September 1940 by Eugène Deloncle. This movement was an offshoot of the prewar Cagoule and maintained close contacts with the Germans. These facts have no particular bearing on Mitterrand himself (as even Catherine Nay acknowledges implicitly on pp. 198–199 of her book), but that has not prevented the extreme right from alluding to them repeatedly. Alain Madelin, a former leader of Occident, was no doubt following the instincts of his youth.

40. Evelyne Largueche, *L'Effet-injure. De la pragmatique à la psychanalyse* (Paris: Presses Universitaires de France, 1983).

41. Figure reported by Hervé Hamon and Patrick Rotman, *Les Intellocrates. Expédition en haute intelligentsia* (Paris: Seuil, 1981), p. 247. On the new right, see also *Mots* 12 (March 1986), special issue on "Right, New Right, Extreme Right. Discourse and Ideology in France and Italy," in particular the articles by Pierre-André Taguieff.

42. Alain de Benoist, *Vu de droite. Anthologie critique des idées contemporaines* (Paris: Copernic, 1977).

43. Figures cited in "L'Extrême Droite nazie et fasciste: menace et riposte," report submitted to the 62nd Congress of the Ligue des Droits de l'Homme (Lille, February 1982) by Madeleine Rébérioux and prepared in 1981 in conjunction with the MRAP and the Association Henri Curiel, p. 3.

44. Alain de Benoist, "Droite, l'ancienne et la nouvelle," *Item*, January 1976-April 1977, reprinted in *Les Idées à l'endroit* (Paris: Editions Libres/Hallier, 1979), p. 57.

45. *Le Monde diplomatique*, January 1977, quoted by de Benoist, *Les Idées*, p. 59.

46. This analysis is based largely on Rémond, *Les Droites en France*.

47. Alexis Carrel, who won the Nobel Prize for Medicine in 1912, wrote the bestseller *L'Homme, cet inconnu* (Paris: Plon, 1935). Although he was not only a forerunner of modern social science but a renowned surgeon, he held rather dubious ideas about biological selection: "The use of eugenics to create a hereditary biological aristocracy would mark an important step toward the solution of today's major problems" (p. 414 of

the paperback reprint of *L'Homme*). In 1941 Vichy made him director of the Fondation Française pour l'Etude des Problèmes Humains, the forerunner of Jean Stoetzel's IFOP and of the INED (1945). See Alain Drouard, "Les Trois âges de la Fondation française pour l'étude des problèmes humains," *Population* 6 (1983).

48. De Benoist, *Les Idées*, p. 74.

49. Interviewed by Kathleen Evin, *Le Nouvel Observateur*, 23 April 1979.

50. See the report on the "springtime university" debates held by the Club de l'Horloge in *L'Evénement de jeudi*, 29 May 1986.

51. See Club de l'Horloge, *Socialisme et fascisme, une même famille?* (Paris: Albin Michel, 1984), and Alain Griotteray, *1940: La Droite était au rendez-vous* (Paris: Laffont, 1985).

52. *Rivarol*, 19 November 1982, p. 4.

53. Bruno Viala, "La Question électorale," *Militant*, September 1982.

54. Based on Edwy Plenel's report in *Le Monde*, 19 October 1983, reprinted in Edwy Plenel and Alain Rollat, *L'Effet Le Pen* (Paris: *Le Monde*/La Découverte, 1984). The newspaper reported certain statements allegedly made by Romain Marie, who won a suit for libel.

55. "Les Habits neufs de la droite française" and "Pétain sans képi," *Le Nouvel Observateur*, 2 July 1979.

56. *Le Monde*, 17 December 1985.

57. For a biographical approach in a profuse literature of uneven quality, see Ladislas de Hoyos, *Barbie* (Paris: Laffont, 1987); Jacques Delarue, "Un SS nommé Barbie," *L'Histoire* 82 (1985), together with a document presented by Pierre Assouline in the same issue; and Guy Morel, *Barbie pour mémoire* (Paris: FNDIRP, 1986). Above all, there is Ophuls' film *Hôtel Terminus*.

58. *Le Monde*, 16 February 1983. A note from a detachment of the French Sûreté in the Palatinate, dated 7 November 1963, reported "definite manipulation" of Barbie by the United States and West Germany and called for the DST or SDECE to intervene.

59. *Le Monde*, 13–14 February 1983.

60. Robert Badinter expressed the wish that "racism, dripping with pride and blood, at last appear before the bar of mankind." See *L'Express*, 6 April 1961.

61. Poll by IFRES/VSD, conducted 5–7 February 1983 and published in *VSD*, 10 February 1983.

62. Interview with *Le Nouvel Observateur*, 11 February 1983.

63. Quoted by Claude Lévy, "L'Affaire Barbie à travers la presse nationale," typescript, 8 pages, lecture at Institut d'Histoire du Temps Présent, 4 March 1983.

64. Raymond Barre before the "Grand Jury RTL/*Le Monde*," 13 February 1983, *Le Monde*, 15 February 1983.

65. Quoted in *Le Monde*, 9 February 1983.

66. She is the author of *J'étais la femme de Jean Moulin* (1977), a book that was widely denounced for its mystification of the subject.

67. On these connections, in addition to the works cited, see the investigative reports by Guillaume Darcell and Guy Konopnicki, *Globe* 1 (November 1985), and Jacques Derogy in *L'Express*.

68. On this event see Serge Klarsfeld, *Les Enfants d'Izieu, une tragédie juive* (Paris: AZ Repro, 1984).

69. Jacques Delarue in a lecture at the Institut d'Histoire du Temps Présent, 21 October 1985.

70. On these events see Erna Paris, *L'Affaire Barbie. Analyse d'un mal français* (Paris: Ramsay, 1985), which is interesting for the portraits that Paris, as a good reporter, gives of the protagonists: Klarsfeld, Vergès, Genoud, and so on.

71. See Jacques Vergès and Etienne Bloch, *La Face cachée du procès Barbie* (Paris: Samuel Tastet, 1983), p. 16, for a report on the Ligoure debates (19 June 1983). This more or less confidential document (to which Jacques Delarue called my attention) reveals the assistance that Vergès received from various intellectuals, but it also indicates what widespread doubts were felt, particularly on the extreme left, about Vergès, Barbie's "wily" attorney. At times the document reminds one of ultra-leftist support for Faurisson.

72. Ibid., p. 23. A fallacious and polemical argument that nevertheless touches on an aspect of the truth: the 1964 vote to suspend the statute of limitations for crimes against humanity took place at the same time as the first vote on an amnesty for the "events" of Algeria (see Chapter 2).

73. Ibid., pp. 32–33.

74. Ibid., p. 35.

75. Arendt, *Eichmann in Jerusalem*, chap. 4.

76. Le Pré-aux-Clercs, 1983. The same argument was put forward in the documentary made for television by Claude Bal but never broadcast, *Que la vérité est amère*, whose polemical intent is clear.

77. Among the spate of books on the subject see René Hardy, *Derniers Mots. Mémoires* (Paris: Fayard, 1984), in which Hardy, probably manipulated by Vergès, attempts to evade responsibility; Lucie Aubrac, *Ils partiront dans l'ivresse. Lyon, mai 43, Londres, février 44* (Paris: Seuil, 1984), one of the most sensitive accounts of underground life; and Henri Noguères, *La Vérité aura le dernier mot* (Paris: Seuil, 1985).

78. *Le Monde*, 11 July 1986.

79. In *Le Monde:* Henri Noguères, 3 January 1986; Serge Klarsfeld, 15 January 1986; Vercors, 22 January 1986. Vergès, delighted, told *Libération* (21 December 1985) that the decision of the appellate court was "a slap in the face for the Chancellery."

80. In *Le Quotidien de Paris,* 7 February 1983.

81. Hearing of 1 July 1987, *Le Monde,* 3 July 1987.

82. Hearing of 23 June 1987, *Le Monde,* 25 June 1987.

83. Alain Finkielkraut, *La Mémoire vaine. Du crime contre l'humanité* (Paris: Gallimard, 1989), p. 76.

84. Christine Ockrent and Comte de Marenches, *Dans le secret des princes* (Paris: Stock, 1986), pp. 84–85.

85. Daniel Cordier, *Jean Moulin. L'Inconnu du Panthéon,* vol. 1: *Une Ambition pour la république. Juin 1899-juin 1936;* vol. 2: *Le Choix d'un destin. Juin 1936-novembre 1940* (Paris: Lattès, 1989). Four other volumes have yet to be published. On the controversy see, for example, the incendiary articles of Henri Noguères and General Chevance-Bertin (*Le Monde,* 15 and 25 November 1989), astonishing for their bad faith, and the articles by Jean-Pierre Azéma and Daniel Cordier (*Le Monde,* 7 and 29 November 1989).

86. Hearing of 18 June 1987, *Le Monde,* 20 June 1987.

87. Finkielkraut, *La mémoire vaine,* p. 125.

88. Bernard-Henri Lévy, ed., "Le Masochisme de Vergès. Entretien avec Claude Lanzmann," *Archives d'un procès. Klaus Barbie* (Paris: *Globe*/Le Livre de Poche, 1987), p. 191.

89. "*Shoah* et la shoah," interview with Claude Lanzmann, in Lévy, ed., *Archives d'un procès,* p. 51.

6. Vectors of Memory

1. Prost, *Les Anciens Combattants et la société française, 1914–1939,* vol. 3, pp. 62ff.

2. *La Mémoire des français.* I participated in this study, but the brief analysis of 8 May given here is based largely on Frank, "Bilan d'une enquête," p. 371, and on work done by correspondents of the IHTP.

3. Law of 7 May 1946, *Journal officiel,* 8 May 1946.

4. Quoted by Marie-Thérèse Frank, Marie-Thérèse Viaud, and Eugène Martres in *La Mémoire des français,* pp. 128, 275, 287.

5. Article 1, law of 20 March 1953, *Journal officiel,* 21 March 1953.

6. See Vaïsse, ed., *8 May 1945.*

7. Report of minister of the interior concerning decree of 11 April 1959, *Journal officiel,* 15 April 1959, as amended by decree of 17 January 1968.

8. On this point see Namer, *Batailles pour la mémoire.*

9. Frank, "Bilan d'une enquête," p. 377.

10. Quoted by François Garçon, *De Blum à Pétain. Cinéma et société française, 1936–1944* (Paris: Cerf, 1984), p. 28.

11. The figures in this paragraph are derived largely from two invaluable sources: Jean-Pierre Jeancolas, "Fonction du témoignage (les années 1939–1945 dans le cinéma d'après-guerre)," *Positif* 170 (June 1975), 45–60, which covers the period 1944–1975; Jean-Michel Andrault, Jean-Pierre Bertin-Maghit, and Gérard Vincent, "Le Cinéma français et la seconde guerre mondiale," *La Revue du cinéma* 378 (December 1982), 71–111, a thorough survey of the period 1969–1979. For the period 1980–1989 I followed the lead of these two authors and used the statistics published regularly by the weekly magazine *Le Film français.* The figures for total production from 1947 to 1987 are based on data collected by the INSEE (X-rated films are not included because of their disproportionate numbers). Although the samples are small and no claim is made as to "statistical significance," a clear evolution is evident. The listing probably is not complete because the films were classified on the basis of synopses. (It would have been financially and technically impossible to view 200 films, some of which have been lost or destroyed.) The analyses of the films (or passing remarks) are based, finally, on a historical approach, and no consideration is given to the technical or cinematic qualities of the works.

12. Jacques Siclier, *La France de Pétain et son cinéma* (Paris: Henri Veyner, 1981), p. 247.

13. François Truffaut, *Les Films de ma vie* (Paris: Flammarion, 1975), quoted by Annette Insdorf, *L'Holocauste à l'écran* (Paris: CinemAction/ Cerf, 1985), p. 43 (a convenient but inaccurate and incomplete source).

14. Louis Pergaud, *La Guerre des boutons* (Paris: Mercure de France, 1963), p. 55 of the Folio paperback edition.

15. Gilles le Morvan, *L'Humanité,* 31 October 1983; Michel Pérez, *Le Matin de Paris,* 28 October 1983.

16. Interview with the author, February 1989.

17. Alain Finkielkraut, *Le Quotidien de Paris,* 30 April 1985.

18. François Garçon, "Le Retour d'une inquiétante imposture: *Lili Marleen* et *Le Dernier Métro,*" *Les Temps modernes* 422 (September 1981), 547.

19. On this point see Annette Wieviorka, "Un Lieu de mémoire: le mémorial du martyr juif inconnu," *Pardès* 2 (1985).

20. Charles de Gaulle, *Le Salut, 1944–1946* (Paris: Plon, 1959), p. 178.

21. Ibid., p. 236.

22. Ibid., p. 38.

23. Ibid., p. 112.

24. Ibid., p. 250.

25. Robert Aron, *Fragments d'une vie* (Paris: Plon, 1981), p. 241.

26. Aron's papers are now held at the BDIC, and the conservators obligingly permitted me to consult them. Yvette Garnier-Rizet, who was his closest collaborator from 1955 on, confirms that Aron's network of contacts was indeed extensive. In particular, it was largely thanks to Raymond de Balazy, the employers' representative on the Commission Nationale Interprofessionnelle d'Epuration (responsible for the purge in industry), that Aron was able to write *Histoire de l'épuration,* vol. 2, part 1: *Le Monde des affaires* (Paris: Fayard, 1974). Balazy turned over to Aron copies of many records whose originals were kept in the Archives Nationales and closed to researchers until 1980.

27. Letter of 3 January 1960, Charles de Gaulle, *Lettres, notes et carnets. Juin 1958–décembre 1960* (Paris: Plon, 1985), pp. 311–312.

28. In particular Marie Kaan, widow of Pierre Kaan, a resistance fighter who died in the camps, who served as an intermediary with resistance circles; Claude Lévy, the secretary-general; Françoise Mercier, at the archives; Dominique Veillon, documentation; Marianne Ranson, photographic archives; Michel Rauzier, library; Annick Besnard, his collaborator; and also Jean Leclerc and many others, including all the historians who worked closely with the CHGM (such as Marie Granet, Marcel Baudot, François Boudot, Jean-Marie d'Hoop).

29. See Henri Michel, "Pour une chronologie de la résistance," *Revue historique,* October 1960; "Chronologie de la résistance, directives-modalités," *Bulletin spécial du CHGM,* July 1966; and for a progress report, Claude Lévy, "La Chronologie de la résistance, état des travaux au 31 décembre 1981," *Bulletin de l'Institut d'histoire du temps présent* 7 (1982).

30. See the archives of the CHGM, Archives Nationales, 78AJ, as well as its *Bulletin.* The investigation continued after the committee was disbanded: see *Bulletin de l'IHTP* 25 (September 1986).

31. Stéphane Courtois, "Luttes politiques et élaboration d'une histoire: le PCF historien du PCF dans la deuxième guerre mondiale," *Communisme* 4 (1983).

32. René Rémond, *Le Gouvernement de Vichy, 1940–1942. Institutions et politiques* (Paris: Armand Colin, 1972), p. 16.

33. Stanley Hoffmann, "Collaboration et collaborationisme," *Preuves,* July-September 1969, and "La Droite à Vichy," *Revue française de science politique,* January-March 1956. All of Hoffmann's articles on Vichy are reprinted in *Decline or Renewal? France since the 1930s* (New York: Viking, 1974). Hoffmann, director of Harvard's Center for European

Studies, was born in Austria but became a naturalized citizen of France, where he lived from the late 1920s to the early 1950s; as a Jew, he experienced the anxieties of the Occupation. Although he later emigrated to the United States, he cannot be considered "foreign" in France.

34. *La France de Vichy,* the French translation of Paxton's book, was published in the "Univers historique" series directed by Jacques Julliard and Michel Winock, who, along with Jean-Pierre Azéma, played a large part in making sure that the book was quickly published in France, unlike many other foreign works such as Novick's on the purge, which was translated and published by Balland seventeen years after its original publication in the United States. Other books have yet to be translated.

35. Marc Ferro, "Maréchal, nous sommes toujours là," *La Quinzaine littéraire,* 16 February 1973.

36. *L'Agent de liaison,* March 1973.

37. Paxton, *Vichy France,* p. 38. When Paxton's book came out in paperback in France, the press coverage was also large. At that time, however, owing to the prominence of Giscardism, many articles stressed the technocratic aspects of the Vichy regime more than collaboration.

38. Dominique Jamet, "L'Oeuf de Columbia," *L'Aurore,* 9 February 1973.

39. Michel Denis, *La France catholique,* 18 May 1973.

40. *Le Monde,* 17 May 1973.

41. In *Le Maréchal* 90 (April-May 1973).

42. During the *Dossiers de l'écran* television debate on Pétain, 25 May 1976. The American historian, faced with three representatives of the Resistance, including Pierre-Henri Teitgen and three dyed-in-the-wool Pétainists (Auphan, Isorni, and Girard), had a hard time getting a word in edgewise; the scholarly (and official) point of view was expressed by Henri Michel. At any rate, that is the memory of the event in the mind of one young student, who had just recently embarked on the study of Vichy because his passion had been kindled by *Vichy France.* In the preface to a 1982 edition of his book (Columbia University Press), Paxton discusses the furor aroused by his work when it was first published in France. Sticking by his conclusions, he rejects the accusation that he wrote in "a mood of easy moral superiority" owing to his distance from French passions and his position as a "victor": "In fact [my book] was written in the shadow of the war in Vietnam, which sharpened my animosity against nationalist conformisms of all kinds. Writing in the late 1960s, what concerned me was not the comparison with defeated France but the confident swagger of the Germans in the summer of 1940."

43. See *Bulletin de l'Association pour défendre la mémoire du maréchal Pétain* 11 (January 1955), 10, which characterizes Aron as a man "who

wants to pass for someone more hostile to the Vichy regime than he really was." Six years later he was no longer even a heretic: *Le Maréchal* 19 (February 1961) printed one of his articles on the "Jewish question," one of the few ever to appear in that publication. Finally, in 1973, Auphan, also writing in *Le Maréchal*, called Aron one of "the more moderate" historians. As the citadel collapses, its faithful defenders cling to the least damaging interpretations, sacrificing a bit more each time they take up a new defensive position.

44. Henri Michel in *Revue d'histoire de la deuxième guerre mondiale* 93 (January 1974).

45. Janine Bourdin, *Revue française de science politique* 23 (June 1973).

46. Alain-Gérard Slama, "Les Yeux d'Abetz," *Contrepoint* 10 (April 1973), the same issue in which Stanley Hoffmann published an article on *The Sorrow and the Pity*.

47. The author wishes to confess that he himself was influenced by this state of mind and no doubt contributed to it with his early writings.

48. Letter of 4 December 1978, from René Descubes, *Le Maréchal* 113 (1979).

49. "Répertoire des chercheurs sur la seconde guerre mondiale," *Cahiers de l'IHTP* 2 (October 1985).

50. See François Bédarida, "L'Histoire de la résistance, lectures d'hier, chantiers de demain," *Vingtième Siècle* 11 (July-September 1986), special issue on "Nouveaux enjeux d'une décennie. Fascismes, antifascismes, 1935–1945." On testimony by résistants and Daniel Cordier's book, see note 85, Chapter 5, and note 55 below.

51. See Hervé Villeré, *L'Affaire de la Section spéciale* (Paris: Fayard, 1973). Letter from René Pleven, 10 February 1972, p. 17.

52. Article 7, law of 3 January 1979, *Journal officiel*, 5 January 1979.

53. Report of the Commission des Affaires Culturelles, no. 536, session of 18 May 1978, *Journal officiel, Sénat, débats parlementaires*. Henri Fréville, the author of *Archives secrètes de Bretagne, 1940–1944* (Rennes: Ouest-France, 1985), confirmed this remarkable omission. On this law see also another report by the same commission, no. 146, session of 13 December 1978; *Journal officiel*, sessions of 4 and 5 December 1978, pp. 8769ff; and the analysis by Ariane Ducrot, "Comment fut élaborée et votée la loi sur les archives du 3 janvier 1979," *La Gazette des Archives* 104 (1979).

54. Pierre Cézard, for a long time the head of the contemporary section, was one of them. Since the Liberation, when he braved bullets with a wheelbarrow to gather up files from the Gestapo and the Hotel Majestic, until his retirement in 1984, he more than any other individual realized the

enormous value of the millions of documents in the national archives. "He knew everything but said nothing," leaving the telling to historians, though at times aware of the distance between their commentaries and the documents under his protection. His successors, including Chantal de Tourtier-Bonazzi, have carried on his work. Interview with Pierre Cézard conducted by the author and Jean-Pierre Azéma in 1986.

55. Cordier has several times given his views on this issue: see the various interviews he gave when his book was published in 1989 and his paper, "De l'acteur à l'historien," *Bulletin de l'Institut d'histoire du temps présent* 35 (March 1989).

56. In the bibliography he prepared on the subject in *Historiens et géographes* 232 (October 1971), 77.

57. Ibid., pp. 79, 81–84.

58. See the reports of the juries for the agrégation in geography, *Historiens et géographes* 239 (December 1972), 249, 273 (for the 1972 exams), and 245 (December 1973), 265, 289.

59. Ibid., December 1972, p. 283.

60. Ibid., p. 326.

61. Ibid., December 1973, p. 267.

62. Ibid., p. 289.

63. A remark suggested by a candidate at the time, my colleague Michel Margairaz, whom I wish to thank for reminding me of the 1972–73 agrégation.

64. Here I am considering only the content of final-year textbooks; I venture no judgment concerning what was actually taught, nor do I place any weight on differences between authors. See, for example, Antoine Bonifacio, *Le Monde contemporain* (Paris: Hachette, 1966), or Bouillon, Sorlin, and Rudel, *Le Monde contemporain* (Paris: Bordas, 1968). On their silences see Serge Klarsfeld, *Le Monde,* 26 April 1982, and *L'Enseignement de la Shoah* (Paris: CDJC, 1982), the proceedings of a round-table discussion held on 14 March 1982 under the auspices of the CDJC and the Association des Professeurs d'Histoire et de Géographie. See also Pierre Assouline, "Faut-il brûler les manuels d'histoire?" *L'Histoire* 59 (September 1983).

65. Antoine Prost, ed., *Histoire. Classe de terminale* (Paris: Armand Colin, 1983).

66. Sentou, Aldebert, and Phan, *Histoire, classe terminale* (Paris: Delagrave, 1983).

67. Ibid., p. 45.

68. Serge Wolikow, ed. *Histoire du temps présent, 1939–1982* (Paris: Messidor/Editions Sociales, 1983): "The Munich capitulation left Czechoslo-

vakia to be dismantled by the Nazis" (p. 21), and "threatened with finding itself alone at war on two fronts, the USSR agreed to sign a nonaggression pact with Germany. With the danger of a three-way antifascist alliance again eliminated, one week later Hitler invaded Poland" (p. 22).

69. Dominique Borne, "L'Histoire du XXe siècle au lycée: le nouveau programme de terminale," *Vingtième Siècle* 21 (January-March 1989).

70. See *Le Monde de l'éducation*, September 1983, p. 40.

71. Memorandum reproduced in "La Déportation," *Textes et documents*, Institut Pédagogique National, 17, 1st trimester 1964, p. 1.

7. Diffuse Memory

1. See *Le Film français;* Andrault, Maghit, and Vincent, "Le Cinéma français."

2. Special insert in *Le Film français,* 1986.

3. My thanks to Eric Vigne of Fayard for making available figures that most publishers are reluctant to give out, as well as to Yvette Garnier-Rizet, Robert Aron's secretary. Figures provided by authors have been rounded off to correct for different accounting procedures used by different publishing houses.

4. These figures were made available to me by Editions du Seuil thanks to Michel Winock and through the patient efforts of Anne Sastourné, who collected them.

5. See note 7.

6. Information kindly provided by Olivier Béressi, head of marketing for ALP (a subsidiary of Hachette), who allowed me to consult his files, particularly reports of discussions and market surveys prior to the introduction of the series.

7. Polls used, in chronological order, are: IFOP (*Sondages,* 9 June 1966, on Pétain); SOFRES/*Le Figaro,* November 1970, in *Histoire Magazine* 10 (1980) (commentary by René Rémond); SOFRES/*Sud-Ouest,* in *Le Maréchal* 85 (November 1971); "Les Français et la commémoration du 8 mai 1945," SOFRES/*L'Express,* 13 May 1975; "Les Jeunes (15–20 ans) se prononcent sur de Gaulle," SOFRES/*L'Express,* 10 November 1975; "Débats autour du maréchal Pétain," IFOP, *Sondages* 3–4 (1976); on *Holocaust, Télé 7 jours,* 21 March 1979, cited by Ménudier, "*Holocauste* en France"; SOFRES/Atlas, conducted in October 1979 (unpublished), see *L'Histoire* 19 (January 1980); "Ce que pensent les Français 35 ans après," Publimétrie/*Les Nouvelles littéraires,* 21 Febru-

ary 1980; "66% des Français ne condamnent pas Pétain," SOFRES/*Figaro Magazine*, 17 May 1980; "Les Français jugent de Gaulle," SOFRES/ *Histoire Magazine*, 1980, issue cited; SOFRES/*Journaux de guerre* (unpublished), December 1982; "Quarante ans après: les Français et la libération," Louis Harris France/*L'Histoire* 67 (May 1984) (commentary by Robert Frank and Henry Rousso). Among polls carried out by historians, in addition to the last one cited, credit should be given to the pioneers: Jean-Louis Crémieux-Brilhac and G. Bensimhon, "Les Propagandes radiophoniques et l'opinion publique en France de 1940 à 1944," *Revue d'histoire de la deuxième guerre mondiale* 101 (January 1976), based on a questionnaire about the occupation years, and Pierre Guillaume, "Résistance et collaboration devant l'opinion actuelle," *Bulletin de la Société d'histoire moderne et contemporaine* 3 (1976); also polls conducted by the group MEMOR, including Jean-Paul Thuillier, "Quarante ans après: mémoires de guerre en zone interdite" (unpublished, 1985), which covered northern France, and Jean-Jacques Girardot and François Marcot, "Au Musée de la résistance et de la déportation de Besançon. Enquêtes par questionnaires," *La Mémoire des français*.

8. Thanks to Judith Saymal and Pascal Krop for allowing me to see these letters, some of which were published in the early September issues. Following the program *Droit de réponse* on Pétain in January 1986, TF1 received roughly 320 letters, briefly summarized by Eric Le Vaillant in *Vingtième Siècle* 13 (1986).

9. Letter published and signed, *L'Evénement du jeudi*, 5 September 1985, p. 64.

10. Ibid.

11. Ibid., p. 63.

12. *Bulletin d'information de l'IFOP, 1944–1945* (Parisian studies). The question asked was: "Should Marshal Pétain be punished?" Possible answers were "death," "another punishment," "no punishment." In SOFRES/*Sud-Ouest*, November 1971, the question was: "In 1945 Marshal Pétain was sentenced to death for 'high treason,' a sentence then commuted because of his age. Do you think that in his case the punishment was not severe enough (he should have been executed as others were), just, too severe (a moral censure would have sufficed), completely unjust (he should not have been found guilty)?" In *Sondages*, 1976, the question was: "Marshal Pétain was sentenced to death . . . In principle, do you think it was proper that he be tried after the war?" In *L'Histoire*, 1983, the question was virtually identical to the one asked in 1971.

13. See Rioux, *La IVe république*, vol. 1, pp. 56–57.

Conclusion

1. Winock, *La Fièvre hexagonale,* p. 383.
2. See my essay in Geoffrey Hartman, ed., *Bitburg in Moral and Political Perspective* (Bloomington: Indiana University Press, 1986).
3. Prosecutor-General Mornet, *Quatre ans à rayer de notre histoire* (Paris: Self, 1949). The quote stands as the epigraph of Mornet's book, with the final words italicized by the author.

Acknowledgments

I should like to express my deep gratitude to Jean-Pierre Azéma, Jean-Pierre Rioux, and Michel Winock, whose continuing advice and close scrutiny helped to make this book a reality.

I should also like to thank my colleagues at the Institut d'Histoire du Temps Présent, an institution that for some years now has been exploring the history and memory of World War II: François Bédarida, Karel Bartosek, Claude Lévy, Michael Pollak, Denis Peschanski, Marianne Ranson, Dominique Veillon, and Danièle Voldman. Jean Astruc, Françoise Mercier, Lucienne Nouveau, and Anne-Marie Pathé helped with the documentation, and Valérie Arigon, Claude Cherrier, Brigitte David, Jean-Marie Guillon, and Eugène Martres, all associates of the IHTP, provided useful leads.

I am especially grateful to a number of individuals who agreed to provide oral or written accounts of their experience, in particular Pierre Cézard, Jacques Chambaz, Jacques Delarue, René Descubes, Jean Favier, Henri Fréville, Yvette Garnier-Rizet, Génia Gemahling, Stanley Hoffmann, Jacques Isorni, Jean-François Kahn, Georges Lamirand, François Lehideux, Louis Malle, Joe Nordmann, Marcel Ophuls, Robert Paxton, Gilbert Renault (known as Rémy), Georges Rouchouze, and Philippe Viannay.

Various people aided me in locating sources: Renée Bédarida, Olivier Béressi, Georges Bonopéra, Yvan Charron, Robert Frank, Etienne Fouilloux, Pascal Krop, Sigrid and Fred Kupferman, Carine Marcé, Guillaume Malaurie, Michel Margairaz, Martine Rousso, Anne Sastourné, Judith Saymal, Jean-François Sirinelli, Chantal de Tourtier-Bonazzi, Pierre Vidal-Naquet, Eric Vigne, Jean-Pierre Vittori, Annette Wagner, and Olivier Wieviorka.

Nathalie and Claudine Larguier, Sébastien Verdoliva, and Jean-Pierre Gouailhardou accorded me a warm welcome in Dover and Chablis.

I also wish to express my profound gratitude to my parents, Annette and Albert Rousso, the first readers of this work in manuscript form and staunch supporters throughout.

INDEX